6—

Ornaments

Natascha Kubisch
Pia Anna Seger

Ornaments

Patterns for Interior Decoration based on
Muster für die Innendekoration aus
Motifs pour décorer son intérieur de

The Practical Decorator and Ornamentist
by George Ashdown Audsley and Maurice Ashdown Audsley

h.f.ullmann

Frontispiece/Frontispiz/Frontispice:
Detail of illustration: Panel decorations using palmette motifs (page 67, top left)
Detail der Abbildung: Paneelverzierungen mit Palmettendekor (Seite 67, oben links)
Détail de l'illustration : Décors de panneaux à palmettes (page 67, en haut à gauche)

Endpapers/Vorsatzpapier/Papier de garde:
© Tandem Verlag GmbH, Königswinter / Photo: Werner Stapelfeldt (based on pattern on page 49, bottom)

Acknowledgements
The editor and publishers would like to thank Deffner & Johann, Röthlein, for putting pigments and brushes at their disposal; Keimfarben, Diedorf, for providing colors and paints; Damian Werner, Kalbach/Rhön and their colleague Doris Unger, Fulda, for producing the stencils and executing the color borders; and Isabel Kühn, Berlin, for her expert advice on the texts accompanying the plates.

Danksagung
Herausgeber und Verlag bedanken sich bei der Firma Deffner & Johann, Röthlein, für die Bereitstellung von Pigmenten und Pinseln; bei der Firma Keimfarben, Diedorf, für die Bereitstellung von Farbmaterial; bei der Firma Damian Werner, Kalbach/Rhön, und deren Mitarbeiterin Doris Unger, Fulda, für die Anfertigung von Schablonen und die entsprechende Ausführung der Ornamentbänder sowie bei Isabel Kühn, Berlin, für das Fachlektorat zu den Tafeltexten.

Remerciements
L'éditeur et la maison d'édition remercient l'entreprise Deffner & Johann, Röthlein, pour la mise à disposition de leurs pigments et pinceaux ; l'entreprise Keimfarben, Diedorf, pour la mise à disposition de leur peinture ; l'entreprise Damian Werner, Kalbach/Rhön et leur collaboratrice Doris Unger, Fulda, pour la fabrication des pochoirs et la réalisation des bandeaux ornementaux ainsi qu'Isabel Kühn, Berlin, pour sa relecture des textes des planches.

The patterns in this book were first published in 1892 by Blackie & Son, Limited, Glasgow under the title
The Practical Decorator and Ornamentist by George Ashdown Audsley and Maurice Ashdown Audsley.

© 2007 Tandem Verlag GmbH
h.f.ullmann is an imprint of Tandem Verlag GmbH

Editor: Peter Delius

For Delius Producing Berlin:
Project coordination and editing: Jens Tewes
Assistants: Hanna Kerstin Buhl, Landy Siemssen
Graphic design: Wolfgang-E. Kaemmer
Picture research: Florence Baret,
Katleen Krause, Jacek Slaski
Typesetting: Delius Producing Berlin

For the publisher:
Project management: Sally Bald
Coordination: Hannah Jarvis
Translation into English: Michael Scuffil
Translation into French: Françoise Chardonnier

Printed in China

ISBN 978-3-8331-4035-8

10 9 8 7 6 5 4 3 2 1
X IX VIII VII VI V IV III II I

Contents Inhalt Sommaire

Introduction
Einleitung

The Audsleys – A Family of Artists and Architects in Victorian Britain
Die Audsleys – eine Architektenfamilie im viktorianischen England
Les Audsley – une famille d'architectes dans l'Angleterre victorienne

The present book is based on *The Practical Decorator and Ornamentist* by George Ashdown Audsley and his son Maurice Ashdown Audsley. George Ashdown Audsley was born in Elgin in north-east Scotland in 1838. Together with his elder brother William James Audsley, he trained as an architect in Glasgow. Scotland being relatively poor, the two brothers sought to improve their career prospects by moving south of the border to Liverpool in 1863. Here they set up an architectural practice together, and it was in Liverpool that Maurice Ashdown Audsley, George's second child and eldest son, was born in 1865. The two brothers – George and William – concentrated on religious buildings in various parts

Das vorliegende Buch basiert auf der Vorlagensammlung *The Practical Decorator and Ornamentist* von George Ashdown Audsley und seinem Sohn Maurice Ashdown Audsley. George Ashdown Audsley wurde 1838 in Elgin im Nordosten Schottlands geboren. Zusammen mit seinem älteren Bruder William James absolvierte er eine Architektenausbildung in Glasgow. Da die Karriereaussichten im ärmeren Schottland schlecht waren, zogen die Brüder 1863 nach Liverpool, wo sie ein Architekturbüro gründeten. Hier in Liverpool wurde 1865 Georges zweites Kind und ältester Sohn Maurice geboren. George und William entwarfen in verschiedenen Liverpooler Stadtteilen vorrangig Kirchen: das Gotteshaus der Pres-

Ce livre se base sur le recueil de motifs *The Practical Decorator and Ornamentist* de George Ashdown Audsley et de son fils, Maurice Ashdown Audsley. George Ashdown Audsley est né en 1838 à Elgin dans le nord-est de l'Écosse. Avec son frère aîné, William James, il fit ses études d'architecture à Glasgow. Comme les perspectives de carrière dans une Écosse plutôt pauvre étaient mauvaises, les deux frères s'installèrent en 1863 à Liverpool où ils ouvrirent un bureau d'architecte. C'est à Liverpool que naquit Maurice, deuxième enfant et fils aîné de George Ashdown Audsley. George et William James Audsley conçurent surtout des plans d'églises pour différents quartiers de Liverpool : l'église de la

St Mary's Church in Ellel, Lancashire, 1873
In keeping with the spirit of the times, this church by George Ashdown Ashley and his brother William is in the neo-Gothic style, which was especially popular in England.

St. Mary's Church in Ellel, Lancashire, erbaut 1873
Die von George Ashdown Audsley und seinem Bruder William erbaute Kirche ist dem Zeitgeist entsprechend im neugotischen Stil gehalten, der sich vor allem in England großer Beliebtheit erfreute.

St. Mary's Church à Ellel, Lancashire, construite en 1873
L'église dont George Ashdown Audsley et son frère William ont été les architectes reflète l'esprit de l'époque, à savoir le style néogothique qui jouissait d'une grande popularité surtout en Angleterre.

of the city: the Presbyterian church in Toxteth (1865–1867), Christ Church in Kensington, (1870), St Margaret's Church in Anfield (1873), and a synagogue, also in Toxteth (1874). In addition, they built St Mary's Church for a merchant in the village of Ellel near Lancaster (1873). Apart from a synagogue in St Petersburgh Place in London's West End, on which they collaborated with other architects, and the design of a golf course, these are the only buildings dating from their Liverpool period. The Audsleys became better known through their ornamental pattern books. Thus William James Audsley published a manual on the symbolism of Christian art as early as 1865, which was followed by further treatises published by his brother, including a two-volume work on Japanese pottery and a multi-volume work on Japanese crafts which dealt in particular with ornamentation. In addition, the two brothers concerned themselves with the decorative arts of the Middle Ages, which at that time were undergoing a fashionable revival. This enthusiasm for medieval art was also, incidentally, reflected in the Audsleys' architectural designs, for their buildings are in "Victorian High Gothic" and thus fully in line with the taste of the time. In general, for all their intensive involvement with ornamentation, it is true to say that the Audsleys remained architects first and foremost, for they always regarded ornament as a decorative addition to buildings, and thus as ancillary to architecture, and in this spirit, the orientation of their treatises was heavily practical. *The Practical Decorator and Ornamentist*, published in 1892 by George Ashdown Audsley and his son Maurice Ashdown Audsley, is no exception. It is a professional guide to the use of ornament, aimed above all at architects and decorative painters. This pattern-folder contained 100 color lithographs of ornamental designs by the Audsleys, which were originally available in fifteen parts on a subscription basis and served as patterns for interior decoration. The

byterianischen Gemeinde in Toxteth (1865–1867), die Christ Church in Kensington (1870) und die St. Margaret's Church in Anfield (1873) sowie eine Synagoge ebenfalls in Toxteth (1874); außerdem errichteten sie unweit Lancasters in der Ortschaft Ellel für einen Händler die St. Mary's Church (1873). Abgesehen von einer Synagoge am St. Petersburgh Place im Londoner West End, die sie zusammen mit anderen Architekten entwarfen, und dem Entwurf eines Golfplatzes sind dies die einzigen belegten Audsley-Bauten ihrer Liverpooler Zeit. Bekannter wurden die Audsleys durch ihre ornamentalen Vorlagenwerke. So hatte William bereits 1865 ein Handbuch zur Symbolik der christlichen Kunst veröffentlicht, dem George mehrere Abhandlungen folgen ließ, darunter ein zweibändiges Werk zur japanischen Keramik und ein mehrbändiges zum japanischen Kunstgewerbe, das sich insbesondere der Ornamentik zuwandte. Außerdem beschäftigten sich die beiden Brüder mit der Ornamentik des Mittelalters, die zu jener Zeit eine modische Wiederbelebung fand. Diese Begeisterung für die Kunst des Mittelalters fand übrigens auch in den Architekturentwürfen der Audsleys ihren Niederschlag, denn ihre Bauten sind dem Zeitgeschmack entsprechend im Stil der „viktorianischen Hochgotik" gehalten. Überhaupt kann man feststellen, dass die Audsleys trotz ihrer intensiven Beschäftigung mit der Ornamentik vor allem Architekten blieben, denn sie betrachteten das Ornament stets als Baudekor im Dienste der Architektur und richteten ihre Abhandlungen in diesem Sinne stark praxisorientiert aus. So gab George zusammen mit seinem Sohn Maurice ab 1892 *The Practical Decorator and Ornamentist* heraus – eine berufsorientierte Anleitung für die Verwendung von Ornamenten, die sich vor allem an Architekten und Dekorationsmaler wandte. Diese Vorlagensammlung beinhaltete 100 Farblithografien mit Ornamententwürfen der Audsleys, die ursprünglich in fünfzehn Teilen auf Subskriptionsbasis erworben werden konnten und als Vorlagen für die

communauté presbytérienne à Toxteth (1865–1867), la Christ Church à Kensington (1870) et la St. Margaret's Church à Anfield (1873), ainsi qu'une synagogue à Toxteth (1874) et, pour le compte d'un marchand, la St. Mary's Church dans la localité d'Ellel non loin de Lancaster (1873). Abstraction faite d'une synagogue sur la St. Petersburgh Place dans le West End londonien, dont ils firent les plans en collaboration avec d'autres architectes, et un projet de terrain de golf, ce sont les seuls bâtiments Audsley répertoriés durant leur séjour à Liverpool. On connaît davantage les Audsley par leurs recueils de modèles ornementaux. William James Audsley avait, par exemple, publié dès 1865 un manuel sur la symbolique dans l'art chrétien, auquel succédèrent plusieurs traités publiés par George Ashdown Audsley, dont un ouvrage en deux tomes sur la céramique japonaise et un volume consacré aux ornements dans les arts décoratifs japonais. Les frères Audsley s'intéressèrent également à l'art ornemental du Moyen Âge qui revenait alors à la mode. Cet engouement pour l'art médiéval se manifesta du reste aussi dans leurs œuvres d'architectes; leurs constructions sont en effet réalisées dans le style du « haut gothique victorien » conformément au goût de l'époque. De manière générale les Audsley, malgré leur intérêt extrême pour l'art ornemental, demeurèrent avant tout des architectes, car ils ne cessèrent de considérer l'ornement comme un élément décoratif au service de l'architecture; c'est dans cet esprit qu'ils donnèrent à leurs traités une nette orientation pratique. George Ashdown Audsley publia par exemple, à partir de 1892, avec son fils Maurice *The Practical Decorator and Ornamentist* – un manuel d'utilisation d'ornements principalement destiné aux professionnels, architectes et peintres décorateurs. Ce recueil de modèles contenait 100 lithographies en couleurs avec des projets d'ornements des Audsley; les motifs rassemblés en 15 tomes vendus en

George Ashdown Audsley, 1838–1925
This Scottish architect and polymath attained an international reputation largely on account of his treatises on Japanese art and his ornamental designs for interior decoration. His books on organ-building, written after his emigration to the USA, became standard works there.

George Ashdown Audsley, 1838–1925
Der schottische Architekt und Universalgelehrte erlangte vor allem durch seine Abhandlungen zur japanischen Kunst und seine Ornamententwürfe zur Innenraumgestaltung einen Ruf, der über England hinausging. Seine nach der Übersiedlung in die USA verfassten Schriften zum Orgelbau wurden dort zu Standardwerken.

George Ashdown Audsley, 1838–1925
L'architecte écossais et esprit universel s'est forgé une réputation qui a dépassé les frontières de l'Angleterre, surtout grâce à ses traités sur l'art japonais et à ses esquisses d'ornements destinés à la décoration intérieure. Ses écrits sur la construction d'orgues, rédigés après son émigration aux USA, sont devenus des ouvrages de référence.

designs were created in particular for friezes, wall surfaces, and ceilings. Evidently they proved so useful that the folder was published in Germany the following year, albeit without the Audsleys' introductory text. *The Practical Decorator and Ornamentist* was the last major pattern-book to be produced by any of the Audsleys before George Ashdown Audsley emigrated to the United States to pursue a highly successful career as both practitioner and theoretician of the art of organ-building. While his handbooks on organ-building achieved the status of standard works, and have been frequently reprinted in the United States in recent years, the pattern folders are only gradually being rediscovered. George Ashdown Audsley died in 1925; nothing is known of the subsequent careers of his brother or son.

Dekoration von Innenräumen gedacht waren. Die Muster waren vor allem für Friese, Wandflächen und Decken entworfen worden und waren offenbar tatsächlich derartig nützlich, dass die Mappe schon im folgenden Jahr auch in Deutschland herausgebracht wurde, wenngleich ohne die beigefügten Erläuterungstexte der Audsleys. *The Practical Decorator and Ornamentist* stellt die letzte große Vorlagensammlung dar, bevor George in die Vereinigten Staaten auswanderte, um dort seine bereits in Großbritannien begonnene Karriere als Orgelbauer und -theoretiker sehr erfolgreich fortzusetzen. Während seine Handbücher zum Orgelbau den Rang von Standardwerken erlangten und in den USA gerade in der jüngsten Vergangenheit in zahlreichen Neuauflagen erschienen, werden die Vorlagensammlungen erst allmählich wieder entdeckt.
George Ashdown Audsley starb 1925. Über die weitere Karriere seines Bruders und seines Sohnes ist nichts bekannt.

souscription devaient servir de modèles pour décorer des intérieurs. Ils avaient surtout été conçus pour la décoration de frises, de murs et de plafonds et se sont en fait avérés si utiles que le recueil parut aussi en Allemagne l'année suivante, mais sans les notes explicatives des Audsley. *The Practical Decorator and Ornamentist* représente le dernier grand recueil de modèles des Audsley avant l'émigration de George Ashdown Audsley aux États-Unis où il mena une carrière très réussie de facteur d'orgues et de théoricien de ce métier. Si ses manuels sur la fabrication d'orgues sont devenus des ouvrages de référence et ont fait l'objet de nombreuses rééditions récentes aux États-Unis, la redécouverte des recueils de modèles ne s'effectue que peu à peu.
George Ashdown Audsley mourut en 1925. On ignore tout de la carrière que son frère et son fils ont poursuivie.

View of Liverpool, late-19th century
This picture shows Liverpool Town Hall. Already an important trading center in the 18th century, Liverpool had become a major port by the late 19th. The expanding city became a magnet for architects like George Ashdown Audsley and his brother William, who set up a practice here in the 1860s. Alongside individual commissions – mainly for churches – George designed interiors for the mansions of the upper-middle classes, and eventually, together with his son Maurice, published the pattern folders which form the basis of the present book.

Ansicht von Liverpool, spätes 19. Jh.
Diese historische Aufnahme zeigt das Rathaus der im Zuge der Industrialisierung zum bedeutenden Produktions- und Handelszentrum angewachsenen Stadt Liverpool. Die rege Bautätigkeit und die Gründung zahlreicher Manufakturen bewogen auch George Ashdown Audsley und seinen Bruder William, sich mit ihrem Architekturbüro in der Großstadt niederzulassen. Neben einzelnen gemeinsamen Aufträgen, die vorrangig den Bau von Kirchen betrafen, entwarf vor allem George Interieurs vornehmer Bürgerhäuser und brachte schließlich gemeinsam mit seinem Sohn Maurice jene Vorlagenmappe für Innendekorateure heraus, die im vorliegenden Buch reproduziert ist.

Vue de Liverpool, fin du XIXᵉ siècle
Cette vue historique montre la mairie de la ville de Liverpool, devenue un important centre de commerce et de production au cours de l'industrialisation. L'activité intense que connaissait le bâtiment et la construction de nombreuses manufactures incitèrent aussi George Ashdown Audsley et son frère William à ouvrir un bureau d'architecte dans cette grande ville. En dehors des différentes commandes qui concernaient principalement la construction d'églises, George Ashdown Audsley conçut des intérieurs de demeures bourgeoises élégantes et publia finalement, avec son fils Maurice, ce recueil de modèles destiné aux architectes d'intérieur et qui est reproduit dans le présent ouvrage.

The Practical Decorator and Ornamentist – A Unique Pattern-Book
Ein einzigartiges Musterbuch – The Practical Decorator and Ornamentist
The Practical Decorator and Ornamentist – Un recueil de motifs exceptionnel

The Practical Decorator and Ornamentist – the title of the original edition of the collection of designs presented here – first appeared in Britain in 1892 as a pattern-book for architects, restorers, decorative painters, and artists. But even the introduction to the 1893 German edition pointed expressly to the fact that this work was not only addressed to the groups mentioned, but also to sculptors and wood carvers, cabinet makers and modelers, potters and engravers. In addition, the patterns could also be used by designers of wallpapers, carpets and furnishing fabrics, and thus fell into the – then still young – category of industrial design, and to this extent fulfilled a totally new need for information.

The Practical Decorator and Ornamentist – so der Titel der Originalausgabe der vorliegenden Ornamentesammlung – erschien 1892 erstmalig in England als Musterbuch für Architekten, Restaurateure, Dekorationsmaler und Künstler. Doch schon im Einleitungstext der 1893 herausgebrachten deutschen Ausgabe wurde ausdrücklich darauf hingewiesen, dass sich dieses Werk nicht nur an die erwähnten Berufsgruppen wendet, sondern ebenso an Stein- und Holzbildhauer, Kunsttischler und Modelleure, Keramiker und Graveure. Überdies ließen sich die Ornamentvorlagen auch für die Entwürfe von Tapeten, Teppichen und Möbelstoffen verwenden und fielen damit in die Kategorie des

The Practical Decorator and Ornamentist – tel est le titre de l'édition originale du présent ouvrage d'ornements – parut pour la première fois en 1892 en Angleterre sous la forme d'un recueil de motifs à l'usage des architectes, restaurateurs, peintres décorateurs et artistes. Le texte d'introduction de l'édition allemande parue dès 1893 précise toutefois que cet ouvrage s'adresse non seulement aux catégories professionnelles mentionnées, mais aussi aux sculpteurs sur pierre et sur bois, aux ébénistes et modeleurs, aux céramistes et graveurs. Les modèles d'ornements servirent en outre à créer des tapisseries, tapis et tissus d'ameublement. Ils entraient de ce

The Practical Decorator and Ornamentist,
published in 1892
The pattern book by George and Maurice Audsley, which forms the basis of the present work, was a collection of expensively-produced, large-format chromo-lithographs, sold on a subscription basis in 15 parts. Intended for practical use, most of the designs could be transferred directly to the wall or other surface without change of scale. The reverse sides of the folders carry advertisements. While this seems curious to us, it was normal practice at the time, and gives an indication of the Audsleys' business sense.

The Practical Decorator and Ornamentist,
veröffentlicht 1892
Das ornamentale Musterwerk von George und Maurice Audsley, das dem vorliegenden Buch zu Grunde liegt, wurde in Form großformatiger Chromolithografien – aufwändiger Mehrfarbdrucke – auf Subskriptionsbasis in 15 Teilen vertrieben. Im Sinne der praktischen Handhabung waren die meisten Ornamententwürfe so angelegt, dass sie ohne Maßstabsveränderung von der Vorlage auf die Wand übertragen werden konnten. Einen kurios anmutenden – jedoch durchaus üblichen – Beweis für die Geschäftstüchtigkeit der Audsleys liefern die Rückseiten der Sammelmappen, die mit Werbeanzeigen bedruckt sind.

The Practical Decorator and Ornamentist,
publié en 1892
Le recueil de motifs ornementaux de George et Maurice Audsley, qui sert de base au présent ouvrage, a été commercialisé par souscription en 15 parties sous la forme de grandes chromolithographies (impressions polychromes coûteux). La disposition choisie dans un souci de meilleur maniement de la plupart des esquisses ornementales permet de transférer celles-ci sur un mur sans modifier l'échelle du modèle. Les dos des chemises portant des annonces publicitaires, pratique singulière et cependant courante, prouvent à quel point les Audsley ont le sens des affaires.

Gabinetto eseguito in Venezia

Above: Division of wall and ceiling for interior-decoration purposes. Engraving after a drawing by Giuseppe Borsato, early-19th century
Design drawings were often copied on to printing plates by copperplate engravers for the purpose of widespread duplication. These found their way to all parts of Europe.

Oben: Wand- und Deckengliederung für die Innenraumgestaltung, Kupferstich nach einer Zeichnung von Giuseppe Borsato, frühes 19. Jh.
Entwurfszeichnungen wurden häufig von Kupferstechern auf Druckplatten übertragen, dann vervielfältigt und europaweit vertrieben.

En haut : Décors de murs et plafonds pour intérieurs. Eau-forte d'après un dessin de Giuseppe Borsato, début du XIXᵉ siècle.
Des graveurs sur cuivre ont souvent transféré et reproduit des esquisses sur des planches à imprimer. Ces motifs furent commercialisés dans toute l'Europe.

Left: Carolingian book of gospels, Parchment, Prague Castle archives, c. 870
From the 8th century on, pattern books were developed which set out the symbolic significance of the various colors and motifs.

Links: Karolingisches Evangeliar, Pergament, Archiv der Prager Burg, um 870
Ab dem 8. Jahrhundert wurden Musterbücher entwickelt, die insbesondere die symbolische Bedeutung von Farben und Bildmotiven für Evangeliare wie dieses festlegten.

À gauche : Évangéliaire carolingien, parchemin, archives du Château de Prague, vers 870
Les ouvrages de motifs qui déterminèrent notamment la signification symbolique des couleurs et des motifs d'évangéliaires tels que celui-ci se sont développés à partir du VIIIᵉ siècle.

Pattern-books and pattern-collections have a tradition going back to the Middle Ages. It is known, for example, that the monks of the 9th century had books of patterns according to which they produced their richly decorated handwritten gospels. Among architects and builders, by contrast, it was for a long time usual to regard many things as trade secrets, to be passed down within the guild from generation to generation. This knowledge included not just the physical laws relating to building (the principles of statics, for example), but also suggestions for decorative motifs. It was only when guildsmen started working at an international level, and in particular with the invention of printing (c. 1455) that the flow of information accelerated, so that drawings or engravings became quickly accessible to a large circle.

noch jungen Industriedesigns, womit sie einem ganz neuen Informationsbedürfnis nachkamen. Dabei haben Musterbücher und -sammlungen eine Tradition, die bis ins Mittelalter zurückreicht. So weiß man beispielsweise, dass schon die Mönche des neunten Jahrhunderts Vorlagen- und Anweisungsbücher hatten, nach denen sie reich verzierte, handgeschriebene Evangelien anfertigten. Unter Baumeistern dagegen war es lange Zeit üblich, Erkenntnisse über architektonische Gesetzmäßigkeiten – wie zum Beispiel die Regeln der Statik –, aber auch Motiv-Vorschläge für den Baudekor von Generation zu Generation als wohlgehütetes Geheimnis der Bauhütte weiterzugeben. Erst mit dem Herausbilden von Handwerkergilden, deren Mitglieder auch international tätig waren, und spätestens seit der Erfindung des Buchdrucks

fait dans la catégorie du design industriel naissant et répondaient ainsi à un tout nouveau besoin de documentation.
Il faut dire que la tradition des livres et recueils de motifs remonte au Moyen Âge. On sait par exemple que les moines du IXᵉ siècle possédaient déjà des livres de modèles dont ils se servaient pour réaliser des évangiles manuscrits, richement enluminés. Parmi les bâtisseurs par contre, on avait depuis longtemps coutume de se transmettre de génération en génération, comme un secret bien gardé, des connaissances sur les lois architectoniques – par exemple, les règles de la statique –, mais aussi des propositions de motifs pour le décor architectural. Ce n'est qu'avec la formation de guildes d'artisans dont les membres étaient actifs dans plusieurs pays, et depuis l'invention de l'imprimerie (vers 1455), que s'est accéléré et amplifié le flux d'informations, ce qui devait permettre à un cercle élargi de personnes intéressées d'accéder rapidement aux modèles dessinés ou gravés. Ainsi apparurent les « planches ornementales » sous la forme de feuilles volantes ou d'ouvrages reliés dont les artisans d'art s'inspirèrent pour leurs propres esquisses d'ornements. Par la suite, une multitude de recueils de modèles fut mise en circulation – des études détaillées dessinées à la main aux planches d'encyclopédies retraçant l'histoire des styles. Enfin, la diffusion des recueils de modèles atteignit son apogée au XIXᵉ siècle avec la fondation de nombreuses écoles d'arts décoratifs et la multiplication d'emplois que l'ornementation a permis de créer dans des corporations entières, sur les chantiers, dans les entreprises artisanales, manufactures et ateliers. Un immense besoin d'ouvrages sur les styles et de modèles de motifs, publiés en polychromie souvent à grands frais en raison des nettes améliorations des techniques d'impression, se faisait désormais sentir.
Outre *The Grammar of Ornament* (Grammaire des ornements) d'Owen Jones, le recueil de motifs des Audsley est une des publications

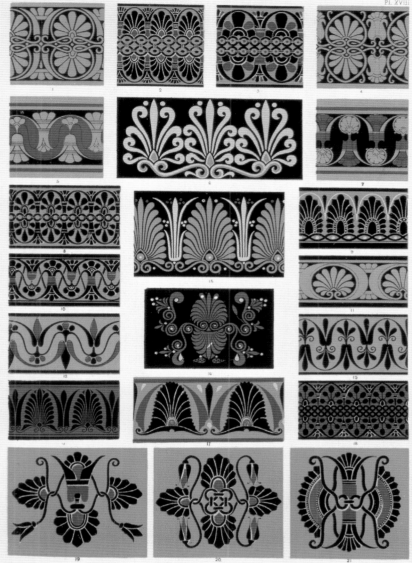

Thus "ornamental prints" began to appear, sometimes as loose leaves, and sometimes bound, which served craftsmen as inspiration for their own ornamental designs. The result was that numerous pattern-books came to be in circulation, ranging from hand-drawn detailed studies to surveys of the history of style in encyclopedias. The distribution of the pattern-book reached its zenith in the 19th century, when numerous craft schools were founded and ornamentation occupied whole trades on construction sites, in craft workshops, and in factories large and small. There was now a great demand for works on style and for pattern-books, which substantial improvements in printing technology now allowed to be published in what were in some cases very expensive multi-color editions.

(um 1455) beschleunigte und erweiterte sich der Informationsfluss, so dass gezeichnete Vorlagen oder Kupferstiche schnell einem größeren Interessentenkreis zugänglich wurden. So entstanden „ornamentale Drucke", die den Kunsthandwerkern teils in Form von Einzelblättern, teils in gebundener Form als Anregung für ihre eigenen Ornamententwürfe dienten. In der Folge kursierte eine Vielzahl von Vorlagenwerken – von handgezeichneten Detailstudien bis zu stilgeschichtlichen Übersichtstafeln in Enzyklopädien. Schließlich erreichte die Verbreitung von Vorlagenwerken im 19. Jahrhundert einen Höhepunkt, als zahlreiche Kunstgewerbeschulen gegründet wurden und das Ornamentieren ganze Berufsstände auf Baustellen, in Handwerksbetrieben, Manufakturen und in Fabriken beschäftigte. Jetzt bestand großer

les plus complètes et les plus importantes de cette époque. Leur recueil était structuré selon des critères stylistiques historiques et se distinguait par des conseils pratiques sur les couleurs et l'utilisation, placés en regard de chaque échantillon. Les motifs étaient principalement conçus pour décorer des bandeaux ornementaux ou des frises qui délimitaient le haut des murs et constituaient ainsi le raccord entre le mur et le plafond. Comme les pièces étaient le plus souvent décorées ou tapissées avec du papier de couleur, selon le goût de l'époque, les bandeaux ornementaux consistaient en dessins relativement dominants pour marquer un contraste avec le reste des murs. De plus, comme les pièces où l'on devait appliquer ces motifs étaient souvent spacieuses et hautes, on peut en quelque sorte parler

Left: Late 18th-century ornamental designs
These designs served as patterns for the decoration of weapons and other craft artifacts.

Links: Ornamententwürfe des späten 18. Jh.
Diese Ornamente dienten als Vorlage zur Verzierung von Waffen und kunsthandwerklichen Gegenständen.

À gauche : Esquisses d'ornements de la fin du XVIIIᵉ siècle
Ces ornements servirent de modèle pour la décoration d'armes et d'objets artisanaux.

Right: Extract from *The Grammar of Ornament* by Owen Jones, London, 1868
These patterns, inspired by the motifs of Greek Antiquity may well have stimulated the Audsleys to publish their own work.

Rechts: Auszug aus *The Grammar of Ornament* von Owen Jones, London, 1868
Diese von Motiven der griechischen Antike inspirierten Entwürfe dürften auch den Audsleys als Anregung für ihre Muster gedient haben.

À droite : Extrait de *The Grammar of Ornament* d'Owen Jones, Londres, 1868
Ces esquisses imitent des motifs de l'Antiquité grecque. Ils ont également dû inspirer les Audsley pour leurs propres esquisses.

Alongside *The Grammar of Ornament* by Owen Jones, the Audsleys' collection is one of the most comprehensive and most important publications of this period. Their folder was arranged by style-historical criteria, and was distinguished by the practical hints on coloration and use with which the Audsleys accompanied every design. The patterns were very largely intended as decorations for ornamental bands or friezes, or as crestings for walls, thus providing a transition between wall and ceiling. As the rooms themselves, in accordance with contemporary taste, generally had patterned or colored wallpaper, the ornamental bands tend to be fairly dominant, in order to stand out against these strong backgrounds. Moreover the rooms for which these patterns were intended were mostly large and high, so that in a sense it can be said that the patterns were designed to be seen from a distance.

The patterns in this edition are reproduced 20% smaller than the

Bedarf an stilkundlichen Werken und Mustervorlagen, die nach deutlichen Verbesserungen in der Drucktechnik in teilweise aufwändigen Vielfarbdrucken herausgebracht wurden.

Neben *The Grammar of Ornament* (Grammatik der Ornamente) von Owen Jones stellt die Mustersammlung der Audsleys eine der umfangreichsten und bedeutendsten Publikationen dieser Zeit dar. Ihre Sammelmappe war nach stilgeschichtlichen Kriterien geordnet und zeichnete sich durch die praktischen Hinweise zu Farbgebung und Verwendung aus, die die Audsleys einem jeden Entwurf zur Seite gestellt hatten. Die Muster waren überwiegend als Dekor für Ornamentbänder oder Friese gedacht, die als oberer Abschluss einer Wand angebracht wurden und somit zwischen Wand und Decke vermittelten. Da die Räume dem Zeitgeschmack entsprechend meist gemustert oder farbig tapeziert waren, fielen die Ornamentbänder verhältnismäßig dominant aus, um sich von der jeweiligen

d'une volonté de créer, avec ces ornements, un effet de trompe-l'œil. Les modèles présentés dans cette édition sont des reproductions réduites de 20 % par rapport aux originaux. On a donc tenu compte du fait que des ornements de ce type sont aujourd'hui plus rarement applicables dans des grands bâtiments publics et sont davantage destinés à de petits intérieurs privés, et qu'il faut donc réduire l'échelle pour obtenir l'effet désiré. Il va de soi que le recueil original n'est pas indispensable dans ce cas ; d'ailleurs, les Audsley, toujours soucieux de fournir des indications précises, ont signalé à plusieurs reprises que leurs esquisses pouvaient être agrandies ou réduites selon les proportions de la pièce concernée.

Contrairement à des réimpressions précédentes, le présent ouvrage ne se contente pas de reproduire purement et simplement les esquisses ornementales, mais il les commente en s'inspirant des notes explicatives des Audsley. Le lecteur

Wallpaper-printing press, England, 19th century
From the middle of the 19th century, the development of the rotary press made possible the production of printed wallpapers. They found a ready market, and created a demand for pattern-books which in turn provided a stimulus in the field of utilitarian design which was not confined to wallpaper and led to the establishment of colleges of applied art.

Tapetenpresse, England, 19. Jh.
Die Entwicklung von Papier- und Rotationsdruckmaschinen ermöglichte ab Mitte des 19. Jahrhunderts die Fertigung von bedruckten Papiertapeten, die schnell regen Zuspruch fanden. Der daraus erwachsende Bedarf an Musterzeichnungen führte zu einer Belebung des Gebrauchs-Designs, die auch in anderen Bereichen zu verzeichnen war und schließlich die Gründung von Kunstgewerbeschulen nach sich zog.

Presse à papiers peints, Angleterre, XIXe siècle
Le développement des presses à imprimer et rotatives permit de fabriquer, à partir du milieu du XIXe siècle, des papiers peints imprimés qui firent l'objet d'un vif engouement. Le besoin de motifs qui en résulta encouragea le développement du design utilitaire qui se manifesta aussi dans d'autres domaines et aboutit à la création d'écoles des arts décoratifs.

originals. This takes account of the circumstance that ornamentation is more likely to be used these days in smaller private rooms than in large public buildings, and that to this extent the scale of the ornaments must be reduced in order to achieve the desired effect. It goes without saying that the pattern-book in no way lays down the law in this respect. The Audsleys, always at pains to provide precise introductions, pointed out that their designs could be enlarged or reduced in scale to conform to the proportions of the room in which they were to be used.

Unlike earlier reprints, the present book does not confine itself to mere reproduction of the ornamental designs, but also provides a commentary on the basis of the Audsleys' own explanatory material. Thus readers are given hints on the use of the individual ornaments, on their stylistic background and on possible color schemes. In addition, the book has been expanded by the addition of art-historical introductions in which the stylistic and cultural background is investigated. And finally, the appendix provides detailed practical hints on the transfer and execution of the designs, thus enabling readers to use the patterns to decorate their own homes.

Hauptfläche abzuheben. Überdies waren die Räume, in denen diese Muster zur Anwendung kommen sollten, meist weitläufig und hoch, so dass man in gewisser Weise von einer bezweckten Fernwirkung der Ornamente sprechen kann.

Bei den in dieser Ausgabe abgebildeten Vorlagen handelt es sich um Reproduktionen, die um 20 % gegenüber der Größe der Originalentwürfe verkleinert sind. Damit wurde dem Umstand Rechnung getragen, dass in heutiger Zeit Ornamente dieser Art seltener in öffentlichen Großbauten als vielmehr in kleineren Privaträumen angebracht werden und dass insofern auch der Maßstab der Ornamente reduziert werden muss, um die angestrebte Wirkung zu enfalten. Selbstverständlich ist das Musterbuch in dieser Hinsicht nicht verbindlich, und so notierten schon die um präzise Anleitungen bemühten Audsleys immer wieder, dass ihre Entwürfe entsprechend den jeweiligen Raumproportionen vergrößert oder verkleinert werden könnten.

Das vorliegende Buch beschränkt sich im Gegensatz zu früheren Reprints nicht auf die reine Reproduktion der Ornamententwürfe, sondern kommentiert diese in Anlehnung an die Erläuterungstexte der Audsleys. So erhält der Leser Hinweise zur Verwendbarkeit der jeweiligen Ornamente, zu ihrem Stil und zu möglichen Farbgebungen. Darüber hinaus wurde das Buch um kunsthistorische Einleitungen ergänzt, in denen das stilgeschichtliche und kulturelle Umfeld der Ornamentik untersucht wird. Und schließlich werden im Anhang detaillierte praktische Anleitungen zur Übertragung und Ausführung der Ornamente gegeben, die es dem Leser ermöglichen, die vorgestellten Muster selber zur Dekoration seiner Wohnung zu verwenden.

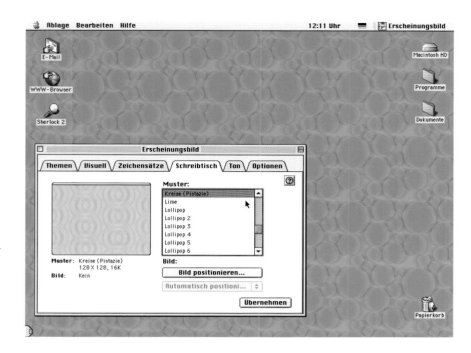

reçoit donc des conseils sur l'utilisation des ornements concernés, sur leur style et sur les combinaisons de couleurs possibles. De plus, l'ouvrage a été complété par des introductions sur l'histoire de l'art, qui évoquent le contexte culturel et stylistique de l'art ornemental. L'annexe contient enfin des indications pratiques et détaillées sur la transposition et l'exécution des ornements ; celles-ci permettront au lecteur d'utiliser les motifs proposés pour décorer son propre intérieur.

Background pattern for a computer screen, 2000
Late-20th century computer graphics have led to a revival of interest in ornamentation. Computers, for example, often come with a selection of pre-programmed graphic designs, allowing users a wide choice of individual screen background displays.

Hintergrundmuster für einen Computer-Bildschirm, 2000
Computer-Grafiker des 20. Jahrhunderts haben die Freude am Ornament neu aufleben lassen: So werden Computer oftmals mit vorprogrammierten Musterkatalogen ausgeliefert, die es dem Nutzer erlauben, aus einer breiten Palette ein individuelles Rapportmuster für den Bildschirmhintergrund seines Computers auszuwählen.

Motif d'arrière-plan pour écran d'ordinateur, 2000
Des infographistes du XXe siècle ont fait revivre l'ornement et les joies qu'il procure : les ordinateurs sont, par exemple, souvent fournis avec des catalogues de motifs préprogrammés permettant à l'utilisateur de sélectionner un motif individuel répétitif dans une palette étendue pour l'arrière-plan de son écran d'ordinateur.

A Short History of Ornament
Kleine Ornamentgeschichte
Bref historique de l'art ornemental

The development and heyday of ornamentation

Since time immemorial, one of mankind's characteristics has been a pleasure in beauty and in decorative objects. As early as the later part of the paleolithic period, or Old Stone Age (c. 30,000 BC), there is evidence of horn and stone utensils with ornamental scratched drawings – simple lines, in other words, which generate particular patterns. In all the millennia since then, this marked iconic character has been one of the determining features of ornament. The ornamentation of the early historical period was based exclusively on simple geometric forms, including circles, squares and triangles, from which ovals, rectangles and lozenges were derived. In addition, rhythmic line-drawings can be seen, along with zigzag bands, wavy lines, and a whole variety of spiral forms, to which a symbolic meaning is often attributed. Almost all early civilizations and all non-urban cultures used these motifs. They can be found as decorations on pottery, and when metalworking first appeared during the Bronze Age (c. 3000 BC), on metallic utensils, weapons and personal adornments too. It can also be assumed that early people employed some simple form of painting the body, probably applied in the context of religious ceremonies.

Interior decoration in the broadest sense – the subject of this book – can be documented since the age of the early cave-dwelling peoples, who invoked fortune in the chase by painting their intended quarry on the walls of their caves and often depicted themselves as hunters. Thus from prehistory and early history we are familiar with a whole

Entstehung der Ornamentik

Seit jeher ist beim Menschen ein Hang zum Schönen und Schmückenden ausgeprägt. Bereits im Jungpaläolithikum (etwa 30 000 v. Chr.) sind einfache Gerätschaften aus Horn und Stein belegt, die mit ornamentalen Ritzzeichnungen verziert sind, mit einfachen Linien also, die bestimmte Muster erzeugen. Dieser ausgeprägte Zeichencharakter gehört mit zu den bestimmenden Wesensmerkmalen des Ornaments, der auch in den folgenden Jahrtausenden erhalten blieb. Die frühgeschichtliche Ornamentik basiert fast ausschließlich auf einfachen geometrischen Formen, zu denen Kreise, Quadrate und Dreiecke gehören, von denen sich Ovale, Rechtecke und Rauten ableiten. Außerdem sieht man rhythmische Strichzeichnungen und Reihungen sowie Zickzack-Bänder, Wellenlinien und die unterschiedlichsten Ausprägungen von Spiralen, denen häufig ein Symbolcharakter zugesprochen wird. Nahezu alle frühen Kulturen und alle Naturvölker haben sich dieser Motive bedient. Sie finden sich als Keramikdekor und mit dem Aufkommen der Metallverarbeitung seit der Bronzezeit (etwa 3000 v. Chr.) auch auf Gerätschaften, Waffen und Schmuck. Ebenso ist anzunehmen, dass die Menschen der Frühzeit schon eine einfache Form der Körperbemalung kannten, die sie wahrscheinlich im Rahmen von Zeremonien vornahmen. Innenraumverzierungen im weitesten Sinne – Thema des vorliegenden Buches – sind ab der Zeit der frühen Höhlenmenschen belegt, die ihr Jagdglück beschworen, indem sie die zu erlegenden Tiere an die Wände ihrer Höhlen malten und sich selber häufig als Jäger darstellten. So kennen

Naissance et apogée de l'art ornemental

L'homme a toujours eu un penchant pour tout ce qui est beau et décoratif. Dès le paléolithique inférieur (environ 30 000 ans avant J.-C.), de simples outils de corne et de pierre sont garnis de dessins ornementaux gravés, de simples traits formant des motifs particuliers. Ce caractère linéaire prononcé constitue un des éléments-clés de l'ornement, qui s'est conservé au cours des millénaires suivants. L'art ornemental préhistorique se base presque exclusivement sur des formes géométriques simples, par exemple des cercles, carrés et triangles, qui donneront naissance aux ovales, rectangles et losanges. On rencontre en outre des dessins au trait rythmés et des alignements, ainsi que des bandeaux en zigzag, des lignes ondulées et les expressions les plus diverses de spirales auxquelles on attribue

Stone-age wall paintings in the Grotta dei Cervi, Apulia
The walls of the Grotta dei Cervi are decorated with painted motifs both abstract and figurative. They include hunting scenes with archers shooting at stags, together with labyrinthine patterns reminiscent of spirals – probably the most common motif in prehistory and early history, and one that has been taken up by all subsequent cultures.

Steinzeitliche Wandmalereien in der Grotta dei Cervi, Apulien
Die Wände der Grotta dei Cervi sind mit Malereien ausgestattet, die sowohl figürliche als auch abstrakte Motive zeigen. So erkennt man Jagdszenen, in denen Jäger mit Pfeil und Bogen auf Hirsche schießen und daneben labyrinthische Gebilde, die formal an die Spirale erinnern – das wohl häufigste Ornament der Vor- und Frühgeschichte, das auch in allen späteren Kulturen fortlebte.

Peintures rupestres de l'âge de la pierre dans la Grotta dei Cervi, Apulie
Les parois de la Grotta dei Cervi sont recouvertes de peintures qui présentent des motifs aussi bien figuratifs qu'abstraits. On y reconnaît des scènes où des chasseurs tirent à l'arc sur des cervidés et à côté, des sortes de labyrinthes qui, par leur forme, rappellent la spirale – l'ornement le plus courant de la préhistoire et de la protohistoire qui s'est également perpétué dans des cultures ultérieures.

Photograph donated by Ninì Ciccarese

series of cave drawings, such as the austerely linear depictions in the Grotta dei Cervi cave in southern Italy, whose abstract character is such that particularly in our own day they command great admiration, now that 20th-century art has itself experienced practically every stage of abstraction. But from prehistory and early history onwards, ornamentation has accompanied mankind through every stage of our development, and has never lost contact with the mental attitudes and concepts of art that characterized each particular epoch.

wir aus der Vor- und Frühgeschichte eine ganze Reihe von Höhlenzeichnungen, wie zum Beispiel die figurativen, streng linearen Darstellungen aus der Grotta dei Cervi in Süditalien, denen ein so hoher Abstraktionsgrad zugrunde liegt, dass sie uns gerade in heutiger Zeit ein Höchstmaß an Bewunderung abverlangen, nachdem die Kunst des 20. Jahrhunderts fast alle Stufen der Abstraktion durchlaufen hat. Die Ornamentik aber hat sich von der Vor- und Frühgeschichte durch alle Entwicklungsstufen der Menschheit gezogen und dabei stets einen Bezug zur Geisteshaltung und Kunstauffassung der jeweiligen Epoche gefunden.

souvent un caractère symbolique. Presque tous les peuples et cultures primitifs se sont servis de ces motifs qui se retrouvent dans les décors de céramiques et, avec le travail des métaux depuis l'âge du bronze (environ 3000 avant J.-C.), dans les outils, les armes et les bijoux. On est également en droit de supposer que les hommes préhistoriques connaissaient déjà une forme simple de peintures corporelles qu'ils réalisaient probablement dans le cadre de cérémonies.
La décoration intérieure dans le sens le plus large du terme, et c'est le propos de ce livre, existe depuis l'époque des premiers hommes qui, pour se porter chance, peignaient les animaux à abattre sur les parois de leurs grottes et se représentaient souvent eux-mêmes en chasseurs. C'est ainsi que la protohistoire et la préhistoire nous ont livré toute une série de peintures rupestres, par exemple les représentations figuratives, strictement linéaires de la « Grotta dei Cervi » (grottes aux cerfs) au sud de l'Italie, basées sur un degré d'abstraction tel qu'elles suscitent chez nous un émerveillement extrême alors qu'aujourd'hui, justement, l'art du XXe siècle a passé par presque tous les échelons de l'abstraction. L'art ornemental a toutefois suivi, depuis la préhistoire et la protohistoire, toutes les phases de l'évolution de l'humanité et y a toujours trouvé une référence à la tournure d'esprit et à la conception artistique de l'époque concernée.

Antiquity

Antike

L'Antiquité

The beginnings of early Greek ornamentation lie in Cretan and Mycenean art (c. 2900–1600/1200 BC), and above all in the (in many cases) well-preserved pottery of the period. In vase-painting, there developed an individual style characterized by geometrically linear shapes, for which reason it is also known as the "geometric style". Alongside simpler shapes, spirals soon appeared, and above all the family of patterns variously known as the meander, Greek key, or fret – an ornamental band typical of

Die Anfänge der antiken griechischen Ornamentik liegen in der kretisch-mykenischen Kunst (etwa 2900–1600/1200 v. Chr.) und hier vor allem in der teilweise gut erhaltenen Keramik. In der Vasenmalerei hatte man einen eigenen Kunststil geprägt, der von geometrisch linearen Formen bestimmt wurde, weshalb er auch „geometrischer Stil" genannt wird. Neben einfachen Formen bildeten sich bald auch Spiralen und vor allem der Mäander heraus, jenes für die Antike charakteristische Ornamentband mit sich recht-

Les débuts de l'art ornemental grec antique remontent à l'art mycénien et crétois (environ 2900–1600/1200 avant J.-C.) et surtout à la céramique en partie bien conservée. C'est dans la peinture des vases que s'est exprimé un style artistique spécifique, déterminé par des formes géométriquement linéaires, d'où le nom de « style géométrique ». À côté de formes simples, on vit bientôt apparaître aussi des spirales et surtout le méandre, bandeau ornemental caractéristique de l'Antiquité avec ses lignes brisées à

Left: Gold beaker, Archaeological Museum, Chara, 6th century BC
This elaborate beaker was a grave-gift to accompany the deceased into the next world. This explains the rich ornamentation – waves were a symbol of water and of life.

Links: Goldener Becher, Archäologisches Museum, Chara, 6. Jh. v. Chr.
Bei diesem kostbaren Becher handelt es sich um eine Grabbeigabe, die der Verstorbene mit ins Jenseits nehmen sollte. Aus diesem besonderen Zweck erklärt sich die reiche Ornamentierung mit Wellenmotiven, dem Symbol des Wassers und des Lebens.

À gauche : Gobelet en or, Musée archéologique, Chara, VIe siècle avant J.-C.
Ce précieux gobelet est une urne que le défunt était censé emporter dans l'au-delà. La destination particulière de cet objet explique la riche décoration avec des motifs de vagues, symbole de l'eau et de la vie.

Classical Antiquity, consisting of lines "twisting" at right angles. The name "meander" comes from a river famous for its twists and turns, the Meandros. In the succeeding period, geometric patterns were joined by vegetal motifs, which increased in importance from the 8th century BC onward. The influence of oriental and Egyptian art was the inspiration behind the vegetal motifs characteristic of the Hellenistic period – the ancient Egyptian lotus blossom and lily motifs, for example, which in slightly altered form reappear in the architectural decoration of Classical Antiquity. However, the most important "nature" motif in the whole history of ornament is probably the acanthus, a thistle-like plant found in the Mediterranean region, whose deeply indented pointed leaves underwent numerous stylizations before the Classical period was out, and in the form of the palmette often decorated the pediments of Classical temples. The "lotus-and-palmette frieze", also known as the "anthemion", became a popular design element and achieved what is probably its most beautiful manifestation on the

winklig brechenden Linien, das seinen Namen von dem windungsreichen Fluss Mäandros ableitet. Zu den geometrischen Motiven traten in der Folgezeit pflanzliche Ornamente, die ab dem 8. Jahrhundert v. Chr. zunehmend an Bedeutung gewannen. Unter dem Einfluss der orientalischen und ägyptischen Kunst bildete sich der vegetabile Dekor des Hellenismus heraus, so etwa die alt-ägyptischen Motive der Lotusblüte und der Lilie, die sich in leicht abgewandelter Form beim antiken Baudekor wiederfinden. Das wohl bedeutendste aus der Natur entlehnte Motiv in der Geschichte der Ornamentik ist jedoch der Akanthus, ein distelartiges Gewächs des Mittelmeerraumes, das mit seinen spitzzackigen Blättern bereits in der Antike die unterschiedlichsten Stilisierungen erfuhr und in Form einer Palmette oft Giebel und Stirnziegel antiker Tempel schmückte. Der „Lotus- und Palmettenfries", der auch als „Anthemion" bekannt ist, wurde zu einem beliebten Gestaltungselement und fand seine wohl schönste Ausführung im 4. Jahrhundert vor Chr. am Erechtheion in Athen. Neben Friesen und Gesims-

angle droit qui doit son nom au fleuve sinueux, le Méandre. Des ornements végétaux qui ont pris de plus en plus d'importance à partir du VIIIe siècle avant J.-C. ont succédé aux motifs géométriques. Le décor végétal de l'hellénisme est né sous l'influence de l'art oriental et égyptien, par exemple les motifs égyptiens anciens de la fleur de lotus et du lis, qui se retrouvent sous une forme légèrement modifiée dans le décor architectural antique. L'acanthe, plante ressemblant au chardon qui pousse dans le bassin méditerranéen, est le principal motif emprunté à la nature dans l'histoire de l'art ornemental ; avec ses feuilles dentelées, elle a connu les stylisations les plus diverses pendant l'Antiquité et orna souvent les frontons et antéfixes de temples antiques sous la forme d'une palmette. La « frise de lotus et de palmettes », également connue sous le nom d'« anthémion », devint un élément architectural très prisé et trouva sa plus belle expression au IVe siècle dans l'Erechthéion à Athènes. À côté des frises et ornements de corniches, on rencontre l'acanthe à partir du IVe siècle avant J.-C., surtout

Opposite, top left: Acanthus, etching, 1713
The acanthus, with its jagged-toothed leaves, is one of the most frequent ornamental motifs. It was widely used in Classical Antiquity for Corinthian capitals and elsewhere. The acanthus provides the basis for the leaf-and-tendril motifs, which became increasingly important in the art of the Middle Ages.

Gegenüberliegende Seite oben links: Akanthus, Kupferstich von 1713
Der spitzzackige Akanthus stellt eins der am häufigsten verwendeten Motive der Ornamentik dar. Bereits in der Antike diente er als Vorbild für korinthische Kapitelle und andere Dekorationselemente. Vom Akanthus leitet sich die Blattranke ab, die vor allem in der Kunst des Mittelalters zunehmend an Bedeutung gewann.

Page ci-contre, en haut à gauche : Acanthe, eau-forte de 1713
L'acanthe aux feuilles dentelées est l'un des motifs les plus fréquents de l'art ornemental. Dans l'Antiquité déjà, elle servait de modèle pour des chapiteaux corinthiens et d'autres éléments décoratifs. L'entrelacs de feuilles est dérivé de l'acanthe et occupa une place de plus en plus importante surtout dans l'art médiéval.

Opposite, bottom: Ivory tablet with lotus blossoms, Samaria, 9th–8th century BC
This ivory tablet has a frieze of alternating lotus blossoms and buds. According to ancient Egyptian mythology, the lotus was a symbol of eternal life.

Gegenüberliegende Seite unten: Elfenbeintafel mit Lotusblüten, Samaria, 9./8. Jh. v. Chr.
Diese Elfenbeintafel zeigt einen Fries rapportierender Lotusblüten und -knospen. Der Lotus galt nach alt-ägyptischem Mythos als Sinnbild des ewigen Lebens.

Page ci-contre, en bas : Plaque d'ivoire à fleurs de lotus, Samaria, IXe-VIIIe siècle avant J.-C.
Cette plaque d'ivoire montre une frise de fleurs et de boutons de lotus récurrents. Dans la mythologie de l'Egypte ancienne, le lotus était le symbole de la vie éternelle.

Acanthus Spinofus.

Erechtheion in Athens, built in the 4th century BC. While common in friezes and cornice decorations, the acanthus is seen most often, from the 4th century BC onward, in the capitals of Corinthian columns, which were readopted time and again by architects in succeeding centuries. The actual significance of the acanthus can be seen in the fact that this motif, like almost no other, keeps recurring throughout the

verzierungen sieht man den Akanthus jedoch ab dem 4. Jahrhundert v. Chr. vor allem an den korinthischen Säulenkapitellen, die über Jahrhunderte hinweg in der Baukunst immer wieder aufgegriffen werden sollten. Die tatsächliche Bedeutung des Akanthus lässt sich auch daran ablesen, dass sich dieses Motiv wie kaum ein anderes durch die gesamte Entwicklungsgeschichte des europäischen Ornaments

dans les chapiteaux corinthiens de colonnes qui allaient être repris quelques siècles plus tard dans l'art architectural. Le fait que ce motif soit un des rares éléments à figurer dans toute l'histoire de l'évolution de l'ornement européen dévoile la signification réelle de l'acanthe. Des stylisations de l'acanthe se rencontrent donc non seulement dans l'art romain que l'Antiquité grecque a adapté à partir du IIe siècle

Above: Acanthus capital, Gerasa, c. 2nd century AD
Unlike the Corinthian capital, this example has just one ring of acanthus leaves carved in high relief. It is one of the best examples of provincial Roman capital sculpture from the Near East in the period of Late Antiquity.

Oben: Akanthus-Kapitell, Gerasa, ca. 2. Jh. n. Chr.
Dieses Kapitell zeigt im Gegensatz zum korinthischen Kapitell nur einen einzigen Blattkranz tief eingeschnittener, plastisch hervortretender Akanthusblätter. Seine Ausarbeitung zählt mit zu den besten Leistungen spätantiker Kapitellskulptur in der römischen Provinzialkunst des Nahen Ostens.

En haut : Chapiteau à feuilles d'acanthe, Gerasa, environ IIe siècle après J.-C.
Contrairement au chapiteau corinthien, ce chapiteau ne présente qu'un entrelacs de feuilles d'acanthe sculptées en relief. Son exécution compte parmi les meilleures réalisations de la sculpture de chapiteaux de l'Antiquité finissante dans l'art provincial romain du Proche-Orient.

Cornice of the Erechtheion on the Acropolis, Athens, 421–406 BC
This cornice is decorated with the Classical anthemion, an alternation of palmettes with lotus blossoms. Above can be seen the Classical egg-and-dart frieze.

Gesims des Erechtheion auf der Akropolis, Athen, 421–406 v. Chr.
Dieses Gesims wird vom Anthemion, einem klassischen Ornament, geziert, bei dem sich Palmetten mit Lotusblüten abwechseln. Darüber sieht man den klassischen Eierstab.

Corniche de l'Erechthéion sur l'Acropole, Athènes, 421–406 avant J.-C.
Cette corniche est ornée d'un « anthémion », ornement classique présentant une alternance de palmettes et de fleurs de lotus. Au-dessus, on peut voir l'ove classique.

Below: Column with capital and cornice, designed by G. A. and M. A. Audsley, 1892
This design by the Audsleys, though highly stylized, is clearly inspired by Classical Antiquity.

Unten: Säule mit Kapitell und Gesims, Entwurf von G. A. und M. A. Audsley, 1892
Bei diesem Entwurf haben sich die Audsleys trotz aller Stilisierung erkennbar an antiken Vorbildern orientiert.

En bas : Colonne avec chapiteau et corniche, esquisse de G. A. Audsley et M. A. Audsley, 1892
Malgré la stylisation, on reconnaît dans cette esquisse une nette inspiration des modèles antiques.

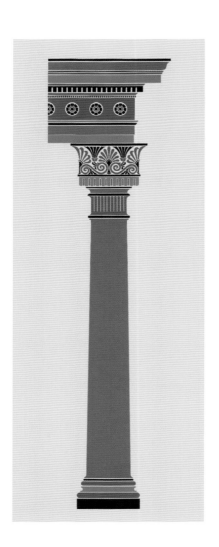

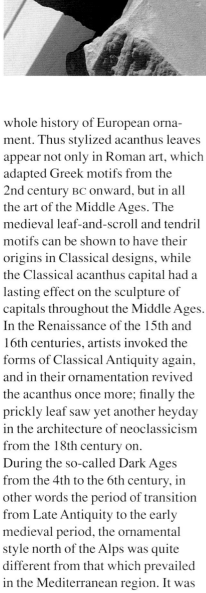

whole history of European ornament. Thus stylized acanthus leaves appear not only in Roman art, which adapted Greek motifs from the 2nd century BC onward, but in all the art of the Middle Ages. The medieval leaf-and-scroll and tendril motifs can be shown to have their origins in Classical designs, while the Classical acanthus capital had a lasting effect on the sculpture of capitals throughout the Middle Ages. In the Renaissance of the 15th and 16th centuries, artists invoked the forms of Classical Antiquity again, and in their ornamentation revived the acanthus once more; finally the prickly leaf saw yet another heyday in the architecture of neoclassicism from the 18th century on.
During the so-called Dark Ages from the 4th to the 6th century, in other words the period of transition from Late Antiquity to the early medieval period, the ornamental style north of the Alps was quite different from that which prevailed in the Mediterranean region. It was characterized by animal figures,

zieht. So sieht man Stilisierungen des Akanthus nicht nur in der römischen Kunst, die ab dem 2. Jahrhundert v. Chr. die griechische Antike adaptierte, sondern auch in der gesamten Kunst des Mittelalters: Der mittelalterliche Rankendekor leitet sich in seinem Ursprung von der klassischen Akanthus-Wellenranke ab, während das antike Akanthus-Kapitell die gesamte Kapitellplastik des Mittelalters nachhaltig beeinflusste. In der Renaissance besann man sich im 15. und 16. Jahrhundert auf die antike Kunst und ließ in der Ornamentik besonders das Akanthusmotiv wieder aufleben, und schließlich erlebte der Akanthus eine neuerliche Blüte im Baudekor des Klassizismus ab dem 18. Jahrhundert.
Während der Völkerwanderungszeit, die vom 4. bis 6. Jahrhundert n. Chr. den Übergang von der Spätantike zum frühen Mittelalter markierte, herrschte nördlich der Alpen ein vollkommen andersartiger Ornamentstil als im Mittelmeerraum vor. Er zeigte stilisierte Tierfiguren, die

avant J.-C., mais aussi dans tout l'art du Moyen Âge : l'entrelacs médiéval est à l'origine dérivé de l'entrelacs classique de vagues et d'acanthes, tandis que le chapiteau antique à feuilles d'acanthe a exercé une influence durable sur toute la sculpture de chapiteaux du Moyen Âge. À l'époque de la Renaissance, c'est-à-dire aux XVᵉ et XVIᵉ siècles, on se souvint de l'art antique et on remit en définitive le motif de l'acanthe au goût du jour dans l'art ornemental ; l'acanthe connut enfin à partir du XVIIIᵉ siècle un nouvel âge d'or dans le décor architectural du néoclassicisme.
Au cours des grandes invasions qui, du IVᵉ au VIᵉ siècle après J.-C., ont marqué la transition entre l'Antiquité et le Moyen Âge, un style ornemental totalement différent de celui du bassin méditerranéen prédomina au nord des Alpes. Il présentait des figures animales stylisées fréquemment entrelacées et révélant un degré d'abstraction élevé. Du point de vue de la forme, ce style est dérivé de

often mutually intertwined, and evincing a high degree of abstraction. This style derives its forms from Celtic exemplars, in which spiral and plaited elements are frequent motifs, often in combination with animals in what is called the zoomorphic style.

The Middle Ages

The Celtic style also had a direct effect on early medieval book illumination. In the 9th century AD, Irish monks founded a monastery on the island of Iona off the western coast of Scotland. Here the famous *Book of Kells* was written, which is now kept in the library of Trinity College, Dublin. This book of the gospels is richly decorated with interlaced scrolls, latticework and stylized animal and human figures, and represents one of the most beautiful examples of medieval book illustration ever created. The initials are particularly richly illuminated: they depict latticework and scrolls alienated almost past recognition; they too are often interlaced with human and animal figures. The forms of Classical Antiquity also found their way into medieval book illumination, however. The monks not only translated Classical texts, but adopted the decorative elements of Antiquity, such as the acanthus, which, stylistically developed, was to leave its mark on medieval ornamentation over the centuries. It was used to decorate portals, columns, friezes and cornices, as well as for the sculptural elements of capitals, where it attained its most beautiful manifestation.

In the Gothic period, geometric elements, such as tracery, are increasingly found alongside leaf-and-tendril ornamentation. Tracery is the openwork patterning in stone, constructed by means of plumb line and dividers, used to decorated windows, whether round, or in the form of pointed arches. This austere tracery was not supplanted by vegetal designs until the late-Gothic period, when motifs such as the trefoil, quatrefoil and cinquefoil are frequent, along with the flamelike

häufig miteinander verschlungen sind und einen hohen Grad an Abstraktion aufweisen. Formal leitet er sich von der keltischen Ornamentik ab, die oft Spiralen und Flechtbandmuster zeigt, und in Verbindung mit den Tierfiguren den so genannten Tierstil ausprägt.

Mittelalter

Der keltische Stil hatte auch einen unmittelbaren Einfluss auf die frühmittelalterliche Buchmalerei. Irische Mönche gründeten im 9. Jahrhundert n. Chr. auf der Insel Iona, an der Westküste Schottlands, ein Kloster, in dem das berühmte *Book of Kells* geschrieben wurde, das sich heute in der Bibliothek des Trinity College in Dublin befindet. Dieses reich mit Flechtbandornamentik, mit stilisierten Tierfiguren und Menschendarstellungen verzierte Evangeliar stellt eines der schönsten Exemplare mittelalterlicher Buchmalerei dar. Vor allem die Anfangsbuchstaben der Texte – die Initialen – wurden besonders prächtig verziert: Sie zeigen fast bis zur Unkenntlichkeit verfremdete Flechtbänder und Rankenmotive, die oft von Menschen und Tierfiguren durchdrungen werden.

Ebenso kam es in der mittelalterlichen Buchmalerei aber auch zu einer Auseinandersetzung mit der Antike. Die Mönche in den Klöstern übersetzten nicht nur antike Schriften, sondern sie verwandten auch die Ornamente der Antike, wie zum Beispiel die Akanthusranke, die als Blattranke stilistisch weiterentwickelt über Jahrhunderte hinweg die mittelalterliche Ornamentik prägen sollte. Sie wurde als Dekor von Portalen, Säulen, Friesen und Gesimsen verwandt sowie in der Kapitellplastik, wo sie ihre schönsten Ausprägungen fand.

In der Gotik treten neben das Laub- und Rankenwerk wieder zunehmend geometrische Formen, wie zum Beispiel das Maßwerk, jene mit Lot und Zirkel „gemessenen", d. h. konstruierten Ornamente, die als Füllung von Fensterrosetten und Spitzbogenfenstern zu sehen sind. Diese strenge Ornamentik sollte erst in der Spätgotik von vegetabilen Formen

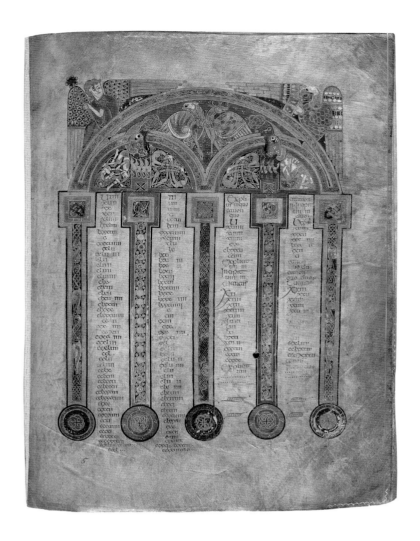

l'art ornemental celtique qui fait souvent appel aux spirales et aux rinceaux et qui, en association avec les figures animales, a marqué ce qu'on appelle le style animalier.

Le Moyen Âge

Le style celtique avait aussi exercé une influence directe sur l'enluminure du début du Moyen Âge. Au IXe siècle après J.-C., des moines irlandais fondèrent sur l'île d'Iona, sur la côte ouest de l'Écosse, un cloître dans lequel fut écrit le célèbre *Book of Kells* qui se trouve aujourd'hui à la bibliothèque du Trinity College à Dublin. Cet évangéliaire richement orné de rinceaux, de figures animales stylisées et de représentations humaines est un des plus beaux exemples d'enluminure médiévale. Les initiales des textes surtout étaient décorées d'une manière somptueuse avec des rinceaux et des entrelacs souvent traversés par des figures humaines et animales insolites et si chargés qu'ils les rendaient presque illisibles.

Book of Kells, Trinity College, Dublin, 8th–9th century
The collection of gospels known as the *Book of Kells* was originally intended for use at the altar. It is characterized by exuberant ornamentation in the typical Celtic style, with interlaced patterns and stylized representations of animals, angels, and the evangelists.

Book of Kells, Trinity College, Dublin, 8./9. Jh.
Das als *Book of Kells* bekannte Evangeliar war ursprünglich für den Gebrauch am Altar bestimmt. Es zeichnet sich durch seine überreiche Ornamentik aus, die vom keltischen Stil beeinflusst ist. So sieht man Flechtbandornamente und Blattranken neben stilisierten Tierfiguren, Engeln und Evangelistendarstellungen.

Book of Kells, Trinity College, Dublin, VIIIe–IXe siècle
L'évangéliaire connu sous le nom de *Book of Kells* devait, à l'origine, être utilisé à l'autel. Il se distingue par ses ornements extrêmement riches, influencés par le style celtique. On y voit par exemple des rinceaux et des entrelacs de feuilles côtoyer des figures animales stylisées, des anges et des représentations évangéliques.

Ceiling of the church of St Maria zur Höhe, Soest, early-13th century
This Romanesque ceiling is characterized by rich decoration on a white plaster background, and in particular by the broad bands of geometric patterns which subdivide the vault in a crosswise fashion. The individual fields are decorated with tree-like tendril motifs and medallions with geometric designs. The spandrels are occupied by little gryphons and depictions of the evangelists.

shapes which gave late Gothic the name of "flamboyant" in France. In addition, cathedrals and other large churches display magnificent ribbed and fan vaulting, which must also be included among the outstanding achievements of the Gothic period. Ornamental art in the West has always been characterized by the presence of regional specialities which have been of greater or lesser

des Maßwerks abgelöst werden, wie zum Beispiel der Fischblase, die den Flamboyant-Stil mit prägten. Außerdem sieht man in den Kathedralen und anderen großen Kirchen herrliche Stern- und Fächergewölbe, die mit zu den herausragendsten Leistungen der Gotik gehören.
Zu allen Zeiten gab es in der Ornamentik des Abendlandes regionale Sonderformen, die für die jeweilige

Mais même dans l'enluminure médiévale, c'est toujours à l'Antiquité qu'on se confronte. Les moines ne traduisaient pas seulement des écrits antiques dans les cloîtres, ils utilisaient aussi les ornements de l'Antiquité, par exemple l'entrelacs d'acanthe, qui devait marquer l'art ornemental de tout le Moyen Âge sous une forme stylistique évoluée de l'entrelacs de feuille. Il a servi à décorer portails, colonnes, frises et corniches, mais c'est dans la sculpture de chapiteaux qu'il trouva ses plus belles expressions.
À l'époque du gothique, on utilise de plus en plus de formes géométriques en combinaison avec les feuillages et entrelacs, par exemple la dentelle de pierre, ces ornements « mesurés » au fil à plomb et au compas, c'est-à-dire « construits », qui servent de raccords aux vitraux à rosaces et aux fenêtres en ogive. Cet art ornemental strict ne devait être supplanté par des formes végétales de la dentelle de pierre qu'à l'époque du gothique tardif, par exemple la vessie de poisson qui a marqué le style flamboyant. De plus, on rencontre dans les cathédrales et d'autres grandes églises de somptueuses voûtes en étoile et en éventail qui appartiennent aux réalisations majeures du gothique.
De tout temps, des formes régionales particulières ont eu, dans l'art ornemental de l'Occident, une importance plus ou moins grande pour l'évolution du style de l'époque. Parmi celles-ci, il faut citer le catalogue de formes extraordinairement riche datant de l'époque de la domination maure (du VIIIe au XVe siècle) et qui s'est surtout maintenu dans le sud de l'Espagne, ainsi que le décor manuélin inventif du Portugal au début du XVIe siècle. Si le style mixte manuélin est demeuré limité dans le temps et dans l'espace, l'influence de l'art ornemental islamique s'est par contre fait sentir dans différents pays d'Europe à des époques ultérieures, notamment dans l'historisme du XIXe siècle.

Gewölbe von St. Maria zur Höhe, Soest, frühes 13. Jh.
Dieses romanische Gewölbe weist eine reiche Ornamentierung auf weißem Putz auf. Bestimmendes Merkmal sind die breiten, mit geometrischen Mustern gezierten Bänder, die das Gewölbe kreuzförmig unterteilen. Die einzelnen Felder werden von baumartigen Rankengebilden und Medaillons mit geometrischem Dekor ausgeschmückt. In den Zwickeln sieht man Evangelistendarstellungen und kleine Greifen.

Voûte de Santa Maria zur Höhe, Soest, début du XIIIe siècle
Cette voûte romane présente de riches ornements sur du crépi blanc. Les larges bandeaux décorés de motifs géométriques en forme de croix qui divisent la voûte sont caractéristiques. Les divers panneaux sont ornés d'entrelacs en forme d'arbres et de médaillons au décor géométrique. On peut voir dans les écoinçons des représentations évangéliques et de petits griffons.

importance further afield. In particular, in this connection, one might note the extraordinary wealth of forms which appeared under Moorish rule in southern Spain (8th–15th century), and the highly original "Manuelan" style in early 16th-century Portugal. While the hybrid Manuelan style was confined to this place and period, the influence of Islamic decorative art made itself felt in various European countries in later periods too, in particular during the era of Revivalism in the 19th century.

Stilentwicklung von mehr oder weniger weit reichender Bedeutung waren. Besonders hervorzuheben sind unter diesen der außerordentlich reiche Formenschatz, der sich vor allem im Süden Spaniens aus der Zeit der maurischen Regierung (8.–15. Jahrhundert) erhalten hat, sowie der phantasievolle manuelinische Dekor Portugals aus dem frühen 16. Jahrhundert. Während der manuelinische Mischstil zeitlich und territorial begrenzt blieb, lässt sich der Einfluss der islamischen Ornamentik auch in späteren Epochen, vor allem im Historismus des 19. Jahrhunderts, in verschiedenen Ländern Europas nachvollziehen.

Renaissance

The Renaissance was characterized by a rediscovery of Classical Antiquity which was to have a lasting effect on the intellectual and artistic history of the West. In the field of decorative art, too, Classical motifs were employed once more, for example the fret and the acanthus. However, a new form of ornamentation was also created, in the form of the "Grotesque", which combined vegetal forms, animals, human figures and fabulous creatures of all kinds, harking back to motifs taken from Roman mural paintings and rediscovered during

Renaissance

In der Renaissance kam es zu einer Wiederentdeckung der Antike, die nachhaltige Auswirkungen auf die Geistes- und Kunstgeschichte des Abendlandes haben sollte. Auch in der Ornamentik nahm man jetzt klassische antike Motive wieder auf, so etwa das Mäanderband und das Akanthusmotiv. Allerdings wurde mit der Groteske auch eine neue Ornamentgattung geschaffen, die pflanzliche Formen, Tiere, menschliche Darstellungen und Fabelwesen aller Art vereint und auf Motive römischer Wandmalereien zurückgeht, die in der Renaissance wieder

La Renaissance

Sous la Renaissance, on redécouvrit l'Antiquité, ce qui devait avoir des répercussions durables sur l'histoire des idées et de l'art en Occident. On reprenait désormais des motifs antiques classiques comme le bandeau de méandres et l'acanthe, jusque dans l'art ornemental. La grotesque donna toutefois lieu à un nouveau genre ornemental qui réunissait toutes sortes de formes végétales, d'animaux, de représentations humaines et de créatures fabuleuses et recourait à des motifs de peintures murales romaines redécouvertes sous la Renaissance.

Octagonal vault of the Chapter House of York Minster, c. 1260
Lofty stained-glass windows with ornamental tracery are just as typical of Gothic church architecture as is the subtle decoration using largely vegetal motifs.

Sterngewölbe im Kapitelhaus der Kathedrale von York, begonnen um 1260
Hochaufragende, farbig und mit Maßwerk gestaltete Fenster sind ebenso typische Merkmale des gotischen Kirchenbaus wie die subtile Ausgestaltung mit zumeist vegetabilen Ornamenten.

Voûte en étoile dans la salle capitulaire de la cathédrale de York, commencée vers 1260
Les fenêtres de couleurs élancées et ornées de broderies en pierre caractérisent les églises gothiques, de même que la décoration subtile avec des ornements le plus souvent végétaux.

the Renaissance. As in Antiquity, many elements of architectural decoration appeared both in two- and three-dimensional manifestations. The cartouche, for example, a medallion-shaped frame decorated with scrolls, was used on coats-of-arms and for inscriptions, but also as a purely decorative element in architecture and the various crafts. In the mid-16th century, Italian decorative painters of the Fontainebleau School developed the cartouche into scrollwork, whose ends roll out, scroll-like, from the surface; quite apart from its ornamental effect, it lives from the contrast between the sculptured decoration and the flat background. It rapidly became popular in architecture and the crafts, and along with the Grotesque, forms one of the characteristic ornaments of the Renaissance. Toward the end of the 16th century, scrollwork developed into strapwork, a two-dimensional symmetrical form of ornamentation, which was originally intended for the decoration of interior wooden

entdeckt wurden. Viele Elemente des Baudekors traten – wie übrigens schon in der Antike – zugleich als plastischer Zierrat und als flächige (gemalte) Ornamente auf. So beispielsweise das Motiv der Kartusche, einem medaillonförmigen, mit Voluten verzierten Rahmenwerk, das für Wappen und Inschriften sowie als reine Zierform in Architektur und Kunsthandwerk verwendet wurde. Mitte des 16. Jahrhunderts entwickelten italienische Dekorationsmaler der Schule von Fontainebleau aus der Kartusche das Rollwerk, das mit seinen schneckenartig sich einrollenden Enden plastisch aus der Fläche heraustritt und neben seinen ornamentalen Formen vor allem von dem Kontrast des flächigen Untergrundes mit den plastischen Ornamenten lebt. Es wurde rasch in Architektur und Kunsthandwerk beliebt und bildet zusammen mit der Groteske eins der charakteristischsten Renaissance-Ornamente. Gegen Ende des 16. Jahrhunderts entstand aus dem Rollwerk das Beschlagwerk, eine flache, symmetrisch angeordnete Ornamentform,

De nombreux éléments du décor architectural – comme du reste dans l'Antiquité déjà – servirent à la fois de décor en relief et d'ornement à plat (peint). C'est le cas par exemple du cartouche, un cadre en forme de médaillon, orné de volutes, qui était utilisé pour les armoiries et épitaphes et représentait une forme ornementale pure dans l'architecture et les métiers d'art. Au milieu du XVIe siècle, des peintres décorateurs italiens de l'école de Fontainebleau mirent au point le cartouche à enroulement qui, avec ses extrémités vrillées à la manière d'un escargot, se détache de la surface par son relief et, en plus de ses formes ornementales, bénéficie surtout du contraste entre le fond à plat et l'ornement en relief. Il fit rapidement fureur dans l'architecture et les métiers d'art et constitua, avec la grotesque, l'un des ornements les plus caractéristiques de la Renaissance. Vers la fin du XVIe siècle, le cartouche à enroulement donna naissance au cloutage, une forme ornementale plate et symétrique qui ornait à l'origine les lambris, mais

TEMPLA DOMVM EXPOSITIS;VICOS FORA MOENIA PONTES;
VIRGINEAM TRIVII QVOD REPARARIS AQVAM.
PRISCA LICET NAVTIS STATVAS DARE COMMODA PORTVS;
ET VATICANVM CINGERE SIXTE IVGVM;
PLVS TAMEN VRBS DEBET;NAM QVAE SQVALORE LATEBAT;
CERNITVR IN CELEBRI BIBLIOTHECA LOCO.

paneling, but subsequently executed in stone, became one of the most common ornaments of the late Renaissance. This in turn was supplanted by the gnarled fleshy curves and powerful scrolls which already pointed the way forward to the Baroque.

die ursprünglich als Dekor für Holz-vertäfelungen in Innenräumen vor-gesehen war, dann aber in Stein aus-geführt zu einem der gängigsten Ornamente der Spät-Renaissance avancierte. Dieses wurde vom Ohr-muschel- und Knorpelwerk abge-löst, das sich durch seine knorpel-förmigen, wulstigen Schwünge und seine kraftvollen Voluten auszeich-nete, mit denen sich bereits der Über-gang zum Früh-Barock ankündigte.

qui, réalisé par la suite en pierre, devint l'un des ornements les plus courants de la Renaissance tardive. Celui-ci a été relayé par les conques et oreilles qui se distinguaient par leurs mouvements protubérants et leurs volutes vigoureuses annonçant déjà le passage au baroque précoce.

Baroque, Régence, Rococo

From the first half of the 17th century onward, the architects of the Italian Baroque gave expressive sculptural emphasis to Renaissance motifs like the acanthus or the cartouche, frequently decorating them with gold and thereby enhancing the effect still further. The austere planning characteristic

Barock, Régence, Rokoko

Die Baumeister des italienischen Barock steigerten Motive der Renaissance wie den Akanthus oder die Kartusche ab der ersten Hälfte des 17. Jahrhunderts ausdrucksstark ins Plastische und verzierten sie häufig mit Gold, wodurch die Wir-kung verstärkt wurde. Die strenge gestalterische Baugliederung der Renaissance lockerte man durch vielfältigen Figurenschmuck und scheinperspektivische Decken-gemälde sowie überreichen Stuck-dekor auf, der vor allem in Deutsch-land und Österreich ausgeprägt war. Das protestantische England zeigte sich an dem fülligen Vokabular barocker Sakral- und Herrschaftsar-chitektur jedoch wenig interessiert, so dass es nicht verwundert, dass die Audsleys in ihrem Vorlagenwerk auf Barock-Ornamente verzichteten. In Frankreich dagegen bildete der Barock mit dem Bau des Schlosses von Versailles schon um 1700 einen zarten flächigen Stil – den Régence-Stil – heraus, der während der Regentschaft von Phillipp von Orléans (1715–1723) maßgeblich das französische Interieur prägte. Der Régence-Stil bevorzugte im Gegensatz zur pathetischen Hof-kunst zierlichere Formen und ersetzte beispielsweise die plasti-sche Säule durch den flachen Pilas-ter. Die bedeutendste Ornamentform des Régence-Stils ist (neben abstrakten Gitterungen) das Bandel-werk, ein vielfältig gebrochener und miteinander verschlungener Ran-kendekor in flächiger Ausprägung. Dieser erfuhr um 1730 eine nochma-lige Verfeinerung und ging elegant-graziös aufgelockert (vom Stil

Le Baroque, la Régence, le rococo

Les architectes du baroque italien intensifièrent à partir du XVIIᵉ siècle l'utilisation du relief dans les motifs de la Renaissance comme l'acanthe ou le cartouche et les peignirent souvent en doré, ce qui les mettait en valeur. On atténua la structure sévère des formes architecturales de la Renaissance par des décors variés de figures et des fresques de plafonds en trompe-l'œil, ainsi que par des décors en stuc exubérants, surtout en Allemagne et en Autriche. L'Angleterre protestante se montra toutefois peu intéressée par le registre profus de l'architecture baroque sacrée et seigneuriale ; il n'est donc pas surprenant que les Audsley aient renoncé aux ornements baroques dans leur recueil de modèles. En France, par contre, le baroque a déjà donné naissance vers 1700, avec la construction du château de Versailles, à un style délicat et plan – le style Régence – qui marqua de façon décisive l'intérieur français sous la régence de Philippe d'Orléans (1715–1723). Le style Régence privilégia des formes plus délicates, contrairement au style pompeux de la cour, et remplaça par exemple la colonne en relief par un pilastre plat. La principale forme ornementale du style Régence est (avec les rinceaux abstraits) la volute, un motif d'entrelacs brisés et diversement imbriqués les uns dans les autres. Ce motif a été une nouvelle fois affiné vers 1730, passant du style Louis XIV au style Louis XV, élégant et gracieux. Quant au « rocaille », ornement en forme de coquillage et s'enroulant à

of Renaissance buildings was enlivened by a wealth of sculptured figures and *trompe-l'œil* perspective ceiling painting along with over-exuberant stucco decoration, which was particularly characteristic of Germany and Austria. Protestant England had little interest, however, in the luxuriant vocabulary of Baroque architecture, whether secular or ecclesiastical, so it is not surprising that there are no Baroque patterns in the Audsleys' collection. In France, by contrast, with the building of the Palace of Versailles, Baroque was transformed as early as c. 1700 into a delicate two-dimensional style, which had a decisive influence on French interior decoration during the regency of Philippe of Orleans (1715–1723) and is hence known as the Régence style. In contrast to the pompous manner of the court style immediately preceding, it preferred delicate forms – sculptured columns, for example, were replaced by flat pilasters. The most important ornamental form of the Régence was (alongside abstract grille forms) a twisting interlaced vine motif in low relief. The style underwent further refinement after about 1730, from when it takes its name – Louis Quinze – from the new king Louis XV.

The 1730s also saw the appearance of the "rocaille" motif, formed of scrolls and scallop-like elements, from which the name "Rococo" for the emerging style was derived. In southern Germany there developed a heavier Rococo style more closely related to Italian Baroque, which exuberantly integrated the whole array of forms into a fantastical, sensuous and colorful total work of art.

Neoclassicism

The highly decorated Rococo was in its turn supplanted around the middle of the 18th century by the austere architectural and decorative forms of neoclassicism, which, harking back to the art of Classical Antiquity, is also known as "Greek Revival". The architectural decor, with its wealth of frieze ornamentation, cornices and acroteria in the

Louis-quatorze) zum Stil Louis-quinze über.

In den dreißiger Jahren des 18. Jahrhunderts entstand außerdem die Rocaille, ein muschelförmiges, sich volutenartig zusammenrollendes Ornament, von dem sich der Stilbegriff Rokoko ableitet.

In Süddeutschland entwickelte sich ein dem italienischen Barock verbundener, schwerer Rokoko-Stil, der die gesamte dekorative Formenwelt in überschäumender Phantasie als ein farben- und sinnenfrohes Gesamtkunstwerk entstehen ließ.

Klassizismus

Der überladene Dekorationsstil des Rokoko wurde Mitte des 18. Jahrhunderts von den strengen Architektur- und Dekorationsformen des Klassizismus abgelöst, der formal auf die klassische Kunst der Antike zurückgeht und deshalb im eng-

la manière de volutes, dont le concept du style rococo est dérivé, il a fait son apparition dans les années 1730.

Un style rococo lourd, apparenté au baroque italien, s'est développé dans le sud de l'Allemagne. Il donna naissance à tout un ensemble de formes décoratives, des œuvres d'art voluptueuses et riches en couleurs, fruit d'une imagination débordante.

Le néoclassicisme

Le style décoratif surchargé du rococo a été remplacé au milieu du XVIIIe siècle par les formes architecturales et décoratives strictes du néoclassicisme qui se réfère, du point de vue des formes, à l'art classique de l'Antiquité et a été

Opposite page: Detail of a fireplace in the drawing room at Syon House, Middlesex, 18th century
This neoclassical white-marble fireplace has a number of ornaments inspired by the motifs of the Ancient World. Alongside the column with its scroll capital, the most striking feature is the broad frieze with its vases and palmettes set in medallion-like frames. In addition, the designer has incorporated ornamental bands with rosettes, spiral tendrils and almost Classical palmettes, along with a narrow gilt egg-and-dart pattern.

Gegenüberliegende Seite: Detail einer Kamineinfassung im Privatsalon von Syon House in Middlesex, 18. Jh.
Diese klassizistische Kamineinfassung aus weißem Marmor zeigt eine Vielzahl von an der Antike orientierten Ornamenten. Neben der Säule mit dem Volutenkapitell fällt vor allem der breite Fries mit den medaillonartig gerahmten Vasen und Palmetten ins Auge. Überdies wurden Ornamentbänder mit Rosetten, Spiralranken und fast klassisch wirkenden Palmetten sowie ein schmaler, in Gold gefasster Eierstab eingearbeitet.

Page ci-contre : Détail d'un manteau de cheminée dans le salon privé de Syon House, Middlesex, XVIIIᵉ siècle
Ce manteau de cheminée classique en marbre blanc présente une multitude d'ornements inspirés de l'Antiquité. La colonne au chapiteau à volutes, de même que la large frise aux vases et palmettes en forme de médaillon attirent particulièrement l'attention. Des bandeaux ornements à rosaces, entrelacs de spirales et palmettes d'aspect presque classique, ainsi qu'un étroit bandeau d'oves de couleur or s'intègrent dans ce décor.

Right: Dining-hall in Neuschwanstein castle near Füssen, constructed 1868–1886
Neuschwanstein symbolizes like no other building of its age the Romantic revival of historical models and styles that characterized the period. The walls of the dining-hall, for example, are decorated with motifs taken from the legends of Wagnerian opera, all set in a surround of gold leaf-and-tendril design.

Rechts: Speisesaal im Schloss Neuschwanstein bei Füssen, erbaut 1868–1886
Schloss Neuschwanstein versinnbildlicht wie kaum ein anderes Gebäude seiner Zeit die romantische Rückbesinnung auf historische Vorbilder und Kunststile, die für den Historismus prägend war. Die Wände des Speisesaals zieren zum Beispiel Gemälde mit Motiven aus dem Sagenkreis der Opern Wagners, die von einem Rahmenwerk aus goldenen Blattranken umgeben sind.

À droite : Salle à manger du château de Neuschwanstein près de Füssen, édifié de 1868 à 1886
Le château de Neuschwanstein est un des rares édifices de son époque à symboliser la réminiscence romantique de modèles et styles artistiques historiques qui ont marqué l'historisme. Des tableaux, aux motifs empruntés au cycle de légendes des opéras de Wagner et au cadre constitué d'entrelacs de feuilles dorées, ornent par exemple les murs de la salle à manger.

form of palmettes, vases and sphinxes, served mainly to emphasize the elements which gave the buildings their visual structure. Alongside the ornaments derived directly from Classical Antiquity, such as fret motifs, acanthus and anthemion friezes, palmettes and acroteria, one also comes across wreaths, garlands and swags of leaves and fruit. They represented a limpid and austere style which was also characteristic of the interior decor of the time.

Revivalism, Art Nouveau

The "Revivalism" of the 19th century represented an effort to find a style. After the harking back to Classical Antiquity which was the hallmark of neoclassicism, there appeared a stylistic pluralism in which all the succeeding periods in decorative art were raided for ideas. Especially popular in this connection was Gothic, which is why the term "Gothic Revival" is also used for much of the period. But the upper-middleclass in particular was eclectic in its predilection for profuse interior decor in one or more historical styles, so that Greek-style rooms might lead on to others in Roman or Egyptian styles, and whole Gothic wings led into others decorated in contemporary 19th-century-style. The interior decoration of the period is characterized also by the heavy use of ornamentation on walls and ceilings together with an often excessive quantity of furniture, textiles and paintings.
While the Revivalist period was primarily focused on earlier styles of decorative art in the West, this did not stand in the way of an interest in non-European cultures, and both Islamic and Far Eastern styles were appreciated. As early as the 18th century, Chinese porcelain had become extremely popular in Europe, and now it was the turn of Japanese art to be discovered by artists and broad sections of the

lischsprachigen Raum auch als „Greek Revival" bezeichnet wird. Der Baudekor mit seinen reichen Ornamentfriesen, Gesimsen und Giebelbekrönungen in Form von Palmetten, Vasen und Sphinxen diente vornehmlich dazu, die gliedernden Teile der Architektur zu betonen. Neben den von der Antike abgeleiteten Ornamenten, wie zum Beispiel den Mäandern, Akanthus- und Anthemionfriesen, Palmetten und Akroterien, sieht man auch Blattkränze, Girlanden und Fruchtgehänge, die als Festons bezeichnet werden. Sie bildeten einen klaren und strengen Stil aus, der unter anderem auch das Interieur prägte.

Historismus, Jugendstil

Der Historismus des 19. Jahrhunderts war von der Suche nach einem Stil geprägt. Nachdem man sich zur Zeit des Klassizismus bereits auf antike Formen rückbesonnen hatte, wandte man sich nun im Rahmen

surnommé pour cette raison « Greek Revival » dans les pays anglophones. Le décor architectural avec ses riches frises ornementales, ses corniches et couronnements de pignons en forme de palmettes, ses vases et ses sphinx servait surtout à mettre en valeur les éléments constitutifs de l'architecture. À côté des ornements dérivés de l'Antiquité, comme les méandres, frises d'acanthe et anthémions, palmettes et acrotères, on rencontre aussi des couronnes de feuilles, des guirlandes et des grappes de fruits qualifiées de festons. Ils formaient un style clair et strict qui marqua entre autres aussi les intérieurs.

L'historisme, l'art nouveau

L'historisme du XIXᵉ siècle s'est caractérisé par une recherche stylistique. Après avoir fait un retour aux formes antiques à l'époque du néoclassicisme, on se tournait une fois de plus au nom d'un pluralisme

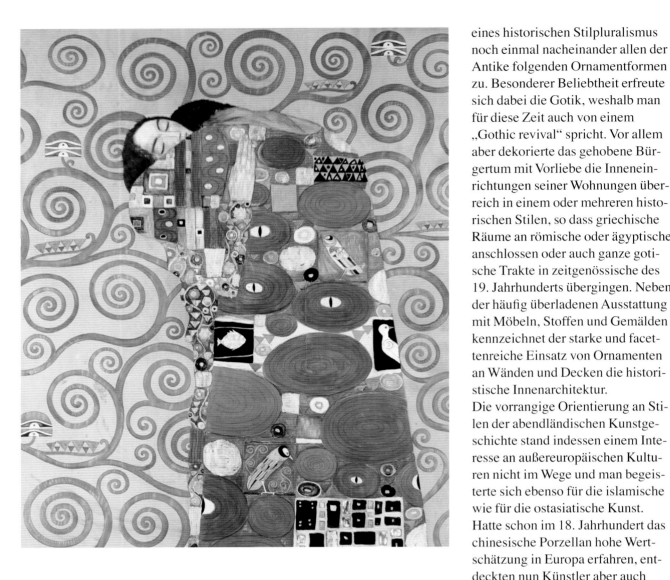

Gustav Klimt, *The Fulfillment*, Musée des Beaux-Arts, Strasbourg, c. 1909
The style known as Art Nouveau was characterized among other things by its predilection for rich ornamentation, as can be seen in this mural.

Gustav Klimt, *Die Erfüllung*, Musée des Beaux-Arts, Straßburg, um 1909
Der Jugendstil zeichnete sich u.a. durch seine Vorliebe für opulente Ornamentik aus, die auch bei diesem Wandbild zum Ausdruck kommt.

Gustav Klimt, *L'Accomplissement*, Musée des Beaux-Arts, Strasbourg, vers 1909
L'art nouveau, mouvement né à la fin du XIXᵉ siècle, se distinguait entre autres par sa prédilection pour un art ornemental opulent. Ce tableau mural en est une illustration.

middle class alike. The simple forms and small decorative objects which were t feature of Japanese crafts inspired both the French Impressionists and the applied artists of the English Arts-and-Crafts movement, with whom the Audsleys were associated. This movement, which as its name makes clear, sought to break down the barriers between fine and applied art, is reckoned to be one of the harbingers of Art Nouveau, and thus of a style which at the dawn of the 20th century created a form of ornamentation which embraced all spheres of art in equal measure.

eines historischen Stilpluralismus noch einmal nacheinander allen der Antike folgenden Ornamentformen zu. Besonderer Beliebtheit erfreute sich dabei die Gotik, weshalb man für diese Zeit auch von einem „Gothic revival" spricht. Vor allem aber dekorierte das gehobene Bürgertum mit Vorliebe die Inneneinrichtungen seiner Wohnungen überreich in einem oder mehreren historischen Stilen, so dass griechische Räume an römische oder ägyptische anschlossen oder auch ganze gotische Trakte in zeitgenössische des 19. Jahrhunderts übergingen. Neben der häufig überladenen Ausstattung mit Möbeln, Stoffen und Gemälden kennzeichnet der starke und facettenreiche Einsatz von Ornamenten an Wänden und Decken die historistische Innenarchitektur.

Die vorrangige Orientierung an Stilen der abendländischen Kunstgeschichte stand indessen einem Interesse an außereuropäischen Kulturen nicht im Wege und man begeisterte sich ebenso für die islamische wie für die ostasiatische Kunst. Hatte schon im 18. Jahrhundert das chinesische Porzellan hohe Wertschätzung in Europa erfahren, entdeckten nun Künstler aber auch breite bürgerliche Schichten die japanische Kunst. Die schlichte Formgebung und kleinteilige Ornamentik, die vor allem ein Merkmal des japanischen Kunsthandwerks sind, regten neben den französischen Impressionisten auch die Kunsthandwerker der englischen Arts-and-Crafts-Bewegung an, der auch die Audsleys nahe standen. Diese Bewegung, die Kunst und Kunstgewerbe zusammenführen wollte, zählt zu den Wegbereitern des Jugendstils und damit jener Kunstrichtung, die an der Wende zum 20. Jahrhundert wieder eine stilbildende Ornamentik schuf, die alle Kunstgattungen gleichermaßen erfasste.

de style historique vers toutes les formes ornementales qui s'étaient succédées depuis l'Antiquité. Le gothique jouissait alors d'une faveur particulière, c'est la raison pour laquelle on parle de la même façon de « Gothic revival » pour qualifier cette époque. Mais c'est surtout la haute bourgeoisie qui aima décorer à l'excès l'intérieur de ses demeures dans un ou plusieurs styles historiques, si bien que le style grec côtoyait le romain ou l'égyptien ou encore que des ailes gothiques entières ouvraient sur des pièces dans le style contemporain du XIXᵉ siècle. À côté d'une surcharge de meubles, d'étoffes et de tableaux, l'introduction massive et systématique d'ornements aux murs et aux plafonds caractérise l'architecture intérieure de l'historisme.

L'orientation prioritaire vers des styles de l'histoire de l'art occidentale n'empêcha toutefois pas l'éclosion d'un intérêt pour des cultures extra-européennes ; on s'enthousiasma aussi bien pour l'art islamique que pour celui de l'Asie orientale. Si la porcelaine chinoise avait remporté un grand succès en Europe dès le XVIIIᵉ siècle, l'art japonais touchait maintenant les artistes, mais aussi des couches plus larges de la population. Les formes simples et les petits ornements très typiques de l'artisanat japonais inspirèrent non seulement les impressionnistes français, mais aussi les artisans du mouvement anglais Arts-and-Crafts, dont les Audsley étaient également proches. Ce mouvement qui voulait réunir art et artisanat est l'un des précurseurs de l'art nouveau et donc de l'orientation artistique qui, au tournant du XXᵉ siècle, recréa une décoration dans un style qui englobait tous les genres artistiques à la fois.

The Modern Age

But the fading of Art Nouveau was accompanied by a general fading of interest in ornamentation. The 20th century was characterized by a fragmentation of values and of

Moderne

Doch mit dem Abklingen des Jugendstils ließ auch das allgemeine Interesse an der Ornamentik nach. Das 20. Jahrhundert war von einem Zerwürfnis der Werte und der politi-

L'art moderne

Mais avec le déclin de l'art nouveau, l'intérêt général pour l'art ornemental faiblit lui aussi. Le XXᵉ siècle a été marqué par un effritement des valeurs et une dégradation de la

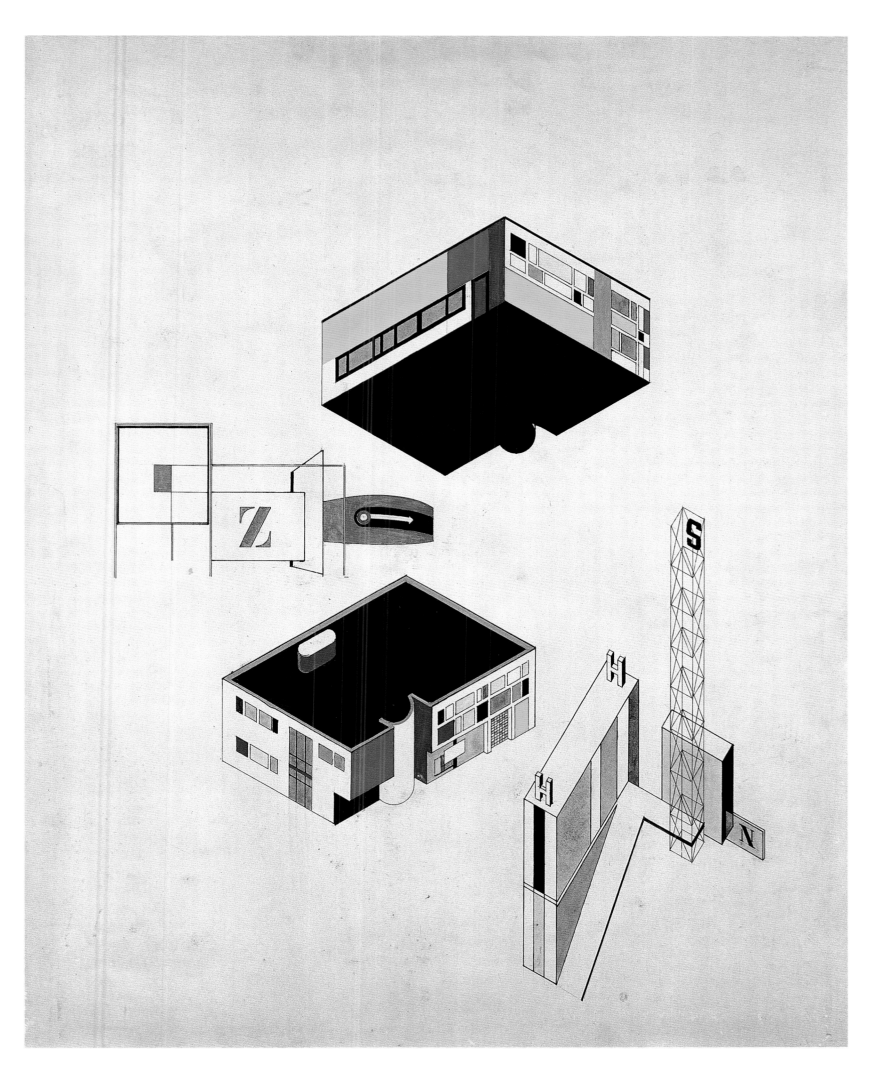

Previous page: Franz Ehrlich, color plans for a building, Bauhaus Foundation, Dessau, 1928
In the spirit of "Neue Sachlichkeit" (New Functionalism), the artists of the Bauhaus design school reduced ornamentation to pure color values and decorated the façades of their buildings with large areas of uniform color.

Vorhergehende Seite: Franz Ehrlich, Farbpläne für ein Gebäude, Stiftung Bauhaus Dessau, 1928
Im Dienste einer neuen Sachlichkeit reduzierten die Bauhaus-Künster das Ornament auf den reinen Farbwert und dekorierten Gebäudefassaden mit großen einheitlichen Farbflächen.

Page précédente : Franz Ehrlich, épure en couleurs d'un bâtiment, Fondation Bauhaus Dessau, 1928
Les artistes du Bauhaus, qui s'étaient mis au service d'une nouvelle objectivité, réduisirent l'ornement à la couleur pure et à des façades décorées de bâtiments portant de grandes surfaces de couleurs uniformes.

Tail-fins of Boeing 747-400 aircraft, London, 1997
During the 20th century, industrial design opened up wholly new fields of ornamentation. Thus British Airways decided to commission large-format designs for the tail-fins of its fleet – each alluding to the national traditions of the various destinations served by the airline. The aircraft in the center, for example, has a design clearly reminiscent of Scottish tartan patterns, while the design on the right consciously evokes connotations with the fauna of Africa.

Seitenleitwerke von Flugzeugen des Typs Boeing 747-400, London, 1997
Im 20. Jahrhundert eröffnete das Industrie-Design der Ornamentik ganz neue Felder. So entschied sich die Fluggesellschaft British Airways, sämtliche Heckflossen ihrer Flugzeuge von Designern mit großflächigen Ornamenten ausstatten zu lassen – und zwar in Anlehnung an nationale Traditionen der unterschiedlichen Zielflughäfen der Fluggesellschaft. Der Entwurf in der Mitte erinnert an die Stoffe Schottlands, während das Muster am rechten Bildrand bewusst Assoziationen zur Tierwelt Afrikas auslösen soll.

Gouvernails d'avions de type Boeing 747-400, Londres, 1997
Au XXe siècle, le design industriel ouvrit à l'art ornemental des horizons entièrement nouveaux. C'est ainsi que la compagnie d'aviation British Airways décida de faire décorer tous les stabilisateurs arrière de ses avions avec des ornements de grande taille par des designers – en empruntant des motifs aux traditions nationales de ses divers pays de destination. Les dessins du milieu font nettement référence aux étoffes ouatinées d'Écosse, tandis que le motif de droite rappelle la faune africaine.

political conditions which was also reflected in art. There was no uniform style which could be said to typify the century, and varied as the different forms of artistic expression were, they rarely had any impact on the decorative arts. The functionalism of the early-20th century succeeded in banishing ornament almost entirely, and thus, apart from popular (folk) art and certain individual exceptions in Europe and the USA, it is only with the Postmodern

schen Verhältnisse geprägt, das sich auch in der Kunst widerspiegelte. Es gibt keinen einheitlichen Stil, der für dieses Jahrhundert bestimmend wäre, und so vielschichtig die künstlerischen Ausdrucksformen auch waren, wirkten sie sich doch nur in den seltensten Fällen auf die Ornamentik aus. Der Funktionalismus zu Beginn des 20. Jahrhunderts hatte das Ornament fast vollständig verdrängt, und so kann man – abgesehen von der Volkskunst und

situation politique qui se sont également reflétés dans l'art. Il n'y a pas de style uniforme déterminant pour ce siècle et malgré leur diversité, les formes d'expression artistiques n'ont influé que très rarement sur l'art ornemental. Le fonctionnalisme du début du XXe siècle avait presque totalement supplanté l'ornement et on ne peut donc parler d'une renaissance de l'art ornemental – hormis l'art populaire et certaines exceptions en Europe et aux États-Unis –

Ornamental band in a restaurant, Berlin, 2000
The closing years of the 20th century saw a revival of interest in classical forms of ornamentation. However the individual motifs were liberated from their artistic context and frequently used as decorative elements in their own right. The essential element of ornamentation, the repetitive motif, serves a different function here, but can still be clearly recognized.

Ornamentband in einem Restaurant, Berlin, 2000
Zum Ende des 20. Jahrhunderts lebt das Interesse an klassischen Ornamentformen wieder auf, jedoch befreit man das Motiv von seinem Kanon und setzt es nun häufig losgelöst von kunsthistorischen Traditionen als eigenständiges raumgestalterisches Element ein. Der Rapport als wesentliches Merkmal des Ornaments wird hier verfremdet, bleibt jedoch nach wie vor erkennbar.

Bandeau ornemental dans un restaurant, Berlin, 2000
À la fin du XXe siècle, les formes ornementales classiques sont revenues au goût du jour, mais on libéra le motif de ses idéaux et on l'utilisa souvent en dehors des traditions historiques et artistiques comme élément individuel de décoration intérieure. Le motif répétitif, élément essentiel de l'art ornemental, a ici une toute autre fonction, mais n'en demeure pas moins apparent.

movement of the 1980s that we can begin to talk once more of a revival of ornamentation. Here, once again, the styles of past epochs serve as patterns, but this time free of much design dogma, which has led to ornamentation being accorded a higher esthetic value in interior decoration than in earlier periods. At the same time, we witness short-lived design fashions, which, put across by the media, quickly spread to saturation point and disappear once more. At the start of the 21st century, then, it is possible to discern a growing interest in the decorative arts on the one hand, while on the other we have no binding esthetic principles which would enable us to speak of a style as such.

bestimmten individuellen Ausnahmen in Europa und den USA – erst seit der Postmoderne in den 80er Jahren von einer Wiederbelebung der Ornamentik sprechen. Dabei dienen wiederum Stile vorangegangener Kunstepochen als Muster, jedoch ist der Umgang mit ihnen heute von vielen gestalterischen Dogmen befreit, was häufig dazu führt, dass der Ornamentik im Rahmen einer Innenraumgestaltung ein höherer ästhetischer Eigenwert zugesprochen wird als in früheren Epochen. Gleichzeitig kommt es zu kurzlebigen Design-Moden, die sich, von Medien transportiert, rasch ausbreiten, um nach einer Übersättigung bald wieder zu verschwinden. Zu Beginn des 21. Jahrhunderts kann deshalb zwar einerseits ein wachsendes Interesse am Dekor festgestellt werden, andererseits aber fehlen jene verbindlichen ästhetischen Grundsätze, die die Definition eines Stils zulassen.

que depuis le post-modernisme des années 80. Une fois de plus, des styles d'époques artistiques antérieures servent de modèles, mais leur approche est aujourd'hui libérée de nombreux dogmes créateurs; de ce fait on attribue souvent à l'art ornemental, dans l'aménagement d'un intérieur, une valeur esthétique propre plus élevée qu'aux époques antérieures. Dans le même temps, des modes de design éphémères voient le jour qui, promues par les médias, se diffusent rapidement pour disparaître aussi vite après saturation. Le début du XXIe siècle est donc marqué par un intérêt croissant pour la décoration, mais aussi par l'absence des principes esthétiques établis qui permettent de définir un style.

Wolfgang-E. Kaemmer, vase, Cologne, 1993
The rapidly changing design fashions of the 1980s and 90s allowed both lively and playful decors and austere and simple ones. The design shown here is derived from the Greek fret, but reinterpreted.

Wolfgang-E. Kaemmer, Vase, Köln, 1993
Die schnell wechselnden Design-Moden der 80er und 90er Jahre ließen sowohl lebendig-spielerischen als auch strengen, schlichten Dekor zu. Der hier gezeigte Entwurf ist vom klassischen Mäander abgeleitet, interpretiert ihn jedoch neu.

Wolfgang-E. Kaemmer, vase, Cologne, 1993
Les modes très changeantes du design des années 80 et 90 ont permis de réaliser des décors vivants et amusants, mais aussi stricts et sobres. L'esquisse illustrée ici est dérivée du méandre classique, mais elle interprète celui-ci de façon inédite.

Ornamental Plates
Ornamenttafeln
Planches d'ornements

Greek Antiquity
Griechische Antike
L'Antiquité grecque

Greek Antiquity is defined as the period from the decline of Mycenaean culture through the Classical and Hellenistic periods until the early centuries AD. This saw the rise of such a sophisticated civilization that one can speak without hesitation of the first cultural blossoming in the West. With the "polis" or city-state, there developed a system of political organization which is regarded as the precursor of democratic forms of government. Its essential characteristic was the importance attached to the individual in his society. Man strove, said Plato, for the Good which he carried within himself and which put his mark on his environment. A similar mental approach also characterized the esthetics of ancient Greece, which declared Man to be the measure of all things, for which reason craftsmen and architects derived ideal proportions from the observation of the human anatomy, which they then transferred to buildings, sculptures and paintings. The regularities they found in nature and the esthetic

Die griechische Antike, die mit dem Untergang der mykenischen Kultur einsetzte und im Hellenismus bis in die ersten nachchristlichen Jahrhunderte reichte, erlebte eine solche zivilisatorische Verfeinerung in allen Bereichen, dass man ohne weiteres von der ersten kulturellen Hochblüte des Abendlandes sprechen kann. So entwickelte sich mit der Polis ein Regierungssystem, das gemeinhin als Vorläufer demokratischer Staatsformen bezeichnet wird, und dessen wesentliches Merkmal in der Bedeutung zu sehen ist, die dem Individuum in seiner Gesellschaft beigemessen wird. Der Mensch strebe, so lehrte Platon, nach dem Guten, das er in sich trage und das auch seine Umwelt präge. Ein ähnlicher gedanklicher Ansatz kennzeichnete die Ästhetik der griechischen Antike, die den Menschen zum Maß der Dinge erklärte, weshalb Kunsthandwerker und Baumeister aus der Beobachtung der menschlichen Anatomie ideale Proportionen ableiteten, die sie auf Bauwerke, Plastiken und Malereien

L'Antiquité grecque qui a débuté avec le déclin de la culture mycénienne et a traversé l'hellénisme jusqu'aux premiers siècles après J.-C. a été marquée par un tel raffinement civilisateur dans tous les domaines qu'on peut carrément parler de la première apogée culturelle de l'Occident. C'est ainsi que s'est développé, avec la polis (cité-État), un système gouvernemental communément qualifié de précurseur des formes de gouvernements démocratiques, se distinguant essentiellement par la prépondérance de l'individu dans sa société. L'homme, professait Platon, aspire au bien qu'il porte en lui et qui reflète aussi son environnement. Un raisonnement identique a marqué l'esthétique de l'Antiquité grecque qui déclarait que l'homme était la mesure de toutes choses ; c'est la raison pour laquelle artisans d'art et bâtisseurs ont tiré de l'observation de l'anatomie humaine des proportions idéales qu'ils ont transposées à des édifices, sculptures et peintures. Les lois qu'ils ont trouvées

Entire complex of the Acropolis in Athens, with view of the Parthenon, 1250 BC
The Acropolis, and especially the Parthenon temple, embodies the essence of Classical Antiquity like no other cultural heritage site. All the architectural elements are logical and harmonized one with another. The result is an organic whole. For millennia, architects have had recourse to the architectural elements of Classical Antiquity.

Gesamtanlage der Akropolis von Athen mit Blick auf den Parthenon, 1250 v. Chr.
Die Akropolis und darauf besonders der Parthenon-Tempel verkörpert wie kaum ein anderes Kulturdenkmal das Wesen der klassischen Antike. Alle Architekturteile sind in ihren Maßverhältnissen logisch aufeinander bezogen und ergeben ein organisches Ganzes. Jahrtausendelang haben Architekten immer wieder auf die Bauformen und Bauelemente der griechischen Antike Bezug genommen.

Site de l'Acropole à Athènes, site avec vue sur le Parthénon, 1250 avant J.-C.
L'Acropole et surtout le temple du Parthénon sont quelques-uns des rares monuments culturels à incarner l'existence de l'Antiquité classique. Tous les éléments architecturaux, à l'organisation logique et aux proportions harmonieuses, forment un ensemble organique. Des siècles durant, des architectes se sont référés aux formes et éléments architecturaux de l'Antiquité grecque.

rules of harmony and dynamics they derived from these regularities have retained their validity over the centuries right up to the present day. By analogy with the mathematical principles of Pythagoras or the constitutional doctrines of Plato, they described a balanced relationship of the individual to the whole, out of which arose beauty and perfection.

The art of Greek Antiquity has been preserved most visibly in its architecture, and in particular (as in almost every culture) in its religious buildings. Magnificent temples, such as that which housed the Oracle at Delphi or those on the Acropolis in Athens, bear witness not only to the craft skills of the builders, but also, and above all, to their sophisticated design sense. It was this design sense, oriented to visual effect, that gave their monumental buildings the serenity, lightness and harmony which have influenced so many succeeding generations in the history of art. From today's point of view, this investigation, adjustment and correction of even the smallest design details is all the more interesting insofar as the temples were reserved for the priests and the ruling class, and to this extent could only be appreciated by the population at large from afar. The exuberant outward decoration of the architecture takes account of this fact; while the temple interiors were traditionally kept plain, the façades were ornamented with decorative architectural elements and relief sculptures. Relatively little is known about the color schemes employed in the temples, or how they were painted, but some of the design elements found in the ornamentation reappear in relief form on the façades of the temples, for example the egg-and-dart motif. Numerous examples of the pictorial abilities of this period can however be found in its crafts, and in particular its pottery. Plates and vases were decorated with scenic images, but also, and above all, with a whole variety of abstract ornamentation.

Secular architecture only came to prominence in the Hellenistic age,

übertrugen. Die von ihnen in der Natur gefundenen Gesetzmäßigkeiten und die daraus abgeleiteten ästhetischen Regeln über Harmonie und Dynamik haben durch die Jahrhunderte bis heute Gültigkeit behalten. In Analogie zu den mathematischen Grundsätzen des Pythagoras oder zur Staatslehre von Platon beschreiben sie das ausgewogene Verhältnis des Einzelnen zum Ganzen, aus dem Schönheit und Vollkommenheit erwachsen.

Am sichtbarsten hat sich die Kunst der griechischen Antike in der Architektur erhalten und zwar (wie in fast allen Kulturen) in der Sakralarchitektur: Großartige Tempelanlagen wie die des Delphischen Orakel-Heiligtums oder der Athener Akropolis bezeugen neben der handwerklichen Qualifikation der Baumeister vor allem ihre gestalterische Raffinesse. Denn erst durch die auf die optische Wirkung ausgerichteten Fassaden erhielten die Kolossalbauten ihre heitere Leichtigkeit und in sich ruhende Geschlossenheit, mit der sie viele nachfolgende Kunstepochen beeinflusst haben. Aus heutiger Sicht ist diese Untersuchung und Abstimmung feinster Gestaltungsmerkmale umso interessanter, als dass Tempelanlagen Priestern und der herrschenden Schicht vorbehalten waren und mithin lediglich in der Fernansicht von der Bevölkerung wahrgenommen werden konnten. Dieser Tatsache trägt die extrovertierte Ausschmückung der Bauwerke Rechnung, denn während das Tempelinnere traditionell einfach gehalten war, wurden die Fassaden mit dekorativem Baudekor und Reliefskulpturen ausgestattet. Über farbliche Gestaltung und Ausmalung der Tempel ist relativ wenig bekannt, doch finden sich einige aus der flächigen Ornamentik übernommene Gestaltungselemente in Reliefform an den Tempelfassaden wieder, so etwa das Eierstabmotiv. Reiche Beispiele für das bildnerische Können dieser Zeit finden sich dagegen im Kunsthandwerk und hier vor allem in der Keramik: Teller und Vasen wurden mit szenischen Bildern, vor allem aber mit variantenreichen Ornamenten geschmückt.

dans la nature et les règles esthétiques sur l'harmonie et le dynamisme qui en découlent ont conservé leur validité au fil des siècles jusqu'à nos jours. Par analogie aux principes mathématiques de Pythagore ou de la politique de Platon, elles décrivent le rapport équilibré entre l'individu et le tout qui donne naissance à la beauté et à la perfection.

L'art de l'Antiquité a subsisté le plus manifestement dans l'architecture, à savoir dans l'architecture religieuse (comme c'est le cas dans presque toutes les cultures): des temples grandioses tels que ceux de l'Oracle de Delphes ou de l'Acropole à Athènes témoignent

Round temple in Delphi, 400 BC
The round temple, to whose imposing size the three reerected Doric marble columns bear witness, displayed a rich architectural ornamentation with vegetal motifs, of which relief fragments on the architrave can still be seen.

Rundtempel in Delphi, 4. Jh. v. Chr.
Der Rundtempel, von dessen imposanter Größe die drei wieder errichteten dorischen Marmorsäulen zeugen, wies einen reichen, mit vegetabilen Motiven verzierten Baudekor auf, von dem am Gebälk noch Relieffragmente zu sehen sind.

Temple rond à Delphes, IVᵉ siècle avant J.-C.
Le temple rond à la taille imposante, comme en témoignent les trois colonnes doriques de marbre reconstruites, présentait un riche décor architectural à motifs végétaux dont il ne reste que des fragments de relief au niveau de l'entablement.

that is to say, the period which followed the Classical age in the narrower sense. The Hellenistic period can be said to have started with the conquest of the Persian Empire by Alexander the Great and the occupation of Persepolis (334 BC), and to have eventually merged into Graeco-Roman culture. Compared with the preceding Classical age, Hellenism is characterized by the increase in oriental influences, resulting from the vast eastward expansion of the Greek culture and the cosmopolitan attitudes of Alexander the Great. These influences made themselves felt first of all in philosophy and sciences, but soon in art and architecture as well. As far as architecture was concerned, the

Die Profanarchitektur kam im Hellenismus zur vollen Blüte, jener Epoche, die auf die klassische folgte. Mit der Eroberung des Perserreiches durch Alexander den Großen und der Einnahme von Persepolis (334 v. Chr.) setzte die Periode des Hellenismus ein, die von der griechisch-römischen Kultur aufgenommen wurde. Der Hellenismus zeichnete sich im Vergleich zur klassischen Epoche durch das vermehrte Aufnehmen orientalischer Einflüsse aus, die sich infolge der gewaltigen Gebietserweiterung der griechischen Kultur nach Osten und der kosmopolitischen Haltung Alexanders des Großen auswirkten. Sie machten sich zunächst in Philosophie und Wissenschaft, bald aber auch in Kunst und Architektur

non seulement du savoir-faire artisanal des bâtisseurs, mais surtout de leur raffinement inventif. Car seul le « design », visant à un effet optique, a conféré aux édifices colossaux une légèreté sereine et une homogénéité harmonieuse par lesquelles ils ont influencé de nombreuses époques artistiques postérieures. Avec le recul, cette exploration et cette harmonisation des formes les plus raffinées semblent d'autant plus intéressantes que les temples étaient réservés aux prêtres et à la classe dirigeante et ne pouvaient donc être aperçus que de loin par la plèbe. La décoration extravertie des édifices tient compte de ce phénomène, car si l'intérieur des temples était traditionnellement simple, les façades, en revanche, s'ornaient de décors architecturaux et de sculptures. On sait relativement peu de choses sur les couleurs et les décors peints des temples, même si quelques éléments décoratifs typiques se présentant sous la forme de reliefs ornent les façades des temples, par exemple le motif de l'ove. D'abondants exemples du savoir-faire inventif de cette époque se retrouvent toutefois dans l'artisanat, et surtout dans la céramique : assiettes et vases représentaient des scènes, mais étaient surtout ornés de motifs aux nombreuses variantes. L'architecture profane n'a connu son apogée qu'à l'époque de l'hellénisme qui a succédé au classicisme. La conquête de la Perse par Alexandre le Grand et la prise de Persépolis (334 avant J.-C.) ont beaucoup marqué le début de l'hellénisme qui a été intégré dans la culture gréco-romaine. L'hellénisme se distingue de l'époque classique par l'assimilation intensive d'influences orientales, due à la prodigieuse expansion territoriale de la culture grecque vers l'est et au cosmopolitisme d'Alexandre le Grand. Ces influences se sont tout d'abord fait sentir dans la philosophie et les sciences et très vite aussi dans l'art et l'architecture. Dans cette dernière discipline, on conçut de plus en plus l'intérieur comme le lieu d'une activité créatrice et accorda désormais une attention accrue aux mosaïques, fresques,

Below: Column with capital and ledge, original design by G.A. and M.A. Audsley, 1892
In this design George Ashdown Audsley takes up Classical forms and recombines them to reflect Classical ideals.

Unten: Säule mit Kapitell und Gesims, Entwurf von G. A. und M. A. Audsley, 1892
Dieser Audsley-Entwurf nimmt den Formenschatz der Antike auf und stellt die Elemente idealtypisch zusammen.

En bas : Avec chapiteau et corniche, esquisse de G. A. et M. A. Ausdley, 1892
Cette esquisse des Audsley reprend le registre de formes de l'Antiquité et réunit les éléments dans une composition conforme à leur idéal.

interior increased in importance as a design sphere, which led to greater importance being attached to mosaics, frescoes, coffered ceilings and architectural decoration.

The high esteem in which Greek culture was held found its expression in the way the art of Greece was adapted by Roman artists in the first three centuries AD. This esteem then reappeared in the Renaissance, the "Rebirth of Antiquity", which started in 14th-century Italy and went on to spread across the whole of Europe. In the 18th and 19th centuries, Greek art underwent a fashionable revival in the movement known as "neoclassicism", which adopted the forms of Classical architecture, and its influence was also apparent among 20th-century architects, for example in the Postmodern movement of the 1980s.

The ornaments of the Audsleys' "Greek style" are not faithful reproductions, but new creations in the style of Graeco-Roman Antiquity. They are mostly based on variations of the acanthus, a thistle-like plant found in the Mediterranean region, whose deeply indented leaves were adopted as the exemplar for Corinthian capitals and other decorative elements, for example friezes. The stylization of the

bemerkbar. In der Baukunst wurde zunehmend der Innenraum als gestalterische Aufgabe entdeckt, was dazu führte, dass nun verstärkt Wert auf Mosaike, Fresken, Kassettendecken und Baudekor gelegt wurde.

Die hohe Wertschätzung der griechischen Kunst und Kultur fand ihren Ausdruck in den Adaptionen durch die römische Kunst (1. Jahrhundert n. Chr. – 3 Jahrhundert n. Chr.). Sie fand aber auch ihren Niederschlag in der Renaissance, jener „Wiedergeburt der Antike", die im 14. Jahrhundert in Italien aufkam und sich über ganz Europa ausbreiten sollte. Im 18. und 19. Jahrhundert erlebte sie eine modische Wiederbelebung durch den „Klassizismus", der sich auf klassische Architekturformen besann, und nicht zuletzt griffen auch die Architekten des 20. Jahrhunderts, etwa in der Postmoderne der 80er Jahre, auf die Formensprache der griechischen Antike zurück.

Die Ornamente des „Griechischen Stils" der Audsleys sind keine originalgetreuen Reproduktionen, sondern Nachschöpfungen im Stil der griechisch-römischen Antike. Sie basieren zumeist auf Variationen des Akanthus, einem distelartigen Gewächs des Mittelmeerraumes, dessen spitzzackige Blätter als Vorbild für korinthische Kapitelle und

plafonds à caissons et décors architecturaux.

La haute considération dont jouissaient l'art et la culture grecs s'exprima dans les adaptations de l'art romain (du Ier au IIIe siècle après J.-C.). Elle se manifesta encore dans la Renaissance, cette « régénération de l'Antiquité » apparue au XIVe siècle en Italie et qui devait s'étendre à toute l'Europe. Aux XVIIIe et XIXe siècles, elle revint au goût du jour grâce au « néoclassicisme » qui rappelait les formes architecturales classiques, mais ce sont aussi les architectes du XXe siècle, se réclamant par exemple de la tendance post-moderne des années 80, qui se sont référés au langage des formes de l'Antiquité grecque.

Les ornements du « style grec » des Audsley ne sont pas de fidèles reproductions, mais plutôt des créations inspirées du style de l'Antiquité gréco-romaine. Elles se basent principalement sur des variations de l'acanthe, une plante épineuse du Bassin méditerranéen et dont les feuilles très découpées ont servi de modèles pour la réalisation des chapiteaux corinthiens et d'autres éléments de décoration, par exemple des frises. La stylisation de l'acanthe a donné forme à la palmette souvent utilisée comme élément décoratif de frises, d'antéfixes ou de couronnements

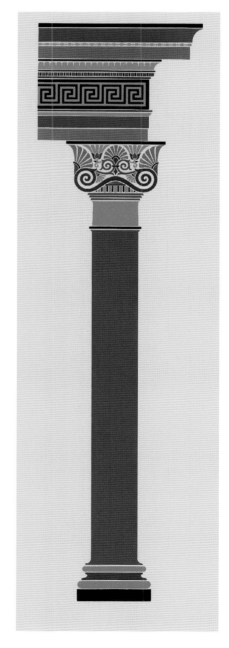

acanthus led to the palmette, which was widely used as a decorative element on the friezes, antesixas and acroteria of Classical temples. If the palmette alternated with a stylized lotus blossom, the result was the anthemion, an ornamental band which often decorates friezes, entablatures and soffits of Hellenistic buildings. Sometimes these motifs were also combined with acanthus rosettes, or else the rosette

andere Dekorationselemente wie zum Beispiel Friese dienten. Die Stilisierung des Akanthus führte zur Palmette, die oft als Dekorationselement von Friesen, Stirnziegeln oder Giebelbekrönungen (Akroterion) von Tempeln verwendet wurde. Kombiniert man die Palmette mit einer stilisierten, rapportierenden Lotusblüte, erhält man das Anthemion, ein Ornamentband, das häufig Friese, Gesimse und Balkenunter-

de frontons (acrotère) de temples. Associée de façon récurrente à une fleur de lotus stylisée, la palmette évolue vers l'anthémion, bandeau ornemental récurrent des frises, corniches et dessous de poutres d'édifices hellénistiques. Ces motifs sont associés de temps à autre à des rosaces d'acanthes; la rosace peut aussi constituer le motif central, comme c'est le cas dans les plafonds à caissons antiques. Perles et oves,

Ancient mosaic from the Attalos II Palace in Pergamon, Pergamon Museum, Berlin, 159–138 BC
The notable wealth of motifs and the elaborate construction of this mosaic reflect the esthetic value placed on ornamentation. The mosaic is bordered at the top by a fret band. This in turn is followed by a narrow zigzag band and a broad strip bearing an arabesque in contrasting colors. This latter stands out by the strength of its color and its perspective, something seldom found in the art of Antiquity. The mosaic is borderd by a plaited band.

Antikes Mosaik aus dem Palast Attalos II. in Pergamon, Pergamon Museum, Berlin, 159–138 v. Chr.
Der auffällige Motivreichtum und die kunstvolle Machart dieses Mosaiks belegen die Wertschätzung, die dem Ornament als Schmuckelement zukam. Das Mosaikfeld wird nach oben von einem breiten Mäanderband begrenzt. Es folgt ein schmales Zickzack-Band und darunter ein breites Wellenband, an das ein breiter Streifen mit einer farbig abgesetzten Arabeske anschließt. Sie besticht durch ihre Farbigkeit und ihre perspektivische Darstellung, die in der Antike selten ist. Das Mosaik wird von einem Flechtband abgeschlossen.

Mosaïque antique provenant du Palais d'Attale II à Pergame, Musée Pergamon, Berlin, 159–138 avant J.-C.
La richesse évidente et la composition artistique de cette mosaïque attestent de l'importance qui était accordée à l'ornement en tant qu'élément décoratif. Le panneau de mosaïque est limité dans le haut par un large bandeau de méandres, suivi par un étroit bandeau de zigzags et en dessous par un large bandeau d'arabesques de couleurs. Cette mosaïque séduit par sa composition de couleurs et son effet de perspective quel'on rencontre rarement dans l'Antiquité. Elle se termine par un bandeau de rinceaux.

was emphasized as the central element, as is the case with the coffered ceilings of Antiquity. Another popular decorative motif was the egg-and-dart, which was often applied to linking elements in architecture, for example the base and capital of columns, abacus and the cornice. Other characteristic patterns of the Greek style are the meander or fret, including swastika motifs, and also the vitruvian scroll

sichten hellenistischer Gebäude ziert. Mitunter werden diese Motive auch mit Akanthusrosetten kombiniert oder die Rosette wird als Zentralmotiv ausgeprägt, wie dies etwa bei antiken Kassettendecken der Fall ist. Ein beliebtes Schmuckmotiv sind auch Perl- und Eierstäbe, die häufig Zwischenglieder der Architektur, wie zum Beispiel Säulenbasis und -hals, Kapitell, Abakus und Gesimsprofile zieren. Zu den charak-

autres motifs ornementaux courants, décorent fréquemment les éléments intermédiaires de l'architecture, par exemple la base et le gorgerin des colonnes, le chapiteau, l'abaque et les profils de corniches. Les méandres et svastikas sont également des motifs caractéristiques du style grec, de même que le bandeau ornemental qualifié de « bande de vagues », évolution ultérieure du méandre classique. Le nom

or "running dog", an ornamental band motif which developed from the Classical fret. The word "meander" in English is more generally applied to rivers which twist and turn, and is in fact derived from the River Meandros in Asia Minor. The connection with rivers points to a certain symbolic connection of the fret pattern with water as the source of life. It is striking that most of the motifs of Antiquity are based on

teristischen Mustern des griechischen Stils gehören überdies Mäander- und Swastikamotive sowie ein als „laufender Hund" bekanntes Ornamentband, eine Weiterentwicklung des klassischen Mäanders. Die Bezeichnung Mäander für ein Ornamentband mit rechtwinklig gebrochenen, fortlaufenden Linien leitet sich von dem kleinasiatischen Fluss Mäandros ab, der besonders windungsreich ist und damit dem Mäan-

« méandre », désignant un bandeau ornemental à lignes continues se pliant à angle droit, est dérivé de Méandre, fleuve d'Asie Mineure particulièrement sinueux. Ce motif souligne en même temps l'importance de l'eau comme origine de la vie. Il est frappant de voir que la plupart des motifs antiques font un retour aux formes naturelles dont la stylisation a été de plus en plus marquée au fil du temps.

Corinthian acanthus capital, now in the local Archaeological Museum of Epidauros, c. 500 BC
The Corinthian acanthus capital is probably the best known of all the capitals of Antiquity. The decor is derived from the acanthus, a thistle-like plant of the Mediterranean region. The Corinthian capital consists of two rings of acanthus leaves, one above the other, in high relief. The open leaves alternate with slender closed leaves elegantly rolled up at the ends, forming scrolls which take the weight of the roof above.

Korinthisches Akanthuskapitell, heute im Archäologischen Museum von Epidaurus, ca. 5. Jh. v. Chr.
Das korinthische Akanthuskapitell ist die heute wohl bekannteste Kapitellform der Antike. Der Dekor ist vom Akanthus, einem distelartigen Gewächs des Mittelmeerraumes, abgeleitet, und wurde hier in zwei übereinander liegenden, plastisch ausgearbeiteten Blattkränzen herausgearbeitet. Zwischen den Akanthusblättern ragen schlanke Blatthülsen hervor, die sich an ihren Enden elegant zusammenrollen und in den Ecken als Voluten ausgeprägt werden, auf denen die Last der aufliegenden Deckplatte ruht.

Chapiteau corinthien à feuilles d'acanthe, aujourd'hui au Musée archéologique d'Épidaure, environ Vᵉ siècle avant J.-C.
Le chapiteau corinthien à feuilles d'acanthe est la forme de chapiteau de l'Antiquité la plus connue aujourd'hui. Le décor est dérivé de l'acanthe, plante ressemblant au chardon et poussant dans le bassin méditerranéen, et il se compose ici de deux entrelacs de feuilles en relief et superposés. On aperçoit entre les feuilles d'acanthe des hampes élancées qui s'enroulent élégamment à leur extrémité et qui prennent la forme de volutes dans les angles sur lesquels l'abaque prend appui.

natural models which were increasingly stylized over the years.

dermotiv gleicht. Der Ursprung dieses Motivs macht zugleich auch auf die Bedeutung des Wassers als Ursprung des Lebens aufmerksam. Es ist auffällig, dass die meisten antiken Motive auf Naturformen zurückgehen, die mit der Zeit immer stärker stilisiert wurden.

Cornice decorations with variations on the egg-and-dart and leaf-and-tongue patterns
Simsverzierungen mit Variationen von Blatt- und Eierstäben
Décorations de corniches avec des variantes de feuilles et d'oves

The seven borders with their continuous motifs illustrated here are particularly suitable for cornice decorations. The top pattern is based on the Classical egg-and-dart, an ornamental band consisting of a series of oval forms. This type of ornamental band was typically used in Antiquity for the undersides of cornices, and thus provided a link between the support and the supported element. The Classical egg-and-dart pattern can be seen here in its original form, presented in dark colors on a pale background. Shown below are variations of the same motif. On the one side the ovals are replaced by triangles and given a colored edge, while in on the other side the ovals are pointed, and likewise with multiple colored edging, giving the pattern greater vitality. A leaf-and-tongue pattern follows. Its form is derived from a series of leaves pointing upwards, but bent back by the weight of the burden they are supporting, thus giving the pattern its final shape. The colored accentuation of the individual elements gives this ornamental band additional plasticity. Presented below are possible decorative variations of the egg-and-dart motif. The bottom picture shows a variation bordered with an astragal.

The patterns can be used for various purposes. They are suitable both as the borders of wall surfaces, or else to accentuate unprofiled ledges or cornices. In addition to the colors depicted on the plates, these ornaments can also be reproduced in a light color on dark background.

Die hier gezeigten sieben Bordüren mit fortlaufenden Motiven eignen sich besonders für Simsverzierungen. Das Muster oben basiert auf dem klassischen Eierstab, einem Ornamentband, bei dem ovale, eiförmige Gebilde aneinander gereiht sind und das auch ionisches Kymation genannt wird. Es zierte in der Antike meist die Unterglieder von Gesimsplatten und vermittelte somit zwischen Stütze und Last. Hier ist der Eierstab in seiner ursprünglichen Form zu sehen, dargestellt in dunklen Farben auf hellem Grund. Darunter werden zwei Varianten desselben Motivs gezeigt: Zum einen sind die Ovale durch Dreiecke ersetzt und farbig umrandet und zum anderen werden sie mit kleinen Spitzen versehen, deren Konturen ebenfalls mehrfach umrandet sind, wodurch das Muster an Vitalität gewinnt. Es folgt eine Blattwelle, die auch als „lesbisches Kymation" bezeichnet wird. Seine Form leitet sich von einer Reihe aufwärts gerichteter Blätter ab, die unter der zu tragenden Last bis zum unteren Ende zurückgekrümmt werden, wodurch das Muster seine endgültige Form erhält. Durch die farbige Akzentuierung der einzelnen Glieder gewinnt dieses Ornamentband zusätzlich an Plastizität. Darunter werden mögliche Varianten des Eierstabmotivs in einer formschönen Ausprägung präsentiert. Die letzte Abbildung zeigt eine Abwandlung des dorischen Kymations mit abschließendem Perlband, auch Perlstab genannt.

Die Muster sind für verschiedene Zwecke verwendbar. So eignen sie sich sowohl als Bordüre für Wandflächen als auch zur Hervorhebung unprofilierter Gesimse. Neben der hier vorgeschlagenen Farbwahl können diese Ornamente auch in einer hellen Farbe auf dunklem Untergrund wiedergegeben werden.

Les sept bordures présentées ici avec des motifs répétitifs conviennent parfaitement à la décoration de corniches. Le motif du haut se base sur la rangée d'oves, un bandeau ornemental formé d'une succession de figures ovales, ovoïdes, appelés également « cymaise ionique ». Dans l'Antiquité, il décorait le plus souvent les sous-moulures de corniches et se trouvait ainsi pris entre l'étai et la charge. La première illustration présente l'ove classique, dans sa forme originale, en couleurs sombres sur fond clair. On reconnaît deux variantes du même motif : les ovales sont d'une part remplacés par des triangles avec une bordure de couleur et d'autre part, pourvus de petites pointes aux contours plusieurs fois bordés, qui confèrent une grande vitalité au motif. On voit une ondulation de feuilles également appelée « cymaise de Lesbos ». Elle emprunte sa forme à une rangée de feuilles pointant vers le haut qui se recourbent vers l'extrémité inférieure sous la charge qu'elles portent, donnant ainsi sa forme définitive au motif. Ce bandeau ornemental gagne encore en plasticité par la couleur qui accentue les différents composants. Des variantes possibles du motif de l'ove sont représentées dans une expression très esthétique. La dernière illustration montre une évolution de la « cymaise dorique » se terminant par un bandeau de perles également appelé « fusarolle ». Les motifs conviennent à diverses applications. Ils serviront ainsi de bordures tant pour les murs que pour rehausser des corniches non profilées. Il est possible de reproduire ces ornements dans les couleurs proposées ici ou d'utiliser d'autres combinaisons, par exemple : de couleur claire sur fond sombre.

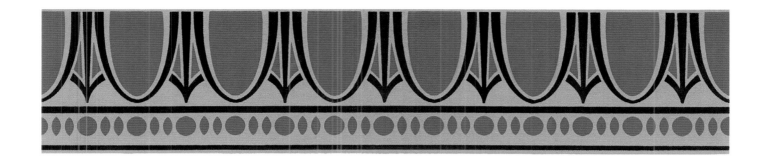

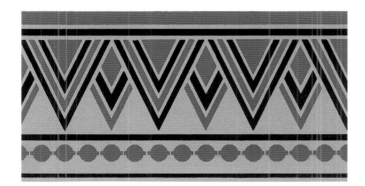

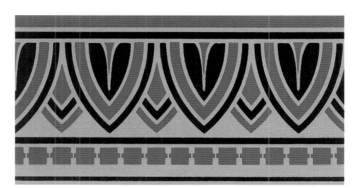

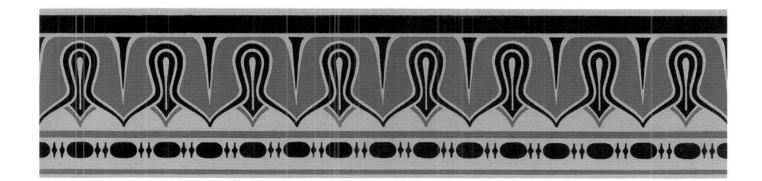

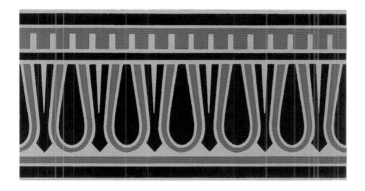

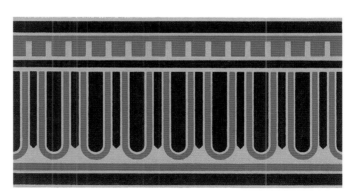

Ornamental bands with variations on the fret
Ornamentbänder mit Variationen des Mäanders
Bandeaux ornementaux avec des variantes du méandre

Shown here are five variations on the Classical fret, probably the best-known of all the ornamental devices of Antiquity. The first band shows a running pattern with inscribed swastikas. The second decorative band restricts itself to a repetition of a simple oblique pattern. The third band shows a particularly splendid example of the fret, while the fourth repeats the swastika, this time in a light color on a dark ground, and slanting to the right. Finally, the fifth shows a fret in combination with rosettes.

The five decorative bands depicted here could be used in a whole range of colors.

Dargestellt sind fünf Variationen des klassischen Mäanders, dem wohl bekanntesten antiken Ornament, in Form von Ornamentbändern. Das erste Band zeigt einen Mäander mit eingeschriebenen Hakenkreuzen, auch Hakenkreuzmäander genannt. Das zweite Ornamentband beschränkt sich auf die Wiedergabe eines schräg angelegten Mäanders. Das dritte Band zeigt einen besonders prächtig gestalteten Mäander. Das vierte Band stellt einen schräg gestellten Hakenkreuzmäander dar. Das fünfte Band zeigt schließlich den Mäander in Verbindung mit Rosetten.

Farblich können die hier vorgestellten Ornamentbänder ganz frei gestaltet werden.

Cette planche présente cinq variations du méandre classique, l'ornement antique traditionnel, sous la forme de bandeaux ornementaux. Le premier bandeau montre un méandre de croix gammées imbriquées, également appelé « méandre aux croix gammées ». Le deuxième bandeau ornemental se limite à reproduire un méandre incliné vers la gauche, le troisième montre un méandre particulièrement riche, le quatrième un méandre à croix gammées incliné vers la droite et enfin le cinquième un méandre associé à des rosaces. Il va sans dire que ces bandeaux ornementaux peuvent être réalisés dans d'autres couleurs que celles présentées ici.

Horizontal ornamental bands with fret motifs
Horizontale Ornamentbänder mit Mäandermotiven
Bandeaux ornementaux horizontaux à motifs de méandres

This plate depicts two elaborate fret patterns. The pattern at the top shows a fret in combination with palmettes reminiscent of the acroterion which might crown the pediment of a Classical temple. The pattern below is reproduced in two variants: on the left-hand side of the picture a swastika fret alternates with rosettes, while on the right the rosettes are replaced by small squares.

Both patterns are suitable as decorations for broad horizontal ornamental bands. The top pattern could also be used to decorate vertical bands or pilasters, provided the palmettes were also made to point upwards. The lower example is suitable for use as a decorative band to demarcate the top of a wall from the ceiling, or else for the underside of a beam. It is not absolutely essential to use two colors as illustrated here. The patterns could be dark against a light background, or alternatively, gold or some similar light color on a dark background.

Diese Tafel präsentiert zwei aufwändig gestaltete Mäanderentwürfe. Das Muster oben zeigt Mäander in Verbindung mit Palmetten, die formal an die Giebelbekrönung antiker Tempel erinnern, die auch Akroterion genannt wird. Das untere Muster wird in zwei Versionen wiedergegeben: In der linken Bildhälfte sieht man Hakenkreuzmäander, die mit Rosetten abwechseln, während in der rechten Bildhälfte kleine Quadrate an die Stelle der Rosetten treten.

Beide Muster eignen sich als Dekor für breite horizontale Ornamentbänder. Das Muster oben kann auch für die Verzierung vertikaler Bänder oder Pilaster angewandt werden, vorausgesetzt, die Palmetten werden senkrecht gestellt. Das untere Beispiel eignet sich als Schmuckband für den oberen Wandabschnitt als Abgrenzung von Zimmerdecken wie auch zur Dekoration der Unterseite von Balken. Es ist nicht unbedingt erforderlich, die Ornamente wie auf der Tafel in zwei Farben auszuführen. Sie können in einer dunklen Farbe auf hellem Grund oder auch in Gold oder einer ähnlichen, hellen Farbe auf dunklem Untergrund aufgetragen werden.

Cette planche présente deux motifs de méandres aux formes riches. Le motif du haut se compose de méandres associés à des palmettes qui, par leur forme, rappellent le couronnement des frontons de temples antiques, également appelé « acrotère ». Le motif du bas est proposé dans deux versions : dans la partie gauche, des méandres à croix gammées alternent avec des rosaces, tandis que des carrés de petite taille remplacent les rosaces dans la partie droite.

Les deux motifs serviront à décorer de larges bandeaux ornementaux horizontaux. Le motif du haut pourra aussi décorer des bandeaux verticaux ou des pilastres, à condition de disposer les palmettes verticalement. Le motif du bas servira de bandeau ornemental pour délimiter la partie supérieure du mur et le plafond d'une pièce et pourra aussi décorer le dessous de poutres. La réalisation en deux couleurs proposée ici n'est pas impérative. On pourra exécuter ces ornements dans une couleur foncée sur fond clair, mais aussi en doré ou dans une couleur claire similaire sur fond sombre.

Horizontal ornamental bands with palmette motifs
Horizontale Ornamentbänder mit Palmettendekor
Bandeaux ornementaux horizontaux à palmettes

What we see here are two horizontal ornamental bands with palmette designs. The Classical palmette which inspired these designs is reproduced in a slightly stylized fashion. The example at the top shows two palmettes – one upright and the other upside-down but otherwise identical – repeating alternately. The two types are linked by elegantly curved lines and thus reminiscent of the Classical palmette frieze. The bottom pattern is based on a palmette in combination with a form incorporating pointed stylized leaves reminiscent of lotus blossoms, which means that this pattern can be seen as a variation on the Classical anthemion band. The coloration – black, ox-blood, and ochre – is reminiscent of Etruscan murals, which were retained for centuries in Roman decorative art. These ornamental bands emphasize the transition from a dark wall to a light ceiling and are also suitable for framing large areas of wall space. Both patterns can be implemented in whatever colors are desired on a light background, or in gold or a similar light color on a dark background.

Hier sind zwei horizontale Ornamentbänder mit Palmettenentwürfen zu sehen. Die klassische Palmette, von der diese Entwürfe inspiriert sind, ist leicht stilisiert wiedergegeben. Das obere Beispiel zeigt zwei Palmetten – eine aufrechte und eine kopfständige – im Rapport. Beide Palmettentypen sind durch elegant geschwungene Linien miteinander verbunden und erinnern daher an den klassischen Palmettenfries. Das Muster unten basiert auf einer Palmette in Verbindung mit ihrer spitzzackigen Stilisierung, die formal an eine Lotusblüte erinnert, so dass dieser Entwurf als eine Variante des klassischen Lotus- und Palmettenbandes gewertet werden kann, der auch als „Anthemion" bekannt ist. Die Farbgebung – Schwarz, Ochsenblut bzw. Dunkelrot und Ocker – erinnert an die der etruskischen Wandmalereien, die in der römischen Kunst über Jahrhunderte hinweg erhalten blieb. Diese Ornamentbänder betonen den Übergang von einer dunklen Wand zu einer hellen Decke und eignen sich auch zur Umrandung größerer Wandflächen. Beide Muster lassen sich in jeder beliebigen Farbe auf hellem Grund oder in Gold oder einem ähnlich hellen Farbton auf dunklem Grund ausführen.

Cette planche présente deux bandeaux ornementaux horizontaux à palmettes. La palmette classique dont ces motifs sont inspirés est légèrement stylisée ici. Le motif du haut montre deux palmettes récurrentes, l'une verticale et l'autre tête-bêche. Les deux types de palmettes sont reliés entre eux par des lignes élégamment incurvées et rappellent de ce fait la frise de palmettes classique. Le motif du bas se compose d'une palmette associée à des feuilles stylisées dentelées dont la forme rappelle une fleur de lotus ; on peut donc considérer ce motif comme une variante du bandeau classique de fleurs de lotus et de palmettes, également connue sous le nom d'« anthémion ». La gamme de couleurs – noir, « sang de bœuf », c'est-à-dire rouge foncé et ocre – rappelle celle des peintures murales étrusques qui, à travers l'art romain, ont subsisté au cours des siècles.
Ces bandeaux ornementaux soulignent la transition d'un mur sombre à un plafond clair et peuvent aussi border de grands murs. Ces deux motifs pourront être réalisés dans n'importe quelle couleur sur fond clair, mais aussi en doré ou dans une teinte claire similaire sur fond sombre.

Horizontal ornamental bands with vitruvian scroll motifs
Horizontale Ornamentbänder mit Wellenornamenten
Bandeaux ornementaux horizontaux à décor de vagues

This plate shows two variations on the vitruvian scroll. The pattern at the top is based on a spiral tendril reminiscent of the Classical form (sometimes known colloquially as the "running dog"). At the ends of the breaking "waves" there are small rosettes, while the resulting spandrels are filled out with stylized calyxes. The lower pattern shows a vitruvian scroll with diagonally opposed palmettes, giving the design a particular dynamism. Both patterns are suitable for use in horizontal or vertical directions, for example in halls, staircases or corridors, and can also be used to separate strongly patterned wall-surfaces. Unlike the top pattern, the one at the bottom cannot be used on decorated wall-surfaces with a preponderance of diagonal elements, as its own oblique palmettes would form too strong a contrast. All the color combinations suggested in connection with the preceding patterns are possible here too.

Diese Tafel zeigt zwei Varianten von Wellenranken. Das obere Muster basiert auf einer spiralförmig geschwungenen Ranke, die an das klassische „Wellenband" erinnert, das volkstümlich auch als „laufender Hund" bezeichnet wird. Am Ende der brechenden Wellen sind kleine Rosetten angeordnet, während die entstehenden Zwickel von stilisierten Kelchblüten geziert werden. Das Ornamentband unten zeigt ein Wellenornament mit sich diagonal gegenüberstehenden Palmetten, die schräg wiedergegeben sind, wodurch das Muster eine besondere Dynamik erhält.
Beide Muster sind für horizontale oder vertikale Wandbänder zu verwenden, wie sie etwa in Sälen, Treppenhäusern oder Gängen vorkommen. Sie können aber auch stark gemusterte Wandflächen voneinander trennen. Im Gegensatz zum oberen Ornament lässt sich das untere nicht an verzierten Wandflächen anbringen, in denen schräge Linien vorherrschen, weil die eigene Neigung einen zu starken Kontrast mit den schrägen Linien der Wandfläche bilden würde. Alle im Zusammenhang mit den vorigen Tafeln erwähnten Farbkombinationen sind auch hier möglich.

Cette planche présente deux variantes de décors de vagues. Le motif du haut se base sur un entrelacs incurvé en spirale qui rappelle la « bande de vagues » classique, couramment appelée « motif à volute ». Des petites rosaces sont disposées à l'extrémité des vagues qui se brisent, tandis que la spirale naissante est ornée de fleurs stylisées en forme de calices. Le bandeau ornemental du bas se compose de vagues à palmettes disposées tête-bêche et en diagonale, ce qui confère au motif un dynamisme particulier.
On utilisera les deux motifs pour des bandeaux horizontaux ou verticaux réalisés sur des murs, tels qu'on en voit par exemple dans des pièces, cages d'escaliers ou couloirs. Mais ils peuvent aussi séparer des murs richement décorés. Contrairement à l'ornement du haut, celui du bas ne convient pas à des murs décorés avec des lignes obliques prédominantes, car leur propre inclinaison contrasterait trop brutalement avec les lignes obliques du mur. Toutes les combinaisons de couleurs en rapport avec les planches précédentes sont possibles ici aussi.

Ornamental bands with tendril motifs
Ornamentbänder mit Rankengebilden
Bandeaux ornementaux à entrelacs

Pictured here are five possibilities for vertical decorative bands. The one in the center shows a variation on the anthemion band, which is particularly attractive on account of its discreet coloration in combination with gold. This pattern suggests itself for broad vertical bands or narrow wall cladding elements, or else as a decoration for pilasters or pilaster strips. If used for wall cladding, its outer borders can be omitted, their functions being taken over by the edges of the cladding element. This band is also suitable for use as a decoration for the undersides of ceiling beams or roofing rafters.

The bands at the sides have a variety of tendril motifs. Top left, is a pattern with slightly curved lanceolate leaves, reminiscent of an olive branch. Below, is a tendril with slim, heart-shaped leaves alternating with red berries, which may represent a variation on the laurel. Top right, is a composition with a very static effect: a tendril with heart-shaped leaves, presumably derived from ivy. By contrast, bottom right, is a dynamic design. These ornamental bands are extremely versatile, both as free-standing decorative elements and together with other ornamental forms. They can be used for example to decorate pillars and columns. In addition, they can also be used on wall surfaces with diagonal patterns and on molded elements. Unlike the preceding patterns, the four narrow tendril patterns on this plate can be cut down the central line, and only one side (with one row of leaves) used.

Dargestellt sind fünf Varianten für vertikale Dekorbänder. Das mittlere Ornamentband zeigt eine Variation eines Palmettenbandes, der durch seine zurückhaltende Farbgebung in Verbindung mit Gold besticht. Dieses Muster kommt für die Gestaltung breiter vertikaler Bänder sowie für schmale Wandverkleidungen oder als Dekor für Pilaster und Lisenen in Frage. Wird es für Wandverkleidungen verwendet, können die äußeren Begrenzungslinien fortgelassen werden, deren Funktion dann die Randleisten übernehmen. Dieses Band ist auch als Dekoration der Unterseite von Deckenbalken oder Dachsparren geeignet. Die seitlichen Bänder werden von unterschiedlichen Ranken geziert. Links oben sind Ranken mit lanzettförmigen, leicht geschwungenen Blättern zu erkennen, die an die Form des Ölzweigs erinnern. Darunter sieht man eine Ranke mit schlanken, herzförmigen Blättern im Wechsel mit roten Beeren, die vielleicht eine Variante des Lorbeers darstellen. Rechts oben ist eine sehr statisch wirkende Komposition wiedergegeben: eine Ranke mit Herzblättern, deren Form sich vermutlich vom Blatt des Efeu ableitet. Darunter ist eine Ranke mit einer dynamischen Linienführung abgebildet.

Diese seitlichen Ornamentbänder können vielfältig verwendet werden, sowohl als allein stehende Dekorationselemente als auch zusammen mit anderen Schmuckformen. So werden sie zum Beispiel zur Dekoration von Säulen und plastischen Leisten eingesetzt und lassen sich überdies auf schräg gemusterten Wandflächen anbringen. Im Gegensatz zu den bereits präsentierten Mustern sind die vier seitlichen Rankenbänder auch als Stängel mit Blättern auf lediglich einer Seite, also in halber Breite, ausführbar.

Cette planche présente cinq variantes de bandeaux décoratifs verticaux. Le bandeau central montre une variante du bandeau de palmettes qui séduit par ses couleurs discrètes associées à du doré. Ce motif convient pour la réalisation de panneaux muraux étroits ou la décoration de pilastres et de lésènes. S'il est utilisé pour des panneaux muraux, on pourra supprimer les lignes de séparation externes dont les listels assureront la fonction. Ce bandeau est idéal aussi pour la décoration de dessous de poutres ou de chevrons.

Les bandeaux latéraux se composent de différents entrelacs. En haut à gauche, des entrelacs à feuilles légèrement incurvées et en forme de lancettes rappellent le rameau d'olivier. En bas, un entrelacs de feuilles élancées, en forme de cœur alternant avec des baies rouges représente peut-être une variante du laurier. En haut à droite, la composition crée une impression de très grande immobilité : un entrelacs de jeunes feuilles dont la forme dérive probablement de la feuille de lierre. Le bandeau du bas présente un entrelacs aux lignes dynamiques.

Ces bandeaux ornementaux peuvent avoir de multiples applications, individuellement ou avec d'autres formes décoratives. Ils peuvent servir à décorer des colonnes et des listels en relief. On peut en outre les réaliser sur des murs à motifs obliques. Contrairement aux motifs déjà présentés, ces quatre bandeaux latéraux d'entrelacs pourront aussi se présenter sous la forme de tiges avec des fleurs d'un seul côté, c'est-à-dire sur la moitié de la largeur.

Broad ornamental bands with stylized palmettes including spiral tendril elements
Breite Ornamentbänder mit stilisierten, geschwungenen Palmettenranken
Larges bandeaux ornementaux à entrelacs de palmettes incurvés stylisés

This plate depicts two broad vertical ornamental bands whose pattern is based on stylized palmettes with scroll elements. The pattern on the left has a conspicuous central stem decorated by a series of palmettes one above the other. Each palmette emerges from a slender calyx between spiral tendrils or scroll-like elements. These provide a frame for the central palmette. The spandrels and other areas not filled by the palmettes or tendrils are occupied by calyx-like motifs reminiscent of the Classical semi-palmette.

The pattern on the right is a variation of that on the left. Particularly striking here is the shape of the spiral tendrils, which form a heartshaped pattern framing the palmette. The vacant spaces are larger, and filled by correspondingly larger palmette-like elements.

Both compositions are highly elaborate. They are suitable for use as broad decorative bands either vertically or horizontally (an appropriate end-piece would be needed). The color scheme of coordinated shades of green used here is particularly attractive, but a more lively coloration would also be possible.

Diese Tafel zeigt zwei breite vertikale Ornamentbänder, deren Muster auf stilisierten, geschwungenen Palmetten beruhen. Das Motiv links verfügt über einen deutlich ausgeprägten Zentralstamm, der von mehreren übereinander angeordneten Palmetten geziert wird. Die den Zentralstamm flankierenden Halbpalmetten entwachsen einem schlanken Blütenkelch, von dem sich stilisierte Ranken abspalten. Diese Ranken rollen sich spiralförmig ein und rahmen die zentrale Palmettenkomposition. Als Füllformen dienen kelchförmige Blattgebilde, die sich formal an der klassischen Halbpalmette orientieren.

Das Muster rechts stellt eine Variante des linken Ornamentbandes dar. Auffällig ist die Form der spiralförmigen Ranken, die eine zentrale, einem Blütenkelch entspringende Palmette herzförmig umschließen. Als seitliche Füllformen sind große Halbpalmetten eingefügt, die sich flächendeckend auffiedern.

Beide Kompositionen sind sehr aufwändig gestaltet. Sie eignen sich als breite Dekorbänder in horizontaler wie vertikaler Ausrichtung, wobei die Endstücke eigens entwickelt werden sollten. Besonders schön ist die hier gewählte Farbgebung Ton in Ton, aber auch eine wesentlich farbigere Gestaltung wäre möglich.

Cette planche présente deux bandeaux ornementaux verticaux, dont les motifs reposent sur des palmettes incurvées stylisées. Le motif de gauche se compose d'une tige centrale très prononcée, ornée d'une succession de palmettes. Les demi-palmettes qui flanquent la tige jaillissent d'un calice de fleur élancé dont se détachent des entrelacs stylisés. Ces entrelacs s'enroulent en spirale et encadrent la composition centrale de palmettes. Des feuilles en forme de calice qui, par leur aspect, rappellent la demi-palmette classique rempliront les espaces vides.

Le motif de droite représente une variante du bandeau ornemental gauche. Le mouvement de ces entrelacs en spirales qui forment un cœur et entourent une palmette sortant d'un calice est particulièrement frappant. Des demi-palmettes de grand format, ajoutées sur les côtés en guise de raccord, s'ouvrent en éventail.

Ces deux compositions ont des formes très riches. Elles serviront de larges bandeaux décoratifs dans le sens horizontal ou vertical et il conviendra dans ce cas de compléter les extrémités. Les couleurs ton sur ton choisies ici sont particulièrement attrayantes, mais une réalisation dans des couleurs plus vives est bien sûr possible.

Corner decorations using palmettes
Eckverzierungen mit Palmetten
Décors d'angles à palmettes

These two decorative suggestions show four distinct palmette compositions designed for the ornamentation of the corners of large wall areas. For the decoration of coffered ceilings on the Classical model, one of the patterns should be chosen and placed in the four corners of the coffer. The coffer would then require in addition a central motif, for example a rosette formed by rotating the corner element about its corner point.

Diese beiden Ornamentvorschläge zeigen vier verschiedene Palmettenkompositionen, die zur Verzierung der Ecken großer Wandflächen bestimmt sind. Zur Ausstattung von Kassettendecken nach antikem Vorbild sollte eins der Muster ausgewählt und an den vier Ecken der Kassette angebracht werden. Die Kassette verlangt überdies nach einem Zentralmotiv, beispielsweise einer Rosette, die sich ergibt, wenn man das Eckornament um seinen Eckpunkt dreht.

Ces deux propositions d'ornements présentent quatre compositions de palmettes différentes destinées à la décoration d'angles de grands murs. On choisira un de ces motifs pour décorer des plafonds à caissons selon le modèle antique et on l'appliquera aux quatre angles du caisson. Le caisson exige en outre un motif central, par exemple une rosace, qu'on obtient en faisant tourner le motif d'angle autour de son angle.

Corner decorations with colored palmette designs
Eckverzierungen mit farbigem Palmettendekor
Décors d'angles à palmettes de couleurs

This plate shows two examples of designs suitable for the corners of ceilings. They each consist of a combination of a rich variety of elaborately drawn palmettes. While the smaller pattern at the top right shows palmettes in combination with tendril, rosette and fret motifs, the pattern at the bottom left is conspicuous by its elegant lines and its general lightness. The coloration is reminiscent of the Etruscan manner.

Both designs are suitable as corner elements for large ceilings where these are subdivided into sizable rectangular fields, as is usual in neoclassical interior decoration schemes. In order to achieve a particularly elegant effect, the ceiling can be surrounded by a fret or palmette band. The Etruscan coloration is not essential; other color schemes are also possible.

Diese Tafel präsentiert zwei Beispiele für Eckverzierungen von Decken. Sie zeigen aufwändig gestaltete Palmetten, die variantenreich miteinander kombiniert sind. Während das kleinere Muster oben rechts Palmetten in Verbindung mit Ranken, Rosetten und Mäandern zeigt, besticht das Motiv unten links vor allem durch seine elegante Linienführung und seinen leichten Charakter. Die Farbgebung erinnert an die etruskische Kolorierung.

Beide Ornamente eignen sich als Eckelemente für große Decken, wenn diese in größere rechteckige Felder unterteilt sind, wie dies bei Zimmerdekorationen im klassischen Stil üblich ist. Um eine besonders elegante Wirkung zu erreichen, kann zusätzlich ein Mäander- oder Palmettenband um die Decke geführt werden. Die etruskische Farbgebung ist nicht bindend, auch andere Farbkombinationen sind möglich.

Cette planche présente deux exemples de décors d'angles pour plafonds. Des palmettes aux formes riches associées entre elles présentent de nombreuses variantes. Si le motif plus petit en haut à droite montre des palmettes avec des entrelacs, rosaces et méandres, le motif en bas à gauche séduit surtout par ses lignes élégantes et sa légèreté. Les couleurs rappellent les tons étrusques. Les deux ornements serviront d'éléments d'angles pour de grands plafonds, si ceux-ci sont subdivisés en panneaux rectangulaires assez grands, comme c'était l'usage dans les décorations de pièces de style classique. Pour produire un effet particulièrement élégant, on peut ajouter un bandeau de méandres ou de palmettes autour du plafond. Des combinaisons de couleurs différentes des tons étrusques présentés ici sont également possibles.

Wall panels with palmette designs
Wandpaneele mit Palmettendekor
Panneaux muraux à palmettes

These four patterns depict palmettes in combination with fret motifs. The two designs at the top are particularly suitable for the decoration of the corners of wall panels, while the two at the bottom are best used as central motifs.

The pattern top left combines three Classical motifs: the fret, the vitruvian scroll – spiral tendrils from which palmettes emerge – and the acanthus leaf. The motif above right is striking by dint of its exuberant scrolls, which are not constrained by the outer edge of the design. The pattern below left shows a Classical palmette, formally reminiscent of the acroterion. Here it is flanked by scroll motifs. The pattern below right shows scroll motifs emerging from a semi-rosette, bordered by two fret designs.

These patterns are primarily intended for the decoration of narrow horizontal panels or other horizontal surfaces demarcated by lines – nameplates for example. The coloration of these panels in gold on a dark ground is very striking, but other monochrome or polychrome color schemes are conceivable.

Diese vier Muster zeigen Palmetten in Verbindung mit Mäandermotiven. Die beiden Motive oben eignen sich besonders zur Ausschmückung der Ecken von Wandpaneelen, während die beiden Muster unten als Zentralmotiv zu verwenden sind.

Das Muster links oben kombiniert drei klassische Motive: den Mäander, die spiralförmige Ranke, aus der Palmetten entspringen, und ein liegendes, spitzzackiges Akanthusblatt. Das Motiv rechts oben bezaubert aufgrund seiner schwungvollen Ranken, die der Randbegrenzung entspringen. Das Motiv links unten zeigt eine klassische Palmette, die formal an das Akroterion, die Giebelbekrönung antiker Tempel, erinnert. Es wird hier von stilisierten Ranken umspielt. Das Muster rechts unten zeigt eine stark stilisierte Ranke, die einer Halbrosette entwächst. Sie wird seitlich von zwei flachen Mäandern begrenzt.

Diese Muster sind vorrangig für die Dekoration schmaler horizontaler Paneele oder anderer horizontal ausgerichteter, von Linien begrenzter Flächen bestimmt – wie beispielsweise Namensschilder. Die Farbgebung dieser Tafel in Gold auf dunklem Grund ist sehr prägnant, es sind jedoch auch andere ein- oder mehrfarbige Umsetzungen denkbar.

Ces quatre motifs présentent des palmettes associées à des méandres. Les deux motifs du haut serviront à décorer les angles de panneaux muraux, tandis que les deux motifs du bas seront utilisés comme décor central.
Le motif en haut à gauche se compose de trois éléments classiques : le méandre, l'entrelacs en spirale d'où jaillissent des palmettes et une feuille d'acanthe dentelée. Le motif en haut à droite fascine par ses entrelacs dynamiques qui sortent de la bordure. Dans le motif en bas à gauche, une palmette classique rappelle, par sa forme, l'acrotère qui couronne le fronton de temples antiques. Il est encadré ici par des entrelacs stylisés. Le motif en bas à droite présente un entrelacs très stylisé d'où jaillit une demi-rosace. Celle-ci est limitée sur le côté par deux méandres plats.
Ces motifs sont essentiels pour la décoration de panneaux horizontaux étroits ou d'autres surfaces horizontales, délimitées par des lignes, par exemple des plaques de maisons. La combinaison de couleurs, doré sur fond sombre, de ces panneaux est très frappante ; des transpositions dans une ou plusieurs couleurs sont toutefois possibles.

Panel decoration with palmette and rosette motifs
Paneelverzierung mit Palmettendekor und Rosetten
Décoration de panneaux à palmettes et rosaces

This complete panel design is based on a Classical palmette, which is used as a central motif. It is framed by stylized spiral tendrils, which are what give this design its particular charm. The whole composition is edged at the bottom with a border of rosettes, while at the top, the rosettes are halved.

The design is particularly suitable for high wall surfaces, as well as for the decoration of pilasters. In general, the pattern is intended for flat surfaces of almost any size.

The border of half-rosettes can be used to edge long horizontal surfaces and also for the undersides of beams. Numerous other design possibilities suggest themselves; almost any color combination is possible.

Dieses flächenfüllende Muster basiert auf einer klassischen Palmette, die als Zentralmotiv verwendet ist. Sie wird von stilisierten Spiralranken gerahmt, welche den besonderen Reiz dieses Ornamententwurfes ausmachen. Die ganze Komposition wird unten von einer Bordüre mit Rosetten begrenzt, während die Rosetten der Bordüre am oberen Rand halbiert sind.

Der Entwurf eignet sich besonders für hochformatige Wandflächen sowie zur Verzierung von Pilastern. Generell ist das Muster für ebene Flächen fast jeder Größe bestimmt.

Die Verzierungen mit den Halbrosetten eignen sich sowohl als Abschluss langer waagerechter Flächen als auch für die dekorative Gestaltung von Balkenuntersichten. Es bieten sich noch viele weitere Gestaltungsmöglichkeiten an, die in nahezu jeder Farbkombination gehalten sein können.

Ce décor qui occupe toute la surface d'un panneau se base sur une palmette classique servant de motif central. Cette palmette est encadrée d'entrelacs en spirale stylisés qui font le charme particulier de cette esquisse ornementale. La composition est délimitée dans le bas par une bordure de rosaces, tandis que la bordure du haut est ornée de demi-rosaces.

Ce motif est idéal pour la décoration de murs hauts, ainsi que de pilastres. Il convient en général aux surfaces planes de pratiquement toutes les dimensions.

Les motifs à demi-rosaces termineront des surfaces longues et horizontales et décoreront des dessous de poutres. Il existe de nombreuses autres réalisations possibles dans presque toutes les combinaisons de couleurs.

Panel decorations using palmette motifs
Paneelverzierungen mit Palmettendekor
Décors de panneaux à palmettes

The four designs illustrated here show variations on the palmette motif. While the first is highly Classical in form, the second already shows a stylized variant. The third design extends the motif, making it a highly decorative composition, reminiscent in form of the acroterion, a decorative element used in Antiquity, and widely used in neoclassical architecture, especially during the first half of the 19th century. The final motif is likewise inspired by the acroterion, although here it takes the form of a free, purely ornamental variation. Thus the palmettes of the central stem are replaced by a strongly stylized blossom on a long stalk, which may perhaps represent a lily.

These motifs are particularly suitable for the ends of narrow vertical areas and for pilasters. The two motifs at the bottom can additionally be used for horizontal areas or borders, in which case the designs should be placed at the two ends of the panels.

The patterns illustrated here can be executed in two colors or else in a single dark color on a light or gold background, as in the illustration. If a decision is taken in favor of two colors on a light ground, the darker color should be used for the dominant motifs.

Die hier abgebildeten vier Ornamente zeigen Varianten von Palmetten. Während die erste Palmette sehr klassisch dargestellt ist, wird sie im zweiten Ornament bereits stilisiert wiedergegeben. Der dritte Entwurf erweitert das Motiv zu einer äußerst dekorativen Komposition, die formal an das Akroterion erinnert, ein Schmuckelement der Antike, das in der Architektur des Klassizismus vor allem in der ersten Hälfte des 19. Jahrhunderts wieder vermehrt verwendet wurde. Das letzte Motiv ist ebenfalls vom Akroterion inspiriert, wenn es sich hierbei auch um eine freie, rein ornamentale Ausprägung handelt. So sind die Palmetten des Zentralstammes durch eine langstielige, stark stilisierte Blüte ersetzt, die möglicherweise eine Lilie darstellt.

Diese Motive eignen sich besonders als Abschluss schmaler vertikaler Felder wie auch für Pilaster. Die beiden Motive unten können darüber hinaus als Dekor horizontaler Felder oder Bordüren verwendet werden, wobei die Ornamente an den beiden Enden der Paneele angebracht werden sollten.

Die hier dargestellten Ornamente lassen sich in zwei Farben oder auch in nur einer dunklen Farbe auf hellem oder goldenem Grund ausführen, ähnlich wie auf der Abbildung. Wenn man sich für zwei Farben auf hellem Grund entscheidet, sollte die dunklere Farbe für die bestimmenden Motive verwendet werden.

Les quatre ornements représentés ici sont des variantes de palmettes. Tandis que la première palmette est très classique, la deuxième est déjà stylisée. La troisième étend le motif à une composition très décorative qui rappelle par sa forme un acrotère, élément décoratif de l'Antiquité, revenu au goût du jour dans l'architecture du néo-classicisme, en particulier pendant la première moitié du XIXe siècle. Le dernier motif est également inspiré de l'acrotère, même s'il s'agit ici d'une expression libre, purement ornementale. Les palmettes de la tige centrale sont remplacées dans ce cas par une fleur à longue tige, très stylisée qui représente peut-être un lis.

Ces motifs termineront des panneaux verticaux étroits, ainsi que des pilastres. Les deux motifs du bas peuvent en outre servir de décor à des panneaux horizontaux ou à des bordures ; il conviendra dans ce cas de disposer ces motifs aux deux extrémités des panneaux. On réalisera les ornements représentés dans deux couleurs ou dans une seule couleur foncée sur fond clair ou doré, comme dans l'illustration. Si on choisit de les exécuter dans deux couleurs sur fond clair, il conviendra d'utiliser la couleur plus foncée pour les motifs principaux.

Panel ornamentation with elaborate palmette design
Paneelverzierung mit aufwändigem Palmettendekor
Panneaux à palmettes richement ornées

The design illustrated here shows a stylized palmette emerging from an acanthus leaf. From the palmette, there emerge a further three palmettes flanked by spiral tendrils. The whole composition is framed by narrow bands which form frets in the corners. This pattern combines Graeco-Roman models with Egyptian influences, which are apparent above all in the central palmette.

This pattern is particularly suitable for vertical decorations on almost any scale. In order to achieve an appropriate esthetic effect, the pattern should fill practically the total breadth of the wall surface. The size of the undecorated field above is by contrast of little importance. The pattern suggests numerous possibilities of coloration. Both dark colors on a light ground, and gold or light colors on a dark ground are possible. A simple coloration in the Etruscan style, in other words in black and dark red on an ocher ground as displayed on pages 49 and 79, is ideally suitable for this kind of design.

Das hier vorgestellte Ornament zeigt ein spitzzackiges Akanthusblatt, dem eine stilisierte Palmette entspringt. Diese bringt als Zentralmotiv drei weitere Palmetten hervor, die von Spiralranken flankiert sind. Die ganze Komposition ist von schmalen Bändern umrahmt, die in den Ecken Mäander formen. Dieses Muster vereint antike griechisch-römische Vorbilder mit ägyptisch anmutenden Einflüssen, die vor allem bei der zentralen Palmette sichtbar sind.

Dieses Muster ist besonders für hochformatige Dekorationen fast jeden Maßstabs geeignet. Um eine angemessene ästhetische Wirkung zu erzielen, sollte das Muster fast die gesamte Breite der Wandfläche ausfüllen; die Größe des darüber befindlichen, nicht ornamentierten Feldes spielt hingegen kaum eine Rolle. Das Muster bietet hinsichtlich seiner Farbgebung viele Variationsmöglichkeiten. Sowohl dunkle Farben auf hellem Grund als auch Gold bzw. helle Farben auf dunklem Grund sind möglich. Eine einfache Kolorierung im etruskischen Stil, d. h. in Schwarz und Dunkelrot auf einem ockerfarbenen Grund, die auch auf den Seiten 49 und 79 angewandt wurde, passt vorzüglich zu dieser Art von Ornamenten.

Le motif présenté ici montre une feuille d'acanthe dentelée d'où jaillit une palmette stylisée. Servant de motif central, celle-ci donne naissance à trois autres palmettes flanquées d'entrelacs en spirale. La composition est encadrée de bandeaux étroits qui forment des méandres dans les angles. Ce motif associe des modèles gréco-romains antiques avec des influences sans doute égyptiennes, surtout visibles sur la palmette centrale.

Ce motif est idéal pour la décoration de panneaux en hauteur de pratiquement toutes les dimensions. Pour obtenir un effet esthétique approprié, un motif doit occuper presque toute la largeur du mur ; en revanche, la dimension du panneau non décoré, situé au-dessus, n'a guère d'importance.

Le motif offre de nombreuses variantes de couleurs : teinte foncée sur fond clair, doré ou teintes claires sur fond sombre, par exemple. Les couleurs de style étrusque, c'est-à-dire noir et rouge foncé sur fond ocre, comme le montrent les pages 49 et 79, conviennent à merveille pour ce type d'ornements.

Palmette design for the ornamentation of octagonal surfaces
Palmettendekor zur Ausschmückung achteckiger Flächen
Palmettes pour la décoration de surfaces octogonales

The two patterns illustrated in this plate go back to the Classical palmette, which is here repeated in a circle around a central rosette. This design is suitable for the central motif of octagonal surfaces such as are found, for example, in coffered ceilings. While in the lower design the palmette circle is easily recognizable as such, the motif at the top has been heavily stylized. Its vegetal forms are more like an Egyptian papyrus than the Classical palmettes from which this design is derived. The two triangles or diagonally bisected squares which fill the spaces between the coffers, are decorated with stars which likewise go back to Classical models – comparable motifs are known from Roman coffered ceilings.

The color combination for these two designs can be chosen according to taste. It could range from the simplest of treatments, for example the use of two shades of a single color – light on dark or dark on light – to elaborate multicolor versions, in which unmixed colors such as gold could also be used. Decorations like these are particularly effective if a coloration in the style of Etruscan murals is chosen, that is to say, black, dark red, and ocher, as illustrated on pages 49 and 79. Another color composition which would suit these patterns is the one shown on the next page.

Die beiden Muster dieser Tafel gehen auf das klassische Palmettenband zurück, das hier kreisförmig um eine zentrale Rosette gelegt ist. Dieser Entwurf eignet sich als Zentralmotiv achteckiger Flächen, wie sie beispielsweise bei Kassettendecken auftreten. Während bei dem Muster unten das Palmettenband durchaus als solches zu erkennen ist, wird es bei dem oberen Motiv weitgehend stilisiert wiedergegeben. Seine vegetabilen Formen gleichen aufgrund ihrer starken Auffiederung eher dem ägyptischen Papyrus, als dass sie an die klassische Palmette erinnern, von der sich dieser Entwurf ableitet. Die beiden Dreiecke bzw. halbierten Quadrate, die sich als Füllformen zwischen die Kassetten schieben, sind von Sternen geziert, die ebenfalls auf antike Vorbilder zurückgehen, da vergleichbare Motive vom Dekor römischer Kassettendecken überliefert sind.

Die Farbkombination dieser Muster ist frei wählbar. Sie reicht von der einfachsten Behandlung, wie zum Beispiel der Verwendung von zwei Schattierungen einer Farbe – hell auf dunkel oder dunkel auf hell –, bis hin zu aufwändigen mehrfarbigen Fassungen, bei der auch ungemischte Farben wie Gold eingesetzt werden können. Besonders wirkungsvoll erscheinen solche Ornamente, wenn man die Farbgebung im Stil der etruskischen Wandmalereien wählt, d. h. Schwarz, Dunkelrot und Ocker, wie auf den Seiten 49 und 79 präsentiert. Eine weitere zu diesen Entwürfen passende Farbkomposition bietet die nachfolgende Tafel an.

Les deux motifs de cette planche se réfèrent au bandeau à palmettes classique disposé ici en cercle autour d'une rosace centrale. Cette esquisse servira de motif central pour des surfaces octogonales telles qu'on en rencontre par exemple dans les plafonds à caissons. Si le bandeau de palmettes est tout à fait reconnaissable dans le motif du bas, il est par contre très stylisé dans celui du haut. Avec leurs feuilles pennées, les formes végétales ressemblent plus au papyrus égyptien qu'à la palmette classique dont cette esquisse est dérivée. Les deux triangles, ou plutôt demi-carrés, qui rempliront les espaces entre les caissons sont ornés d'étoiles qui se réfèrent également à des modèles antiques, car des motifs similaires se trouvaient dans les plafonds à caissons romains.

La combinaison de couleurs de ces motifs est libre. Elle varie du traitement le plus simple, par exemple l'utilisation de deux dégradés d'une couleur – clair sur foncé ou foncé sur clair – aux riches couleurs qui permettront d'utiliser aussi des teintes telles que le doré. Ces ornements seront du plus bel effet si on choisit une combinaison de couleurs dans le style des peintures murales étrusques, c'est-à-dire noir, rouge foncé et ocre, comme le montrent les pages 49 et 79. La planche suivante présente une autre combinaison de couleurs idéale pour ces esquisses.

Palmette decor for square coffers
Palmettendekor für quadratische Kassetten
Décor de palmettes pour caissons carrés

The two patterns show palmettes arranged in a circle around a central rosette. In the bottom motif, the rosette is clearly recognizable as such. Four large palmettes are grouped around it, each within a heart-shaped frame formed by the "tails" of spiral tendrils. The points of these hearts point into the corners of the coffer. Filling the spaces between the hearts are small stylized papyrus plants, which betray an Egyptian influence. The top pattern shows a variation of the one just described. The strongly stylized palmettes have shifted from the corners to the sides of the square, and are likewise framed by heart-shaped elements formed by the tails of spiral tendrils. Here, the hearts point towards the center of the ensemble. The spandrels are occupied by lanceolate lotus leaves.

These patterns are particularly suitable for the decoration of square coffers or ceilings. The notes on coloration given for the previous plate are equally valid here, in other words two shades of the same color can be recommended. If a highly elaborate coloration is chosen, the most important elements should be emphasized. For example, if gold is used in combination with light colors, one must make sure that the balance of the pattern is retained in all lighting conditions.

Die beiden Ornamente zeigen Palmetten, die sich kreisförmig um eine zentrale Rosette legen. Bei dem Motiv unten ist die Rosette eindeutig als solche zu erkennen. Um sie herum gruppieren sich vier große Palmetten, die von Spiralranken herzförmig gerahmt sind und mit ihren Spitzen in die Ecken des quadratischen Ornamentfeldes weisen. Dazwischen sieht man kleine Papyrusstauden als Füllformen. Sie lassen einen ägyptischen Einfluss erkennen. Das Muster oben zeigt eine Variation des unteren Motivs. Die stark stilisierten Palmetten, die hier von den Ecken an die Seiten des Quadrates gerückt sind, werden von herzförmigen Spiralranken gerahmt, die mit ihren Spitzen zur Mitte des Ornamentfeldes zeigen. Die Ecken werden hier von spitzblättrigen Lotusblüten ausgefüllt.

Diese Muster sind besonders für die Verzierung quadratischer Kassetten oder Zimmerdecken geeignet. Für die Farbwahl gelten die Bemerkungen zur vorhergehenden Tafel, d. h. zwei Schattierungen von einer Farbe wären empfehlenswert. Bei einer sehr aufwändigen farbigen Gestaltung sollten die wichtigsten Formen hervorgehoben werden. Wird zum Beispiel Gold in Zusammenhang mit hellen Farben verwendet, muss darauf geachtet werden, dass dieses Muster bei jeder Beleuchtung ausgewogen wirkt.

Les deux ornements présentent des palmettes disposées en cercle autour d'une rosace centrale. La rosace est nettement reconnaissable dans le motif du bas. Quatre grandes palmettes regroupées autour d'elle sont encadrées par des entrelacs en spirales et en forme de cœur, et pointent avec leur extrémité vers les coins du panneau ornemental carré. De petits papyrus révélant une influence égyptienne remplissent les espaces entre les motifs de cœurs. Le motif du haut est une variante de celui du bas. Les palmettes très stylisées qui sont passées des angles aux côtés du carré sont encadrées par des entrelacs en spirales et en forme de cœurs qui pointent vers le milieu du panneau ornemental. Des fleurs de lotus aux feuilles pointues garnissent les angles.

Ces motifs serviront à décorer des caissons carrés ou des plafonds. Les observations relatives à la planche précédente concernant le choix des couleurs sont valables ici aussi, c'est-à-dire que deux dégradés d'une couleur sont recommandés. Si on utilise des couleurs riches, il conviendra de mettre les principales formes en évidence. Si on choisit du doré par exemple avec des couleurs claires, il faudra veiller à ce que ce motif soit équilibré sous n'importe quel éclairage.

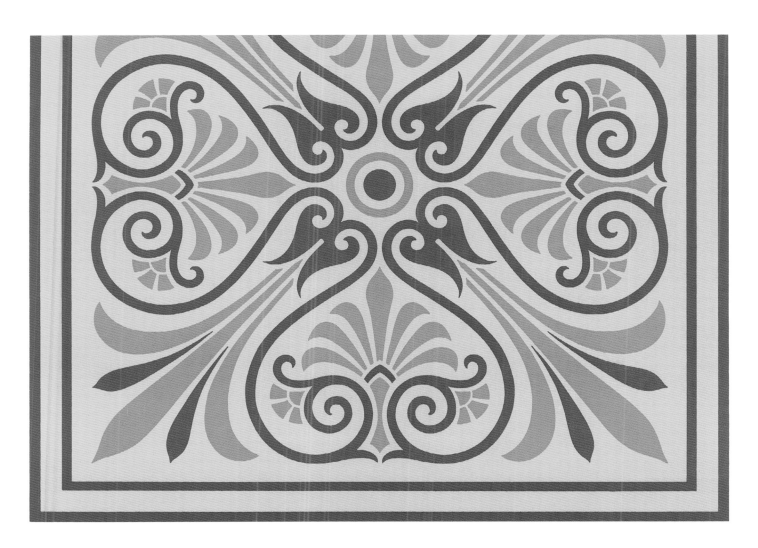

Palmette decor for the ornamentation of round coffers or as the central motif for a large ceiling
Palmettendekor zur Verzierung runder Kassetten oder als Zentralmotiv einer großen Decke
Palmettes pour la décoration de caissons ronds ou comme motif central d'un grand plafond

This design is based on the form of the Classical anthemion, the lotus-and-palmette band, here placed like a garland around a central star. The whole composition is encircled by an astragal and a leaf-and-tongue band. All the motifs mentioned can be derived directly from Classical exemplars. The separate corner motifs can be used to fill the spandrels between the round central motif and the corners of the ceiling.

The pattern is best suited to the ornamentation of large round coffers or comparable areas. If the corner elements are dispensed with, it can also be used as the central motif for a ceiling. The corner designs illustrated here can be used alone or in combination with the large central motif in all appropriate positions. In combination with the round pattern, the top corner element is to be preferred. Other suitable corner ornamentations to supplement a central motif can be seen on page 61. With regard to coloration, the schemes illustrated on pages 71 and 73 can also be followed here.

Dieser Entwurf basiert formal auf dem Anthemion, dem antiken Lotus- und Palmettenband, das hier kranzartig um einen zentralen Stern gelegt ist. Umrandet wird die ganze Komposition von einem Perlstab und einer Blattwelle, einem „lesbischen Kymation". Alle genannten Motive lassen sich direkt von klassischen Vorbildern ableiten. Die abgesetzten Eckmotive können als Füllformen zwischen dem runden Zentralmotiv und den Ecken der Decke benutzt werden.

Das Muster eignet sich vornehmlich zur Verzierung großer runder Kassetten oder vergleichbarer Flächen. Unter Verzicht auf die Randverzierungen kann es auch als Zentralmotiv für eine Decke verwendet werden. Die hier dargestellten Eckentwürfe können allein oder zusammen mit dem großen Zentralmotiv an allen geeigneten Stellen angebracht werden. In Verbindung mit dem runden Muster wäre das obere Eckornament vorzuziehen. Weitere geeignete Eckverzierungen zur Ergänzung des zentralen Motivs bietet der Ornamentvorschlag auf Seite 61. Bezüglich der Farbgebung bietet sich auch die Kolorierung auf den Seiten 71 und 73 an.

Par sa forme, ce motif rappelle l'anthémion, le bandeau antique de lotus et de palmettes, disposé ici en couronne autour d'une étoile centrale. Toute la composition est entourée d'un rang de perles et d'une ondulation de feuilles, une « cymaise de Lesbos ». Tous les motifs cités sont directement dérivés de modèles classiques. Les motifs d'angle dissociés peuvent remplir les espaces entre le motif central rond et les angles du plafond.

Le motif servira à décorer de grands caissons ronds ou des surfaces similaires. Il pourra servir aussi de motif central pour un plafond, mais sans les bordures décorées. Les motifs d'angle présentés ici peuvent être réalisés individuellement ou avec le grand motif central à tous les endroits appropriés. On préférera dans ce cas l'ornement d'angle supérieur associé au motif rond. La planche à la page 61 propose d'autres décors d'angles appropriés pour compléter le motif central. Les planches aux pages 71 et 73 présentent d'autres combinaisons de couleurs.

Broad ornamental band with elaborate palmettes and rosette border
Breites Ornamentband mit aufwändig gestalteten Palmetten und abschließender Rosettenbordüre
Large bandeau ornemental avec palmettes aux formes riches et bordure de rosaces

This plate shows a broad palmette band, in which Classically inspired palmettes alternate with playful leaf-like elements, from which lotus blossoms emerge. The lower border of the composition is formed by a narrow band decorated with rosettes.
The pattern is suitable as the decor for a frieze. Its lightness of character means that it can also be upscaled. If the pattern is used as the decoration for the frieze of an entablature, only the broad palmette band should be used, omitting the rosette border entirely, or else it can be used as the border of the architrave. In addition, the pattern can serve as the crowning ornamental band of a room or for any other important frieze. The choice of colors is subject to no constraint.

Diese Tafel zeigt ein breites Palmettenband, bei dem sich klassisch anmutende Palmetten mit verspielten Blattgebilden abwechseln, aus denen Lotusblumen entspringen. Den unteren Abschluss der Komposition bildet ein schmales, von Rosetten geziertes Band.
Das Muster eignet sich als Dekor für Friese. Aufgrund seines leichten Charakters kann es auch in einen größeren Maßstab übertragen werden. Verwendet man das Muster als Dekor für den Fries eines Gebälks, sollte nur das breite Palmettenband benutzt werden, während das Rosettenband entweder komplett weggelassen oder als Abschluss des Architravs eingesetzt werden kann. Außerdem eignet sich dieses Muster als bekrönendes Ornamentband eines Raumes sowie für jeden anderen wichtigen Fries. Die Auswahl der Farben unterliegt keinerlei Beschränkungen.

Cette planche présente un large bandeau de palmettes dans lequel des palmettes rappelant le style classique alternent avec des formes de feuilles trop décorées d'où jaillissent des fleurs de lotus. Un étroit bandeau décoré de rosaces constitue la limite inférieure de la composition.
Le motif servira à décorer des frises. Sa légèreté permet de le reproduire à plus grande échelle. Si on veut réaliser une frise sur des poutres avec ce motif, on choisira le large bandeau de palmettes, tandis qu'on ignorera totalement le bandeau de rosaces ou qu'on l'utilisera pour terminer l'architrave. Ce motif est en outre idéal comme bandeau ornemental servant de couronne, ainsi que pour toute autre frise importante. Le choix des couleurs ne fait l'objet d'aucune restriction.

Broad ornamental band with Classical motifs for decorating friezes
Breites Ornamentband mit klassischen Motiven zur Dekoration von Friesen
Large bandeau ornemental à motifs classiques pour la décoration de frises

The design of this pattern goes back to the anthemion, the Classical frieze in which palmettes alternate with stylized lotus blossoms. At the bottom, the pattern is bordered by a narrow fret band.

The pattern is particularly suited to the ornamentation of wall friezes. The color scheme illustrated here is that found on ancient Etruscan pottery, from which this ornamental type is derived. Other, more magnificent colors can also be used, however. These patterns create a particularly impressive effect if executed in gold on black or another dark ground.

Dieses Muster geht in seiner Gestaltung auf das Anthemion, den klassischen Fries zurück, bei dem sich Palmetten mit stilisierten Lotusblüten abwechseln. Nach unten wird das Muster von einem schmalen Mäanderband abgeschlossen.

Das Muster eignet sich zur Ausschmückung von Wandfriesen. Die hier dargestellte Farbgestaltung entspricht der antiken etruskischen Töpferware, von der dieser Ornamenttypus abgeleitet ist. Es lassen sich jedoch auch andere, prächtigere Farben einsetzen. Diese Muster entfalten eine besonders eindrucksvolle Wirkung, wenn sie in Gold auf Schwarz oder einem anderen dunklen Untergrund ausgeführt werden.

Par sa forme, ce motif rappelle l'anthémion, la frise classique dans laquelle les palmettes alternent avec des fleurs de lotus stylisées. Il se termine dans le bas par un étroit bandeau de méandres.

Ce motif servira à décorer des frises murales. La combinaison de couleurs présentée ici correspond à celle des poteries étrusques antiques dont ce type d'ornement est dérivé. Il est toutefois possible de choisir d'autres couleurs plus somptueuses. Le motif sera du plus bel effet s'il est réalisé en doré sur fond noir ou d'une autre couleur sombre.

Masonry pattern with Classical motifs for decorating large surfaces
Ziegelmuster als Flächendekoration mit klassischen Motiven
Dessin de briques pour la décoration de surfaces à motifs classiques

This decor is based on rectangles which each contain two palmettes reflecting each other across a central rosette. They are flanked by spiral tendrils. The spaces between the rectangles are filled by fret patterns. This design can be called a "masonry pattern" because the rectangular fields are arranged like the bricks in a wall, each row being staggered relative to the adjacent one.
This pattern is suitable for the ornamentation of large wall surfaces. The coloration should be kept simple and reticent, in order not to allow the pattern to dominate. If only the base of the wall is to be decorated with this pattern, stronger colors can be used, for example gold (either alone or in combination with strong colors) on a dark ground. Coloration in the Etruscan style, as illustrated on pages 49 and 79, would also be possible.

Diese Flächendekoration basiert auf Rechtecken, die zwei Palmetten enthalten, welche sich an einer zentralen Rosette spiegeln. Sie werden von stilisierten Spiralranken flankiert. Als Füllformen zwischen den Rechtecken werden Bänder verwendet, die sich zu Mäandern formen. Dieser Entwurf kann als „Ziegelmuster" bezeichnet werden, da sich die rechteckigen Felder ähnlich wie die Ziegelsteine einer Mauer aneinander reihen, wobei die Reihen horizontal gegeneinander verschoben werden.
Dieses Muster eignet sich zur Verzierung großer Wandflächen, wobei die Farbgebung einfach und zurückhaltend sein sollte, um das Ornament nicht zu dominant wirken zu lassen. Wenn nur die Sockelzone einer Wand mit diesem Muster verziert werden soll, können kräftigere Farben verwendet werden, wie zum Beispiel Gold (allein oder in Verbindung mit kräftigen Farben) auf dunklem Grund. Auch eine Farbgebung des etruskischen Stils wie auf den Seiten 49 und 79 wäre möglich.

Cette décoration de surface se base sur des rectangles qui contiennent deux palmettes placées tête-bêche de chaque côté d'une rosace centrale. Elles sont en outre flanquées d'entrelacs stylisés en spirale. Des bandeaux se transformant en méandres servent de raccords entre les rectangles. Cette esquisse peut être qualifiée de « motif de briques », car les panneaux rectangulaires sont disposés à la manière des briques d'un mur, les rangées étant décalées horizontalement les unes par rapport aux autres.
Ce motif servira à décorer de grands murs et dans ce cas, la combinaison de couleurs devra être simple et discrète afin que l'ornement ne soit pas trop prédominant. Si ce motif ne doit décorer que le soubassement d'un mur, on pourra utiliser des couleurs plus vives, par exemple du doré (uniquement en association avec des couleurs vives) sur un fond sombre. Une combinaison de couleurs dans le style étrusque serait possible, comme le montrent les planches aux pages 49 et 79.

Masonry pattern with stylized motifs as a decoration for large surfaces
Ziegelmuster als Flächendekoration mit stilisierten Motiven
Motif de briques pour la décoration de surfaces avec des dessins stylisés

In the center of each of the individual ornamental fields, which are arranged like bricks in a wall, is an upright palmette emerging from an acanthus. The composition is flanked by spiral tendrils. In place of space-filling elements, there are squares with star-shaped rosettes, placed at the corners (or on the sides, as the case may be) of the "bricks" or ornamental fields.

This pattern is particularly suited to the ornamentation of wall surfaces which permit elaborate decoration, like for example the bases of the walls of large halls, staircases and large corridors, such as are found in public buildings. The elaborate color-scheme depicted here could be replaced by a far simpler scheme, for example different shades of the same color. In well-lit locations, the coloration could follow the Etruscan pattern to good effect.

Die einzelnen, wie Ziegel aneinander gereihten Ornamentfelder werden in ihrem Zentrum von einer aufrecht stehenden Palmette geziert, die einem spitzblättrigen Akanthus entspringt. Die Komposition wird von Spiralranken flankiert. Anstelle von Füllformen werden hier Quadrate mit sternförmigen Rosetten bzw. Vielpässen als Verzahnung der rechteckigen Ornamentfelder benutzt.

Dieses Muster eignet sich besonders für die Gestaltung von Wandflächen, die eine reiche Ornamentierung zulassen, wie zum Beispiel die Sockelzonen von Sälen, Treppenhäusern und großen Gängen, wie sie in öffentlichen Gebäuden vorkommen. Die hier präsentierte aufwändige farbliche Gestaltung des Musters lässt sich auch durch eine wesentlich einfachere Ausführung, zum Beispiel Ton in Ton, ersetzen. An gut belichteten Orten kann die Farbgebung im etruskischen Stil durchaus effektvoll sein.

Les panneaux ornementaux juxtaposés comme des briques sont ornés, en leur centre, d'une palmette verticale d'où jaillit une feuille d'acanthe dentelée. La composition est flanquée d'entrelacs en spirale. Des carrés avec des rosaces en forme d'étoiles ou des motifs multilobes figurant les angles des panneaux ornementaux rectangulaires remplacent ici les raccords.

Ce motif servira à décorer des murs pouvant recevoir de riches ornements, par exemple les soubassements de pièces, cages d'escaliers et grands couloirs, tels qu'on en rencontre dans des bâtiments publics. Le motif aux riches couleurs présenté ici peut aussi s'exécuter de façon beaucoup plus simple, par exemple ton sur ton. Dans des endroits bien éclairés, une composition de couleurs dans le style étrusque sera du plus bel effet.

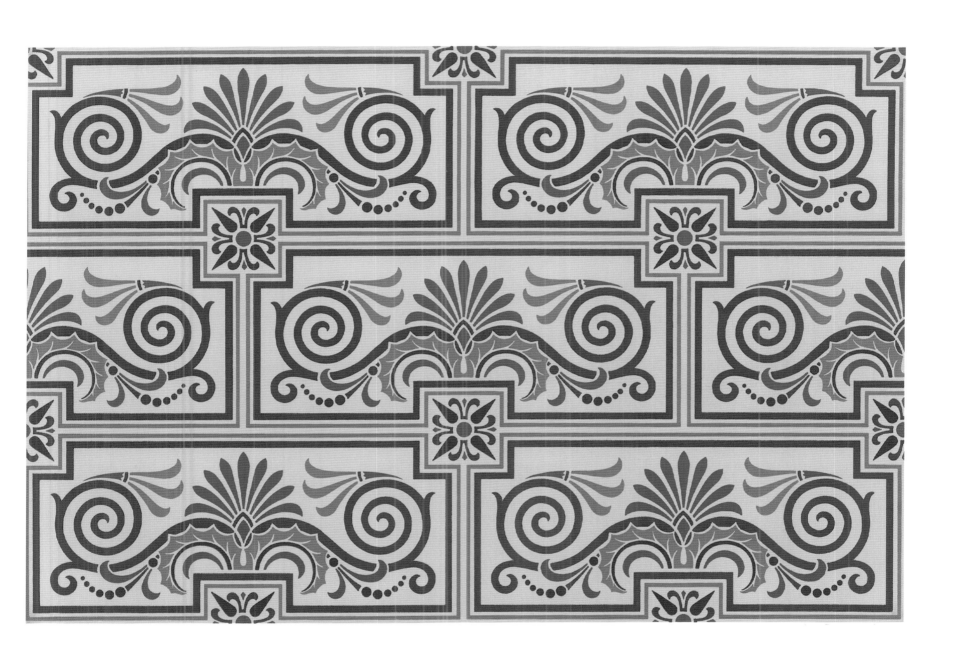

Diaper pattern of arches and palmettes
Flächendekoration aus Bögen mit eingeschlossenem Palmettendekor
Décoration de surfaces avec arcs et palmettes intégrées

This all-over pattern shows staggered rows of pointed arches; where the bases of two adjacent arches in one row meet the cusp of an arch in the row beneath, there is a rosette. Thus a pattern is formed like the scales of a fish, adorned with the Classical composition of acanthus, palmette and vitruvian scroll.
This pattern is suited to the decoration of walls, panels and other flat surfaces. It can be reproduced on any scale and in any color scheme. For large areas of wall, it can be reproduced, using a stencil, on a light ground in a single color, which should be no more than a hint darker than the ground. If the intention is to achieve a more striking ornamental effect, two shades of the same color can be used, as illustrated here. In this case, two separate stencils will be necessary. For smaller surfaces which permit elaborate decoration, a stencil can be used to execute the pattern in black or another dark color on a gold ground or else in gold on a dark ground.

Dieses flächendeckende Muster zeigt gegeneinander verschobene Reihen von spitz zulaufenden Bögen, deren Verbindungspunkte von Rosetten geziert werden. Sie bilden ein schuppenförmiges Muster, in das die klassische Komposition von Akanthus, Palmetten und Spiralranken eingesetzt ist.
Dieses Muster eignet sich zur Dekoration von Wandflächen, Paneelen und anderen ebenen Flächen. Es lässt sich in jedem beliebigen Maßstab und in jeder beliebigen Kolorierung anwenden. Bei größeren Wandflächen kann es in einer einzigen Farbe, die nur wenige Nuancen dunkler als der Untergrund sein sollte, mit der Schablone auf einen hellen Grund aufgetragen werden. Soll die Ornamentierung prächtiger wirken, können zwei Schattierungen einer Farbe wie auf der Abbildung gewählt werden. In diesem Falle sind jedoch zwei Schablonen erforderlich. Für kleinere Flächen, die eine aufwändige Verzierung zulassen, lässt sich das Muster in Schwarz oder einer anderen dunklen Farbe auf goldenem Grund oder in Gold auf dunklem Grund mit der Schablone auftragen.

Ce motif destiné à décorer des surfaces présente des rangées d'arcs décalées se terminant en pointe et dont les points d'intersection sont ornés de rosaces. Ces arcs forment un motif d'écailles dans lequel s'intègre la composition classique de feuilles d'acanthe, de palmettes et d'entrelacs en spirale.
Ce motif servira à décorer des murs, panneaux et autres surfaces planes. Il est réalisable dans n'importe quelles dimensions et couleurs. Si la surface des murs est plus grande, on pourra le transposer au pochoir sur un fond clair, dans une seule couleur qui devra être légèrement plus foncée que le fond. Si l'objectif est d'obtenir une décoration plus somptueuse, on pourra choisir deux dégradés d'une couleur comme le montre l'illustration. Dans ce cas, il conviendra d'utiliser deux pochoirs. Pour des surfaces plus petites permettant de réaliser une riche décoration, on transposera le motif au pochoir en noir ou dans une autre couleur foncée sur fond doré ou en doré sur fond sombre.

The Middle Ages
Mittelalter
Le Moyen Âge

The Middle Ages – covering the art-historical periods known as Romanesque (c. 900–1200) and Gothic (c. 1200–1550) – represent an important slice of European cultural history. After the collapse of the Roman Empire in the West (AD 476), the Church became the chief repository of culture in western Europe. Monks collected the knowledge of Antiquity in their monastic libraries, they researched and taught and, from Italy outwards, spread the architectural style which we know as Romanesque throughout Europe.
Typical of Romanesque church architecture is the basilica, a long building with a central nave flanked by aisles on either side, with

Das Mittelalter mit den Epochen der Romanik (ca. 900–1200) und Gotik (ca. 1200–1550) stellt einen wichtigen Abschnitt der europäischen Kunstgeschichte dar. Nach dem Zusammenbruch des Römischen Reiches (476 n. Chr.) war vor allem die Kirche Träger des Kulturschaffens in Europa geworden. Mönche sammelten und übersetzten in ihren Klosterbibliotheken das Wissen der Antike, sie forschten und lehrten und verbreiteten von Italien ausgehend die Bauformen der Romanik über ganz Europa.
Typisch für die romanische Architektur ist die dreischiffige Basilika mit ihren massiven Mauern, die von außen den Eindruck einer wahren „Gottesburg" macht. Im Inneren

Le Moyen Âge représente, avec l'époque de l'art roman (environ 900–1200) et gothique (environ 1200–1550), un chapitre important de l'histoire européenne de l'art. Après l'effondrement de l'Empire romain (476 après J.-C.), l'Église devint la principale représentante de la culture en Europe. Des moines accumulaient et traduisaient le savoir de l'Antiquité dans les bibliothèques des monastères ; ils étudièrent, enseignèrent et répandirent depuis l'Italie les formes architecturales de l'art roman dans toute l'Europe.
La basilique à trois nefs, avec ses murs massifs qui, vus de l'extérieur, font l'effet d'une véritable « forteresse de Dieu », est

Church of Notre Dame, Malay, Saône et Loire, 11th century
Typical of Romanesque church architecture is the basilica, a low building with raised central nave and side aisles, and in many cases a conspicuous transept. The round-arched windows and almost fort-like character of this example are also typical features of the Romanesque style.

Notre-Dame in Malay, Saône-et-Loire, 11. Jh.
Typisch für die romanische Architektur ist die Basilika, ein gedrungener, meist dreischiffiger Kirchenbau mit erhöhtem Mittelschiff und ausgeprägtem Querschiff. Die Rundbogenfenster und der fast wehrhafte Charakter dieser Anlage sind weitere typische Merkmale des romanischen Baustils.

Notre-Dame de Malay, Saône-et-Loire, XIe siècle
La basilique, cet édifice religieux trapu souvent composé de trois nefs, avec la nef centrale rehaussée et un transept mis en valeur, est caractéristique de l'architecture romane. Les fenêtres à arcs en plein cintre et l'allure d'église fortifiée de cet édifice sont d'autres attributs typiques du style architectural roman.

massively thick walls, giving the impression from outside of a veritable "castle of God". Inside, the space is structured vertically with arcades and both free-standing and embedded columns, while horizontal accents take the form of heavily ornamented cornices and friezes. Columns, pillars and arches were generally covered with ornaments or sculpted figures, whose original brightly-colored paint has survived only in very few cases. The round-arched windows are often richly framed with vegetal ornamentation and sometimes with figures, too.

A characteristic feature of 12th-century Romanesque ornamentation is the tendril motif with its freely designed and independently evolving leaves, which bear only a distant resemblance to the acanthus of Classical Antiquity, from which they took their original inspiration. The tendrils or vines which often appear as decoration on the sculpted columns of Romanesque stepped portals came increasingly to be inhabited by animal and human figures, dragons, birds, and fantastical fabulous beasts, and they are at their most beautiful on the capitals of columns. Ornaments as illustrative decoration were also of importance in other spheres, however. In particular, liturgical accessories, ivory and wood carvings, gospels and bibles were often richly decorated. Initials, for instance, were often so profusely illuminated with stylized tendrils, animals, human figures and other, fantastical, beings that this form of illustration can be said to constitute a separate genre within that of medieval miniature painting. The walls of churches and palaces were hung as a matter of course with tapestries and embroideries, but few have survived, due to the perishable materials they were made from. The transition from Romanesque to Gothic was apparent in France as early as the mid-12th century; in England it began around 1175, and in Germany shortly after 1200. Far-reaching political changes had taken place throughout Europe. Millions of people had fallen victim to

werden die Kirchenräume durch Arkaden, Säulen und Lisenen gegliedert, während die Horizontale vielfach durch ornamentierte Friese und Gesimse akzentuiert wird. Säulen, Pfeiler und Bögen bedeckte man gewöhnlich mit Ornamenten oder mit Figurenschmuck. Deren ursprünglich farbige Bemalung hat sich in den wenigsten Fällen erhalten. Die Rundbogenfenster weisen häufig eine reiche Umrahmung mit Pflanzenornamenten und mitunter auch mit Figuren auf.

Charakteristisch für die Ornamentik der Romanik des 12. Jahrhunderts ist der Rankendekor mit seinen frei und selbstständig sich entwickelnden Blättern, die nur noch entfernt den antiken Akanthus erkennen lassen, von dem sie inspiriert sind. Das Rankenwerk, das vielfach als Zierde an skulptierten Säulen romanischer Stufenportale zu sehen ist, wird zunehmend von Tier- und Menschengestalten sowie Drachen, Vögeln und phantasievollen Fabelwesen durchzogen und findet schließlich in der Kapitellplastik seine schönste Ausprägung. Ornamente als illustrativer Schmuck waren jedoch auch in anderen Bereichen von Bedeutung; vor allem wurden lithurgische Geräte, Elfenbein- und Holzschnitzereien sowie Evangeliare und Bibelabschriften reich verziert. Initialen – die jeweiligen Anfangsbuchstaben eines Textes – wurden beispielsweise oftmals mit so aufwändig stilisiertem Rankenwerk, Tier- und Menschengestalten oder anderen phantastischen Wesen ausgeschmückt, dass sich damit ein eigenes Genre innerhalb der mittelalterlichen Miniaturmalerei herausbildete. Als gewöhnlichen Wandschmuck wählte man in Kirchen und Palästen üblicherweise kunstvolle Wandbehänge mit Web- und Stickarbeiten, die sich aufgrund der hohen Anfälligkeit des Materials jedoch kaum erhalten haben.

Der Übergang von der Romanik zur Gotik bahnte sich in Frankreich schon etwa Mitte des 12. Jahrhunderts an; in England begann er gegen 1175 und in Deutschland kurz nach 1200. Tief greifende politische Wandlungen hatten sich in ganz Europa vollzogen; Millionen von

caractéristique de l'architecture romane. À l'intérieur, arcades, colonnes et lésènes séparent les différents espaces de l'église, tandis que des frises et corniches souvent décorées accentuent l'horizontale. Les colonnes, piliers et voûtes étaient la plupart du temps agrémentés d'ornements ou de statues, dont la peinture d'origine ne s'est conservée que très rarement. Les fenêtres en plein cintre présentent souvent un riche encadrement d'ornements végétaux alternant avec des statues.

L'entrelacs avec ses feuilles qui se déploient, libres et indépendantes, et ne rappellent plus que vaguement l'acanthe antique dont elles sont inspirées, caractérise l'art ornemental roman du XIIᵉ siècle. L'entrelacs, qui sert souvent à décorer les statues-colonnes des portails à gradins romans, est de plus en plus parcouru de formes animales et humaines, de même que de dragons, oiseaux et créatures fabuleuses imaginaires et finit par trouver sa plus belle

Royal tomb at San Isidoro, León, c. 1063–1100
The Pantheón de los Reyes, the tomb of the kings of León, is characterized both by the medieval sculpture of its capitals and by its magnificent murals, which constitute one of the most complete picture cycles of the whole Middle Ages. Alongside figurative bible scenes, the barrel vault is also decorated by tendril motifs derived from the acanthus, and reproduced here in stylized form.

Königliches Grabmonument von San Isidoro in León, um 1063–1100
Das so genannte Pantheón de los Reyes der Könige von León zeichnet sich sowohl durch seine mittelalterliche Kapitellplastik als auch durch seine herrlichen Wandmalereien aus – einen der am vollständigsten erhaltenen Bilderzyklen des Mittelalters. Neben figürlichen Szenen der Bibel sieht man an den Gurtbögen Rankendekor, der sich formal vom Akanthus ableitet und hier in einer sehr stilisierten Form wiedergegeben wurde.

Monument funéraire royal de San Isidoro à León, vers 1063–1100
Le tombeau des rois de León, dit Pantheón de los Reyes, se distingue tant par ses chapiteaux médiévaux en relief que par ses splendides peintures murales – un des cycles de tableaux du Moyen Âge presque entièrement conservés. À côté des scènes figurées de la Bible, les arcs-doubleaux sont décorés par un entrelacs dérivé de la feuille d'acanthe et reproduit ici sous une forme stylisée.

expression dans les sculptures de chapiteaux. Les décors dits historiés jouèrent toutefois un rôle important dans d'autres domaines ; ce sont surtout les instruments liturgiques, pièces d'orfèvrerie, ivoires et sculptures sur bois, ainsi que les évangéliaires et copies de la Bible qui firent l'objet de riches ornements. Les initiales – premières lettres d'un texte – étaient par exemple souvent décorées d'une telle profusion d'entrelacs, de figures animales et humaines ou d'autres créatures fantastiques stylisées qu'un genre particulier se créa à l'intérieur de l'art médiéval de la miniature. Des tapisseries tissées et brodées, réalisées avec art, mais rarement conservées en raison de la grande fragilité du matériau, constituaient le décor mural ordinaire des églises et palais.

La transition du roman au gothique s'amorça en France dès le milieu du XIIe siècle ; elle débuta en Angleterre vers 1175 et en Allemagne peu après 1200. Des bouleversements politiques profonds s'étaient opérés dans toute l'Europe ; des millions de personnes avaient été victimes d'épidémies et l'Inquisition

Book of Gospels of Henry the Lion, Duke Augustus Library, Wolfenbüttel, 1185–1188
This richly illuminated manuscript is one of the outstanding achievements of Romanesque book illustration. St Mark the evangelist is depicted sitting on a throne giving the sign of blessing. Conspicuous features include the Romanesque architecture in the background, the richly decorated letters and the ornamental border with its stylized fret patterns. Late Classical traditions are visibly still alive here; they are however adapted and fused with Christian symbolism.

Evangeliar Heinrichs des Löwen, Herzog-August-Bibliothek, Wolfenbüttel, 1185–1188
Diese reich illuminierte Handschrift zählt zu den herausragenden Leistungen romanischer Buchkunst. Der Evangelist Markus wird auf einem Thron sitzend im Segensgestus wiedergegeben. Auffällig ist die romanische Architektur im Hintergrund, die reich verzierten Lettern und die ornamental gestaltete Bordüre mit ihren stilisierten Mäandern. Spätantike Traditionen leben hier erkennbar weiter, werden jedoch adaptiert und mit der christlichen Figurensymbolik verschmolzen.

Évangéliaire de Henri le Lion, Bibliothèque Herzog August, Wolfenbüttel, 1185–1188
Ce manuscrit richement enluminé est une des plus belles réalisations de l'art du livre. Marc l'évangéliste est représenté assis sur un trône et faisant un geste de bénédiction. L'architecture romane à l'arrière-plan, les lettres richement décorées et la bordure ornementale aux méandres stylisés sont particulièrement frappantes. Les traditions de l'Antiquité finissante sont clairement perpétuées ici, mais elles sont adaptées et se fondent dans la symbolique des figures chrétiennes.

Reliquary of St Stephen from Limoges, Guinel-les-Cascades, c. 1160–1170
The enamelwork of Limoges is world-famous. The sides of this reliquary depict the twelve apostles, framed in a richly-ornamented round arch, while the lid is decorated with angels, each framed in a kind of medallion. The background to the figures is also ornamented.

Reliquienschrein des Heiligen Stephanus aus Limoges, Guinel-les-Cascades, um 1160–1170
Die Emailarbeiten aus Limoges sind weltberühmt. Dieser Reliquienschrein zeigt an den Seitenwänden die zwölf Apostel, die von reich ornamentierten Rundbögen gerahmt sind, während der Deckel von medaillonartig gerahmten Engeln geschmückt wird. Der Hintergrund der figürlichen Szenen ist ornamental ausgeschmückt.

Reliquaire de saint Stéphane de Limoges, Guinel-les-Cascades, vers 1160–1170
Les émaux de Limoges sont célèbres dans le monde entier. Ce reliquaire présente, sur ses faces latérales, les douze apôtres encadrés d'arcs en plein cintre richement décorés, tandis que le couvercle est orné d'anges formant une sorte de médaillon. L'arrière-plan des scènes figurées est également décoré.

epidemics, and the Inquisition, which started its activities in the years after 1230, threatened every section of the population. In their distress and uncertainty, people increasingly sought personal help from God and the saints, so that by 1300, mysticism had sprung up as a strong counter-movement to Scholasticism. The cathedrals and the schools attached to them were the places in which these changes in the world and the image of the world were most immediately reflected. The increasing height of their walls and the vertical emphasis of all the space-structuring elements pointed to an esthetic which bore the stamp of the new piety and the ecstatic search for God that characterized mysticism. The brilliant invention of the pointed arch allowed the construction of arches of different spans but the same height, which in turn created the precondition for rib vaulting above rectangular spaces.

Menschen waren Epidemien zum Opfer gefallen und die nach 1230 einsetzende Inquisition bedrohte alle Bevölkerungsschichten. In ihrer Not und Unsicherheit suchten die Menschen zunehmend persönlichen Beistand bei Gott und den Heiligen, so dass um 1300 die Mystik als starke Gegenbewegung zur Scholastik entstand. Die Kathedrale aber wurde der Ort, in dem sich diese Wandlungen der Welt und des Weltbildes am direktesten widerspiegelten: Die wachsende Höhe ihrer Wände, der Vertikalismus aller gliedernden Elemente deuten auf einen Formwillen hin, der von der neuen Frömmigkeit und von der ekstatischen Gottsuche der Mystik geprägt ist. Die geniale Erfindung des Spitzbogens erlaubte es, Bögen mit unterschiedlichen Spannweiten bei gleicher Scheitelhöhe zu bauen, womit die Voraussetzung für Grat- und Rippengewölbe über rechteckigen Räumen und Raumkompartimenten

instaurée vers 1230 menaçait toutes les couches de la population. En proie à la détresse et à l'incertitude, les gens cherchaient de plus en plus une assistance personnelle auprès de Dieu et des saints, d'où l'apparition du mysticisme vers 1300, mouvement massif de réaction à la scolastique. La cathédrale fut cependant le lieu où ces transformations du monde et de l'image du monde se sont reflétées le plus directement : la hauteur croissante de ses murs, la verticalité de tous les éléments indiquent une intention formelle marquée par la nouvelle dévotion et par la recherche extatique de Dieu à travers le mysticisme. La géniale invention de l'arc ogival permit de construire des arcs de travées différentes avec des flèches identiques, ce qui facilita tout naturellement la création de voûtes d'arête et à nervures au-dessus de salles rectangulaires et d'espaces compartimentés. Les cathédrales de

Wooden ceiling of St Michael's Church, Hildesheim, with 13th-century painting
The wooden ceiling of St Michael's Church, Hildesheim, is a masterpiece of medieval monumental painting. The middle section represents the rod of Jesse; it is flanked by two strips depicting the apostles and other saints. The spaces between are filled with intertwined tendril motifs doubtless derived from book illustration.

Holzdecke der Michaeliskirche, Hildesheim, Deckenmalerei aus dem 13. Jh.
Die Holzdecke der Michaeliskirche in Hildesheim stellt ein Meisterwerk mittelalterlicher Monumentalmalerei dar. Der mittlere Streifen zeigt die Wurzel Jesse; sie wird von zwei seitlichen Streifen mit Apostel- und Heiligendarstellungen flankiert. Als Füllformen erkennt man dicht ineinander verschlungene Blattranken, die vermutlich von der Buchmalerei abgeleitet sind.

Plafond en bois de l'église Saint-Michel, Hildesheim, peinture de plafond du XIIIᵉ siècle
Le plafond en bois de l'église Saint-Michel à Hildesheim est un chef-d'œuvre de la peinture monumentale du Moyen Âge. La bande centrale présente l'Arbre de Jessé ; elle est flanquée de deux bandes latérales représentant les apôtres et les saints. Des entrelacs de feuilles étroitement imbriqués qui sont probablement dérivés de l'enluminure s'inscrivent entre les motifs principaux.

North choir ambulatory of St Mary's church, Stargard, c. 1400

St Mary's in Stargard in Western Pomerania is a fine example of Gothic church architecture. The characteristic feature of Gothic architecture is the increased height of the walls in combination with pointed arches, which arise from a new esthetic and give expression to a new piety. The ceilings too were often given an ornamental treatment. Here, for example, we have folksy depictions of flowers. Columns and pilasters were frequently decorated with stars or with vegetal tendril motifs which continued into the intrados of the arches. Thus we have an harmonious fusion of decorative ceilings with mural paintings in contrasting colors, which together make the house of God a "total work of art".

Nördlicher Chorumgang der Marienkirche, Stargard, ausgebaut um 1400

Die Marienkirche von Stargard in Westpommern ist ein schönes Beispiel gotischer Sakralarchitektur. Charakteristisch für die Architektur der Gotik ist die zunehmende Höhe der Wände in Verbindung mit Spitzbögen, die einem neuen Formwillen entspringen und eine gesteigerte Frömmigkeit zum Ausdruck bringen. Die Gewölbe wurden oftmals ornamental ausgeschmückt. So sieht man hier volkstümlich wiedergegebene Blumen. Pfeiler und Dienste wurden häufig mit Sternen oder mit Blattrankenornamenten dekoriert, die sich bis in die Laibungen fortsetzten. So kommt es auch hier zu einer harmonischen Verschmelzung dekorativer Gewölbeformen mit farbig abgesetzten Wandmalereien, die das Gotteshaus als Gesamtkunstwerk erscheinen lassen.

Déambulatoire nord de l'église Notre-Dame, Stargard, achevée vers 1400

L'église Notre-Dame de Stargard en Poméranie occidentale est un bel exemple d'architecture religieuse gothique. La hauteur croissante des murs associée à des arcs en ogive qui résultent d'une nouvelle volonté de forme et expriment une piété exacerbée, caractérisent l'architecture du gothique. Les voûtes étaient souvent décorées. On voit ici, par exemple, des représentations de fleurs. Des piliers et perches colonnettes étaient fréquemment ornées d'étoiles ou d'entrelacs de feuilles qui se poursuivaient jusque dans les intrados. Les formes de voûtes décoratives et les peintures murales de couleurs, qui donnent à la maison de Dieu l'apparence d'une œuvre d'art à part entière, fusionnent de façon harmonieuse.

The most beautiful works of French Gothic include the cathedrals in Paris (1163–1360), Rheims (1211–1250) and Rouen (1212–1280). The walls of the cathedrals were increasingly perforated by tall pointed windows decorated with tracery, that is to say, geometrical patterns constructed with plumblines and set-squares. The windows were glazed with stained glass, while the gables of the nave and transepts were filled with great rose-windows. Alongside the richly ornamented tracery with its purely geometric decoration, vegetal motifs were also of importance. Stylized foliage and vine tendrils decorated not only friezes and cornices, but also gables and consoles and the richly ornamented keystones in the vaulting. Vegetal decoration was particularly striking in quatrefoil tracery and finials, as well as in the features known as crockets, where the vegetal elements

geschaffen wurde. Zu den schönsten Werken der französischen Gotik zählen die Kathedralen zu Paris (1163–1360), Reims (1211–1250) und Rouen (1212–1280). Die Wände der Kathedralen wurden zunehmend von hohen Spitzbogen-fenstern durchbrochen, die mit Maßwerk, d. h. mit jenen mittels Lot und Winkelmaß „gemessenen" bzw. konstruierten geometrischen Mustern, geziert waren. Die Fenster waren mit farbigem Glas ausge-schmückt, während die Giebel-wände des Haupt- und Querschiffs mit großen Fensterrosetten ausge-füllt wurden. Neben dem reich orna-mentierten Maßwerk mit seinen rein geometrischen Ornamenten war auch der vegetabile Dekor von Bedeutung. Stilisiertes Laub- und Rankenwerk zierte nicht nur Friese und Gesimse, sondern auch Giebel-schrägen und Konsolen sowie die reich verzierten Schlusssteine der Gewölbe. Eine besondere Auspra-

Paris (1163–1360), Reims (1211–1250) et Rouen (1212–1280) sont quelques-uns des plus beaux ouvrages de l'art gothique français. Les murs des cathédrales furent de plus en plus souvent percés de hautes fenêtres en ogive ornées de broderies de pierre, c'est-à-dire de motifs géométriques « au compas », créés à l'aide d'un fil à plomb et d'une équerre. Des vitraux de couleurs décoraient les fenêtres, tandis que de grandes rosaces occupaient les pignons de la nef principale et du transept. À côté des broderies de pierre aux riches motifs purement géométriques, le décor végétal revêtait lui aussi une grande importance. Rinceaux et entrelacs stylisés ornaient non seulement les frises et corniches, mais aussi les biseaux des pignons et consoles, ainsi que les clés de voûtes richement décorées. Le motif végétal trouva une expression particulière dans la réalisation de

Cathedral of Notre Dame, Paris, mid-13th century
The famouse cathedral of Notre Dame ("Our Lady") is regarded as one of the masterpieces of Gothic. A basilica with a galleried nave and two aisles to either side, it is notable for the austerity of its architecture and for its decor, in particular the filigree tracery and large rose windows with their radial arrangement of lucid geometric forms.

Notre-Dame, Paris, Mitte 13. Jh.
Die weltberühmte Notre-Dame gilt als eines der Meisterwerke der Gotik. Die fünfschiffige Emporenbasilika besticht durch ihre strenge Architektur und ihren Baudekor, insbesonde-re das filigran ornamentierte Maßwerk und die großen Fensterrosetten. Deren Muster setzen sich aus klaren geometrischen Grund-elementen zusammen, die radial in Rosen-form angeordnet sind.

Notre-Dame, Paris, milieu du XIIIᵉ siècle
Notre-Dame, l'église mondialement célèbre, passe pour être l'un des chefs-d'œuvre de l'art gothique. La basilique à tribunes et à cinq nefs séduit par son architecture austère et son décor, notamment les dentelles de pierre en filigrane et les immenses rosaces. Les motifs de celles-ci se composent de figu-res géométriques fondamentales aux lignes pures qui, par leur disposition radiale, pren-nent la forme de roses.

Tilman Riemenschneider, Altar of St Mary, Herrgottskirche, Creglingen, c. 1502–1505
The gables with the notable altar are full of intertwined vines and tendrils which seem to break out of the available space and to penetrate the frame. This work of art heralds the approaching Renaissance.

Marienaltar von Tilman Riemenschneider, Herrgottskirche in Creglingen, um 1502–1505
In den Giebelfeldern des beeindruckenden Altars sieht man virtuos ineinander verschlungenes Rankenwerk, das den gegebenen Raum zu sprengen scheint. Mit diesem Werk kündigt sich bereits der Übergang zur Renaissance an.

Autel de la Vierge de Tilman Riemenschneider, Herrgottskirche à Creglingen, vers 1502–1505
Les tympans de l'impressionnant autel sont ornés d'entrelacs interrompus avec art et imbriqués les uns dans les autres avec virtuosité, qui semblent agrandir l'espace intérieur. Cet ouvrage annonce déjà le passage à la Renaissance.

appear to creep along. A conspicuous feature of medieval vegetal ornamentation is that the designs are frequently based on oak and beech leaves, vines, ivy, thistles and roses – in other words, native plants. During the 15th century, the leaf-and-tendril motifs became increasingly stylized and lost their dynamism.

The rise of a bourgeoisie in the 14th and 15th centuries represented the appearance of a self-confident social class with a strong awareness of its own status. This class supported the construction and decorating of cathedrals and regarded them as symbols of civic prestige. In addition, a large number of secular buildings were erected in the Gothic

gung erlangte der vegetabile Dekor bei der Ausführung von Kreuzblumen und Fialen sowie den so genannten Kriechblumen. Auffällig beim vegetabilen Dekor der Gotik ist, dass die Blattformen vielfach Eichen- und Buchenlaub, Weinblatt und Efeu, Disteln und Rosen darstellen und somit den Pflanzen der heimischen Vegetation entlehnt sind. Im 15. Jahrhundert erstarren die Blattranken zunehmend und werden immer stärker schematisiert.

Mit dem Aufstieg des Bürgertums im 14. und 15. Jahrhundert bildete sich eine neue Gesellschaftsschicht mit einem ausgeprägten Standes- und Selbstbewusstsein heraus, die in den Kathedralen Wahrzeichen ihrer Städte sah und deren Bau und Aus-

fleurons, de pinacles et de ce qu'on appelle les crosses. Le plus frappant dans le décor végétal du gothique, c'est que les formes représentées sont souvent des feuilles de chêne et de hêtre, de vigne et de lierre, des chardons et des roses, c'est-à-dire qu'elles sont empruntées à la végétation locale. Au XVe siècle, les entrelacs de feuilles se figent et se schématisent à l'excès.

L'essor de la bourgeoisie aux XIVe et XVe siècles a donné naissance à une nouvelle couche sociale qui a une conscience plus marquée de son rang et de soi-même et voit dans les cathédrales dont elle favorise la construction et l'ornementation, l'emblème de sa ville. De plus, de nombreux édifices profanes gothiques furent érigés, mairies et maisons bourgeoises par exemple, présentant un décor similaire à celui des églises. L'art ornemental du gothique s'exprime surtout dans les autels, chaires, tabernacles et stalles ainsi que dans les objets du culte, comme les reliquaires, croix, calices et ciboires. Cette valorisation des ornements entraîna une explosion de métiers artisanaux tels que la sculpture, la taille de la pierre, la sculpture sur bois et le travail du bronze, l'orfèvrerie et la miniature. En Angleterre, le gothique fit son apparition à la fin du XIIe siècle avec la construction du chœur de Cantorbéry (1175–1184) par Maître Guillaume de Sens et prit fin vers 1550 avec la Réforme. Le premier gothique anglais (« Early English Style »), dont les exemples les plus frappants sont peut-être les cathédrales de Salisbury (1220–1258) et d'Oxford (vers 1250), se caractérise par une stricte organisation de l'église en plusieurs espaces avec trois nefs exagérément longues et des transepts saillants, derrière lesquels se trouve le déambulatoire emprunté à l'architecture romane avec la chapelle centrale, la « Lady Chapel ».

Le décor du haut gothique anglais (« Decorated Style ») du XIVe siècle est surtout marqué par de somptueuses voûtes d'arête, ainsi que par des dentelles de pierre décorées à l'excès, dont la richesse a donné son nom au « Decorated Style ». La

style, such as city halls and town houses of the wealthy, whose decoration resembled that of the churches. Gothic ornamentation found its expression first and foremost in altars, pulpits, choir stalls, tabernacles, as well as for liturgical accessories such as reliquaries, crosses and chalices. This up-valuing of ornament led in turn to a blossoming of craft skills, such as sculpture, stone-masonry, decorative woodcarving, bronze-casting, gold work and miniature-painting.

In England, the Gothic period started in the late-12th century with the building of the choir of Canterbury Cathedral (1175–1184) by Master William of Sens, and ended in the mid-16th century with the Reformation. The finest examples of the earliest period of Gothic in England, known as "Early English style", are probably Salisbury Cathedral (1220–1258) and Christ Church Cathedral, Oxford (c. 1250). The style is characterized by a strict division of the interior by means of a lengthened nave flanked by aisles on either side, and clearly demarcated transepts, beyond which the choir is surrounded by an ambulatory – taken over from the Romanesque style, or "Norman" as it is known in England – at the center of which is a chapel dedicated to the Virgin and hence known as a "Lady Chapel". The English High Gothic of the 14th century is known as "Decorated style", largely on account of the profusely ornamented tracery and magnificent star patterns resulting from the ribbed vaulting. Among the outstanding examples of this style is Exeter Cathedral (1257–1369). The final phase of English Gothic is known as "Perpendicular style"; by the time it started, in the mid-15th century, the Renaissance was already under way in Italy, and when it came to an end, a century later, the High Renaissance was already on the wane elsewhere. The Perpendicular style is characterized by, and derived its name from, the strong vertical elements which structured the walls of the building: pillars and engaged columns which

schmückung unterstützte. Außerdem entstanden zahlreiche gotische Profanbauten, wie zum Beispiel Rathäuser und Bürgerhäuser, die einen ähnlichen Dekor wie die Kirchen aufwiesen. Die Ornamentik der Gotik drückt sich vor allem bei Altären, Kanzeln, Sakramentshäuschen und dem Chorgestühl sowie bei lithurgischen Geräten aus wie zum Beispiel Reliquienkästchen, Kreuzen und Pokalen. Durch diese Aufwertung der Ornamentik kam es zu einer Blüte von Berufen des Kunsthandwerks wie der Bildhauerei, der Steinmetzkunst, der Bildschnitzer und der Bronzegießer sowie der Goldschmiedekunst und der Miniaturmalerei.

In England setzte die Gotik Ende des 12. Jahrhunderts mit dem Bau des Chors von Canterbury (1175–1184) durch Meister Wilhelm von Sens ein und endete um 1550 mit der Reformation. Die englische Frühgotik („Early English Style"), deren einprägsamste Beispiele vielleicht die Kathedrale von Salisbury (1220–1258) und die Christ Church in Oxford (um 1250) sind, zeichnet sich durch eine strenge Gliederung des Kirchenraums mittels drei überlängter Längsschiffe und deutlich abgesetzter Querschiffe aus, an die sich der von der romanischen Architektur übernommene Chorumgang mit der Zentralkapelle, der „Lady Chapel", anschließt.

In der englischen Hochgotik („Decorated Style") des 14. Jahrhunderts werden hinsichtlich des Dekors vor allem prächtige Rippengewölbe sowie überreich verziertes Maßwerk ausgeprägt, deren reicher Dekor dem „Decorated Style" seinen Namen gab. Zu den herausragendsten Bauwerken dieses Stils zählt die Kathedrale von Exeter (1257–1369). Die englische Spätgotik („Perpendicular Style") setzte etwa Mitte des 15. Jahrhunderts ein, zu einem Zeitpunkt, als in Italien bereits die Renaissance aufkam. Der „Perpendicular Style" endete Mitte des 16. Jahrhunderts, als andernorts die Hochrenaissance ihre Blüte überschritten hatte. Dieser Stil zeichnet sich durch eine strenge Gliederung der Wände mittels Pfei-

cathédrale d'Exeter (1257–1369) est un des édifices les plus remarquables de ce style. Le gothique tardif anglais (« Perpendicular Style ») a débuté à peu près au milieu du XVᵉ siècle, à une époque où la Renaissance faisait déjà son apparition en Italie. Le « Perpendicular Style » s'est achevé au milieu du XVIᵉ siècle tandis qu'ailleurs, la Renaissance amorçait déjà son déclin. Ce style se distingue par une organisation stricte des murs au moyen de piliers et de perches colonnettes qui supportent des voûtes en étoile et en éventail typiques du gothique anglais. De plus, les églises possèdent un chœur qui se termine par un rectangle orné d'une imposante fenêtre à dentelles

This reliquary is notable for its enchantingly accurate architectural imitation, and its graceful figures, but also for its elegant ornamentation. Tracery, finials and quatrefoils are all in evidence, taken from the inventory of Gothic architectural decoration, and here reproduced in precise detail.

Karlsreliquiar, Aachener Domschatz, um 1350
Das Reliquiar bezaubert nicht nur wegen seiner gelungenen Architekturnachbildung und seiner anmutigen Figuren, sondern auch durch seine feine Ornamentik. So sieht man Maßwerk, Fialen und Kreuzblumen, die dem gotischen Baudekor entnommen sind und hier minutiös wiedergegeben wurden.

Reliquaire de Charlemagne provenant du trésor de la cathédrale d'Aix-la-Chapelle, vers 1350.
Ce reliquaire séduit non seulement par son imitation architecturale réussie et ses gracieuses représentations figurées, mais aussi par ses délicats ornements. On peut voir, par exemple, des dentelles de pierre, des pinacles et des fleurons empruntés au décor architectural gothique et reproduits minutieusement ici.

supported the characteristically English ribbed vaults. Perpendicular churches tend to have a rectangular East end, with a very large East window with tracery. The enthusiasm for this style was so great that older churches were often rebuilt in the Perpendicular style, or else given new and larger windows. Apart from the elaborate vaulting and windows, Perpendicular ornamentation is in fact if anything somewhat reticent, and based exclusively on vegetal forms, with leaf and calyx motifs for capitals, and tendril motifs for friezes, along with the usual Gothic array of crockets, finials and decorated gables.

All these elements were given new life for a while during the 19th century Gothic revival, which was also reflected in the Audsleys' ornamental designs, many of them derived from the architectural ornamentation of the Middle Ages, whose models, originally in relief, were translated with the help of color into two dimensions.

lern und Diensten aus, die für die englische Gotik charakteristische Stern- und Fächergewölbe tragen. Außerdem besitzen die Kirchen einen rechteckigen Chorschluss, der von einem großen Fenster mit Maßwerk geziert wird. Die Begeisterung für diesen neuen Stil war so groß, dass ältere Kirchen im „Perpendicular Style" umgebaut wurden oder zumindest neue, breite Fenster erhielten. Die Ornamentik ist, abgesehen von den aufwändigen Gewölben und Fenstern, zurückhaltend und basiert ausschließlich auf vegetabilen Formen, zu denen Blatt- und Kelchkapitelle sowie Rankenfriese ebenso gehören wie die für die gotische Architektur typischen Krabben, Fialen und Wimpergen.

All diese Elemente fanden in der Architektur des Historismus gegen Ende des 19. Jahrhunderts, dem „Gothic Revival", eine zeitweilige Wiederbelebung, die sich auch in den Ornamenttafeln der Audsleys widerspiegelt. Ihre Entwürfe sind vielfach dem mittelalterlichen Baudekor entlehnt, dessen reliefartige Vorbilder hier als flächige Ornamenttafeln nur mit dem Gestaltungsmittel der Farbe umgesetzt werden.

de pierre. Ce nouveau style souleva un enthousiasme tel qu'on se mit à transformer des églises plus anciennes en « Perpendicular Style » ou du moins qu'on y perça de nouvelles fenêtres plus larges. L'ornementation est plutôt modeste, à l'exception des riches voûtes et fenêtres, et se base exclusivement sur des formes végétales auxquelles participent les chapiteaux à feuilles et à tambour, les frises d'entrelacs, ainsi que les crosses, pinacles et guimberges caractéristiques de l'architecture gothique.

Tous ces éléments revinrent temporairement au goût du jour vers la fin du XIXᵉ siècle dans l'architecture de l'historisme, le « Gothic Revival », qui se manifeste à travers les planches ornementales des Audsley. Ceux-ci ont souvent emprunté leurs planches ornementales au décor architectural du Moyen Âge, dont la transposition à plat des modèles en relief n'est réalisable ici qu'au moyen de la couleur.

Friezes with decoration inspired by Gothic style
Friese mit gotisch inspiriertem Dekor
Frises à décor d'inspiration gothique

These six designs represent two-dimensional stylized adaptations of medieval moldings. The two patterns at the top are derived respectively from a billet molding in Binham Priory, Norfolk and a cubed molding in St Augustine's Priory in Canterbury. The elaborate zigzag frieze is based on a molding in Lincoln Cathedral. These three patterns are characteristic of the Norman style of medieval architecture.

The band in the middle shows the typically Gothic quatrefoil and crocket motifs. The latter is a vegetal design that appears to creep along the ribs of medieval vaults. It is typical especially of the Early English style. The next band shows a simple variation on the trefoil motif; it is typical of English High Gothic (Decorated style), and should thus be used only in this austere and highly stylized form. The band at the bottom shows a series of squares decorated with quatrefoils, typical of the final phase of English Gothic, known as the Perpendicular style, and commonly found in buildings of the period.

Diese sechs Entwürfe stellen flächig umgesetzte Stilisierungen mittelalterlicher Friese dar. Die beiden Muster oben leiten sich von einem Rollenfries aus Binham Priory in Norfolk sowie einem Würfelfries von St. Augustin in Canterbury ab. Der aufwändig gestaltete Zickzack-Fries ist der Kathedrale von Lincoln entnommen. Diese drei Muster sind charakteristisch für die normannische Stilrichtung der mittelalterlichen Architektur.

Das mittlere Ornamentband zeigt die für die gotische Architektur charakteristischen Kleeblattmotive in Verbindung mit Krabben, jenen vegetabilen Gebilden, die an den Rippen mittelalterlicher Gebäude entlangzukriechen scheinen, weshalb sie auch als „Kriechblumen" bezeichnet werden. Sie sind typisch für die englische Frühgotik (Early English Style). Das vorletzte Ornamentband präsentiert in Kreisen vertiefte Dreipässe, die als „Ballenblumen" bezeichnet werden. Diese einfachen Motive sind für die englische Hochgotik (Decorated Style) charakteristisch und sollten daher nur in einer strengen und stark stilisierten Form angewendet werden. Das untere Band zeigt eine Abfolge von Quadraten, die von vierblättrigen Blumen geziert werden. Sie sind für die englische Spätgotik (Perpendicular Style) typisch und finden sich daher häufig als Dekor in spätgotischen Gebäuden.

Ces six esquisses présentent des stylisations à plat de frises médiévales. Les deux motifs du haut sont dérivés d'une billette du Prieuré de Binham dans le Norfolk, ainsi que d'une frise à damiers de St. Augustin à Cantorbéry. La frise en zigzag aux formes riches est empruntée à la cathédrale de Lincoln. Ces trois motifs reflètent l'influence du style normand sur l'architecture médiévale.

Le bandeau ornemental central présente des feuilles de trèfle, motif caractéristique de l'architecture gothique, en association avec des crosses, ces formes végétales qui semblent ramper le long des nervures des édifices médiévaux, d'où leur nom de « fleurs rampantes ». Ces motifs sont typiques du premier gothique anglais (Early English Style). L'avant-dernier bandeau ornemental présente des trilobes insérés dans des cercles et qui portent le nom de « fleurs en boule ». Ces motifs simples caractérisent le haut gothique anglais (Decorated Style) et ne doivent donc être utilisés que sous une forme sévère et très stylisée. Le bandeau du bas présente une succession de carrés ornés de fleurs à quatre feuilles. Ces motifs sont typiques du gothique tardif anglais (Perpendicular Style) et décorent donc souvent des édifices de cette époque.

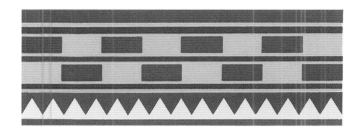

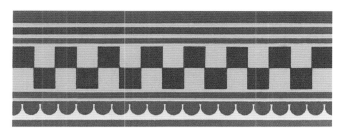

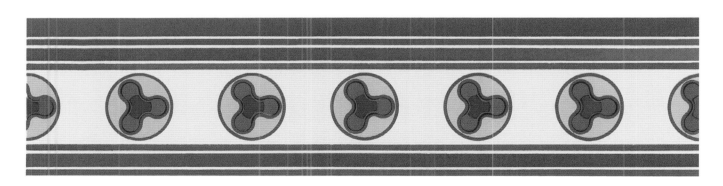

Horizontal ornamental bands with tendril motifs
Horizontale Ornamentbänder mit feingliedrigen Ranken
Bandeaux ornementaux horizontaux à entrelacs délicats

These two ornamental bands are decorated with slender tendrils. The top pattern is based on a stylized lily, flanked symmetrically by palmette-like motifs. The lower pattern is a version of the vitruvian scroll; the insides of the curves based on a sinuous tendril are filled by highly stylized leaves on elegantly spiraling shoots. The top edge of both bands is formed by narrow borders clearly inspired by the cubed molding, while the lower edge is formed by a narrow border of three-quarter circles and semicircles respectively.

These patterns can be used equally well in religious or secular buildings. They are particularly suitable for use as horizontal ornamental bands on walls decorated with some kind of masonry pattern. They can also be used as crestings for walls or for the base zones of walls, where these are decorated with some simple repeating pattern. The designs can be executed either in subdued tones, or else in bright colors.

Die beiden Ornamentbänder werden von feingliedrigen Ranken geziert. Das obere Muster basiert auf einer stilisierten Lilie, von der sich spiegelbildlich Palmetten abspalten. Das Muster unten zeigt eine Wellenranke mit schlanken, stark stilisierten Blättern, die sich elegant einrollen. Als obere Begrenzung beider Ornamentbänder dienen schmale, offensichtlich vom Würfelfries abgeleitete Ornamentstreifen, während der untere Abschluss von Bändern aus kleinen Halb- und Dreiviertelkreisen gebildet wird.

Diese Muster sind gleichermaßen für sakrale und profane Bauwerke verwendbar. Sie eignen sich besonders als Dekor für horizontale Ornamentbänder auf Wänden, die mit dem Ziegelmuster geschmückt sind. Auch als obere Begrenzung von Wand- und Sockelzonen sind sie einsetzbar, wenn diese mit einem einfachen oder gesprenkelten Motiv in der Art eines Tüpfelmusters verziert sind. Die Muster können sowohl farblich zurückhaltend als auch bunt gestaltet werden.

Les deux bandeaux sont ornés d'entrelacs délicats. Le motif du haut se base sur un lis stylisé dont se séparent des palmettes qui se font face. Le motif du bas présente un entrelacs de vagues aux feuilles élancées, très stylisées qui s'enroulent avec élégance. Des bandes ornementales manifestement dérivées de la frise à damiers servent de limite supérieure aux deux bandeaux, tandis que de petits demicercles ou trois quarts de cercles constituent la limite inférieure.

Ces motifs sont utilisables dans des édifices tant sacrés que profanes. Ils serviront à décorer des bandeaux ornementaux sur des murs ornés du motif de briques. Ils formeront aussi la limite supérieure entre murs et soubassements, si ceux-ci sont décorés d'un motif simple ou tacheté à la manière d'un mouchetis. Ces motifs pourront être réalisés dans des couleurs discrètes ou vives.

Horizontal ornamental bands with tendril and oak leaf patterns
Horizontale Ornamentbänder mit Ranken und Eichenlaub
Bandeaux ornementaux horizontaux à entrelacs et feuilles de chêne

These two designs depict highly expressive leaf patterns. While the top design is based on a vitruvian scroll with leaves reminiscent of oak-leaves, the lower composition represents a stylization of various kinds of leaves. These ornamentations are derived from the architectural decoration of the 13th-century cathedral in Laon, France.

The coloration illustrated here is very elaborate, but simpler color schemes are possible. Thus both patterns can be applied in a single color on a simple ground, for example in a light color or gold on a dark ground or vice versa. In both cases, the borders can be executed in a different color from the main design. The basic color of these borders can also differ from the color of the wall. Both designs are appropriate not only to churches, but also to secular buildings.

Diese beiden Ornamentbänder zeigen sehr ausdrucksvoll gestaltete Blattranken. Während das obere Muster auf einer Wellenranke basiert, deren Blätter an Eichenlaub erinnern, zeigt der untere Entwurf eine Stilisierung unterschiedlicher Blattformen. Diese Ornamente lassen sich vom Baudekor der Kathedrale von Laon (13. Jh.) in Frankreich ableiten.

Die hier dargestellte farbige Umsetzung ist sehr aufwändig; es ist jedoch auch eine einfachere Gestaltung möglich. So können zum Beispiel beide Muster in einer einzigen Farbe auf einem einfarbigen Grund aufgetragen werden, etwa in einer hellen Farbe oder Gold auf dunklem Grund oder in einer dunklen Farbe auf hellem Grund. In beiden Fällen dürfen die Randleisten in einer anderen Farbe gestaltet sein als das Ornamentband. Die Grundfarbe dieser Leisten darf sich überdies von der Grundfarbe der Wand unterscheiden. Beide Entwürfe können sowohl in Kirchen als auch in Profanbauten umgesetzt werden.

Ces deux bandeaux présentent des entrelacs de feuilles aux formes très expressives. Si le motif du haut se base sur un entrelacs de vagues dont les feuilles rappellent celles du chêne, celui du bas montre par contre une stylisation de formes de feuilles différentes. Ces ornements sont inspirés du décor architectural de la cathédrale de Laon (XIIIe siècle) en France.

La transposition en couleurs présentée ici est très riche ; une exécution plus simple est toutefois possible. On peut par exemple réaliser les deux motifs en une seule couleur sur un fond monochrome : teinte claire ou doré sur fond sombre ou teinte foncée sur fond clair. Dans les deux cas, on choisira une couleur différente de celle du bandeau ornemental pour les listels, dont la couleur de fond devra se distinguer de celle du mur. Ces deux motifs pourront s'utiliser dans des églises aussi bien que dans des édifices profanes.

Horizontal ornamental bands with tendril motifs
Horizontale Ornamentbänder mit Ranken
Bandeaux ornementaux horizontaux à entrelacs

The three designs illustrated here show tendril patterns derived from early Gothic exemplars. As there is no symbolism attached to these motifs, they can be used both for churches and for secular buildings. Patterns like these can be used for horizontal, vertical, raking or indeed curved bands.

The designs of these bands are very rich in detail, but nevertheless balanced. They can therefore be used in a larger format, up to 30 centimeters in breadth. In elevated locations, on church walls for example, they can be made even bigger. The best effect is achieved by executing them either in a dark color on a light ground, or in a light color on a dark ground.

Die hier abgebildeten drei Entwürfe zeigen Ranken, die sich von Vorbildern des frühgotischen Baudekors ableiten lassen. Da diesen Motiven kein Symbolgehalt zugrunde liegt, können sie als Dekor für Kirchen und Profanbauten gleichermaßen verwendet werden. Solche Muster eignen sich vor allem für horizontale, vertikale, schräge und geschwungene Bänder.

Die Muster dieser Bänder sind sehr detailreich, aber trotzdem ausgewogen. Sie können daher auch in einem größeren Maßstab mit einer Breite bis zu 30 cm ausgeführt werden. An erhöhten Stellen, an Kirchenwänden etwa, können sie auch darüber hinausgehend vergrößert werden. Die schönste Wirkung erzielen sie in einer dunklen Farbe auf hellem Grund oder in einer hellen Farbe auf dunklem Grund.

Les trois motifs illustrés ici présentent des entrelacs dérivés des modèles du décor architectural du premier gothique. Comme ces motifs n'ont pas de contenu symbolique, ils pourront s'utiliser dans des églises et dans des édifices profanes. Ils permettront de réaliser des bandeaux horizontaux, verticaux, obliques et arqués.

Les motifs de ces bandeaux sont très détaillés, mais équilibrés. Il est donc possible de les reproduire sur une largeur de 30 cm au maximum. On les agrandira davantage encore pour les placer en hauteur, par exemple sur des murs d'église. Ils seront du plus bel effet dans une couleur foncée sur fond clair ou dans une couleur claire sur fond sombre.

Vertical ornamental bands with scroll motifs
Vertikale Ornamentbänder mit Wellenranken
Bandeaux ornementaux verticaux à entrelacs de vagues

These two patterns show elaborate vitruvian scroll motifs. The left-hand design consists of two wave meanders staggered so that they form ovals decorated with elegant leaf-tendrils and small rosettes sprouting from the main stems. As the tendrils from each stem are almost, but not quite, identical, the result is a pleasing complexity in the symmetry. The right-hand design is similar, but here the two waves are reflected, fully symmetrically, about the central axis, giving scope for additional ornamentation.

Both patterns are suitable for the decoration of broad vertical wall bands, as well as for the intrados of pointed arches. If the patterns are used in churches, a further application is possible. In roof structures where the rafters are visible, the interstices are often plastered, providing an opportunity for decoration. As a rule, these areas are 30–35 centimeters broad, and can easily be decorated with the help of a stencil. In pale yellow on an off-white or white ground, they produce a light, well-balanced effect.

Diese beiden Entwürfe zeigen aufwändig gestaltete Ranken. Der linke Entwurf besteht aus zwei gegenläufigen Wellenranken, die sich überkreuzen und dabei ovale Medaillons bilden, die von eleganten Blattranken und kleinen Rosetten geziert sind. Die Ranke rechts stellt eine Variation desselben Themas dar. Die beiden Wellen spiegeln sich an der Mittelachse, wodurch ein neues Ornament entsteht. Beide Muster eignen sich als Dekor breiter vertikaler Wandbänder sowie als Zierde der Laibungen von Spitzbögen. Bei der Ausschmückung von Kirchen ist noch eine weitere Verwendung dieser Ornamente möglich: Bei Dachkonstruktionen, deren Holzbalken sichtbar sind, werden häufig die Zwischenräume der Dachsparren verputzt und bieten sich daher zur Dekoration an. Diese Felder haben in der Regel eine Breite von 30 bis 35 cm und lassen sich problemlos mit der Schablone bearbeiten. In einem blassgelben Farbton auf hellem, pergamentfarbenem oder auch weißem Grund aufgetragen, haben sie eine leichte und ausgwogene Wirkung.

Ces deux esquisses présentent des entrelacs aux formes riches. Le motif de gauche se compose de deux entrelacs de vagues qui se déroulent en sens contraire, s'entrecroisent et forment des médaillons ovales ornés d'élégants entrelacs de feuilles et de petites rosaces. Le motif de droite présente une variante du même thème. Les deux entrelacs de vagues se font face de chaque côté de l'axe central, donnant ainsi naissance à un nouvel ornement.

Les deux motifs serviront à décorer de larges bandes de murs verticales, ainsi que les intrados d'arcs en ogive. Une autre utilisation de ces ornements est possible lorsqu'il s'agit de décorer des églises : dans les systèmes de toits avec des poutres en bois visibles, les intervalles entre les chevrons sont souvent crépis et se prêtent donc parfaitement à la décoration. Ces panneaux ont en général 30 à 35 cm de large et peuvent être traités sans problème au pochoir. Ils produiront une impression de légèreté et d'équilibre s'ils sont réalisés dans un ton jaune pâle sur un fond clair, couleur parchemin ou sur du blanc.

Panel ornamentation with a vegetal motif
Paneelverzierung mit vegetabilem Dekor
Panneau à décor végétal

This very elaborate design is based on an acanthus plant with highly stylized leaves. The use of different shades of the same color is particularly attractive.

The design is suitable above all for the ornamentation of small rectangular surfaces or as the top or bottom element of long vertical decorations. Although the panel has a rectangular frame, it does not necessarily have to be used for rectangular surfaces. On the contrary, it is very suitable for panels ending in a round or pointed arch. There is a free choice of color schemes with this pattern – dark on a light ground, or else light or gold on a dark ground.

Dieser sehr aufwändig gestaltete Entwurf basiert auf einer Akanthuspflanze, deren Blätter stark stilisiert sind. Besonders ansprechend ist die farbige Gestaltung dieses Motivs Ton in Ton.

Dieses Muster eignet sich vor allem als Dekor kleiner, rechteckiger Flächen oder als unterer oder oberer Abschluss lang gezogener Füllungen. Obwohl das Paneel rechteckig gerahmt ist, lässt sich dieses Muster keineswegs ausschließlich für rechteckige Flächen verwenden, im Gegenteil: Es passt auch sehr gut zu Paneelen, die in einem Spitzbogen oder einem Rundbogen enden. Farblich kann dieser Entwurf ganz frei gestaltet werden – in einer dunklen Farbe auf hellem Grund oder auch in einem hellen Farbton oder Gold auf dunklem Grund.

Cette esquisse aux formes très riches se base sur une acanthe aux feuilles stylisées. La composition ton sur ton de ce motif est particulièrement esthétique.

Ce motif servira avant tout à décorer de petites surfaces rectangulaires ou à terminer le haut ou le bas de panneaux longs. Même si le panneau a un cadre rectangulaire, ce motif n'est pas exclusivement destiné à des surfaces rectangulaires, bien au contraire : il convient aussi à des panneaux se terminant par un arc en ogive ou en plein cintre. Toutes les combinaisons de couleurs sont possibles : teinte foncée sur fond clair ou teinte claire ou dorée sur fond sombre.

Horizontal ornamental band with elaborate vitruvian-scroll motif
Horizontales Ornamentband mit aufwändig gestalteten Ranken
Bandeau ornemental horizontal à entrelacs aux formes riches

The broad ornamental band illustrated here shows an elaborate, highly stylized acanthus whose main – horizontal – stem produces spiral shoots at equal intervals. Each shoot ends in an acanthus bud of exaggerated length, flanked by acanthus leaves. In addition, from the top of each shoot there sprouts an upright shoot crowned by a stylized acanthus palmette.

This design is suitable for use as a dividing frieze between a dark base zone and a light wall surface above. In the case of highly elaborate wall decorations, this frieze can be applied above a broad ornamental band or some other relief-like frieze. Whether the pattern is executed in polychrome or monochrome should be decided on the basis of the color scheme of the whole room.

Das hier vorgestellte breite Ornamentband zeigt eine aufwändig gestaltete, stark stilisierte Akanthusranke, deren liegender Stängel sich in gleichmäßigen Abständen einrollt. Den Ausläufer der Ranke ziert eine längliche Akanthusknospe, die von spitzzackigen Blättern umspielt wird. Nach oben hin spaltet sich von der Ranke ein aufrechter Stängel ab, den eine stilisierte Akanthuspalmette bekrönt. Dieses Muster eignet sich als trennender Fries zwischen einer dunklen Sockelzone und einer hellen darüber liegenden Wandfläche. Bei sehr aufwändig gestalteten Wanddekorationen kann dieser Fries oberhalb eines breiten Ornamentbandes oder eines anderen reliefartigen Frieses aufgetragen werden. Die ein- oder mehrfarbige Gestaltung des Musters sollte sich an der Farbgebung des gesamten Raumes orientieren.

Le large bandeau illustré ici présente un entrelacs de feuilles d'acanthe très stylisé, aux formes riches et dont la tige posée à plat s'enroule à intervalles réguliers. Un bouton d'acanthe oblong, encadré par des feuilles aux pointes découpées, orne le stolon de l'entrelacs. Une tige droite couronnée par une palmette d'acanthe stylisée s'élance vers le haut en se séparant de l'entrelacs. Ce motif servira de frise de séparation entre un soubassement sombre et une surface de mur claire au-dessus de lui. Si les décorations murales présentent des formes riches, on pourra transposer cette frise au-dessus d'un large bandeau ornemental ou d'une autre frise donnant l'impression de relief. La réalisation monochrome ou polychrome du motif dépend des couleurs utilisées dans l'ensemble de la pièce.

Corner ornaments with leaf and scroll motifs for ceiling decoration
Eckornamente mit Blatt- und Rankenmotiven zur Verzierung von Decken
Ornements d'angles à feuilles et entrelacs pour la décoration de plafonds

The two designs show leaf and scroll motifs suitable as corner decorations for large ceilings. The actual size of the execution would depend on the dimensions of the ceiling in question. If the corner decorations are to be so large that their diagonal exceeds 60 centimeters in length, or they are to be executed in dark or powerful colors, the version illustrated at the top is preferable, with its more slender tendrils and delicate leaves. On a smaller scale, these ornaments can also be used as decorations for wooden panels or wall surfaces.

The simple color scheme illustrated here, using a medium shade on a light ground, is not binding; the patterns can also be executed in other colors. If the ceiling is basically dark, a good effect can be achieved by executing the designs in a light color or in gold.

Die beiden Entwürfe zeigen Blatt- und Rankenmotive, die als Eckornamente für die Verzierung großer Decken geeignet sind. Die maßstäbliche Umsetzung richtet sich nach den Dimensionen der jeweiligen Decke. Wenn die Eckornamente so groß ausgeführt werden sollen, dass ihre Diagonale eine Länge von 60 cm übersteigt, oder wenn eine Gestaltung in dunklen oder kräftigen Farben geplant ist, so ist das feingliedrigere Ornament oben auf der Tafel vorzuziehen. In einem kleineren Maßstab lassen sich diese Ornamente auch als Dekoration für Holzpaneele oder Wandflächen verwenden.

Die auf der Abbildung dargestellte einfache Kolorierung in einem mittelkräftigen Farbton auf hellem Grund ist nicht bindend, die Muster lassen sich auch in aufwändigeren Farben umsetzen. Hat die Decke einen dunklen Grundton, so können die Ornamente wirkungsvoll in einer hellen Farbe oder Gold ausgeführt werden.

Ces deux esquisses présentent des motifs de feuilles et d'entrelacs qui serviront d'ornements d'angles pour la décoration de grands plafonds. Leur transposition à l'échelle s'effectuera selon les dimensions du plafond. S'il est nécessaire d'agrandir ces ornements d'angles afin que la longueur de leur diagonale dépasse 60 cm ou si on envisage une composition dans des couleurs sombres ou vives, on préférera l'ornement plus délicat présenté dans le haut de la planche. À échelle réduite, ces ornements serviront aussi à la décoration de panneaux de bois ou de murs.

Il n'est pas impératif d'adopter la combinaison de couleurs simple illustrée ici, c'est-à-dire un ton moyen sur un fond clair ; on peut très bien utiliser des couleurs plus riches pour ces motifs. Si la couleur de fond du plafond est sombre, les ornements réalisés en couleur claire ou en doré seront du plus bel effet.

Corner and intermediate ornaments with vegetal motifs for panels or other wall elements
Eck- und Zwischenstücke mit vegetabilem Dekor für Paneele oder Wandfüllungen
Pièces d'angles et raccords à décor végétal pour panneaux ou pans de murs

Ten different patterns for corners and two more for intermediate spaces are illustrated here. They show various leaf and scroll motifs, whose forms are derived from English Gothic. The designs are suitable both for the decoration of panels and for larger wall surfaces. Although the patterns are shown here in two colors, a livelier color scheme is also possible.

Hier sind zehn verschiedene Muster für Ecken und zusätzlich zwei für Zwischenstücke dargestellt. Sie zeigen verschiedene Blatt- und Rankengebilde, deren Formen der englischen Gotik entlehnt sind.
Die Motive eignen sich sowohl zur Verzierung von Paneelen als auch zur Dekoration großer Wandflächen. Obwohl die Muster hier in zwei Farben vorgestellt werden, ist auch eine farbigere Gestaltung möglich.

Cette planche présente dix motifs différents pour angles et deux autres pour raccords. Il s'agit de divers thèmes de feuilles et d'entrelacs dont les formes sont empruntées au gothique anglais.
Ces motifs serviront à décorer des panneaux aussi bien que de grandes surfaces de murs. Il est possible de les réaliser dans d'autres couleurs que celles présentées ici.

Square paterae with rosette motifs
Quadratische Felder mit Rosettendekor
Panneaux carrés à rosaces

These six designs show vegetal forms derived from rosettes but adapted to fill a square patera. Highly stylized, these motifs are derived from the decoration of medieval timber roofs which can be seen in English churches.

These patterns are intended for execution in two dimensions and in lively color. They can be used for panel decoration, but also for ceilings, as illustrated on page 119. For comparable vegetal patterns, see page 243.

Diese sechs Entwürfe zeigen ins Quadrat umgesetzte pflanzliche Gebilde, die sich formal von der Rosette ableiten. Die stark schematisierten Motive lassen sich vom Dekor mittelalterlicher Holzdecken ableiten, wie sie in englischen Kirchen zu sehen sind. Diese Muster sind für eine flache, farbige Umsetzung bestimmt. Sie können als Paneelverzierungen verwendet werden, eignen sich aber auch als Deckenverzierung, wie auf Seite 119 veranschaulicht. Zu vergleichbaren vegetabilen Mustern siehe Seite 243.

Ces six esquisses présentent des formes végétales intégrées dans des carrés qui, par leur forme, sont dérivées de la rosace. Les motifs très schématisés sont inspirés du décor de plafonds en bois médiévaux, tels qu'on en rencontre dans certaines églises anglaises. Ces motifs pourront être transposés à plat et en couleurs et serviront à décorer des panneaux, mais aussi des plafonds comme le montre la planche à la page 119. La planche à la page 243 présente des motifs végétaux similaires.

Roof or ceiling decoration with vitruvian-scroll motif
Dach- oder Deckendekoration mit Rankendekor
Entrelacs destinés à la décoration de toits ou de plafonds

The two designs, which are identical apart from their coloration, show an elaborate tendril design in the form of a vitruvian scroll. The tendrils sprout from a massive central stem, which is itself decorated by striking rosette designs. These highly detailed patterns are intended for the ornamentation of rafters in church roofs or ceilings. In these roof constructions, the underside of the beams or rafters is frequently visible, while the spaces between are either plastered or decorated. The ornamental bands illustrated here are suitable both for the rafters and for the spaces between. The narrow black border with the quatrefoil designs is intended for the ornamentation of the undersides of the rafters. The broader bands with the scroll motif are suitable for the spaces in between the rafters.

The rafters and intermediate spaces can also be decorated in these patterns but on a ground of a single color – parchment or some similar shade – on which the patterns can be painted in one or more colors. A further pattern for the ornamentation of the spaces between rafters is shown on page 105.

Die beiden Entwürfe, die sich lediglich in der Farbgebung unterscheiden, zeigen aufwändig gestaltete Blattranken. Sie spalten sich von einem massiven Zentralstamm ab, der von ausdrucksstarken Rosetten geziert wird. Diese sehr detailreichen Entwürfe sind für die Verzierung der Holzbalken von Kirchendächern oder -decken bestimmt. Bei solchen Dachkonstruktionen ist häufig die Unterseite der Dachsparren sichtbar, die Felder zwischen den Sparren werden meist verputzt oder dekoriert. Die hier gezeigten Ornamentbänder sind sowohl für die Verzierung der Sparrenunterseiten als auch für die Zwischenräume geeignet. Das schmale schwarze Band mit den in einem Kreis eingeschriebenen Vierpässen dient zur Dekoration der Balkenuntersichten. Die beiden hellen Ornamentstreifen mit dem Rankendekor schmücken die Felder zwischen den Dachsparren.

Balken und Zwischenräume können abweichend von der Darstellung auch in einem einheitlichen Farbton – pergamentfarben oder in einem ähnlichen Ton – gestrichen werden. Auf diesen Untergrund werden dann die ein- oder mehrfarbigen Muster aufgetragen. Ein weiteres Muster zur Ausschmückung von Balkenzwischenräumen ist auf Seite 105 zu sehen.

Ces deux esquisses qui se distinguent par leur combinaison de couleurs présentent des entrelacs de feuilles aux formes riches, se détachant d'une tige centrale massive ornée de rosaces expressives. Ces motifs très détaillés serviront à décorer les poutres en bois de toits ou de plafonds d'églises. Dans ces systèmes de toits, le dessous des chevrons est souvent visible et les panneaux entre les chevrons sont en général crépis ou décorés. Les bandeaux ornementaux illustrés ici conviennent pour la décoration de dessous de chevrons aussi bien que pour les surfaces intermédiaires. La bande noire étroite aux quadrilobes inscrits dans un cercle servira à décorer les dessous de poutres. Les deux bandes ornementales claires à entrelacs décoreront les panneaux situés entre les chevrons. On pourra peindre les poutres et surfaces intermédiaires dans une couleur homogène différente de celle présentée ici, par exemple un ton parchemin ou similaire. Le motif monochrome ou polychrome sera alors transposé sur ce fond. La planche à la page 105 présente un autre motif destiné à la décoration d'espaces entre des poutres.

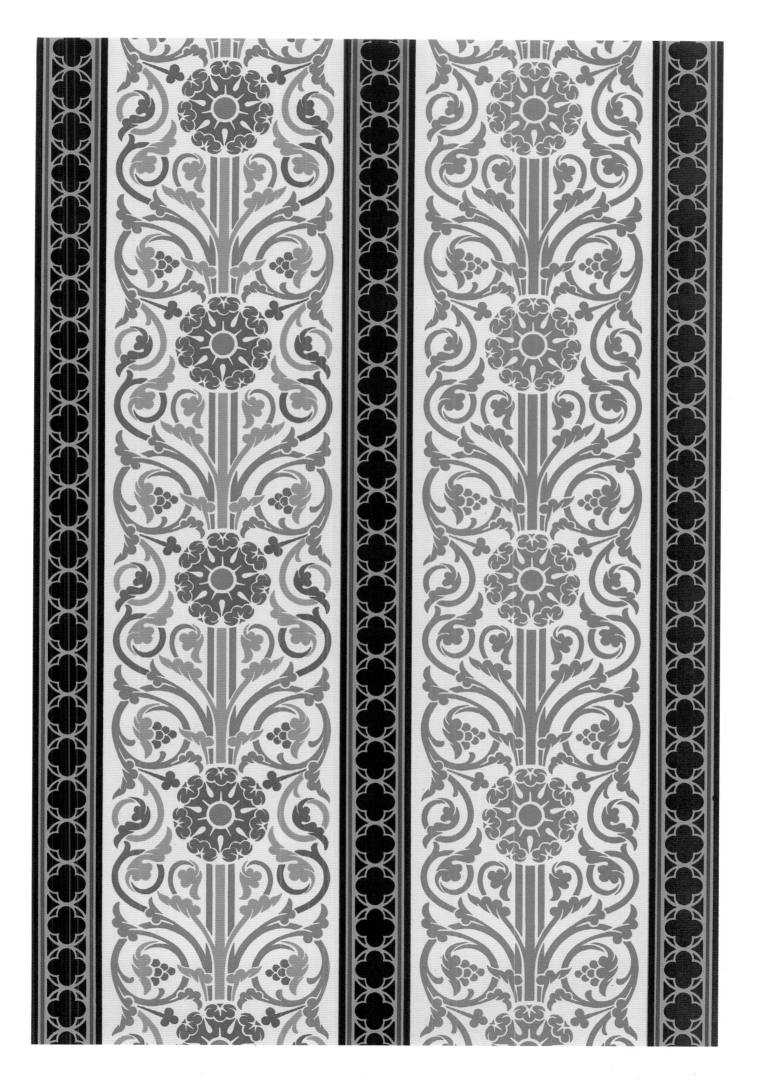

Rosette decoration for a coffered ceiling
Dekoration einer Kassettendecke mit Rosetten
Décoration d'un plafond à caissons avec rosaces

This plate depicts a large-format ceiling decoration. It is based on large rosettes framed by squares consisting of narrow ornamental bands. The charm of the design lies primarily in the interplay of the rosettes with the elaborate borders. At the corners of the squares there are somewhat smaller rosettes expanded into small squares. They are derived from the keystones found in medieval churches. These patterns are also suitable for the decoration of ceilings which are visibly subdivided into square coffers. In this case, only the large rosettes need to be inserted into the coffers. Ceilings of this kind are suitable both for religious and for secular buildings.

Diese Tafel präsentiert eine großflächige Deckendekoration. Sie basiert auf großen Rosetten, die von schmalen Ornamentbändern quadratisch gerahmt sind. Der Entwurf besticht vor allem durch das Zusammenspiel der Rosetten mit den aufwändig gemusterten Bändern. An den Kreuzungspunkten der Bänder sieht man etwas kleinere, zum Quadrat erweiterte Rosetten. Sie leiten sich formal von den Schlusssteinen mittelalterlicher Kirchen ab. Diese Muster eignen sich auch zur Gestaltung von Decken, die durch sichtbare Balken in quadratische Kassetten unterteilt sind. Hier werden dann lediglich die großen Rosetten in die Kassetten eingefügt. Decken dieser Art eignen sich sowohl für sakrale als auch für profane Bauten.

Cette planche présente une décoration destinée à un plafond de grande surface. Elle se base sur de grandes rosaces insérées dans des carrés et encadrées par d'étroits bandeaux ornementaux. L'esquisse séduit surtout par la combinaison de rosaces et de bandeaux richement ornés. Aux points d'intersection des bandeaux, on voit des rosaces un peu plus petites qui s'élargissent pour former un carré. Ce motif est dérivé des clés de voûte des églises médiévales ; il sera idéal aussi pour les plafonds subdivisés en caissons carrés par des poutres visibles. Dans ce cas, on n'insérera que les grandes rosaces dans les caissons. Des plafonds de ce type conviendront aux édifices sacrés aussi bien que profanes.

Diaper patterns with tendril and flower motifs
Tapetenmuster mit Blattranken und Blumen
Motif de tapisserie à entrelacs de feuilles et fleurs

These two diaper designs are comparable to wallpaper patterns. The left-hand one shows quatrefoils penetrated by leaves and flowers, while in that on the right, the quatrefoils are replaced by crosses.

These designs are suitable for the ornamentation of wall surfaces. Although they are shown here in polychrome, both can also be executed in one color – either dark on light or light on a dark ground. Some variety can be brought into the coloration of the ground by painting the area inside the crosses or the quatrefoils a different color from the rest.

Die beiden flächendeckenden Muster sind mit Tapetenmustern vergleichbar. Beim linken Muster sieht man Vierpässe, die von Blättern und Blumen durchrankt sind, beim Motiv rechts treten Kreuze an deren Stelle.

Diese Entwürfe sind zur Ausmalung von Wandflächen geeignet. Obwohl hier eine mehrfarbige Umsetzung präsentiert wird, lassen sich beide Muster auch einfarbig ausführen – sowohl in dunklen Farben auf hellem als auch in hellen Farben auf dunklem Grund. In die Färbung des Grundes lässt sich Abwechslung bringen, indem man die Grundflächen der Vierpässe und Kreuze in einem anderen Farbton ausführt als die übrige Fläche.

Ces deux motifs très riches sont comparables aux motifs de tapisserie. Celui de gauche se compose de quadrilobes parcourus par des entrelacs de feuilles et de fleurs et qui sont remplacés par des croix dans le motif de droite.

Ces motifs serviront à décorer des murs. Même s'ils sont présentés dans plusieurs couleurs ici, il est possible de les réaliser dans une seule couleur, c'est-à-dire dans une teinte sombre sur fond clair ou dans une teinte claire sur fond sombre. On peut aussi réaliser le fond des quadrilobes et des croix dans une couleur différente du reste de la surface.

Masonry pattern as diaper decoration with stylized lilies and rosettes
Ziegelmuster als Flächendekoration mit stilisierten Lilien und Rosetten
Motif de briques pour la décoration de surfaces avec des lis et des rosaces

The masonry pattern shown here consists of stylized lilies in combination with small rosettes at the points where the lily stems meet lines running in the other direction. The pattern is suitable for the discreet decoration of wall surfaces.

This pattern is suitable both for churches and for secular buildings; in the latter, for the walls of large rooms, staircases and corridors; in the former for all those wall surfaces which would otherwise remain undecorated. The pattern achieves a convincing effect above a dark monochrome or patterned base zone. In a somewhat subdued, quiet coloration, it can also be used for the base zone itself, with a different, lighter pattern above. Only in exceptional cases is it advisable to cover a whole wall from ceiling to floor with a single masonry pattern.

Das hier vorgestellte Ziegelmuster zeigt stilisierte Lilien in Verbindung mit kleinen Rosetten, die die verschiedenen Felder miteinander verbinden. Die Verzierung eignet sich für eine zurückhaltende Dekoration von Wandflächen.

Das Muster ist sowohl für kirchliche als auch für profane Bauwerke geeignet. In Profanbauten kann es zur Dekoration von Saalwänden, Treppenhäusern und Gängen verwendet werden; in Kirchen hingegen sollte es all jene Wandflächen bedecken, die ansonsten unverziert blieben. Überzeugende Wirkung entfaltet das Muster oberhalb einer dunklen, einfarbigen oder auch gemusterten Sockelzone. In einer etwas gedämpften, ruhigen Farbgebung kann man es auch für die Sockelzone selbst verwenden und darüber ein anderes, helleres Muster anbringen. Nur in Ausnahmefällen ist es empfehlenswert, eine ganze Wand vom Boden bis zur Decke mit einem durchgehenden Ziegelmuster zu gestalten.

Le motif de briques illustré ici présente des lis stylisés associés à de petites rosaces qui relient les différents panneaux entre eux. Ce motif est idéal pour une décoration discrète de murs. Le motif servira à décorer des édifices tant religieux que profanes. Dans les édifices profanes, il pourra être utilisé pour décorer des murs, cages d'escaliers et couloirs; dans les églises, en revanche, il devra couvrir tous les murs qui, sinon, resteront nus. Le motif sera du plus bel effet s'il est réalisé au-dessus d'un soubassement sombre, monochrome, voire décoré. On peut l'utiliser pour le soubassement lui-même dans une combinaison de couleurs légèrement atténuées, neutres, et appliquer en outre un autre motif plus clair. L'utilisation d'un motif de briques continu sur tout un mur, du sol au plafond, n'est recommandée que dans des cas exceptionnels.

Masonry pattern with tendril motif
Ziegelmuster mit Rankenornamenten
Motif de briques à entrelacs

This masonry pattern with its delicate tendril motifs is inspired by medieval designs dating from the 13th and 14th centuries.
Many original patterns of this kind can still be found on church walls today. Some, however, have been whitewashed over in the course of time, never to be rediscovered undamaged, if at all. Other fragments have fallen victim to incompetent restoration, and are disfigured to the point of unrecognizability. The pattern shown here can be considered an example of the grace, simplicity and inspiration which is typical of the most outstanding medieval art of this kind.

Dieses Ziegelmuster mit seinen feinen Ranken-ornamenten ist von mittelalterlichen Entwür-fen des 13. und 14. Jahrhunderts inspiriert.
Viele Originale dieser Art sind heute noch an Kirchenwänden zu entdecken. Etliche sind jedoch zwischenzeitlich übertüncht worden, um niemals oder nur in stark beschädigtem Zustand wieder entdeckt zu werden. Andere Fragmente sind unkundigen Restaurierungen zum Opfer gefallen und bis zur Unkenntlich-keit entstellt worden. Das vorliegende Muster mag als Beispiel für Anmut, Einfachheit und Inspiration gelten, die den herausragendsten Arbeiten des Mittelalters dieser Art zu eigen ist.

Ce motif de briques avec ses délicats entrelacs est inspiré d'esquisses médiévales des XIIIe et XIVe siècles.
On trouve aujourd'hui encore de nombreux exemplaires originaux de ce motif sur des murs d'églises. Certains ont toutefois été badi-geonnés depuis lors pour ne plus jamais être redécouverts, ou seulement dans un piteux état. D'autres fragments ont fait l'objet de restaurations sauvages au point de devenir méconnaissables. Le motif illustré ici peut être considéré comme un exemple de grâce, de simplicité et d'inspiration qu'on peut attribuer aux ouvrages de ce type les plus remarquables du Moyen Âge.

Diaper patterns with lozenges and vegetal motifs
Tapetenmuster mit Rauten und Ranken
Motifs de tapisserie à losanges et entrelacs

The two patterns resemble wallpaper designs. On the left, there is a pattern of crisscross lines forming lozenge shapes. The points where the lines cross are decorated with rosettes, while the lozenges themselves are decorated with elegant spiral tendrils. The pattern on the right is a variation on this theme. Here, the lines form a series of arcs, while from each rosette sprouts a lily pointing upwards.

These patterns are suitable for covering wall surfaces whose decoration is intended to make an impression of splendor, without coming across as over-heavy. They can be executed on practically any scale. Above a dark base zone, or on columns, they can be extremely effective. If they are used to decorate church walls, the threefold breadth of the illustration would be the appropriate format. A monochrome version would be quite acceptable.

Die beiden Muster gleichen Tapetenmustern. Links erkennt man sich kreuzende Linien, die ein Netz von Rauten bilden. Die Kreuzungspunkte dieser Linien werden von Rosetten geziert, während die Rauten selbst von sich spiralförmig einrollenden filigranen Ranken ausgeschmückt sind. Das rechte Muster variiert dieses Thema: Die Linien bilden hier Bögen; aus der Rosette entspringt eine stilisierte Lilie, die sich in die Höhe reckt.

Diese Muster eignen sich als Flächendekoration für Wände, deren Verzierung einen prächtigen und zugleich leichten Eindruck hervorrufen soll. Sie können in fast jedem Maßstab ausgeführt werden. Oberhalb einer dunklen Sockelzone oder an Säulen angebracht, wissen sie zu überzeugen. Verwendet man sie als Dekor für Kirchenwände, so ist etwa die dreifache Breite der Abbildung der passende Maßstab für die Ausführung, die auch einfarbig gehalten sein kann.

Ces deux motifs ressemblent à des motifs de tapisserie. À gauche, des lignes qui s'entrecroisent forment un réseau de losanges. Les points d'intersection sont ornés de rosaces, tandis que des entrelacs en filigrane et qui s'enroulent en spirale parcourent les losanges. Le motif de droite présente une variante de ce thème: les lignes forment des arcs; de la rosace jaillit un lis stylisé qui pointe vers le haut.

Ces motifs serviront à décorer des murs et devront donner une impression à la fois de somptuosité et de légèreté. On pourra les exécuter à n'importe quelle échelle. Ils seront du plus bel effet au-dessus d'un soubassement ou sur des colonnes. Si on en décore des murs d'églises, il conviendra de tripler la largeur de l'illustration; une réalisation monochrome est également possible.

Diaper patterns with squares or quatrefoils and vegetal motifs
Tapetenmuster mit verbundenen Rastern und Ranken
Motifs de tapisserie à quadrillage et entrelacs

The pattern on the left is characterized by squares, turned so that their diagonals are vertical, in vertical columns. Between the columns are vertical stems from which sprout spiral tendrils. In the pattern on the right, the squares are replaced by quatrefoils; these two are decorated with vegetal motifs. Both patterns are derived from French craftsmanship of the 13th and 14th centuries.
These patterns come across with particular effect on the walls of churches and public buildings. Any color scheme is acceptable; the motifs can also be executed in a light color on a dark ground. The interior fields of the squares or quatrefoils can be given a different color from the rest of the ground.

Bei dem linken Muster sieht man auf die Spitzen gestellte Quadrate, die vertikale Reihen bilden. Die Zwischenräume sind von aufrechten Ranken geschmückt, deren Seitentriebe sich spiralförmig einrollen. Beim rechten Muster treten Vierpässe an die Stelle der Quadrate; auch sie werden von Blattranken geziert. Beide Muster lassen sich vom französischen Kunsthandwerk des 13. und 14. Jahrhunderts ableiten.
Diese Muster entfalten eine besonders eindrucksvolle Wirkung an den Wänden kirchlicher und öffentlicher Gebäude. Jede Farbwahl ist zulässig; die Motive können auch in einer hellen Farbe auf dunklem Grund ausgeführt werden. Die Felder der Vierecke bzw. Vierpässe können in einem anderen Farbton gehalten sein als die übrige Grundfläche.

Le motif de gauche présente des carrés disposés sur leurs pointes qui forment des rangées verticales. Les intervalles sont ornés d'entrelacs verticaux dont les stolons s'enroulent en spirales. Dans le motif de droite, des quadrilobes également ornés d'entrelacs de feuilles remplacent les carrés. Ces deux motifs sont dérivés de l'art artisanal français des XIIIᵉ et XIVᵉ siècles.
Ces motifs seront du plus bel effet sur des murs d'édifices religieux et publics. Toutes les combinaisons de couleurs sont permises, par exemple une teinte claire sur un fond sombre. On pourra réaliser les panneaux des carrés ou des quadrilobes dans une autre couleur que celle du fond.

Floral ornaments inspired by textile patterns
Von Textilmustern inspirierte florale Ornamente
Ornements floraux inspirés de textiles imprimés

These patterns show a variety of leaf and flower designs taken from brocade and damask fabrics of the 15th and 16th centuries. Motifs like these are extremely versatile. They can be used in rows or groups to form a large-scale wall pattern, and they are particularly suitable for the decoration of the base zones of walls in small apartments, in which case a more elaborate color scheme is also possible. If on the other hand these patterns are used for large surfaces, for example for the walls of large rooms or staircases, warm but light colors should be used, for example a quiet brownish-yellow on a light parchment or cream ground. An attractive effect can also be achieved by applying these patterns in black or some other dark color on a gold ground, or in gold on a black ground. If the pattern is executed in matt on a semi-gloss ground, the result comes across like silk brocade.

Diese Muster zeigen unterschiedliche Blatt- und Blütengebilde, die von Brokat- und Damaststoffen des 15. und 16. Jahrhunderts übernommen wurden.
Solche Motive sind vielfältig verwendbar. Sie können in Reihung oder Gruppierung aufgetragen, zu einem großflächigen Wandmuster ergänzt werden und sind besonders zur Verzierung von Sockelzonen in kleinen Wohnungen geeignet, wobei in diesem Fall auch eine aufwändigere Kolorierung möglich ist. Werden solche Muster hingegen für große Flächen verwendet, etwa für die Wände von Sälen oder Treppenhäusern, sollte man warme und blasse Farben wählen – beispielsweise ein ruhiges Braungelb auf einem hellen pergament- oder cremefarbenen Grund. Eine schöne Wirkung lässt sich auch erzielen, wenn man diese Muster in Schwarz oder einer anderen dunklen Farbe auf goldenem Grund oder in Gold auf schwarzem Grund aufträgt. Wird das Muster mit matter Farbe auf einem halbglänzendem Grund aufgetragen, wirkt das Resultat wie Seidenbrokat.

Ces motifs présentent diverses formes de feuilles et de fleurs empruntées à des étoffes de brocart et de damas des XVe et XVIe siècles.
Ces motifs sont destinés à des applications diverses. Transposés par rangées ou par groupes, ils pourront couvrir de grandes surfaces de murs et serviront à décorer des soubassements dans de petits intérieurs et dans ce cas, on pourra choisir des couleurs plus riches. Si on utilise par contre ces motifs sur de grandes surfaces, par exemple des murs ou des cages d'escaliers, il faudra choisir des couleurs chaudes et pâles, par exemple un mordoré discret sur un fond clair parchemin ou crème. Ces motifs seront du plus bel effet si on les réalise en noir ou dans une autre couleur foncée sur un fond doré ou en doré sur un fond noir. Une couleur mate sur un fond semi-brillant imitera le brocart de soie.

Diaper patterns based on brocade fabrics
Von Brokatstoffen inspirierte Tapetenmuster
Motifs de tapisserie inspirés d'étoffes de brocart

The two patterns show vegetal motifs derived from the acanthus. These designs are inspired by those of medieval brocade fabrics. While the pattern on the left has the acanthus palmettes framed, medallion-like, by an acanthus-leaf motif, that on the right has the acanthus motifs in staggered columns, giving the composition elegance and dynamism. These patterns are suitable for church decoration, in particular for the pulpit, as well as for the background of blind arcades and other small surfaces. There is no restriction as to color.

Die beiden Muster zeigen Pflanzenornamente, deren vegetabile Formen sich vom Akanthus ableiten. Diese Entwürfe sind von den Mustern mittelalterlicher Brokatstoffe inspiriert. Während bei dem Muster links die Akanthuspalmetten von Blattgebilden medaillonartig gerahmt werden, sind sie beim rechten Muster im versetzten Rapport angeordnet, wodurch der Komposition Eleganz und Bewegung verliehen wird. Diese Muster sind zur Dekoration von Kirchen geeignet, insbesondere für die Verzierung der Kanzel sowie als Hintergrund von Arkaden und anderer kleinerer Flächen. Die Farben können beliebig gewählt werden.

Les deux motifs présentent des ornements végétaux dont les formes sont dérivées de l'acanthe. Ces esquisses sont inspirées de motifs d'étoffes de brocart médiévales. Si les palmettes d'acanthe sont encadrées par des feuilles formant un médaillon dans le motif de gauche, elles se répètent en se décalant dans celui de droite, ce qui confère de l'élégance et du mouvement à la composition. Ces motifs serviront à décorer des églises, en particulier des chaires, ainsi que le fond d'arcades et d'autres surfaces plus petites. Le choix des couleurs est libre.

Crestings with leaf motifs
Bekrönende Ornamentbänder mit Blattdekor
Bandeaux ornementaux à décors de feuilles en forme de couronnes

These four ornamental bands with leaf motifs are based on the characteristic roof-ridge decorations of late-Gothic English architecture, here adapted for two-dimensional designs.

The motifs are suitable for crestings. They can also be used beneath a contoured molding of a different color. The colors need to be chosen to fit the context.

Diese vier Ornamentbänder zeigen Blattfriese, die von den charakteristischen Firstkrönungen der spätgotischen englischen Architektur übernommen wurden und hier in die Fläche umgesetzt sind.

Diese Motive eignen sich als Dekor für bekrönende Ornamentbänder. Fügt man ihnen oben eine farbig abgesetzte Kontur hinzu, lassen sie sich auch als Borten verwenden. Die Farben sollten den Gegebenheiten entsprechend gewählt werden.

Ces quatre bandeaux ornementaux présentent des frises de feuilles empruntées aux faîteaux caractéristiques de l'architecture du gothique tardif anglais et qui sont transposées à plat ici. Ces motifs serviront à décorer des bandeaux ornementaux en forme de couronnes. Si on ajoute un contour en couleur dans le haut, ils pourront aussi servir de galons. Les couleurs seront choisies en fonction de l'environnement.

Ornamental bands with various floral and vegetal motifs
Ornamentbänder mit verschiedenen Rankenmotiven
Bandeaux ornementaux à entrelacs différents

This plate illustrates seven horizontal ornamental bands with various vegetal and floral motifs. At the top is a frieze with stylized vine-leaves and grapes. Next, there is an ivy tendril in two colors. Then we have a broad band with a vegetal motif, followed by a narrow band with rosettes. The next band has a wave-like stem from which sprout highly stylized acanthus leaves; this is followed by another narrow rosette band. At the bottom is a band with rosettes separated by pairs of narrow fields reminiscent of the tracery in Gothic buildings.
These ornamental bands are intended for the decoration of the undersides of rafters, purlins and other timber roof elements. With minor changes in the coloration, they can also be applied to unpainted, though usually varnished wood. Quiet and discreet colors should be chosen.

Auf dieser Tafel werden sieben horizontal verlaufende Ornamentbänder mit verschiedenen Rankenmotiven dargestellt. Oben ist ein Fries mit stilisiertem Weinlaub und Trauben zu erkennen. Darunter schließt sich ein Efeuband in zweifarbiger Gestaltung an. Als Drittes folgt ein breites Band mit vegetabilen Formen, darunter ein schmales Band mit Rosetten. Als Nächstes sieht man eine Bordüre, die von einer Wellenranke mit stilisierten Blattgebilden geziert wird. Sie leiten sich formal vom Akanthus ab. Daran schließt sich wiederum ein schmales Rosettenband an. Das letzte Ornamentband zeigt Rosetten, die mit länglichen Feldern verbunden werden und formal an das Maßwerk mittelalterlicher Gebäude erinnern.
Diese Ornamentbänder sind zur Verzierung von Balkenuntersichten, Pfetten und Trägern eines hölzernen Dachtragewerks bestimmt. Mit geringen Abwandlungen in der Farbgebung lassen sie sich auch auf naturbelassenem, meist gefirnissten Holz auftragen. Zur Ausführung sollte man ruhige und zurückhaltende Farben wählen.

Cette planche présente sept bandeaux ornementaux horizontaux avec différents motifs d'entrelacs. On reconnaît en haut une frise avec des feuilles de vigne et des raisins stylisés. En dessous, un bandeau de lierre en deux couleurs, puis un large bandeau à formes végétales, un étroit bandeau à rosaces. Vient ensuite une bordure ornée d'un entrelacs de vagues à feuilles stylisées dérivées de l'acanthe. Le motif suivant est de nouveau un étroit bandeau de rosaces. Le dernier bandeau ornemental se compose de rosaces associées à des panneaux oblongs et rappelant par leur forme les dentelles de pierre d'édifices médiévaux.
Ces bandeaux ornementaux serviront à décorer des dessous de poutres, des pannes et poutres d'une charpente en bois. Il est également possible de les transposer sur du bois naturel, le plus souvent verni, en changeant très peu les couleurs. On choisira des teintes moyennes et discrètes pour leur réalisation.

Motifs for the decoration of gables and spandrels
Motive zur Dekoration von Giebelfeldern und Zwickeln
Motifs pour la décoration de tympans et de clés de voûtes

These designs show decorations for the visible gables and spandrels of roof structures, such as can be found in Gothic churches and large halls. The decorations make use of palmette, rosette and imitation tracery motifs.
The designs are derived from the Perpendicular style, the characteristic English form of late Gothic, albeit in stylized form. In appropriate colors, they can also be applied to unpainted wood, either in a light color on dark wood, or vice versa.

Diese Entwürfe zeigen Dekorationen für die sichtbaren Giebelfelder und Zwickel von Dachkonstruktionen, so wie man sie in Kirchen und großen Hallen des gotischen Stils vorfindet. Diese Dekorationen enthalten Palmetten, Rosetten und Maßwerknachbildungen.
Die Entwürfe sind den charakteristischen Formen der englischen Spätgotik (Perpendicular Style) entlehnt, wenngleich ihre Formen stilisiert wiedergegeben wurden. In geeigneten Farben lassen sie sich auf unbehandeltem Holz auftragen – entweder in einem hellen Ton auf dunklem Holz oder in einer dunklen Farbe auf hellem Grund.

Ces esquisses présentent des décors pour les tympans et clés de voûtes visibles de toits, tels qu'on en trouve dans les églises et grandes halles de style gothique. Ces décors se composent de palmettes, de rosaces et d'imitations de dentelles de pierre.
Les motifs sont empruntés aux formes caractéristiques du gothique tardif anglais (Perpendicular Style), même si ces formes sont stylisées. Il est possible de les réaliser sur du bois non traité dans des couleurs appropriées – teinte claire sur bois foncé ou teinte sombre sur fond clair.

Renaissance

The Renaissance marked the end of the Middle Ages and the birth of the Modern age in its wider sense. This "rebirth" of Classical Antiquity began in Italy in around 1350, and spread throughout Europe within a few decades. The heyday of the Renaissance was the 16th century; at the start of the 17th century, it was replaced by the Baroque.

Human consciousness in the Renais-

Das Zeitalter der Renaissance markiert das Ende des Mittelalters und den Beginn der Neuzeit; diese „Wiedergeburt" der Antike begann um 1350 in Italien und erreichte innerhalb weniger Jahrzehnte ganz Europa. Ihre Glanzzeit hatte die Renaissance im 16. Jahrhundert; sie wurde zu Beginn des 17. Jahrhunderts vom Barock abgelöst.

Das Bewusstsein der Menschen der

L'époque de la Renaissance marque la fin du Moyen Âge et le début des Temps Modernes ; ce « renouveau » de l'Antiquité a débuté vers 1350 en Italie et s'est étendu à toute l'Europe en quelques siècles. La Renaissance a connu son apogée au XVIe siècle ; le baroque lui a succédé au XVIIe siècle.

La conscience des hommes de la Renaissance était marquée par une

The church of Santa Maria Novella, Florence, 1246–1470
The façade of the church is notable for its strict symmetry, its execution in black and white marble, and its rich ornamentation. After the lower part of the façade had been completed in the mid-14th century, the famous Renaissance architect Leon Battista Alberti added the splendid pediment. "Bellezza ed ornamenti" (beauty and ornament) were for Alberti the chief criteria of architecture, alongside the laws of harmony.

Santa Maria Novella, Florenz, 1246–1470
Die Fassade der Kirche besticht durch ihre strenge symmetrische Gestaltung, die polychrome Ausführung in weißem und schwarzem Marmor und die reiche Ornamentik. Nachdem der untere Teil der Fassade Mitte des 14. Jahrhunderts vollendet war, setzte der berühmte Renaissance-Architekt Leon Battista Alberti 1470 den prächtigen Giebel auf. „Bellezza e ornamenti" – Schönheit und Ornamente – waren neben den Gesetzen der Harmonie für Alberti die Hauptkriterien für Architektur.

Santa Maria Novella, Florence, 1246–1470
La façade de l'église séduit par sa décoration symétrique stricte, l'exécution polychrome en marbre blanc et noir et les riches ornements. Après avoir achevé la partie inférieure de la façade au milieu du XIVe siècle, le célèbre architecte de la Renaissance Leon Battista Alverti y ajouta le somptueux pignon en 1470. « Bellezza e ornamenti » – beauté et ornements – tels étaient, en dehors des règles de l'harmonie, les critères architecturaux essentiels aux yeux d'Alberti.

Opposite page: Raphael, *The Academy at Athens*, fresco. Stanza della Segnatura, Rome, 1510–1511
The theme of this fresco is the rediscovery of ancient philosophy and of ancient science. The scene is placed by Raphael in a richly-ornamented Renaissance building; the picture in turn is framed by large contemporary ornaments.

Gegenüberliegende Seite: Raffael, *Die Schule von Athen*, Fresko, Stanza della Segnatura, Rom, 1510–1511
Das Fresko thematisiert die Wiederentdeckung der antiken Philosophie und Naturwissenschaften. Die Szene wird von Raffael inmitten reich geschmückter Renaissance-Architektur wiedergegeben, das Wandbild seinerseits ist von großen zeitgenössischen Ornamenten eingefasst.

Page ci-contre : Raphaël, *L'École d'Athènes*, fresque, Stanza della Segnatura, Rome, 1510–1511
La fresque a pour thème la redécouverte de la philosophie antique et des sciences de la nature. Raphaël reproduit la scène au milieu d'une architecture Renaissance richement décorée ; le tableau mural est, quant à lui, encadré par des ornements contemporains de grande taille.

sance was marked by an attitude of mind which focused not on God – in contrast to the theocratic view prevailing during the Middle Ages – but Man. Not faith and humility, but knowledge and self-confidence were the watchwords of the new age, which found its ideal expression in the *uomo universale*, the universally-educated Renaissance Man, who was equally at home in philosophy and politics, literature and art, history and science, technology and economics. The genius of Leonardo da Vinci consisted in the creative embodiment of this ideal.
Inspired by archaeological discoveries in Italy, and also by

Renaissance war von einer Geisteshaltung geprägt, deren Zentrum im Gegensatz zur theokratischen Weltanschauung des Mittelalters nicht mehr Gott, sondern der Mensch war. Nicht Glaube und Demut, sondern Wissen und Selbstbewusstsein waren die Maximen der Neuzeit, die ihren idealtypischen Ausdruck im „Uomo universale", dem universell gebildeten Renaissance-Menschen, fanden, der sich gleichermaßen für Philosophie und Politik, Literatur und Kunst, Geschichte und Wissenschaft, Technik und Ökonomie interessierte. Das Genie Leonardo da Vincis bestand in der schöpferischen Verkörperung dieses Ideals.

tournure d'esprit dont le centre n'était plus Dieu mais l'homme, contrairement à la conception théocratique du monde en vogue au Moyen Âge. Les maximes des Temps Modernes, qui trouvèrent leur expression idéale dans « l'Uomo universale », l'homme de la Renaissance à la culture universelle qui s'intéressait au même titre à la philosophie et la politique, à la littérature et l'art, à l'histoire et la science, à la technique et l'économie, n'étaient pas la foi et l'humilité, mais le savoir et la confiance en soi. Le génie de Léonard de Vinci consista à incarner cet idéal par la création.

Classical manuscripts brought to Italy by Byzantine scholars after the capture of Constantinople by the Turks in 1453, there arose a general interest in Antiquity. In order to decipher and discuss Classical texts, people learned Latin and Greek, and many also wrote in Latin. The wealthy commercial city of Florence quickly developed into the center of this movement in the early-15th century; artists, scholars and craftsmen were supported by the nobility and prosperous bourgeoisie – in particular the Medici banking family – and thus the stage was set for a period of lively artistic and intellectual creativity.

The enthusiasm for Antiquity, which had such a marked influence on the philosophy and intellectual life of the Renaissance, was also to have its effect on architecture. There was a rejection of the building styles of the Middle Ages, which went so far that Gothic cathedrals were left unfinished. A new style won acceptance, which derived its forms from Classical exemplars, and at the same time aimed increasingly at a balance of proportions and harmony of architectural elements.

In the area of decoration, the chief

Angeregt durch archäologische Entdeckungen in Italien sowie durch antike Schriften, die byzantinische Gelehrte nach der Eroberung Konstantinopels durch die Türken (1453) nach Italien mitbrachten, begann man sich für die Antike zu interessieren. Um antike Schriften entziffern und diskutieren zu können, eignete man sich Kenntnisse in Latein und Griechisch an und manch einer verfasste selber Texte in Latein. Zum Zentrum dieser Bewegung entwickelte sich zu Beginn des 15. Jahrhunderts schnell die reiche Handelsstadt Florenz, in der Adelige und wohlhabende Bürger – allen voran das Bankiersgeschlecht der Medici – Künstler, Gelehrte und Handwerker förderten und damit die Voraussetzungen zu reger geistiger und künstlerischer Produktion schufen.

Die Begeisterung für die Antike, die so wesentlich die Philosophie und Geistesgeschichte der Renaissance prägte, sollte auch einen unmittelbaren Einfluss auf die Architektur haben. So wandte man sich von den Bauformen des Mittelalters ab und ging sogar so weit, begonnene gotische Kathedralen nicht mehr zu vollenden. Ein neuer Stil setzte sich

Les découvertes archéologiques en Italie, ainsi que des écrits antiques que des érudits byzantins rapportèrent en Italie après la conquête de Constantinople par les Turcs (1453), suscitèrent un intérêt pour l'Antiquité. Pour pouvoir déchiffrer et étudier des écrits antiques, on se mit à apprendre le latin et le grec, et d'aucuns rédigèrent à leur tour des textes en latin. La riche ville commerçante de Florence, où nobles et bourgeois aisés – notamment les Médicis, célèbre famille de banquiers – favorisèrent les artistes, érudits et artisans et créèrent ainsi les conditions nécessaires à une intense production intellectuelle et artistique, devint rapidement le centre de ce mouvement au début du XVᵉ siècle.

L'attrait de l'Antiquité, qui a marqué si fort la philosophie et l'histoire des idées de la Renaissance, devait aussi exercer une influence directe sur l'architecture. C'est ainsi qu'on se détourna des formes architecturales du Moyen Âge au point de ne plus achever les cathédrales gothiques mises en chantier. Un nouveau style s'imposa qui empruntait ses formes architecturales et décoratives au modèle de l'Antiquité et aspirait de

Gallery in the Château Le Lude on the Loire, painted between 1559 and 1585
Italian decorative painters founded the Fontainebleau School in France; its chief decorative element was the scrollwork, derived from the cartouche. Here it can be seen in high relief in the base zone. Above it is the picture itself, depicting Old Testament scenes. The base of the ceiling vault is decorated with acanthus leaves and fret patterns.

Ein Kabinett im Schloss Le Lude an der Loir, ausgemalt zwischen 1559 und 1585
Italienische Dekorationsmaler begründeten in Frankreich die Schule von Fontainebleau, deren wichtigstes Dekorationselement das von der Kartusche abgeleitete Rollwerk war. Hier ist es in der Sockelzone wiedergegeben. Darüber erstreckt sich das eigentliche Bildfeld mit alttestamentarischen Szenen. Den Gewölbeansatz zieren dekorative Bänder mit Akanthusblättern und Mäandern.

Un cabinet au château du Lude sur le Loir, peint entre 1559 et 1585
Des peintres décorateurs italiens fondèrent en France l'école de Fontainebleau dont le principal élément décoratif était le cartouche à enroulement, représenté ici en relief dans le soubassement. Au-dessus, le tableau proprement dit illustre des scènes de l'Ancien Testament. Des bandeaux décoratifs à feuilles d'acanthe et méandres ornent la partie naissante des voûtes.

masterpiece was the pair of bronze doors for the Baptistery of San Giovanni in Florence created by the Florentine sculptor Lorenzo Ghiberti – a work which pointed the way forward for the Renaissance. The leaves and tendrils of this relief depart from the schematic idiom of the Middle Ages and are reproduced in barely stylized form. The tendrils, with their flowers and fruits, are occasionally penetrated by little birds, and demonstrate an attitude of mind full of fresh, pulsing life which was to leave its mark on the whole of Renaissance art.
Richly decorated tendrils with delicate leaves and slender stalks constitute one of the most important of all Renaissance ornamental motifs. They decorate friezes, entablatures, pilasters and columns alike. Alongside ornaments inspired by Antiquity, one sees an increasing number of stylized fruits and flowers along with religious and secular emblems, allegories and grotesqueries. Another typical Renaissance ornament,

durch, der seine Bau- und Dekorformen dem Vorbild der Antike entlehnte und dabei zunehmend auf die Ausgewogenheit der Proportionen und Harmonie aller Bauelemente abzielte.
Auf dem Gebiet der Dekoration war es vor allem der Florentiner Lorenzo Ghiberti, der mit seinen Bronzetüren des Baptisteriums von San Giovanni in Florenz ein Meisterwerk schuf, das für die Renaissance wegweisend war. Die Blattranken dieser Reliefplastik lösen sich vom Schematismus des Mittelalters und werden in nur geringer Stilisierung wiedergegeben. Die Blumen- und Fruchtgewinde, die gelegentlich von einem kleinen Vogel durchdrungen werden, lassen jene neue Geisteshaltung erkennen, die von frischem und pulsierendem Leben erfüllt war und die gesamte Renaissancekunst prägen sollte.
Die reich verzierten Ranken mit ihren zarten Blättern und ihren schlanken Stängeln sind eines der wichtigsten Renaissance-Ornamente. Sie schmücken gleichermaßen Friese und Gesimse wie auch Pilaster und Säulenschäfte. Neben klassisch inspirierten Ornamenten sieht man zunehmend auch stilisierte Frucht- und Blumengewinde sowie religiöse und weltliche Embleme, Allegorien und Grotesken. Ein weiteres typisches Renaissance-Ornament, das auch heute noch an nahezu allen erhaltenen Gebäuden dieser Zeit gefunden werden kann, ist die Rahmung. Zu dieser Gattung zählen Medaillonrahmen ebenso wie reich verzierte Kartuschen mit Beschlag- und Rollwerk.
Die Tatsache, dass Rahmenornamente im Sammelwerk der Audsleys nicht enthalten sind, ist ein interessanter Beleg für die ausschnitthafte Rezeption der Renaissance in England. Denn tatsächlich hatte sich die Renaissance-Kunst von Italien über Frankreich und Deutschland nach Spanien ausgebreitet – doch erreichten lediglich ihre Ausläufer das England der Tudor-Könige. Die Spaltung zwischen dem katholischen Rom und dem seit der Reformation protestantischen England unterband jeden künstlerischen Austausch.

plus en plus à l'équilibre des proportions autant qu'à l'harmonie de tous les éléments architecturaux.
Dans le domaine de la décoration, il faut notamment citer le Florentin Lorenzo Ghiberti, créateur des portes en bronze du baptistère de San Giovanni à Florence, un chef-d'œuvre précurseur de la Renaissance. Les entrelacs de feuilles de cette sculpture délaissent le schématisme du Moyen Âge et ne font plus l'objet que d'une stylisation insignifiante. Les guirlandes de fleurs et de fruits, parfois traversées par un petit oiseau, sont révélatrices de cette nouvelle tournure d'esprit emplie d'une vie inédite et intense et qui devait marquer l'art de la Renaissance tout entier.
Les entrelacs richement ornés, avec leurs feuilles délicates et leurs tiges élancées, constituent un des ornements majeurs de la Renaissance. Ils décorent aussi bien les frises et corniches que les pilastres et fûts de colonnes. En dehors des ornements d'inspiration classique, on rencontre aussi de plus en plus de guirlandes stylisées de fruits et de fleurs, ainsi que des emblèmes religieux et profanes, des allégories et des grotesques. Le cadre, qu'on retrouve aujourd'hui encore sur presque tous les édifices conservés de cette époque, est un autre ornement typique de la Renaissance. Les médaillons appartiennent à ce genre, de même que les cartouches richement ornés de cloutage et d'enroulements.
L'absence des cadres en tant qu'ornements dans le recueil des Audsley est une preuve intéressante de l'accueil fragmentaire de la Renaissance en Angleterre. Car l'art de la Renaissance s'était en effet propagé d'Italie en Espagne en passant par la France et l'Allemagne – mais c'est sous une forme affaiblie qu'il avait fini par s'introduire dans l'Angleterre des Tudor. La scission entre la Rome catholique et l'Angleterre protestante depuis la Réforme empêchait tout échange artistique. Sous la reine Elisabeth Ire, aucun palais Renaissance remarquable ne fut érigé, et même dans l'Écosse catholique des Stuart, le château de

which can be seen to this day on practically all buildings dating from the Renaissance period, is the frame. Under this heading come medallions as well as richly decorated cartouches with strapwork and scrollwork. The fact that framing ornaments are not included in the Audsleys' collected work is an interesting indication of the way the Renaissance was received in somewhat piecemeal fashion in England. In fact, while Renaissance art really did spread from Italy via France and Germany to Spain, it only brushed the England of the Tudors. The split between Catholic Rome and post-Reformation protestant England prevented any artistic exchange. The reign of Queen Elizabeth I saw the construction of no major Renaissance palaces, and even in the Catholic Scotland of the Stuarts, only Stirling Castle can really be called a Renaissance structure. The only significant representative of the Late Renaissance in England was the architect Inigo Jones, a great

Unter Königin Elisabeth I. entstanden keine bedeutenden Renaissance-Paläste und selbst im katholischen Schottland der Stuart-Könige kann allenfalls Stirling Castle als Renaissance-Bau angeführt werden. Als einzig namhafter Vertreter der englischen Spätrenaissance ist der Architekt Inigo Jones zu nennen, der ein großer Bewunderer Palladios war. Er wurde zu Beginn des 17. Jahrhunderts als Generalbauinspektor am englischen Hof eingesetzt und führte mit seinen Bauwerken den Stil Palladios in England ein – zu einem Zeitpunkt, da in Italien bereits der Barock aufkam. Da sich also die Renaissance-Kunst spät und mit relativ wenigen Hauptwerken in England entfaltete, konnte sie dort auch keinen prägenden Einfluss hinterlassen. Mithin war das öffentliche Interesse an der Renaissance auch bei späteren Generationen in England verhalten und der Nutzen von Ornamentmustern im Renaissancestil begrenzt. So erklärt sich, warum die Audsleys bei

Stirling est le seul édifice à pouvoir se réclamer du style Renaissance. L'unique représentant réputé de la Renaissance anglaise finissante est l'architecte Inigo Jones qui était un grand admirateur de Palladio. Il fut nommé inspecteur général des bâtiments à la cour anglaise au début du XVIIe siècle et introduisit, grâce à ses réalisations, le style de Palladio en Angleterre – à une époque où le baroque faisait déjà son apparition en Italie.
Comme l'art de la Renaissance se développait tardivement en Angleterre et avec assez peu d'œuvres majeures, il ne put guère y laisser d'influence marquante. L'intérêt du public pour la Renaissance a donc été modéré en Angleterre, même dans les générations suivantes, et l'utilisation de motifs ornementaux de style Renaissance s'est donc trouvée limitée. Cela explique pourquoi les Audsley ne présentent que peu de motifs de style Renaissance dans leurs esquisses ornementales. Quelques-unes de leurs

Tapestry from the cycle "King Francis Hunting", Château Chambord, near Blois, early-17th century
This wall-hanging is dedicated to the hunt, the pleasure of kings. It depicts King Francis I of France giving instruction to his falconer. The scene is framed by a border of grotesques and acanthus-leaf tendrils, which already point the way ahead to the coming Baroque.

Gobelin aus dem Zyklus „Die Jagd des König Franz" im Schloss Chambord bei Blois, frühes 17. Jh.
Dieser Wandbehang ist dem königlichen Vergnügen, der Jagd, gewidmet. Dargestellt ist König Franz I., der seine Falkner anweist. Die Szene wird von einer Bordüre mit Grotesken und Akanthusranken gerahmt, die bereits auf den aufkommenden Barock verweist.

Tapisserie Gobelin du cycle « La Chasse du Roi François », château de Chambord près de Blois, début du XVIIe siècle
Cette tapisserie est consacrée au plaisir royal, la chasse. Elle représente le roi François Ier donnant des ordres à ses fauconniers. La scène est bordée de grotesques et d'entrelacs d'acanthe qui annoncent déjà le Baroque naissant.

Stirling Castle, 16th century
Stirling Castle was built by the Stuart kings of Scotland in the 16th century. Stylistically, the façade with its window-frames and sculptures leans heavily on French Renaissance models. This is the only Renaissance building that the Audsleys would have been able to see first-hand in their native Scotland, which may explain why relatively little space is devoted to the Renaissance in *The Practical Decorator and Ornamentist*.

Stirling Castle, 16. Jh.
Stirling Castle wurde im 16. Jahrhundert von den Stuart-Königen errichtet und steht stellvertretend für die Renaissance-Architektur in Schottland. Die Fassade mit den Fensterrahmungen und den Skulpturen ist stilistisch dem französischen Geschmack entlehnt. Es handelt sich hierbei um den einzigen Renaissance-Bau, den die Audsleys in ihrer Heimat aus eigener Anschauung kennen lernen konnten. Dies erklärt vermutlich, warum sie dem Renaissance-Stil in ihrem Vorlagenwerk nur ein verhaltenes Interesse entgegenbrachten.

Château de Stirling, XVIᵉ siècle
Le château de Stirling, bâti par les rois Stuart, est le représentant de l'architecture de la Renaissance en Écosse. La façade aux cadres de fenêtres et aux sculptures est, par son style, empruntée au goût français. Il s'agit ici du seul bâtiment Renaissance que George Ashdown Audsley a pu connaître, dans son pays natal, pour l'avoir observé. Cela explique sans doute pourquoi il ne manifesta qu'un intérêt modéré pour le style Renaissance dans son recueil de modèles.

admirer of Palladio. He was appointed Surveyor of Works to the English court at the beginning of the 17th century, and introduced the Palladian style into England at a time when the Baroque was already making its appearance in Italy. As Renaissance art arrived relatively late in England and gave rise to relatively few major works there, it also left no lasting impression. Public interest in the Renaissance in England was only modest, even among later generations, and the use of Renaissance ornamental motifs was not widespread. This explains why the Audsleys included so few Renaissance motifs among their patterns. Some of their individual designs, such as the elegant scroll motifs illustrated on page 163, reveal a clear borrowing from the Italian Renaissance, while other patterns, such as the leaf-and-scroll designs on page 165, still betray a distinct medieval legacy – which in general disappeared with the advent of the new age.

ihren Ornamententwürfen des Renaissance-Stils nur wenig Motive vorstellen. Einzelne Entwürfe der Audsleys, wie zum Beispiel die eleganten Rankengebilde auf Seite 163, lassen deutlich eine Anlehnung an die italienische Renaissance erkennen, während bei anderen Mustern, wie zum Beispiel den Ranken auf Seite 165, noch deutlich ein Vermächtnis des Mittelalters zu verspüren ist, das in der Renaissance mit dem Beginn der Neuzeit überwunden wurde.

esquisses, par exemple les élégantes formes ornementales à la page 163, révèlent un emprunt indubitable à la Renaissance italienne, tandis que dans d'autres motifs, tels que les entrelacs à la page 165, l'héritage du Moyen Âge qui a disparu sous la Renaissance avec l'avènement des Temps Modernes, laisse des traces visibles.

Opposite page: View of the fourth hall of the Galleria Borghese, Rome, late-16th century
Noteworthy alongside the collection of sculpture is the rich decoration of the walls and ceiling. The walls are characterized by niches for statues, pilasters surmounted by capitals, and figurative reliefs. The ceiling painting shows *trompe l'œil* Roman architecture reminiscent of murals in Pompeii and characteristic of the Renaissance.

Gegenüberliegende Seite: Gesamtansicht des vierten Saals der Galleria Borghese, Rom, spätes 16. Jh.
Neben der Skulpturensammlung besticht der überreiche Wand- und Deckendekor. Die Wände werden von skulpturgeschmückten Nischen, kapitellbekrönten Pilastern und figürlichen Reliefs geziert. Das Deckengemälde zeigt römische Scheinarchitekturen, die an pompejanische Wandmalereien erinnern und für die Renaissance charakteristisch sind.

Page ci-contre: Vue d'ensemble de la quatrième salle de la Ghalleria Borghese, Rome, fin du XVIᵉ siècle
La collection de sculptures, mais aussi le décor surchargé des murs et du plafond attirent particulièrement l'attention. Les murs sont ornés de niches contenant des sculptures, de pilastres couronnés de chapiteaux et de reliefs figurés. La fresque du plafond se compose de trompe-l'œil de style romain qui rappellent les peintures murales de Pompéi et sont caractéristiques de la Renaissance.

Horizontal bands with stylized tendrils
Horizontale Bänder mit stilisierten Ranken
Bandeaux horizontaux à entrelacs stylisés

The three ornamental bands are decorated with tendrils which are stylistically close to the Renaissance. The upper design alienates the tendril itself to an austerely geometric form, though decorated with garlands and stylized leaves. The band in the middle shows a frieze with stylized vines and vine leaves, while the one at the bottom shows stylized spiral tendrils ending in acanthus leaves. These patterns are suitable for use as ornamental bands on a wall, and also crestings above monochrome or patterned wall surfaces. They can also form complete borders, in which case suitable corner decorations would have to be found. The color schemes for these ornamental bands are not subject to any restriction. Gold on a very dark ground would have a very elegant effect.

Die drei Ornamentbänder werden von Ranken geziert, die stilistisch der Renaissance nahe stehen. Der obere Entwurf entfremdet die Ranke zur einer streng geometrischen Form, die mit Girlanden und stilisierten Blättern geschmückt ist. Das mittlere Band zeigt einen Fries mit stilisierten Weinlaubranken. Der untere Entwurf präsentiert spiralförmig eingerollte Ranken, die in spitzzackigen Akanthusblättern enden.
Diese Muster eignen sich als Ornamentbänder an der Wand sowie als abschließende Borte über einfarbigen oder gemusterten Wandflächen. Ebenso lassen sie sich als Umrandungen verwenden, wobei zusätzlich entsprechende Eckverzierungen entwickelt werden müssen. Die Ornamentbänder können farblich nach Belieben gestaltet werden. In Gold auf tiefdunklem Grund haben sie eine erlesene Wirkung.

Les trois bandeaux ornementaux sont décorés d'entrelacs dont le style rappelle la Renaissance. Dans le motif du haut, l'entrelacs, détourné de sa forme initiale, devient strictement géométrique et s'orne de guirlandes et de feuilles stylisées. Le motif central présente une frise à feuilles de vigne stylisées et celui du bas, des entrelacs qui s'enroulent sur eux-mêmes en spirale et se terminent par des feuilles d'acanthes très découpées.
Ces motifs serviront de bandeaux ornementaux sur des murs et de bordures de finition sur des surfaces murales monochromes ou décorées. Ils pourront de la même façon servir d'encadrements, mais dans ce cas, il conviendra d'ajouter des décors d'angles appropriés. Les bandeaux ornementaux peuvent être réalisés dans des couleurs au choix. Les motifs dorés sur un fond très sombre sont du plus bel effet.

Curved borders with tendrils, acanthus and lilies
Bogensegmente mit Ranken, Akanthus und Lilien
Segments d'arcs à entrelacs, acanthes et lis

The plate shows four curved borders decorated with vegetal motifs. The design at the top is characterized by a central stem from which flowers and leaves sprout symmetrically to each side. The next design shows an acanthus frieze. The third is marked by a tendril with long stylized leaves twisting in elegant fashion about a central stem. The pattern at the bottom shows stylized lilies connected with a border of semi-circles and small colored disks.
This kind of decoration can be used to frame circular panels or round arches. The coloration can be left to the taste of the user, but it should harmonize with the remaining wall surfaces.

Die Tafel zeigt vier Bogensegmente, die von vegetabilem Dekor geziert werden. Beim oberen Entwurf ist ein Zentralstamm zu erkennen, dem seitlich Blüten und Blätter entwachsen. Darunter folgt ein Akanthusfries. Das dritte Motiv wird von einer Wellenranke mit schlanken, stilisierten Blättern bestimmt, die einen zentralen Stamm elegant umgreifen. Das Muster unten zeigt stilisierte Lilien, die mit einer Borte aus größeren Halbkreisen und kleinen, farblich ausgemalten Kreisen verbunden werden.
Diese Art von Verzierung dient zur Rahmung kreisförmiger Paneele sowie zur Einfassung von Rundbögen. Die farbliche Gestaltung kann frei gewählt werden, sie sollte lediglich mit den übrigen Wandflächen harmonieren.

Cette planche présente quatre segments d'arcs décorés de motifs végétaux. Dans le motif du haut, des fleurs et des feuilles poussent de chaque côté d'une tige centrale. Le deuxième motif se compose d'une frise de feuilles d'acanthe et le troisième se caractérise par un entrelacs de vagues à feuilles stylisées élancées qui s'enroulent avec élégance autour d'une branche principale. Le motif du bas présente des lis stylisés reliés entre eux par une bordure de demi-cercles assez grands et de petits cercles de couleurs.
Ce type de décoration sert à encadrer des panneaux de formes circulaires, ainsi qu'à border des arcs en plein cintre. Les motifs peuvent être réalisés dans des couleurs au choix, à condition toutefois que celles-ci soient en harmonie avec le reste des surfaces murales.

Large-format leaf rosettes with stylized acanthus leaves as ornamentation for panels and coffers
Großflächige Blattrosetten mit stilisierten Akanthusblättern als Dekor von Paneelen oder Kassetten
Rosaces de grande dimension à feuilles d'acanthe stylisées pour panneaux ou caissons

These two designs depict leaf rosettes derived from the acanthus, intertwined with spiral tendrils.
The patterns are suitable for decorating square or octagonal panels and coffers. The pattern at the top can also be used as a central ceiling-decoration, in which case the individual elements simply have to be enlarged. There is no restriction as to coloration: dark colors on a light ground are effective.

Diese beiden Ornamententwürfe präsentieren Blattrosetten, die vom Akanthus abgeleitet und mit spiralförmigen Blattranken verbunden sind.
Die Muster eignen sich als Zierde quadratischer oder achteckiger Paneele und Kassetten. Das Muster oben kann auch als Mittelstück einer Decke verwendet werden, wobei die einzelnen Elemente lediglich vergrößert werden müssen. Die Farbgebung unterliegt keinerlei Auflagen; dunkle Farben auf hellem Grund wirken überzeugend.

Ces deux motifs ornementaux présentent des rosaces de feuilles dérivées de la feuille d'acanthe et reliées entre elles par des entre-lacs de feuilles en forme de spirales.
Les motifs serviront à décorer des panneaux et des caissons carrés ou octogonaux. Le motif du haut peut également constituer la pièce centrale d'un plafond et dans ce cas, il suffira d'agrandir les différents éléments. Le motif peut être réalisé dans des couleurs au choix ; la combinaison de couleurs sombres sur fond clair est irrésistible.

Corner ornaments with palmette decor for square and rectangular panels
Eckornamente mit Palmettendekor für quadratische und rechteckige Paneele
Ornements d'angles à décor de palmettes pour panneaux carrés et rectangulaires

These six corner motifs feature various palmettes derived from the Classical acanthus, a recurrent motif in Renaissance art.
The designs are suitable as decorations for panels or doors. If the panels are very small, the outer border can be omitted. All the patterns can be executed in one or more colors. Gold on a dark ground looks particularly elegant.

Diese sechs Eckmotive werden von unterschiedlichen Palmetten bestimmt, die sich formal vom klassischen Akanthus, einem auch in der Renaissance-Kunst immer wieder auftretenden Motiv, ableiten.
Die Entwürfe eignen sich als Dekor von Paneelen oder Türen. Sind die Paneelfelder sehr klein, können die äußeren Begrenzungslinien der Muster weggelassen werden. Alle Muster lassen sich in einer oder mehreren Farben ausführen. Eine Umsetzung in Gold auf dunklem Grund hat eine erlesene Wirkung.

Ces six motifs d'angles se caractérisent par diverses palmettes qui, du point de vue de leur forme, sont dérivées de la feuille d'acanthe classique, un motif également récurrent dans l'art de la Renaissance.
Les motifs serviront à décorer des panneaux ou des portes. Si les panneaux sont très petits, on pourra ignorer les lignes de séparation extérieures des motifs. Tous les motifs sont réalisés dans une ou plusieurs couleurs. Une exécution en doré sur fond sombre sera aussi du plus bel effet.

Two corner ornaments with palmettes for decorating stucco ceilings
Zwei Eckornamente mit Palmetten zur Dekoration von Stuckdecken
Deux ornements d'angles à palmettes pour la décoration de plafonds en stuc

This plate illustrates two corner ornaments with an opulent palmette decor. In addition, it shows three intermediate elements and two framing borders.

These motifs are intended for the decoration of lightly modeled stucco ceilings. The narrow borders should always be a few centimeters away from the outer cornice, while the corner and intermediate elements in their turn should be an appropriate distance from the border. Here, all the ornaments are shown in a single color on a light ground, but other color compositions can be developed, including for example shading the palmettes, which could be very effective.

Diese Abbildung zeigt zwei Eckornamente mit reichem Palmettendekor. Ferner sieht man drei Zwischenstücke und zwei rahmende Borten.

Diese Motive sind zur Dekoration leicht modellierter Stuckdecken bestimmt. Die schmalen Borten sollten stets einige Zentimeter Abstand zum äußeren Gesims einhalten, während die Eck- und Zwischenstücke wiederum einen angemessenen Abstand zu diesen Borten wahren sollten. Hier sind alle Ornamente in einer Farbe auf hellem Untergrund gezeigt, doch es lassen sich auch andere Farbkompositionen entwickeln, die zum Beispiel eine effektvolle Schattierung der Palmetten einschließen könnten.

Cette planche présente deux ornements d'angles à palmettes richement décorées. On remarquera en outre trois raccords et deux bordures qui forment un cadre.

Ces motifs sont destinés à la décoration de plafonds en stuc légèrement en relief. Les bordures étroites doivent toujours se trouver à quelques centimètres de la corniche extérieure ; on laissera de la même façon un intervalle approprié entre les pièces d'angles, les raccords et ces bordures. Tous les ornements présentés ici sont monochromes sur fond clair, mais d'autres combinaisons de couleurs sont possibles, par exemple un dégradé impressionnant de tons pour les palmettes.

Rosettes
Rosetten
Rosaces

This plate illustrates six large and two small rosettes with variations in the detail of the leaves.

These rosettes are intended for the decoration of panels. The four designs in the corners are particularly suitable for the ornamentation of round or octagonal panels, while the two large rosettes to the left and right are more suited to hexagonal panels. The two smaller rosettes in the middle are intended only to fill square panels.

Diese Tafel präsentiert sechs große und zwei kleine Rosetten mit unterschiedlich gestaltetem Blattwerk.

Die Rosetten sind zur Zierde von Paneelen bestimmt. Die vier Entwürfe in den Ecken eignen sich besonders als Dekor runder oder achteckiger Paneele, während die beiden großen Entwürfe rechts und links eher für sechseckige Paneele verwendet werden sollten. Die beiden kleineren Rosetten in der Mitte sind ausschließlich zur Füllung von Quadraten bestimmt.

Cette planche présente six rosaces de grande taille et deux petites aux feuilles de formes différentes.

Les rosaces serviront à décorer des panneaux. Les quatre motifs d'angles conviennent parfaitement à la décoration de panneaux ronds ou octogonaux, tandis que les deux grands motifs à droite et à gauche s'appliqueront plutôt à des panneaux hexagonaux. Les deux rosaces centrales plus petites sont exclusivement destinées à remplir des carrés.

Composition of stylized acanthus leaves for the ornamentation of panels
Komposition aus stilisierten Akanthusblättern zur Dekoration von Paneelen
Composition de feuilles d'acanthe stylisées pour la décoration de panneaux

This design reproduces a composition of stylized acanthus leaves. A decoratively framed rosette is surmounted by a central stem, which sprouts leaves and spiral tendrils. Also sprouting from the central stem are long highly stylized acanthus leaf shoots stretching elegantly upwards. The whole composition is crowned by a strongly stylized palmette. This pattern is suitable for the ornamentation of panels, and also as the decorative top or bottom element of a pilaster or similar narrow projecting structural element. The design is executed in black on a light ground, and this color scheme is particularly suitable for door panels. Nonetheless, the pattern can also be executed in black on gold or gold on black.

Dieser Entwurf gibt eine Komposition aus stilisierten Akanthusblättern wieder. Oberhalb einer ornamental gerahmten Rosette erhebt sich ein Zentralstamm, dem spiralförmige einrollende Blattranken entwachsen. Außerdem spalten sich vom Zentralstamm lange, stark stilisierte Akanthusblätter ab, die sich elegant in die Höhe recken. Die Komposition wird von einer stark stilisierten Palmette bekrönt. Dieses Muster eignet sich als Dekor von Paneelen sowie als dekorativer oberer oder unterer Abschluss eines Pilasters oder anderer schmaler, vorspringender Gebäudeteile. Der Ornamententwurf ist in schwarz auf hellem Grund gehalten und eignet sich in dieser Farbgebung besonders gut zur Füllung von Türfeldern. Er lässt sich aber auch in Schwarz auf goldenem oder in Gold auf schwarzem Grund auftragen.

Cette planche présente une composition de feuilles d'acanthe stylisées. Une tige centrale d'où émergent des entrelacs de feuilles enroulés en spirale s'élève au-dessus d'une rosace placée dans un médaillon ornemental. De plus, des feuilles d'acanthe excessivement longues et très stylisées, qui pointent avec élégance vers le haut, se séparent de la tige principale. La composition est couronnée d'une palmette très stylisée. Ce motif servira de décor à des panneaux, ainsi que de finition supérieure ou inférieure d'un pilastre ou d'autres parties étroites et saillantes d'un édifice. Le motif ornemental est réalisé en noir sur fond clair et, dans ces tons, c'est un décor idéal pour des panneaux de portes. Une exécution en noir sur fond doré ou en doré sur fond noir est toutefois possible.

Three vertical ornamental bands with elaborate leaf-and-scroll designs
Drei vertikale Ornamentbänder mit aufwändigem Rankendekor
Trois bandeaux ornementaux verticaux à entrelacs richement décorés

These patterns show three imaginative leaf-and-scroll motifs suitable for sizable compositions. The pattern on the left, with its stylized acanthus leaves, the slender capital and the crowning palmette, is reminiscent of Italian Renaissance motifs. The pattern in the center, with the stylized palmette framed at the foot by two scrolls forming a heart, betrays a Classical influence. The design on the right depicts a series of double scrolls each forming a heart-shaped motif around an acanthus bud with leaves.

These patterns are suitable for the decoration of pilasters, narrow panels, intrados, the undersides of beams and vertical ornamental bands. The color scheme can be chosen according to taste.

Diese Muster zeigen drei phantasievolle Rankengebilde, die sich für größere Kompositionen anbieten. Das Motiv links erinnert mit seinen stilisierten Akanthusranken, dem schlanken Blattkapitell und der die Komposition bekrönenden Palmette an Motive der italienischen Renaissance. Das Motiv in der Mitte lässt mit der stilisierten Palmette, die am Fuße des Paneels herzförmig von Spiralranken geziert wird, eine Anlehnung an antike Vorbilder erkennen. Das rechte Motiv zeigt sich herzförmig windende Spiralranken in Verbindung mit Akanthusblättern, in deren Mitte eine aufspringende Akanthusknospe als Zentralmotiv eingebettet ist.

Diese Muster eignen sich als Dekor von Pilastern, schmalen Paneelen, Bogenlaibungen und Balkenuntersichten sowie als Motiv für vertikal verlaufende Ornamentbänder. Die Farbgebung kann frei gewählt werden.

Ces motifs présentent trois formes d'entrelacs inventives qui se prêtent parfaitement à la réalisation de compositions de plus grande taille. Par ses entrelacs de feuilles d'acanthe stylisés, son chapiteau de feuilles élancé et ses palmettes couronnant la composition, le motif de gauche rappelle des motifs de la Renaissance italienne. Le motif central à palmette stylisée décorée par des entrelacs en spirale et formant des cœurs dans le bas du panneau est un emprunt aux modèles antiques. Le motif de droite présente, lui aussi, des entrelacs en spirale et formant des cœurs, associés à des feuilles d'acanthe au milieu desquelles émerge un bourgeon d'acanthe comme motif central.

Ces motifs serviront à décorer des pilastres, des panneaux étroits, des intrados et des dessous de poutres, ainsi que des motifs destinés à des bandeaux ornementaux verticaux. Ils peuvent être réalisés dans n'importe quelle couleur au choix.

Masonry pattern with spiral tendril motif
Ziegelmuster mit Rankendekor
Motif de briques à entrelacs

The masonry pattern depicted here is dominated by a central vase motif (typical of the Renaissance) in each of the rectangular fields. In this case, the vase has an acanthus leaf and a pair of symmetrical spiral tendrils growing out of it, providing a highly effective frame for the composition.

The delicacy of this pattern makes it suitable for the decoration of the walls of entrance halls, staircases and corridors. In very large rooms, it should be executed on a correspondingly larger scale. If a decision is made to execute the motifs and the brick-like frame in a single color not very different in tone from the ground, the total impression is one of harmony. For this purpose, a warm brown on a yellowish-brown ground suggests itself, or else a yellowish-brown on a parchment or cream ground.

Bei dem hier präsentierten Ziegelmuster fällt die Verwendung einer Vasenform auf, die als Zentralmotiv in die rechteckigen Felder eingepasst ist. Das Motiv der Vase entstammt dem Formenschatz der Renaissance. Bei diesem Entwurf entwachsen der Vase ein zentrales Akanthusblatt und ausladende Spiralranken, welche die Komposition effektvoll rahmen. Dieses Muster eignet sich aufgrund seines leichten Charakters besonders als Wanddekor von Eingangshallen, Treppenhäusern und Gängen. In sehr großen Räumen sollte es in einem entsprechend großen Maßstab wiedergegeben werden. Wenn für das Motiv einschließlich der die Felder begrenzenden Konturen ein Farbton gewählt wird, der nur wenig heller oder dunkler als der Untergrund ist, ergibt sich ein harmonischer Gesamteindruck. Zu diesem Zweck eignen sich ein warmes Braun auf gelb-braunem Grund oder ein Gelb-Braun auf pergament- oder cremefarbenem Grund.

Ce qui frappe surtout dans le motif de briques présenté ici, c'est l'utilisation d'une forme de vase intégrée comme motif central dans les panneaux rectangulaires. Le motif du vase est dérivé des formes de la Renaissance. Dans ce motif, une feuille d'acanthe centrale et de larges spirales émergent du vase, en encadrant la composition avec beaucoup d'effet.

En raison de sa légèreté, ce motif servira de décor mural pour des halls d'entrée, des cages d'escaliers et des couloirs. Dans des espaces très grands, il conviendra de le reproduire à l'échelle correspondante. Un ton légèrement plus clair ou sombre que le fond pour le motif dont les contours délimitent les panneaux, donnera une impression d'ensemble harmonieuse. La combinaison de brun chaud sur fond marron-jaune ou de marron-jaune sur fond couleur parchemin ou crème est idéale dans ce cas.

Renaissance 165

Diaper pattern with stylized spiral tendrils
Tapetenmuster mit stilisierten Ranken
Motif de tenture à entrelacs stylisés

This large-format wall decoration shows highly stylized tendrils undulating in a vertical direction in symmetrically reflecting pairs. They form the contours of a uniform pattern whose internal fields are decorated with leaf-and-scroll motifs, small rosettes and acanthus leaves.

As the pattern is primarily intended for wall surfaces, it should be executed in a relatively large format geared to the total area of the wall. Instead of the reticent coloration illustrated in the plate, stronger colors on a dark ground can also be chosen.

Dieses großflächig angelegte Wandmuster zeigt stark stilisierte Ranken, die vertikal in Wellenform verlaufen und spiegelbildlich angeordnet sind. Sie bilden die Kontur eines gleichmäßigen Musters, dessen Innenflächen von Blatt- und Spiralranken sowie kleinen Rosetten und Akanthusblättern ausgeschmückt werden.

Da das Muster vornehmlich zur Verzierung von Wandflächen bestimmt ist, sollte es in einem relativ großen, sich an der Gesamtfläche der Wand orientierenden Maßstab ausgeführt werden. Statt der zurückhaltenden Farbgebung, wie sie die vorliegende Tafel präsentiert, können auch kräftige Farben auf dunklem Grund gewählt werden.

Ce motif mural de grande envergure présente des entrelacs très stylisés qui s'étirent verticalement pour former des vagues et sont disposés de façon symétrique. Les entrelacs forment le contour d'un motif régulier, dont les surfaces intérieures sont décorées de circonvolutions de feuilles et de spirales, ainsi que de petites rosaces et de feuilles d'acanthe. Comme le motif est principalement destiné à décorer des surfaces murales, il convient de le réaliser à une échelle relativement grande, en fonction de la surface totale du mur. Des couleurs vives sur fond sombre peuvent remplacer la couleur discrète présentée dans cette planche.

Neoclassicism
Klassizismus
Le néoclassicisme

The stylistic period known as neo-classicism, in which design harked back to the age of Greek Antiquity, began around the middle of the 18th century and was succeeded in the second half of the 19th century by a more generally oriented Revivalism. In the history of ideas, the Age of Enlightenment is reckoned to have started by the mid-18th century at the latest. The Enlightenment is also known as the Age of Reason, the period when man's critical mental faculties were seen as the

Die Stilepoche des Klassizismus, in der man sich auf die klassische Periode der griechischen Antike besann, setzte etwa Mitte des 18. Jahrhunderts ein und wurde in der zweiten Hälfte des 19. Jahrhunderts durch den Historismus abgelöst. In geisteswissenschaftlichen Zusammenhängen spricht man spätestens ab der Mitte des 18. Jahrhunderts von der Epoche der Aufklärung, in welcher die Vernunft und der kritische Verstand des Menschen als Voraussetzung und zugleich maßgebliche

L'époque du néoclassicisme, marquée par une réminiscence de la période classique de l'Antiquité grecque, a débuté à peu près au milieu du XVIIIᵉ siècle et a été relayée par l'historisme dans la deuxième moitié du XIXᵉ siècle. Dans le domaine des lettres, on parlera de « siècle des Lumières » à partir de la deuxième moitié du XVIIIᵉ siècle, quand la raison et l'esprit critique étaient considérés comme les principes de base et en même temps comme l'autorité

Schauspielhaus (Theater), Karl Friedrich
Schinkel, Berlin, 1818–1821
The Schauspielhaus in Berlin is an imposing
example of neoclassical architecture. The
characteristic feature of this style was its harking back to the models of Classical Antiquity,
and in particular, ancient Greece. Thus the
façade of the Schauspielhaus, with its flight of
steps, its columned portico and its pediment,
is strongly reminiscent of Classical temples.
At the same time, the cuboid structures to the
sides, broken by high windows, and their ste-
reotypical, strictly symmetrical arrangement,
are in accord with the Classical ideal of harmony and beauty.

Schauspielhaus von Karl Friedrich Schinkel,
Berlin, 1818–1821
Das Berliner Schauspielhaus ist ein beein-
druckendes Beispiel klassizistischer Architektur. Kennzeichnend für diesen Architekturstil
ist die Rückbesinnung auf antike, meist griechische Vorbilder. So erinnert die Fassade des
Schauspielhauses mit Freitreppe, Säulenportikus und Dreiecksgiebel deutlich an antike
Tempelvorbilder. Zugleich sieht man aber
auch seitlich ausladende kubische Baukörper,
die von hohen Fenstern durchbrochen sind
und deren streng symmetrische Anordnung
dem klassizistischen Ideal von Harmonie und
Schönheit entspricht.

Théâtre de Karl Friedrich Schinkel, Berlin,
1818–1821
Le théâtre de Berlin est un exemple impressionnant de l'architecture néoclassique. La
réminiscence de modèles antiques, surtout
grecs est caractéristique de ce style architectural. La façade, avec son perron, son portique à colonnes et son pignon triangulaire,
rappelle nettement les modèles de temples
antiques. Mais on voit aussi sur le côté de
larges corps de bâtiments cubiques percés
de hautes fenêtres et dont la disposition purement géométrique répond à l'idéal néoclassique d'harmonie et de beauté.

precondition and authority for all
ethical, political and social action.
The belief in human reason, which
in the nature of things would bring
about what was good and right, led
not only to social changes, but also
to major political upheavals. From
the end of the 18th century, increasing secularization, leading in much
of Europe to confiscation of Church
lands, left the Church in a position
of greatly reduced importance. The
power of monarchs and feudal lords
was thrown into question. The ideas
of the Enlightenment and increasing
dissatisfaction with the prevailing
social order triggered the French
Revolution, whose beginning
was symbolized by the Storming
of the Bastille in 1789. The stated
principles of the Revolution were
"Liberty, Equality, Fraternity".
The most important results of the
Revolution were the elimination of
feudal rights, the formulation of a
declaration of "the Rights of Man
and the Citizen", and the proclamation of a democratic constitution in
1791. This development left its mark
on the whole of continental Europe.
A similar development had already
taken place in the United States,
where a federal democratic constitution was proclaimed in 1787.

Autorität für ethisches, politisches
und soziales Handeln angesehen
wurden.
Der Glaube an die menschliche Vernunft, die naturbedingt das Gute und
Richtige bewirken werde, hatte nicht
nur gesellschaftspolitische Veränderungen zur Folge, sondern leitete
auch schwerwiegende politische
Umstürze ein. Die Kirche verlor mit
der seit dem Ende des 18. Jahrhunderts fortschreitenden Säkularisie-
rung (der Verweltlichung der Gesellschaft und der sich ihr anschließenden Enteignung der Kirche) zuse-
hends an Bedeutung. Die Macht der
Monarchen und Feudalherren wurde
in Frage gestellt. Das Gedankengut
der Aufklärung und die fortschrei-
tende Unzufriedenheit mit den herrschenden sozialen Verhältnissen
lösten 1789 mit dem Sturm auf die
Bastille die Französische Revolution
aus, deren Grundsätze Freiheit,
Gleichheit und Brüderlichkeit
hießen. Wesentliche Ergebnisse der
Revolution waren die Aufhebung
der Feudalrechte, die Formulierung
der Menschen- und Bürgerrechte
sowie die Ausrufung einer demokra-
tischen Verfassung (1791). Diese
Entwicklung prägte ganz Europa.
Sie hatte sich in ähnlicher Weise
auch den Vereinigten Staaten voll-

décisive pour le comportement
éthique, politique et social.
La foi en la raison humaine qui, par
nature, produit le bien et le vrai,
entraîna non seulement des change-
ments socio-politiques, mais aussi
des bouleversements politiques très
profonds. L'Église perdit d'un coup
de son importance avec la séculari-
sation croissante irréversible depuis
la fin du XVIIIᵉ siècle (la laïcisation
de la société et la dépossession de
l'Église qui s'ensuivit). La puis-
sance du monarque et des seigneurs
féodaux fut mise en cause. Les
idées des Lumières et l'insatisfac-
tion croissante due aux conditions
sociales en vigueur déclenchèrent,
avec la prise de la Bastille en 1789,
la Révolution française dont les
principes étaient la Liberté, l'Égalité
et la Fraternité. Certes, ceux-ci
s'imposèrent avec des effusions de
sang, mais ils marquent aujourd'hui
encore notre sens de la démocratie.
Les acquisitions majeures de la
Révolution française furent l'abo-
lition de la féodalité, la Déclaration
des droits de l'homme et du citoyen,
ainsi que la proclamation d'une
constitution démocratique (1791).
Cette évolution marqua toute
l'Europe. Elle s'était accomplie
de la même façon aux États-Unis

Opposite page: Thomas Cole, *The Architect's
Dream*, oil on canvas, The Toledo Museum of
Art, Ohio, 1840
Immersed in a magnificent vision, the
architect dreams of the past architectural
styles on which neoclassicism was based.

Gegenüberliegende Seite: Thomas Cole, *Der
Traum des Architekten*, Öl auf Leinwand, The
Toledo Museum of Art, Ohio, 1840
Versunken in eine großartige Vision träumt der
Architekt von den vergangenen Architekturstil-
en, auf die sich der Klassizismus bezieht.

Page ci-contre: Thomas Cole, *Le Rêve de
l'Architecte*, huile sur toile, Museum of Art
à Toledo, Ohio, 1840.
Au premier plan, l'architecte plongé dans une
vision grandiose rêve des styles architecturaux du passé auxquels se réfère le néoclassicisme.

These socio-political changes were naturally enough reflected in art and architecture. The ideal of education gave rise to numerous museums, libraries, universities and colleges, opera-houses, and theaters; the age also saw the construction of parliament and council buildings, banks and hotels, along with spacious residential neighborhoods and splendid parks. Another characteristic of the neoclassical period was the laying out of extensive street networks, which have put their stamp on such cities as Edinburgh, Stockholm, Munich and Berlin. The

zogen, wo bereits 1787 eine bundesstaatliche, demokratische Verfassung ausgerufen wurde.
Die gesellschaftspolitischen Veränderungen hatten natürlich auch Einfluss auf Kunst und Architektur. Dem Bildungsideal entsprechend entstanden zahlreiche Bibliotheken und Museen, Universitäten und Internate, Opern- und Theaterhäuser, aber auch Rats- und Parlamentsgebäude, Banken und Hotels sowie großzügig angelegte Wohnanlagen und herrliche Parks. Charakteristisch für die Epoche des Klassizismus ist auch die Planung weitläufi-

où une constitution fédérale et démocratique avait été votée dès 1787.
Les bouleversements socio-politiques eurent bien sûr aussi des répercussions sur l'art et l'architecture. Répondant à l'idéal de culture, d'innombrables bibliothèques et musées, universités et internats, opéras et théâtres virent le jour, mais aussi des hôtels de ville et parlements, des banques et hôtels, ainsi que des cités aménagées avec faste et des parcs somptueux. Le tracé de larges artères qui marque l'identité de villes telles

architecture of neoclassicism was limpid and sober. The exuberant forms of the Baroque and Rococo periods, which had characterized the 17th and much of the 18th centuries, had outlived themselves. In view of the fact that the Enlightenment continued the intellectual approach of the Renaissance of the 15th and 16th centuries, the revival of Classical architectural models, which were seen as the epitome of beauty and harmony, was only logical.
One of the characteristic features of

ger Straßenzüge, die das Bild von Städten wie Edinburgh, Stockholm, München und Berlin prägen. Die Architektur des Klassizismus war klar und nüchtern; die überschwängliche Formensprache des Barock und Rokoko, die noch das 17. und große Teile des 18. Jahrhunderts bestimmte, hatte sich überlebt. Angesichts der Tatsache, dass die Aufklärung die geistigen Ansätze der Renaissance des 15. und 16. Jahrhunderts fortführte, war die Wiederaufnahme antiker Baufor-

qu'Édimbourg, Stockholm, Munich et Berlin caractérise aussi l'époque du néoclassicisme. L'architecture du néoclassicisme était pure et sobre ; le langage exubérant des formes du baroque et du rococo qui déterminait encore le XVIIe et une grande partie du XVIIIe siècle avait fait son temps. Comme les Lumières poursuivirent le mouvement intellectuel amorcé par la Renaissance aux XVe et XVIe siècles, la reprise de formes architecturales antiques considérées comme l'incarnation de la beauté et

neoclassical architecture was the temple façade with its columned portico and triangular pediment. In contrast to the Classical models, the cuboid body of the building was structured by the use of cornices and pilasters. The columns, inspired by the so-called "orders" of the Classical temples (where they often served a purely decorative function), now took on a structural, load-bearing function. This sober, clearly-structured architecture was not devoid of ornament, but it was not lavish, taking the form of garlands, swags, urns, rosettes, Classical palmettes and frets, and egg-and-dart moldings.

The Audsleys were very familiar with neoclassical architecture. It comes as no surprise, therefore, that they were particularly interested in ornamentation derived from Classical sources. Their neoclassical designs are remarkably similar to their Greek designs, as demonstrated for example by the palmettes illustrated on pages 183 and 197. They are at most variants on the same theme, drawing attention to the close relationship between neoclassicism and the art of Classical Antiquity. One striking general point is that the broad ornamental bands are now patterned more strongly. In addition, the patterns have a more austerely linear character, as can be seen in the stylized leaf motifs on page 185. The vegetal forms, formally reminiscent in most cases of the Classical palmette, are more strongly stylized (see page 177). Stylized lotus blossoms are another common motif, as illustrated on page 187. They can be put down to "Egyptian influence", which is probably due to the ornamental designs of Owen Jones. With his *Grammar of Ornament* (1856), Jones created a standard work on ornamental design, which was known to the Audsleys and provided them with inspiration.

men, die man als Inbegriff von Schönheit und Harmonie ansah, nur folgerichtig.

Eines der charakteristischsten Merkmale der klassizistischen Architektur ist die Tempelstirnwand mit Säulenportikus und Dreiecksgiebel. Der blockhafte Baukörper wurde im Gegensatz zur antiken Architektur durch Pilaster und Gesimse gegliedert. Die Säulenordnungen, die vom antiken Tempel übernommen wurden, bei dem sie oft rein dekorativ angelegt waren, sind jetzt konstruktiv bedingt und tragen das Gebälk. Als sparsamer Dekor dieser nüchternen und klar gegliederten Architektur dienen neben Girlanden, Urnen und Rosetten die klassischen Palmetten und Mäander sowie Perl- und Eierstäbe.

Die Architektur des Klassizismus war den Audsleys bestens vertraut. Es überrascht daher nicht, dass sie gerade den antik geprägten Ornamenten ein besonderes Interesse entgegenbrachten. Es fällt auf, dass sich ihre Ornamente des klassizistischen Stils kaum von denen des griechischen Stils unterscheiden, wie dies zum Beispiel die Palmettenentwürfe der Seiten 183 und 197 demonstrieren. Sie können allenfalls als eine Variante desselben Motivs bezeichnet werden, was auf die enge Verbindung des Klassizismus mit der antiken Kunst aufmerksam macht. Im Allgemeinen fällt auf, dass die breiten Ornamentbänder jetzt etwas stärker gemustert sind, außerdem weisen die Muster einen strengeren linearen Charakter auf, der bei dem stilisierten Rankendekor auf Seite 185 zu sehen ist.

Die vegetabilen Formen, die sich formal zumeist an der klassischen Palmette orientieren, sind stärker stilisiert (siehe Seite 177). Überdies sind häufig stilisierte Lotusblüten zu erkennen, wie zum Beispiel auf Seite 187. Sie sind als „ägyptischer Einfluss" zu werten, der vermutlich auf die Ornamententwürfe von Owen Jones zurückzuführen ist. Jones hatte mit seiner *Grammar of Ornament* (1856) ein Standardwerk zur Ornamentkunde geschaffen, das auch den Audsleys bekannt war und ihnen als Inspirationsquelle diente.

de l'harmonie était tout à fait logique.

La façade des temples ornée d'un portique à colonnes et d'un fronton triangulaire est une des principales caractéristiques de l'architecture néoclassique. Le corps de bâtiment massif se composait de pilastres et de corniches, contrairement à l'architecture antique. Les colonnes, empruntées au temple antique où elles étaient généralement purement décoratives, dépendent maintenant de la construction et supportent l'entablement. Des guirlandes, urnes et rosaces, mais aussi les palmettes classiques, les méandres, perles et oves sont les seuls ornements de cette architecture sobre et clairement organisée.

Les Audsley avaient une très grande connaissance de l'architecture du néoclassicisme. Il n'est donc pas surprenant qu'ils aient précisément porté un intérêt particulier aux ornements d'inspiration antique. Ce qui frappe particulièrement, c'est le peu de différence entre leurs ornements de style néoclassique et ceux du style grec, comme le montrent les palmettes aux pages 183 et 197. On peut tout au plus les qualifier de variantes d'un même style, ce qui met en évidence le lien étroit entre le néoclassicisme et l'art antique. Les larges bandeaux ornementaux un peu plus accentués retiennent en général l'attention. De plus, ces motifs présentent un caractère linéaire plus strict, par exemple dans les entrelacs stylisés à la page 185.

Les formes végétales qui rappellent pour la plupart la palmette classique sont davantage stylisées (voir page 177). Les fleurs de lotus stylisées sont en outre fréquentes, comme à la page 187. On y reconnaît une « influence égyptienne » probablement due aux esquisses ornementales d'Owen Jones. Ce dernier livra, avec sa *Grammar of Ornament* (1856), un ouvrage capital sur l'art ornemental que les Audsley connaissaient et qui leur servit de source d'inspiration.

Horizontal bands with palmette and rosette motifs
Horizontale Bänder mit Palmetten- und Rosettendekor
Bandeaux horizontaux à palmettes et rosaces

The ornamental bands illustrated here go back in form to stylized palmette bands. The top pattern shows palmettes opening out like fans, alternating with smaller pairs of palmettes reflected about their base. A vitruvian scroll forms the connecting element. The composition is bordered at the base with a narrow band of semi-rosettes.

The lower pattern shows a variant of the rosette based on the acanthus leaf. Each rosette is framed by two pairs of leaves arranged in a semi-circle, each backing on to the "frame" of the next rosette. The resulting spandrels are filled with stylized buds. This composition is bordered at the base with a narrow band depicting a wave motif.

The two patterns illustrated here are suitable for the decoration of horizontal bands; they can also be used as border strips above monochrome or patterned base areas of walls. Both patterns can also be used as borders for ceiling panels, in which case a suitable corner solution must be found. The lower pattern can also be used vertically to form the border of vertical panels. By omitting the wave border, this ornamental band can also be used on the underside of beams or rafters, or on the intrados of an arch. Both patterns can be executed in a single color, either dark on a light ground or vice versa.

Die hier abgebildeten Ornamentbänder gehen formal auf stilisierte Palmettenbänder zurück. Das obere Muster zeigt sich fächerartig aufspaltende Palmetten, die sich mit kleinen, sich gegenüberstehenden Palmetten abwechseln, die durch Spiralranken verbunden sind. Die Komposition wird nach unten von einem schmalen Band mit Halbrosetten abgeschlossen. Das Muster unten zeigt dagegen eine Abwandlung des spitzzackigen Akanthus als Rosette. Diese wird von zwei im Halbrund dargestellten Akanthusblättern gerahmt, die von einer Knospe bekrönt sind. Nach unten wird diese Komposition von einem schmalen Wellenband begrenzt.

Die beiden vorgestellten Muster sind für die Verzierung horizontaler Bänder sowie als Begrenzungsstreifen oberhalb einfarbiger oder gemusterter Sockelzonen geeignet. Beide Muster können auch als Bordüren um Deckentäfelungen eingesetzt werden, wobei lediglich eine passende Ecklösung entwickelt werden muss. Das untere Muster lässt sich überdies in vertikaler Ausrichtung verwenden, so dass es zur Begrenzung vertikaler Paneele oder Wandflächen verwendet werden kann. Unter Verzicht auf die Wellenranke kann dieses Ornamentband auf die Unterseite von Balken und Dachgebälk sowie auf Laibungen von Bögen aufgetragen werden. Beide Muster können in einer einzigen Farbe, dunkel auf hellem oder hell auf dunklem Grund, ausgeführt werden.

Les bandeaux ornementaux représentés ici rappellent par leur forme des bandeaux de palmettes stylisés. Dans le motif du haut, des palmettes s'ouvrent en éventail et alternent avec de petites palmettes disposées tête-bêche et reliées par des entrelacs en spirales. La composition se termine dans le bas par un bandeau étroit de demi-rosaces.

Le motif du bas présente par contre une forme dérivée de l'acanthe dentelée servant de rosace. Celle-ci est encadrée par deux feuilles d'acanthe disposées en demi-cercle et couronnées d'un bouton. Cette composition se termine dans le bas par un étroit bandeau de vagues.

Les deux motifs illustrés serviront de décor pour des bandeaux horizontaux et de bande de séparation au-dessus de soubassements monochromes ou décorés. Ils pourront aussi servir à border des plafonds en lambris et dans ce cas, il conviendra de trouver une solution appropriée pour les angles. Le motif du bas peut s'utiliser en outre dans le sens vertical et délimiter ainsi des panneaux ou murs verticaux. On pourra transposer ce bandeau ornemental, à l'exception de l'entrelacs de vagues, sur la face inférieure de poutres et de charpentes, ainsi que sur des intrados. Les deux motifs peuvent être réalisés en une seule couleur: sombre sur fond clair ou claire sur fond sombre.

Horizontal bands with stylized tendril patterns
Horizontale Bänder mit Rankendekor
Bandeaux horizontaux à entrelacs

Both of the patterns on this plate use tendril motifs. While the stylized palmettes in the lower pattern are still recognizable as such, those in the top pattern are elements of a highly stylized tendril, in which leaf motifs alternate with heraldic lily-like elements. The composition is edged at the bottom by a narrow border with a fret motif.

The lower pattern shows a tendril which appears to lap along the band like a wave; periodically it sprouts stylized leaves. The sideshoots take the form of stylized palmettes reminiscent of heraldic lilies. The fret border of the top pattern is here replaced by an astragal.

Both patterns can be used as ornamental bands above a wall surface. They also provide an esthetically convincing demarcation between a dark base zone and the light area above, irrespective of whether the latter is monochrome or patterned. For these ornamental bands, the color scheme can be chosen to match that of the adjacent surfaces. Gold on a black or other very dark ground, or black on a gold ground, are both very effective with these patterns.

Beide Ornamentbänder zeigen Ranken. Während bei dem Muster unten die stilisierten Palmetten noch als solche zu erkennen sind, werden sie beim Band oben als stark stilisierte Blattranke ausgeprägt. Die den Aufbau des oberen Musters bestimmenden Blattformen rapportieren mit den als Blattranken ausgeprägten Palmetten und gleichen formal einer Lilie. Die Komposition wird nach unten von einem schmalen mäanderartigen Band abgeschlossen.

Das untere Muster zeigt eine Ranke mit wellenförmigem Verlauf, von der sich stilisierte Blätter seitlich abspalten. Den Seitentrieben der Ranke entspringen schematisierte Palmetten, die formal an eine Lilie erinnern. Das begrenzende mäanderartige Band der oberen Komposition ist beim unteren Muster durch ein Perlband ersetzt.

Beide Muster können als Zierbänder oberhalb einer Wandfläche verwendet werden. Sie bieten eine ästhetisch überzeugende Abtrennung einer dunklen Sockelzone von einer darüber liegenden hellen Wandfläche, gleichgültig ob diese einfarbig oder leicht gemustert ist. Für diese Ornamentbänder kann die farbige Gestaltung ganz nach dem Charakter der angrenzenden Dekoration entwickelt werden. Gold auf schwarzem oder einem anderen tiefdunklen Untergrund, aber auch Schwarz auf goldenem Grund wirkt bei diesen Mustern sehr ansprechend.

Ces deux bandeaux ornementaux se composent d'entrelacs. Si les palmettes stylisées dans le motif du bas sont nettement reconnaissables, elles se présentent par contre sous la forme d'entrelacs de feuilles très stylisées dans le bandeau du haut. Les feuilles qui déterminent la composition du motif supérieur sont récurrentes avec des palmettes en guise d'entrelacs de feuilles et ressemblent, par leur forme, à des lis. La composition se termine dans le bas par une bande étroite similaire à un méandre.

Le motif du bas montre un entrelacs avec un tracé de vagues, de chaque côté duquel se détachent des feuilles stylisées. Des palmettes schématisées qui rappellent des lis par leur forme jaillissent des stolons. La bande de séparation en forme de méandre de la composition supérieure est remplacée par des perles dans le motif du bas.

Les deux motifs serviront de bandeaux ornementaux dans le haut d'un mur. Monochromes ou légèrement décorés, ils constitueront une séparation convaincante sur le plan esthétique entre un soubassement sombre et un mur clair. La combinaison de couleurs de ces bandeaux ornementaux peut être choisie selon le type de décoration environnante. Ce motif sera du plus bel effet en doré sur fond noir ou sombre ou en noir sur fond doré.

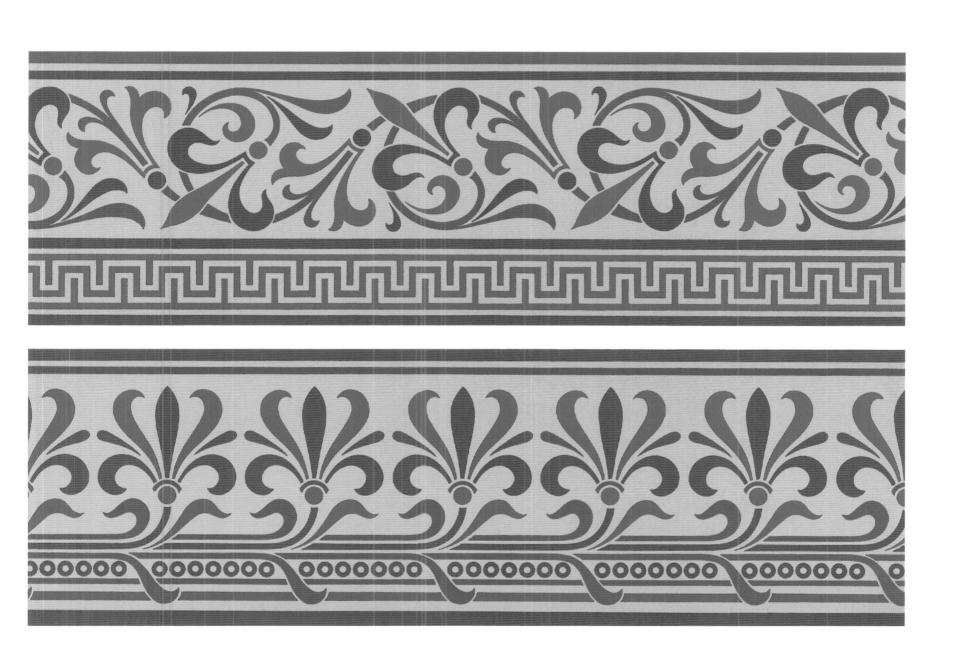

Horizontal bands with stylized palmette motifs
Horizontale Bänder mit stilisiertem Palmettendekor
Bandeaux horizontaux à palmettes stylisées

These two patterns show variations on a palmette band influenced by the Egyptian style. In the top example, we have an alternation of stylized palmettes and splendid lotus blossoms, which here crown bisected stars, and to this extent the design resembles the anthemion frieze. These dominant motifs are linked by a vitruvian scroll. The lower edge is formed by a fret pattern border. The bottom pattern is characterized by a series of elements each consisting of a pair of striking fan-like semi-palmettes framing a slender stylized plant consisting of a column of bell-like flowers tapering towards the top. These palmette elements alternate with ornamental designs each crowned by a five-pointed star. The pattern is edged at the bottom by an oblique fret pattern.

These patterns are ideally suitable for use as horizontal bands and crestings. If they are used to demarcate two surfaces, lines must be added above the ornamental bands in order to delineate the latter at the top. The basic color of this dividing line must be chosen with attention to the color of the base zone, which should always be darker than the area above.

Die beiden Muster zeigen Variationen eines vom ägyptischen Stil beeinflussten Palmettenbandes. Beim Band oben wechseln ähnlich wie beim Anthemionfries stilisierte Palmetten mit prächtigen Lotusblüten ab, die hier einen halbierten Stern bekrönen. Die Elemente sind durch spiralförmige Ranken verbunden. Den unteren Abschluss bildet ein mäanderartiges Band. Beim Muster unten fallen die sich fächerartig aufspaltenden Halbpalmetten auf. Sie rahmen eine schlanke Staude, die sich aus kleinen, sich nach oben hin verjüngenden Glockenblumen zusammensetzt. Dazwischen sieht man ornamentale Kompositionen, die von einem kleinen fünfzackigen Stern bekrönt sind. Das Muster wird nach unten hin von einem schräg gestellten Mäanderband abgeschlossen.

Diese Muster eignen sich hervorragend als horizontale Bänder und Abschlussleisten. Wenn sie zur Abgrenzung zweier Flächen voneinander verwendet werden, müssen oberhalb des Ornamentstreifens zusätzlich Linien angebracht werden, um seine obere Begrenzung zu definieren. Die Grundfarbe dieser Trennlinie muss mit Rücksicht auf die Farbe der Sockelzone gewählt werden, die stets dunkler sein sollte als die darüber liegende Fläche.

Les deux motifs présentent des variantes d'un bandeau de palmettes influencé par le style égyptien. Dans le bandeau du haut, des palmettes stylisées alternent, comme dans l'anthémion, avec de somptueuses fleurs de lotus couronnées ici par une demi-étoile. Les éléments sont reliés entre eux par des entrelacs en spirale. Le motif se termine dans le bas par un bandeau de méandres. Les demi-palmettes s'ouvrant en éventail dans le motif du bas attirent le regard. Elles encadrent une tige élancée, composée de petites campanules qui se rétrécissent vers le haut. Les deux motifs sont séparés par des compositions ornementales couronnées d'une petite étoile à cinq branches. Le motif se termine dans le bas par un bandeau de méandres obliques.

Ces motifs feront merveille comme bandeaux horizontaux et cimaises. Si on les utilise pour séparer deux surfaces, il convient d'ajouter des lignes au-dessus de la bande ornementale afin de définir la limite supérieure. La couleur de fond de cette ligne de séparation doit être choisie en fonction de la couleur du soubassement qui sera toujours plus foncée que la surface supérieure.

Horizontal bands with stylized palmettes
Horizontale Bänder mit stilisierten Palmetten
Bandeaux horizontaux à palmettes stylisées

The upper ornamental band is characterized by highly stylized, fan-like palmettes alternating with slender acanthus-leaf compositions each centering on an acanthus bud. The lower edge of the composition is formed by a fret-like border. The design below is dominated by stylized tendrils crowned alternately by large calyxes and small buds. The lower edge is formed by a border of circles alternating with three vertical lines.

Like the designs on page 179, these patterns are ideally suited as decorations for horizontal bands and crestings. The lower design can also be used, on a larger scale, to decorate concave moldings of ceilings, in which case a suitable corner design must be found.

Beim oberen Ornamentband sieht man stark stilisierte, sich fächerartig aufspaltende Palmetten, die mit schlanken, spitzzackigen Blattkompositionen abwechseln, in deren Mitte sich eine schlanke Akanthusknospe befindet. Nach unten wird die Komposition von einem mäanderartigen Band abgeschlossen. Das untere Muster wird von stilisierten Ranken bestimmt, deren halbrunde Stängel sich überkreuzen. Sie werden abwechselnd von großen Kelchblüten und kleinen Knospen bekrönt. Den unteren Abschluss bildet ein Band aus Kreisen und senkrechten Linien. Diese Muster eignen sich ähnlich wie die Entwürfe auf Seite 179 hervorragend als Zierde horizontaler Bänder und Abschlussleisten. Das untere Ornamentband kann in einem größeren Maßstab auch zur Verzierung der Kehlleisten von Decken verwendet werden, wobei eine passende Eckgestaltung entworfen werden muss.

Le bandeau ornemental du haut présente des palmettes très stylisées, qui s'ouvrent en éventail et alternent avec des compositions de feuilles élancées et dentelées, au milieu desquelles se trouve un élégant bouton d'acanthe. La composition se termine dans le bas par un bandeau de méandres. Le motif du bas se compose d'entrelacs stylisés dont les tiges semi-cylindriques s'entrecroisent et qui sont couronnés d'une alternance de grandes fleurs en forme de calices et de petits boutons. Le motif se termine dans le bas par un bandeau de cercles et de lignes verticales.

Ces motifs similaires à ceux de la page 179 décoreront à merveille des bandeaux et cimaises horizontaux. Il est possible d'agrandir le bandeau ornemental inférieur et d'en décorer les entraits de plafonds ; dans ce cas, il conviendra de trouver une solution appropriée pour les angles.

Panel designs with palmette decor
Paneel mit Palmettendekor
Panneau à palmettes

Here we see two designs for panel ornamentation, derived from Greek exemplars. While the top pattern with its fan-like palmette is relatively simple, the design below is striking by dint of its rich vegetal decoration and the complex fret pattern in the lower corners. A conspicuous feature of the motif is the naturalistic design of the central acanthus leaf, which contrasts strongly with the strictly linear, strongly stylized representation of the vegetal design elements.

These patterns are suitable for the ornamentation of the lower sections of vertical panels. If the simpler design is chosen, the upper section of the panels can remain undecorated; all that is needed are the demarcation lines. If the more elaborate design is chosen, by contrast, the fret pattern in the lower corners must be repeated in the upper corners of the panels. The patterns illustrated on this plate can be executed in monochrome or polychrome according to taste.

Hier sind zwei Beispiele von Palmetten wiedergegeben, die von griechischen Vorbildern abgeleitet sind. Während das obere Muster mit der sich fächerartig aufspaltenden Palmette weniger komplex gestaltet ist, besticht das Muster unten durch seinen reichen vegetabilen Dekor und die Flechtbandornamentik der unteren Ecken. Auffällig bei dem Motiv unten ist die naturnahe Gestaltung des zentralen Akanthusblattes, die im Gegensatz zu der sonst streng linearen, stark stilisierten Darstellungsweise des vegetabilen Dekors steht.

Diese Muster eignen sich für die Verzierung des unteren Teils vertikaler Paneele. Wählt man das einfachere Ornament oben, kann der obere Abschnitt der Paneele unverziert bleiben; lediglich die Begrenzungslinien müssen um das Feld herumgeführt werden. Wählt man hingegen das aufwändigere Muster unten, sollte das Flechtbandornament der unteren Ecken auch in den oberen Ecken der Paneele wiederholt werden. Die Muster dieser Tafel können sowohl ein- als auch mehrfarbig ausgeführt werden.

Cette planche présente deux exemples de palmettes dérivées de modèles grecs. Si le motif du haut a une forme moins complexe avec la palmette s'ouvrant en éventail, le motif du bas, par contre, séduit par son riche décor végétal et les rinceaux placés dans les coins inférieurs. La forme naturelle de la feuille d'acanthe centrale qui contraste avec la présentation par ailleurs strictement linéaire et très stylisée du décor végétal est frappante dans le motif du bas.

Ces motifs serviront à décorer la partie inférieure de panneaux verticaux. Si on choisit l'ornement supérieur plus simple, on pourra se dispenser de décorer la partie supérieure des panneaux ; on ne tracera dans ce cas que les lignes de séparation autour du panneau. Si on choisit par contre le motif plus riche, il faudra répéter le treillis des angles inférieurs dans les angles supérieurs des panneaux. Les motifs de cette planche peuvent être réalisés dans une ou plusieurs couleurs.

Panel with stylized leaf decor
Paneel mit stilisiertem Rankendekor
Panneau à entrelacs stylisés

The design illustrated here has as its central motif a highly stylized composition of leaves on three stems issuing from a semi-rosette, which itself is perched on a fret pattern which forms part of the border of the whole design. The fret is repeated in different versions in the top corners and in the middle of the long sides of the panel.

This pattern is suitable for door ornamentation as well as for vertical panels. The central motif should be positioned in the bottom center of a broad rectangular panel; the corners must be treated appropriately, and the intermediate spaces can be arranged as desired. Patterns of this type can also be executed in black or another dark color. The result resembles marquetry work, and the effect is very distinguished.

Die vorliegende Abbildung präsentiert als Zentralmotiv eine stark stilisierte Blattranke, deren drei Stängel einer Halbrosette entwachsen. Diese wird von zwei Mäandern getragen, die sich aus dem Rand des Ornamentfeldes entwickeln. An den Seiten und den oberen Ecken des Paneels ist diese Idee wieder aufgegriffen, so dass sich aus dem Rand heraus weitere Mäanderformen ergeben.

Dieses Muster eignet sich für Türverzierungen sowie für vertikale Täfelungen. Auf einem breiten rechteckigen Paneel wird die Ranke unten in der Mitte angebracht, während die Ecken eine passende Lösung erhalten müssen und die Zwischenstücke variabel gestaltet werden können. Muster dieses Typs können in Schwarz oder einer anderen dunklen Farbe ausgeführt werden. Die Wirkung ähnelt der von Einlegearbeiten und hat einen erlesenen Charakter.

Le motif central de cette planche est un entrelacs de feuilles très stylisées dont les trois tiges donnent naissance à une demi-rosace. Celle-ci est supportée par deux méandres qui sortent de la bordure du panneau ornemental. Le thème est repris sur les côtés et dans les angles supérieurs du panneau, de sorte que d'autres formes de méandres jaillissent de la bordure. Ce motif est idéal pour la décoration de portes et de lambris verticaux. L'entrelacs occupe la partie centrale et inférieure d'un large panneau rectangulaire ; il conviendra toutefois de trouver une solution appropriée pour les angles et de donner des formes variables aux raccords. Des motifs de ce type peuvent être réalisés en noir ou dans une autre couleur foncée. L'effet de marqueterie obtenu est très raffiné.

Panel with lotus blossoms and spiral tendrils
Paneel mit Lotusblüten und Spiralranken
Panneau à fleurs de lotus et entrelacs en spirale

This design shows three long-stemmed lotus blossoms flanked by spiral tendrils. These latter are also decorated with lotus blossoms, which tend to push the tendrils themselves visually into the background. The tendril motif is loosely based on the Classical palmette and thus betrays Greek influences, while the lotus blossoms are characteristic of Egyptian art. The lotus-blossom motif was taken up again in the mid-19th-century pattern books of Owen Jones, and appears here in a highly original form.

This pattern is suitable not only for the decoration of panels, but thanks to its lightness of character can also be applied to large wall areas and other surfaces. Any color combination is possible, provided the chosen colors do not clash. If this pattern is executed on a small scale, both gold on a dark ground and black on gold would be good combinations.

Dieser Entwurf zeigt drei langstielige Lotusblüten, die von Spiralranken flankiert werden. Diese sind zusätzlich mit Lotusblüten verziert, wodurch das Rankenmotiv zunehmend in den Hintergrund tritt. Während sich die Ranken formal von den antiken Palmetten ableiten und daher einen griechischen Einfluss erkennen lassen, verweisen die Lotusblumen auf die ägyptische Kunst. Das Motiv der Lotusblüte wurde Mitte des 19. Jahrhunderts durch die Vorlagenbücher von Owen Jones wieder aufgenommen und wird hier in einem höchst originellen Entwurf vorgestellt.

Das vorliegende Muster eignet sich nicht nur für die Verzierung von Paneelen, sondern kann aufgrund seines leichten Charakters auch auf große Wandbereiche und sonstige Flächen übertragen werden. Jede Farbkombination ist möglich, solange die gewählten Farbtöne miteinander harmonieren. Wird dieses Muster in einem kleinen Maßstab ausgeführt, überzeugt sowohl Gold auf einem dunklem Grund als auch Schwarz auf Gold.

Cette planche présente trois fleurs de lotus à longues tiges, flanquées d'entrelacs en spirale. Les fleurs de lotus qui ornent l'entrelacs font passer celui-ci au second plan. Si les entrelacs dérivent par leur forme des palmettes antiques et révèlent une influence grecque, les fleurs de lotus se réfèrent à l'art égyptien. Le motif de la fleur de lotus a été repris au milieu du XIXᵉ siècle dans les ouvrages de modèles d'Owen Jones et il est présenté ici dans une esquisse très originale.

Ce motif servira non seulement à décorer des panneaux, mais pourra aussi être transposé sur de grands murs et d'autres surfaces en raison de sa légèreté. Toutes les combinaisons de couleurs sont possibles, dans la mesure où les tons choisis sont harmonieux. Si ce motif est réalisé à échelle réduite, le doré sur fond sombre et le noir sur fond doré seront du plus bel effet.

Vertical bands with stylized palmettes and lotus-blossoms
Vertikale Bänder mit stilisierten Palmetten- und Lotusblüten
Bandeaux verticaux à palmettes et fleurs de lotus stylisées

Here we see two examples of tendril motifs. The ornamental band on the left is edged on the left by a border of stars, which is separated from the main part of the design by a black line. Parallel to this is a robust stem, from whose right-hand side sprout spiral tendrils, each enclosing a small rosette. Between the spiral tendrils are shorter shoots ending in a design formally reminiscent of the Greek lily. In contrast to this dynamic composition, the pattern on the right is highly static. It is based on a central stem, from which lotus blossoms sprout symmetrically. The design is edged on the right by a narrow rosette border separated from the main pattern by a thick black line. Both patterns are suitable as ornamentation for vertical bands and for panels or pilasters. The design on the left can also be used for horizontal bands. By reflecting it about the main stem, this pattern can be doubled in breadth, in which case the star border must either be omitted or itself doubled.

Auf vorliegender Tafel sind zwei Beispiele von Ranken wiedergegeben. Das Ornamentband links wird an seinem linken Rand von einem Sternenband begrenzt. Es folgt eine schwarze Borte, an die sich ein kräftiger Zentralstamm anschließt, von dessen rechter Seite sich spiralförmig Ranken abspalten, die sich ihrerseits um eine kleine Rosette winden. Man erkennt Blatt- und Blütengebilde, die formal von der griechischen Lilie abgeleitet sind. Das rechte Muster wirkt hingegen sehr statisch. Es basiert auf einem Zentralstamm, von dem sich achsensymmetrisch Lotusblüten abspalten. Am rechten Rand wird die Komposition von einem schmalen Band mit gezackten Rosetten begrenzt.
Beide Muster eignen sich als Zierde vertikaler Bänder sowie für Paneele oder Pilaster. Das Muster links lässt sich auch als horizontales Band verwenden. Durch Spiegelung entlang dem Rankenstängel kann dieses Muster auch auf die doppelte Breite erweitert werden, wobei der Streifen mit den Sternen entweder verdoppelt oder ganz fortgelassen werden muss.

Cette planche présente deux exemples d'entrelacs. Le bandeau ornemental de gauche est limité sur son bord gauche par une bande d'étoiles, suivie d'un galon noir, puis d'une épaisse branche centrale donnant naissance sur le côté droit à des entrelacs en spirale qui, à leur tour, s'enroulent autour d'une petite rosace. On reconnaît des feuilles et des fleurs qui, par leur forme, sont dérivées du lis grec. Le motif de droite est par contre très statique. Il se base sur une branche centrale avec des fleurs de lotus disposées de façon symétrique de chaque côté de l'axe. La composition se termine sur le bord droit par un étroit bandeau de rosaces dentelées.
Les deux motifs serviront à décorer des bandeaux verticaux, ainsi que des panneaux ou des pilastres. Le motif de gauche servira aussi de bandeau horizontal. Il est possible de réaliser ce motif sur une double largeur en inversant l'image le long de la tige de l'entrelacs ; dans ce cas, il faudra doubler la bande d'étoiles ou l'abandonner totalement.

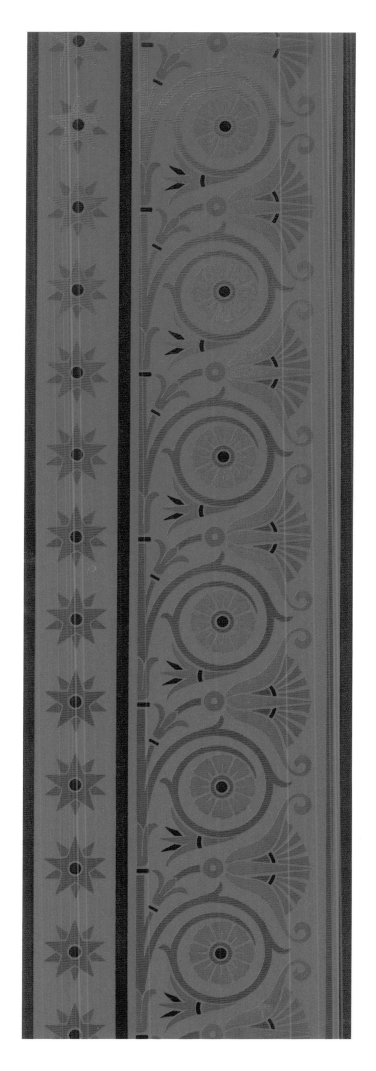

Rosettes
Rosetten
Rosaces

This plate shows six different types of rosette. These patterns are suitable for small round panels or coffers, and also as the central motifs of large, complicated compositions. Repeated at regular intervals, they can also be used to decorate vertical or horizontal fascias.
The rosettes can be executed in a single color. Polychrome versions, for example using gold, are also entirely possible, as taste dictates.

Diese Tafel zeigt sechs verschiedene Typen von Rosetten. Diese Muster eignen sich als Zierde kleiner runder Vertäfelungen und Kassetten sowie als Zentralmotive großer, komplizierter Kompositionen. In regelmäßigen Abständen wiederholt, können sie auch als Dekor horizontaler oder vertikaler Faszien dienen.
Man kann die Rosetten in einer einzigen Farbe ausführen. Es ist aber auch eine mehrfarbige Ausführung, zum Beispiel in Gold, möglich, die ganz individuell gewählt werden kann.

Cette planche présente six types de rosaces différents. Ces motifs décoreront de petits lambris ou caissons ronds et serviront de motifs centraux dans de grandes compositions compliquées. Répétés à intervalles réguliers, ils pourront aussi décorer des fasces horizontales ou verticales.
Les rosaces pourront être monochromes, mais une exécution dans plusieurs couleurs choisies individuellement est aussi possible, par exemple en doré.

Large-format palmette designs for square coffers or panels
Großflächiger Palmettendekor für quadratische Kassetten, Täfelungen oder Paneele
Grand décor de palmettes pour caissons carrés, lambris ou panneaux

The pattern at the top shows a central rosette enclosed in concentric zigzag polygons, while the remainder of the field is occupied by other vegetal motifs. The corners are occupied by triplets of lotus-blossoms, betraying an Egyptian influence probably due to an Owen Jones pattern-book. Between the lotus-blossoms can be seen variations of the Classical acanthus, reminiscent of the acroterion decorations of Classical pediments. The pattern below is a variation of the same motif. The lines here are more elegantly curved, the acanthus leaf more strongly stylized, and the lotus-blossoms more dominant.

The two patterns are suitable for the decoration of square coffers and ceilings or panels. They are shown here in gold on a dark background, but any other color scheme would be possible.

Das Muster oben zeigt eine zentrale Rosette, umgeben von einem zackigen Kranz, an den sich rundherum weitere vegetabile Motive anschließen. In den Ecken sind langstielige Lotusblüten zu sehen, die einen ägyptischen Einfluss erkennen lassen, der vermutlich auf Vorlagen von Owen Jones zurückzuführen ist. Zwischen den Lotusblüten sieht man Varianten des antiken Akanthus, die formal an Verzierungen antiker Tempelgiebel (Akroterion) erinnern. Das Muster unten bildet eine Variante desselben Motivs. Die Linien sind hier eleganter geschwungen, das Akanthusblatt ist stärker stilisiert und die Lotusblüten werden zum bestimmenden Motiv.

Beide Muster sind zur Verzierung von quadratischen Kassetten und Zimmerdecken oder Täfelungen bestimmt. Sie sind hier in Gold auf dunklem Grund gezeichnet, aber auch jede andere Farbwahl ist möglich.

Le motif du haut présente une rosace centrale entourée d'une couronne dentelée, autour de laquelle d'autres motifs végétaux sont disposés. Les angles sont occupés par des fleurs de lotus aux longues tiges qui révèlent une influence égyptienne probablement empruntée aux modèles d'Owen Jones. Entre les fleurs de lotus, on voit des variantes de l'acanthe antique qui rappellent par leur forme des décors de frontons de temples (acrotère). Le motif du bas présente une variante du même thème. Les lignes sont incurvées ici de façon plus élégante, la feuille d'acanthe est davantage stylisée et les fleurs de lotus deviennent le motif prédominant.

Les deux motifs serviront à décorer des caissons et des plafonds carrés ou des lambris. Ils sont représentés ici en doré sur fond sombre, mais toute autre combinaison de couleurs est également possible.

Stylized palmette decor for octagonal coffers or panels
Stilisierter Palmettendekor für achteckige Kassetten oder Paneele
Palmettes stylisées pour caissons octogonaux ou panneaux

These two patterns for octagonal coffers are based on a garland of palmettes around a central rosette. While the palmettes in the top design evince two forms of stylization, in the bottom pattern they are barely recognizable as such and have become purely ornamental devices to fill the spaces between the highly stylized tendrils which dominate the design. These patterns are suitable for the ornamentation of octagonal coffers or panels on ceilings, or for panels in any position. They can also be used for the central portions of rectangular, octagonal or round ceilings. The diagonally bisected squares inserted between the large octagons are decorated with stylized palmettes which are appropriate for a large number of ornamental purposes. Although the illustrations depict an elaborate polychrome color scheme, these patterns lose nothing by being executed in a reticent monochrome version – light on dark or dark on light. Gold on a dark ground, as on page 193, also has a highly pleasing esthetic effect.

Die beiden Muster der achteckigen Kassetten basieren auf einem Palmettenband, das kranz-förmig um eine zentrale Rosette gelegt ist. Während die Palmetten beim oberen Muster zwei Stilisierungsformen aufweisen, sind sie beim unteren Motiv rein ornamental aufgelöst. Sie treten dort nur noch als Füllformen der stark stilisierten Spiralranke in Erscheinung, die den Aufbau des Musters bestimmt. Diese Muster eignen sich zur Verzierung acht-eckiger Kassetten oder Täfelungen an Zim-merdecken sowie für Paneele in beliebiger Position. Sie können aber auch als Mittel-stücke rechteckiger, achteckiger oder runder Decken verwendet werden. Die halbierten Quadrate, die sich seitlich zwischen die großen Achtecke schieben, werden von stili-sierten Palmetten geziert, die sich als Dekor für die unterschiedlichsten Zwecke anbieten. Obwohl die Abbildungen eine aufwändige, mehrfarbige Variante veranschaulichen, lassen sich diese Muster auch in einer zurückhalten-den, einfarbigen Gestaltung überzeugend anwenden – hell auf dunkel oder dunkel auf hell. Auch Gold auf dunklem Grund, wie auf Seite 193 dargestellt, hat eine ausgesprochen angenehme Wirkung.

Les deux motifs de caissons octogonaux se basent sur un bandeau de palmettes disposé en couronne autour d'une rosace centrale. Si les palmettes du motif supérieur présentent deux formes de stylisations, elles sont par contre disposées de façon purement ornementale dans le motif du bas. Elles ne jouent ici que le rôle de raccords entre les entrelacs très stylisés qui déterminent la composition du motif. Ces motifs serviront à décorer des caissons octogonaux ou lambris de plafonds, ainsi que des panneaux dans n'importe quelle position. On peut toutefois les utiliser aussi comme rac-cords pour des plafonds rectangulaires, octo-gonaux ou ronds. Les demi-carrés qui s'insèrent latéralement entre les grands octo-gones sont ornés de palmettes stylisées qui conviendront aux applications les plus di-verses. Même si les illustrations présentent une variante riche en couleurs, ces motifs seront aussi du plus bel effet en une seule teinte discrète – claire sur fond sombre ou foncée sur fond clair. La réalisation en doré sur fond sombre, telle que la présente la page 193, est très attrayante.

Corner ornamentation with palmette decor
Eckverzierungen mit Palmettendekor
Décors d'angles à palmettes

These two designs show palmettes suitable for corner decorations of panels, wall surfaces and coffers. In the case of large panels, these motifs should be repeated in all four corners; smaller panels should by contrast only be decorated in the upper corners, for example in combination with the palmette motifs illustrated on page 183. These patterns can be executed in monochrome or polychrome.

Diese zwei Entwürfe zeigen Palmetten, die sich als Eckverzierung von Paneelen, Wandflächen und Kassetten eignen. Bei großen Paneelen sollten diese Motive an allen vier Ecken wiederholt werden, bei kleineren hingegen nur die oberen Ecken zieren, zum Beispiel in Verbindung mit den Palmettenmotiven auf Seite 183. Diese Muster können ein- oder mehrfarbig gestaltet werden.

Ces deux esquisses montrent des palmettes idéales pour la décoration d'angles de panneaux, murs et caissons. Si les panneaux sont de grande taille, il conviendra de répéter ces motifs aux quatre angles; mais s'ils sont petits, on ne décorera que les angles supérieurs, en association avec les palmettes à la page 183, par exemple. Ces motifs sont réalisables en une ou plusieurs couleurs.

Corner ornamentation with palmette decor
Eckverzierungen mit Palmettendekor
Décors d'angles à palmettes

This plate too shows palmettes as corner decorations. In the lower design, a part of a rosette is used in the lower right-hand corner, its appearance reminiscent of a palmette. These motifs are suitable as decorations for panels, wall surfaces and coffers, and can be executed in monochrome or polychrome.

Auch diese Tafel zeigt Palmetten als Eckornamente. Beim unteren Entwurf wird rechts unten ein Teil einer Rosette verwendet, deren Aussehen formal an eine Palmette erinnert. Diese Motive eignen sich als Dekor von Paneelen, Wandflächen und Kassetten und können ein- oder mehrfarbig ausgeführt werden.

Cette planche présente aussi des palmettes en guise ornements d'angles. Dans le motif du bas, une portion de rosace dont la forme rappelle une palmette est utilisée dans l'angle à droite. Ces motifs décoreront des panneaux, murs et caissons et pourront être réalisés dans une ou plusieurs couleurs.

Wall decorations with stylized palmettes and lotus blossoms
Wanddekorationen mit stilisierten Palmetten und Lotusblüten
Décorations murales à palmettes et fleurs de lotus stylisées

Both designs illustrated here show richly ornamented bands which are broad enough to be used as wall decorations in their own right. While the design at the top is dominated by stylized lilies, that at the bottom is characterized by long-stemmed lotus blossoms, which are presumably derived from an Owen Jones pattern-book.

These ornamental bands can be applied above a dark, patterned or monochrome base zone. They can if desired be separated from the base zone by an eye-catching strip of some kind. These designs can reach a breadth of more than a meter, and for especially high walls the scale can be increased accordingly. There are numerous possibilities of color schemes which would work well.

Beide Entwürfe dieser Abbildung zeigen reich ornamentierte Bänder, die so breit sind, dass sie geradezu zu eigenständigen Wandmustern werden. Während beim oberen Muster stilisierte Lilien die Komposition bestimmen, treten unten langstielige Lotusblüten an ihre Stelle, die vermutlich auf Vorlagen von Owen Jones zurückzuführen sind.

Die Ornamentbänder können oberhalb einer dunklen, einfarbigen oder gemusterten Sockelzone aufgetragen werden. Man kann sie von der Sockelzone auch durch eine Randleiste oder einen anderen markanten Streifen trennen. Diese Ornamentbänder können eine Breite von über einem Meter erreichen und ihr Maßstab kann bei besonders hohen Wänden entsprechend vergrößert werden. Farblich bieten sich viele verschiedene Gestaltungsmöglichkeiten an.

Les deux esquisses de cette planche présentent des bandeaux richement ornés, si larges qu'ils deviennent simplement des décors muraux à eux seuls. Si des lis stylisés composent le motif du haut, des fleurs de lotus à longue tige probablement empruntées aux modèles d'Owen Jones les remplacent par contre dans le motif du bas.

Ces bandeaux ornementaux se placeront au-dessus d'un soubassement sombre monochrome ou à motifs. On pourra les séparer du soubassement à l'aide d'une bordure ou d'une autre bande distincte. Ils pourront avoir plus d'un mètre de large et on les agrandira pour les adapter à des murs particulièrement hauts. De nombreuses combinaisons de couleurs différentes sont possibles.

Diaper decoration using fret and scroll motifs
Flächendekoration mit Rankendekor und Mäandern
Décoration de surfaces avec des entrelacs et des méandres

The design illustrated here is suited exclusively to the decoration of large wall areas, and is thus reminiscent of wallpaper patterns. The design is based on a tessellation of flattened octagons and small squares. While the octagons are decorated with elaborate scroll motifs, the squares have fret patterns.
If this design is executed in a medium tone on a light ground, it can be used to cover the whole surface of the wall. In the colors illustrated here, by contrast, it is more suitable for decorating a base zone. More elaborate color schemes can however be worked out for this pattern.

Das hier abgebildete Muster ist ausschließlich als Zierde von großen Wandflächen geeignet und erinnert daher an ein Tapetenmuster.
Der Entwurf basiert auf gedrungenen Achtecken, die mit prächtigen Ranken ausgeschmückt sind. Als Füllformen werden Quadrate verwendet, die mit vier Mäandern ausgefüllt sind.
Führt man dieses Muster in einem mittelkräftigen Farbton auf hellem Grund aus, so darf es die gesamte Wandfläche einnehmen. In der hier gezeigten Farbgebung eignet es sich hingegen vornehmlich zur Verzierung von Sockelzonen. Es lassen sich aber auch aufwändigere Kolorierungen für diesen Entwurf entwickeln.

Le motif illustré ici sert exclusivement à décorer de grands murs et rappelle donc un motif de tapisserie. L'esquisse se base sur des octogones trapus, ornés de somptueux entrelacs. Des carrés composés de quatre méandres garniront les espaces entre les motifs.
Si on choisit une teinte moyenne sur fond clair, le motif pourra occuper toute la surface du mur. Dans la combinaison de couleurs présentée ici, il est par contre idéal pour décorer des soubassements. Une réalisation dans des couleurs plus riches est, bien sûr, possible.

Japanese Style
Japanischer Stil
Le style japonais

In contrast to almost all the other motifs presented in this book, the ornamental designs summarized in this section are derived not from architecture but from crafts. This can be explained on the one hand by the particularities of Japanese architecture, which is fundamentally different from the architecture of Europe. The other reason is that the Audsleys had no examples of Japanese buildings to go by, which

Die hier zusammengefassten Ornamententwürfe sind im Unterschied zu fast allen anderen gezeigten Motiven nicht von der Architektur, sondern vom Kunstgewerbe beeinflusst. Dies erklärt sich einerseits aus den spezifischen Besonderheiten der japanischen Architektur, die sich grundlegend von der europäischen unterscheidet. Andererseits fehlte es den Audsleys jedoch auch an gebauten Anschauungsobjekten und damit

Contrairement à presque tous les autres motifs présentés, ce n'est pas l'architecture qui exerce une influence sur les motifs ornementaux rassemblés ici, mais bien les arts décoratifs. Cela tient en partie aux particularités de l'architecture japonaise qui se distingue fondamentalement de l'architecture européenne. Par ailleurs, les Audsley ne disposaient pas d'édifice de référence, ni par

Garden Landscape with Couple Making Music, detail of a painted Japanese screen, Burke Collection, New York, 17th century (Edo period)
This screen depicts a garden landscape with little rivers and lakes, where an angler is casting his line. The various parts of the garden are linked by bridges. In the top left quarter, a traditional building on stilts can be seen; its open sliding doors allow a glimpse into the interior, where a couple in tender embrace are playing a koto, the traditional stringed instrument of Japan. The reductionist formal language is characteristic of Japanese art.

Gartenlandschaft mit musizierendem Paar, Ausschnitt aus einem bemalten japanischen Wandschirm, Burke Collection, New York, 17. Jh. (Edo- oder Tokugawa-Zeit)
Auf diesem Wandschirm ist eine Gartenlandschaft mit kleinen Flüssen und Seen dargestellt, in die ein Mann seine Angel zum Fischen auswirft. Eine Brücke verbindet die einzelnen Bereiche des Gartens miteinander. In der linken oberen Bildhälfte sieht man einen traditionellen, auf Pfosten stehenden Ständerbau, dessen offene Schiebetüren den Blick in das Innere freigeben, wo ein Paar in zärtlicher Umarmung auf einer Koto, dem traditionellen japanischen Saiteninstrument, spielt. Die reduzierte Formensprache ist kennzeichnend für die japanische Kunst.

Paysage de jardin avec couple jouant de la musique, panneau de paravent japonais peint, collection Burke, New York, XVIIe siècle (époque Edo ou Tokugawa)
Ce paravent représente un paysage de jardin avec de petits cours d'eau et lacs dans lesquels un homme pêche au lancer. Un pont relie les différentes parties du jardin. Dans la moitié supérieure gauche de l'illustration, on voit une maison traditionnelle sur pilotis dont les portes coulissantes ouvertes permettent d'apercevoir un intérieur où un couple tendrement enlacé joue du koto, l'instrument à cordes traditionnel du Japon. Le langage réduit des formes est caractéristique de l'art japonais.

also deprived them of any field of application for their designs. The characteristic Japanese house was a raised wooden building placed, if space allowed, in the middle of a garden in which there would be streams and ponds. Like the garden, the living area, raised on piers, is asymmetric in plan, and, by virtue of sliding doors, variable in its allocation of space to the various rooms, which are lit by windows and sliding doors in the outer wall. In place of glass, these are fitted with translucent paper. As the sliding doors can be easily removed, the boundary between interior and garden is not fixed, and as a result the living space is experienced as a close-to-nature, continually changing environment in which

zugleich an Einsatzgebieten für ihre Ornamente.
Der charakteristischste Bautypus in der japanischen Wohnkultur ist der aus Holz errichtete Ständerbau, der traditionell – und bei entsprechenden räumlichen Gegebenheiten – inmitten eines Gartens angelegt wurde, der von Flüssen und kleinen Teichen durchzogen war. Der auf Pfeilern errichtete Wohnkomplex hat ähnlich wie der Garten einen asymmetrischen Grundriss und erlaubt mittels Schiebetüren das kurzfristige Herstellen von variablen Raumeinheiten. Diese erhalten ihr Licht durch Fenster und Schiebetüren in der Außenwand, die mit lichtdurchlässigem Papier bespannt sind. Da sich diese Schiebetüren leicht entfernen lassen, ist die

conséquent de domaine d'application pour leurs ornementations.
La construction typique de l'habitat japonais est la maison en bois sur pilotis installée par tradition – et selon l'espace disponible – au milieu d'un jardin traversé par des cours d'eau et parsemé de petits étangs. Tout comme le jardin, la maison sur pilotis a un plan asymétrique et permet de créer rapidement des pièces de superficie variable grâce à des portes coulissantes. Ces pièces reçoivent la lumière du jour à travers des fenêtres et portes coulissant dans le mur extérieur, tendues de papier diaphane. Comme ces portes sont escamotables, la frontière entre l'intérieur et le jardin s'estompe et la surface habitable est vécue

Japanese house with view of garden, Kyoto, late-19th century
Instead of solid walls, the traditional Japanese house has sliding doors of translucent paper. As these doors can be easily removed, the boundary between inside and outside is fluid, and thus the living quarters are experienced as a natural environment subject to constant change, in which man is at one with nature.

Japanisches Wohnhaus mit Blick in den Garten, Kyoto, spätes 19. Jh.
Das traditionelle japanische Wohnhaus besitzt anstelle von massiven Wänden leicht zu entfernende Schiebetüren, die mit lichtdurchlässigem Papier bespannt sind. Die Grenze zwischen Wohnung und Umwelt wird fließend, der Mensch steht der Natur sehr nahe.

Maison japonaise avec vue sur le jardin, Kyoto, fin du XIXe siècle
La maison japonaise traditionnelle possédait des portes coulissantes tendues de papier translucide à la place de murs massifs. Comme ces portes s'escamotent facilement, la frontière entre l'espace habitable et l'environnement est fluctuante, de sorte que l'homme est très proche de la nature.

Man and nature are in harmony. Even the room for the tea ceremony, so important to Japanese culture, is understood not as a place of habitation, but as a vision of an unspoiled nature independent of human beings.

Japanese building tradition has nothing comparable with the architectural decoration found in Europe. Murals were not usual, and the paper doors and walls were decorated at most with a decorative hanging, also of paper, known as a "kakemono". The architecture was unfussy and functional, and the furnishings sparse. It was customary to sit and sleep on mats of rice-straw and thus to dispense with bulky items of furniture. Often the only decorations in the room were a Buddhist altar with a niche for a picture, a flower arrangement or a small writing desk, a bookshelf and a piece of furniture resembling what in Europe might be called a what-not. These objects were frequently commissioned from craftsmen.

Grenze zwischen Innenraum und Garten fließend und so wird der Wohnraum als naturnahe, sich ständig wandelnde Umwelt erfahren, in der der Mensch mit der Natur im Einklang steht. Selbst der für die japanische Kultur so bedeutende Teeraum für die Teezeremonie wird nicht als ein Lebensraum, sondern als Vision einer vom Menschen unabhängigen, intakten Natur verstanden.

Einen der europäischen Architektur vergleichbaren Baudekor kennt die japanische Bautradition nicht. Wandmalereien waren nicht üblich und die mit Papier bespannten Schiebetüren und Wände der Häuser wurden allenfalls von einem ebenfalls aus Papier gefertigten dekorativen Wandbehang („Kakemono") geziert. Die Architektur war klar und sachlich und das Mobiliar karg, da man meist auf Reisstrohmatten saß und schlief und somit auf sperrige Einrichtungsgegenstände verzichtete. Einzige Zierde des Raumes waren oftmals ein buddhistischer

comme un environnement naturel, en constante évolution, dans lequel l'homme est en harmonie avec la nature. Le salon lui-même, si important dans la culture japonaise pour la cérémonie du thé, n'est pas conçu comme un espace vital, mais comme le reflet d'une nature intacte, indépendante de l'homme.

La tradition architecturale japonaise ne connaît pas de décor comparable à celui de l'architecture européenne. Les peintures murales n'étaient pas courantes : les portes coulissantes et murs des maisons tendus de papier étaient tout au plus décorés d'une tapisserie ornementale (« Kakemono »), en papier également. L'architecture était sobre, sans fioriture et le mobilier rare, car on s'asseyait et dormait le plus souvent sur des nattes en paille de riz et renonçait ainsi aux objets d'ameublement encombrants. La seule décoration de la pièce était souvent un autel bouddhiste et une niche cultuelle, une composition florale ou un petit bureau, une planche à livres et une étagère. Ces objets étaient souvent commandés à des artisans d'art.

Les arts décoratifs ont de tout temps été très prisés au Japon. Peintres et artisans d'art étaient au service du clergé, de la noblesse de cour et féodale et, depuis le XVIIᵉ siècle, de la riche bourgeoisie. Ils se trouvaient sous la protection personnelle d'un mentor dont ils dépendaient, mais dont ils recevaient aussi les encouragements. Comme les peintres fournissaient souvent les esquisses de décors pour des céramiques et porcelaines, des laques et motifs pour des textiles, une coopération fructueuse s'instaura entre les « designers » et les artisans d'art. Voulant, à la fin du XIXᵉ siècle, réunir l'art et les arts décoratifs, les réformateurs du mouvement anglais Arts-and-Crafts, de l'art nouveau français et du Jugendstil en Allemagne et en Autriche se réclamèrent du lien étroit entre la création intellectuelle et les réalisations artisanales qui existaient au Japon. Il n'est donc pas surprenant que les Audsley se soient aussi intéressés à l'art japonais et qu'ils aient publié, en plus de leurs esquisses ornemen-

Crafts had always enjoyed a position of great esteem in Japan. Painters and craftsmen were employed by the priests, the court and the nobility, and since the 17th century by the wealthy urban class as well. They were under the personal protection of a patron, on whom they were, it is true, dependent, but by whom they were supported. As painters often supplied the designs for pottery and porcelain decoration, lacquer work and textile patterns, there was fruitful collaboration between designers and craftsmen.

These close links between intellectual creativity and craft production in Japan provided a model for European esthetic reformers of the late 19th century, such as the Arts-and-Crafts movement in England, and the exponents of Art Nouveau on the European continent, who were trying to reunite art and craftsmanship. It need not surprise us, therefore, that the Audsleys concerned themselves with Japanese art, and alongside their ornamental designs in the Japanese style, published various books on Japanese crafts, in particular Japanese porcelain.

Their "Japanese style" ornamental designs are inspired by Japanese craft patterns, for example porcelain vessels, plates and wall decorations. Japanese porcelain was not of significance until the beginning of the 17th century, when kaolin or china clay, which is important in porcelain manufacture, was discovered in Japan. Previously the Japanese had either imported their kaolin from China – particularly as China had possessed a trade monopoly for porcelain, the "white gold", since the 9th century – or else they had done without it and used lacquer utensils instead. Lacquer, the sap of the lacquer or varnish tree, has the property of forming, after a long drying period, a waterproof and heatproof protective layer, which can be chiseled, painted and inlaid with mother-of-pearl. In Japan, lacquerwork was a craft in its own right. For a long time therefore, porcelain did not enjoy the importance it had in neighboring China. Nonetheless, the Japanese

Altar mit einer Bildnische, ein Blumengesteck oder ein kleiner Schreibtisch, ein Bücherregal und eine Etagere. Diese Gegenstände wurden häufig bei Kunsthandwerkern in Auftrag gegeben.

Das Kunstgewerbe erfreute sich in Japan seit jeher hoher Wertschätzung. Maler und Kunsthandwerker standen im Dienst des Klerus, des Hof- und Feudaladels und seit dem 17. Jahrhundert auch des reichen Bürgertums. Sie standen unter dem persönlichen Schutz eines Patrons, von dem sie zwar abhängig waren, durch den sie aber auch gefördert wurden. Da Maler häufig auch die Entwürfe für Keramik- und Porzellandekore, Lackarbeiten und Textilmuster lieferten, kam es zu einer fruchtbaren Zusammenarbeit von „Designern" und Kunsthandwerkern.

Auf die enge Verbindung von geistiger Schöpfung und handwerklicher Ausführung in Japan sollten sich Ende des 19. Jahrhunderts die Reformer der englischen Arts-and-Crafts-Bewegung, des französischen Art Nouveau und des Jugendstils in Deutschland und Österreich berufen, als sie Kunst und Handwerk wieder zusammenführen wollten. Es überrascht daher nicht, dass sich auch die Audsleys mit der japanischen Kunst beschäftigten und neben ihren Ornamententwürfen des japanischen Stils verschiedene Bücher zum japanischen Kunstgewerbe, insbesondere zum japanischen Porzellan veröffentlichten. Ihre Ornamententwürfe des „Japanischen Stils" sind von Vorlagen des japanischen Kunstgewerbes inspiriert, etwa von Porzellangefäßen, -tellern und Wandbehängen. Das japanische Porzellan erlangte erst Anfang des 17. Jahrhunderts Bedeutung, als die für die Porzellanherstellung wichtige Kaolin-Erde auch in Japan entdeckt wurde. Zuvor hatte man sich chinesischen Import-Porzellans bedient – zumal China seit dem 9. Jahrhundert das Handelsmonopol auf das „weiße Gold", das Porzellan, besaß – oder man verwendete Lackgefäße. Der aus dem Lackbaum gewonnene Lacksaft hat die Eigenschaft, nach langem Trocknen eine wasser- und hitzebestän-

tales de style japonais, divers ouvrages sur les arts décoratifs japonais, notamment la porcelaine.

Leurs esquisses ornementales de « style japonais » sont inspirées de modèles des arts décoratifs japonais, par exemple des récipients et assiettes en porcelaine et des tapisseries. La porcelaine japonaise n'a suscité de l'intérêt qu'au début du XVIIᵉ siècle, époque où le kaolin, si précieux pour la fabrication de la porcelaine, fut découvert aussi au Japon. On se servait auparavant de la porcelaine importée de Chine – d'autant plus que la Chine détenait depuis le IXᵉ siècle le monopole commercial de « l'or blanc », la porcelaine – ou de récipients émaillés. La gomme-résine extraite du sumac a la particularité de former, après une longue période de séchage, une couche protectrice imperméable et résistante à la chaleur, qui peut être peinte, ciselée et sertie de perles ; cette fabrication d'émaille a contribué à l'éclosion d'un art décoratif spécifique au

Futon cover with chrysanthemums, cotton, Jeffrey Montgomery Collection, Lugano, late-19th/early-20th century
The traditional Japanese bed, or futon, was normally decorated with a colorful patterned cover. The one illustrated here shows chrysanthemums on an indigo background. The Audsleys chose a similar pattern for their Japanese designs (see pages 221 and 229), but their flowers are more heavily stylized.

Futonüberwurf mit Chrysanthemen, Baumwolle, Sammlung Jeffrey Montgomery, Lugano, spätes 19./frühes 20. Jh.
Das traditionelle japanische Bett, der Futon, wurde gewöhnlich von einer bunt gemusterten Decke geziert. Der hier abgebildete Überwurf zeigt Chrysanthemen auf indigofarbenem Grund. Ein ähnliches Chrysanthemenmotiv wählten die Audsleys für einige ihrer Entwürfe des japanischen Stils (siehe Seite 221 und 229), wobei sie die Blüten jedoch stärker stilisierten.

Housse de futon à chrysanthèmes, coton, collection Jeffrey Montgomery, Lugano, fin du XIXᵉ/début du XXᵉ siècle
Le lit japonais traditionnel, le futon, était en général agrémenté d'une housse à motifs multicolores. La housse illustrée ici présente un motif de chrysanthèmes sur fond indigo. Les Audsley choisirent un modèle similaire pour quelques-unes de leurs esquisses, où les fleurs sont cependant davantage stylisées (voir pages 221 et 229).

porcelain trade quickly caught up, and from 1659 supplied the Dutch East India Company, which had a base in Nagasaki, with export wares destined for the European market. The small motifs, scattered irregularly over a white ground, which characterize Japanese Imari ware, were soon so popular that they were even imitated in Chantilly and Meissen.

As the Audsleys were also collectors of Japanese porcelain, it comes as no surprise to learn that they were inspired by the formal idiom of these patterns when designing their own ornamental motifs. They seized on the geometric and vegetal motifs of the Japanese porcelain, and enlarged them many times over for their own designs. It was a successful experiment, even though it is not always easy to find a fitting frame for these dominant ornaments. They come across to best effect in large rooms and festive halls whose interior decoration is basically oriental. This is particularly true of designs executed in gold on a dark ground, for example the fret patterns on pages 211 and 213, and the stylized leaves and rosettes on page 221 – a design whose coloration is reminiscent of

dige Schutzschicht zu bilden, die bemalt, ziseliert und mit Perlmutt-einlagen versehen werden kann und in Japan zum Aufblühen eines eigenen Kunstgewerbes beigetragen hat. Das Porzellan hatte daher lange Zeit nicht die Bedeutung wie im benachbarten China. Trotzdem holte der japanische Handel schnell auf und belieferte ab 1659 die in Nagasaki ansässige niederländische Ost-indien-Kompanie mit Exportware für den europäischen Markt. Die auf weißem Grund stehenden, kleinteiligen und unregelmäßig über die Fläche verteilten Dekore des japanischen Imari-Porzellans erfreuten sich bald solcher Beliebtheit, dass sie sogar in Meißen und Chantilly nachgeahmt wurden.

Da auch die Audsleys Sammler japanischen Porzellans waren, überrascht es nicht, dass sie sich von der Formensprache dieser Muster in ihren Ornamententwürfen anregen ließen. Sie griffen die geometrischen und vegetabilen Ornamente des japanischen Porzellans heraus und vergrößerten sie für ihre Ornamententwürfe um ein Vielfaches – ein gelungenes Experiment, wenngleich es nicht immer leicht fällt, für diese dominanten Ornamente den geeigneten Rahmen zu finden.

Japon. Pendant longtemps, la porcelaine n'a donc pas eu la même importance que dans la Chine voisine. Le commerce japonais connut toutefois une reprise rapide et fournit, à partir de 1659 à la compagnie hollandaise des Indes orientales établie à Nagasaki, des marchandises d'exportation destinées au marché européen. Les décors sur fond blanc de la porcelaine japonaise Imari, de petit format et irrégulièrement répartis, remportèrent un tel succès qu'ils furent bientôt imités à Meißen et à Chantilly.

Comme les Audsley collectionnaient aussi la porcelaine japonaise, il n'est pas surprenant qu'ils se soient inspirés du langage des formes de ces motifs dans leurs esquisses ornementales. Ils reprirent les ornements géométriques et végétaux de la porcelaine japonaise et les agrandirent plusieurs fois pour leurs propres esquisses – une expérience réussie, même s'il n'est pas toujours facile de trouver le cadre approprié pour une utilisation prépondérante de ce genre d'ornements. Ils sont du plus bel effet dans les pièces spacieuses et les salles de réceptions dont l'intérieur est de style asiatique. C'est le cas

Bowl with chrysanthemum decor, Imari porcelain, National Museum, Tokyo, 17th century
This porcelain bowl is decorated with chrysanthemums, the emblem of Japanese emperors.

Schale mit Chrysanthemendekor, Imari-Porzellan, Nationalmuseum Tokio, 17. Jh.
Diese kostbare Porzellanschale wird von Chrysanthemen geziert, die als Symbol des japanischen Kaisers gelten.

Coupe avec décor de chrysanthèmes, porcelaine Imari, Musée national de Tokyo, XVIIᵉ siècle
Cette précieuse coupe en porcelaine est ornée de chrysanthèmes qui sont le symbole de l'empereur du Japon.

Plate, kutani porcelain, Hatakeyama Collection, Tokyo, mid-17th century
The central motif comprises a bunch of peonies and part of a belvedere whose floor is decorated with geometric ornaments. The Audsleys may well have been inspired by similar pieces for the designs illustrated on pages 213 and 227.

Porzellanteller, Kutani-Keramik, Sammlung Hatakeyama, Tokio, Mitte 17. Jh.
Als Zentralmotiv sieht man einen Pfingstrosenstrauch und den Ausschnitt einer Aussichtsplattform, deren Boden von geometrischen Ornamenten geziert wird. Ähnliche Muster dürften die Audsleys zu ihren Entwürfen auf Seite 213 und 227 inspiriert haben.

Assiette de porcelaine, céramique Kutani, collection Hatakeyama, Tokyo, milieu du XVIIᵉ siècle
Cette assiette a pour motif central un bouquet de pivoines et une plate-forme découpée dont le fond est décoré d'ornements géométriques. Des motifs similaires ont dû inspirer les Audsley pour leurs esquisses présentées aux pages 213 et 227.

Japanese lacquerwork, but in fact is derived from heraldic emblems. Other motifs taken from Japanese ornamental style, like those on pages 227 and 229, for example, show stylized chrysanthemums on a gold ground. These come across as very attractive, but they also have a strongly symbolic aspect: the stylized chrysanthemum – often found as a motif on Japanese porcelain – is the emblem of the Emperor of Japan.

Other ornaments, by contrast, like the purely vegetal patterns on a light ground – for example the bamboo, reed and rose motifs on pages 219, 223 and 225 – are also conceivable in small rooms. In general, the versatility of these exotic ornamental designs is surprising.

Besondere Wirkung entfalten sie in großen Räumen und festlichen Sälen, deren Interieur im asiatischen Stil gehalten ist. Dies gilt besonders für jene Ornamente, die in Gold auf dunklem Grund ausgeführt sind, wie zum Beispiel die Mäanderentwürfe auf den Seiten 211 und 213 und die stilisierten Blüten und Rosetten auf Seite 221 – ein Ornament, das hinsichtlich seiner Farbgebung an japanische Lackarbeiten erinnert, in Wirklichkeit jedoch von heraldischen Emblemen abgeleitet ist. Andere Motive des japanischen Ornamentstils, wie etwa auf den Seiten 227 und 229, zeigen stilisierte Chrysanthemen auf goldenem Grund. Diese wirken sehr lieblich, haben aber einen hohen Symbolwert: Die stilisierte Chrysantheme, die auch häufig als Dekor auf japanischem Porzellan zu finden ist, ist das Emblem des Kaisers von Japan. Andere Ornamente hingegen, wie zum Beispiel die rein vegetabilen Muster auf hellem Grund, zu denen die Bambus-, Schilf- und Rosendarstellungen auf den Seiten 219, 223 und 225 gehören, kann man sich auch in kleinen Räumen vorstellen. Insgesamt überrascht die vielseitige Verwendbarkeit dieser exotischen Ornamententwürfe.

notamment d'ornements réalisés en doré sur fond sombre, par exemple les motifs de méandres aux pages 211 et 213 et les fleurs et rosaces stylisées à la page 221 – qui rappellent les laques japonaises par leurs couleurs, mais qui dérivent en réalité d'emblèmes héraldiques. D'autres motifs du style ornemental japonais, par exemple aux pages 227 et 229, présentent des chrysanthèmes stylisés sur fond doré. Décoratifs à l'extrême, ceux-ci n'en ont pas moins une haute valeur symbolique : le chrysan-thème stylisé souvent représenté sur la porcelaine japonaise est l'emblème de l'empereur du Japon.
En revanche, d'autres ornements conviennent aussi à de petites pièces, tels que les motifs purement végétaux sur fond clair, auxquels appartiennent les représentations de bambous, roseaux et roses aux pages 219, 223 et 225. La variété d'applications de ces motifs ornementaux exotiques est pour le moins surprenante.

Lacquer chest, Freer Gallery of Art, Washington, late-16th century
This lacquer chest, decorated with gold particles and mother-of-pearl inlays, is notable for the exquisite reproduction of the flowers and grasses. The Audsleys were probably inspired by similar pieces for the designs illustrated on pages 219 and 225.

Lacktruhe, Freer Gallery of Art, Washington, spätes 16. Jh.
Bei dieser kostbaren mit Goldpartikeln und Perlmutteinlagen verzierten Lacktruhe besticht die feine Wiedergabe der Blumen und Gräser. Von ähnlichen Motiven ließen sich die Audsleys vermutlich zu ihren Motiven auf den Seiten 219 und 225 inspirieren.

Coffre laqué, Freer Gallery of Art, Washington, fin du XVIe siècle
Ce précieux coffre laqué décoré de particules d'or et d'incrustations de nacre séduit par la délicate reproduction de fleurs et d'herbes. Les Audsley se sont probablement inspirés de motifs similaires pour leurs propres motifs présentés aux pages 219 et 225.

Five fret designs
Fünf Mäanderentwürfe
Cinq motifs de méandres

A surprising feature of ornaments in the Japanese style is the use of the fret motif, which in Europe has always been associated with Classical Antiquity. But the fret is very widespread in Japanese culture and has always given rise to original designs. Here five fret designs are shown, of which the two at the bottom are combined with small semi-rosettes. This combination is unusual in European designs.
Any conceivable color scheme is possible for these designs; they can be executed in dark colors on a light ground or vice versa. Gold on black is particularly elegant.

Bei den Ornamenten des japanischen Stils überrascht die Verwendung des Mäandermusters, das in Europa seit jeher mit der Antike in Verbindung gebracht wird. Aber gerade das Mäandermuster ist in der japanischen Kultur weit verbreitet und hat immer wieder Anlass zu originellen Formschöpfungen gegeben. Hier werden fünf Mäanderentwürfe vorgestellt, von denen die beiden unteren eine Verbindung mit kleinen Halbrosetten eingehen. Eine solche Kombination ist für europäische Entwürfe eher ungewöhnlich.
Für diese Muster bietet sich jede denkbare Farbkombination an; sie können in dunklen Farben auf hellem Grund oder in hellen Farben auf dunklem Grund ausgeführt werden. Gold auf schwarzem Grund hat eine besonders edle Wirkung.

Ce qui surprend dans les ornements du style japonais, c'est l'utilisation du motif du méandre qu'on a de tout temps, en Europe, associé à l'Antiquité. Mais ce même motif de méandre est aussi très répandu dans la culture japonaise et a toujours donné lieu à des formes originales. Cette planche présente cinq motifs de méandres, dont les deux derniers sont associés à des demi-rosaces de petite taille. Cette composition est plutôt inhabituelle pour des motifs européens.
Toutes les combinaisons de couleurs imaginables conviennent pour ce motif ; ils peuvent être réalisés dans des couleurs sombres sur fond clair ou dans des couleurs claires sur fond sombre. Un motif doré sur un fond noir produira un effet particulièrement raffiné.

Diaper patterns using fret motifs
Tapetenmuster mit flächigen Mäandern
Motifs de tapisserie à méandres plats

Shown here are four examples of frets used to cover a whole surface. Unlike the Classical fret band, the designs are positioned at a slant to emphasize the diagonals.

These patterns are suitable for the decoration of large surfaces, but they can also be used as the background to other ornamental motifs (see page 227). A particularly attractive effect is achieved by executing the designs in gold on a dark ground, but other color combinations are also possible.

Hier werden vier Beispiele von Mäandern präsentiert, die als Flächendekoration wiedergegeben sind. Im Gegensatz zum klassischen Mäanderband wird durch die Schrägstellung der Ornamente die Diagonale betont.

Solche Muster bieten sich zur Verzierung großer Flächen an, können aber auch als Hintergrundmotiv für andere Ornamente verwendet werden (siehe Seite 227). Besonders schön ist die Ausführung dieser Ornamente in Gold auf dunklem Grund, wenngleich auch andere Farbkompositionen möglich sind.

Cette planche présente quatre exemples de méandres servant à décorer des surfaces. Contrairement au bandeau classique de méandres, la diagonale est accentuée ici par la position oblique des ornements.

Ces motifs conviennent à la décoration de grandes surfaces de murs, mais peuvent aussi servir de motif de fond à d'autres ornements (voir page 227). Leur réalisation en doré sur fond sombre est particulièrement décorative, mais d'autres combinaisons de couleurs sont également possibles.

Diaper patterns using lozenges, ovals and rosettes
Tapetenmuster mit Rauten, Ovalen und Rosetten
Motifs de tapisserie à losanges, ovales et rosaces

The upper pattern is dominated by overlapping ovals. The fields within the overlaps are executed in gold, as are the rosettes in the centers of the ovals. The lower pattern is based on dark-colored lozenges filled out with rosettes. These motifs are derived from patterns found in Japanese crafts. Comparable motifs are frequently found in Japanese porcelain, lacquer and metalwork, as well as on fabrics. These patterns allow numerous possible applications, for example for the base zones of walls, or for smaller panels. The patterns are shown in a horizontal orientation, but they could also be used vertically. Coloration can be varied to suit the taste of the user.

Das obere Muster wird von Ovalen bestimmt, die sich überlappen. Die dadurch entstehende Fläche ist in Gold gestaltet, ebenso wie die im Zentrum der Ovale angeordneten Rosetten. Das untere Muster zeigt in dunkler Farbe gehaltene Rauten, die mit Rosetten ausgefüllt sind. Diese Ornamente sind von Vorlagen des japanischen Kunstgewerbes abgeleitet. Vergleichbare Motive sieht man häufig bei japanischem Porzellan, bei Lack- und Metallarbeiten sowie auf Stoffen. Diese Muster gestatten eine vielfältige Anwendung. So lassen sie sich zum Beispiel zur Wanddekoration, etwa zur Ausschmückung von Sockelzonen, oder als Dekor kleinerer Paneele verwenden. Die Muster sind hier in horizontaler Ausrichtung gezeigt, sie sind jedoch auch in vertikaler Ausführung denkbar. Die Farbgebung kann frei gewählt werden.

Le motif du haut se caractérise par un chevauchement d'ovales. Le fond est doré, de même que les rosaces disposées au centre des ovales. Le motif du bas présente des losanges d'une couleur sombre soutenue, remplis de rosaces. Ces ornements sont dérivés de modèles des arts décoratifs japonais. Des motifs similaires sont courants dans la porcelaine japonaise, les laques et les ouvrages en métal, ainsi que dans les étoffes. Ces motifs conviennent pour de multiples applications: la décoration murale, par exemple pour orner des socles, ou de panneaux plus petits. Leur présentation pourra être horizontale, comme dans cette planche, ou verticale. Une réalisation dans d'autres couleurs est, bien sûr, possible.

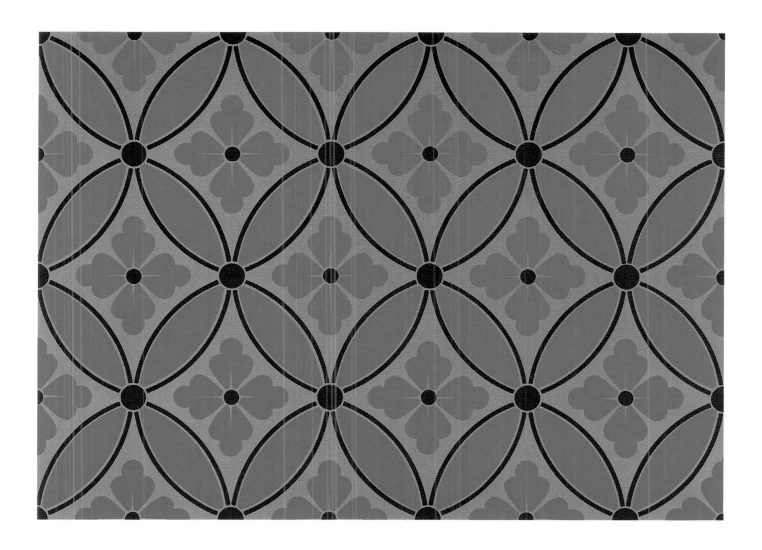

Diaper patterns using lozenges, circles and rosettes
Tapetenmuster mit Rauten, Kreisen und Rosetten
Motifs de tapisserie à losanges, cercles et rosaces

The top design consists of lozenges formed by diagonal strips. The lozenges are filled with rosettes. The lower pattern consists of overlapping circles whose centers are decorated with rosettes. These motifs are derived from small-scale Japanese crafts, but can also be used for large-scale wall decorations.

The color scheme shown here, in gold on a dark ground, is typical of Japanese ornamentation, even though a simpler scheme is possible. To create a balanced impression in a room, the patterns could, for example, be executed in a single color, which should be somewhat darker than the ground. The effect can be enhanced by choosing a gloss or semi-gloss color for the ground, and applying the pattern in matt with a stencil. Of course, the patterns can also be executed in a light color on a dark ground.

Beim oberen Muster sieht man diagonal verlaufende, sich kreuzende Bänder, die Rauten bilden. Die Rauten sind mit Rosetten ausgeschmückt. Im unteren Muster überlappen sich Kreise, deren Zentren von Rosetten geziert werden. Diese Motive sind vom japanischen Kleinkunsthandwerk abgeleitet, lassen sich aber auch als großflächige Wanddekoration verwenden.

Die hier wiedergebene Darstellung in Gold auf dunklem Grund ist für die japanische Ornamentik charakteristisch, wenngleich auch eine einfachere Farbgebung vorstellbar ist. Für einen ausgewogenen Raumeindruck können die Muster zum Beispiel in einer einzigen Farbe, die etwas dunkler als der Untergrund sein sollte, aufgetragen werden. Die Wirkung lässt sich noch verstärken, indem eine glänzende oder halbglänzende Untergrundfarbe gewählt und das Muster in matter Farbe mit einer Schablone aufgetragen wird. Natürlich können die Muster auch in einer hellen Farbe auf dunklem Grund ausgeführt werden.

Le motif du haut présente des bandeaux diagonaux entrecroisés et formant des losanges qui sont ornés de rosaces. Dans le motif du bas, des cercles aux centres décorés de rosaces se chevauchent. Même si ces motifs sont dérivés du petit artisanat japonais, ils peuvent aussi servir à décorer de grands pans de murs. Les motifs reproduits ici en doré sur fond sombre sont caractéristiques de l'ornementation japonaise, mais une combinaison de couleurs plus simple est admise. Des motifs monochromes un peu plus foncés que le fond créeront, par exemple, une impression d'équilibre. Pour renforcer cet effet, on pourra choisir une couleur de fond brillante ou semi-brillante et réaliser le motif au pochoir dans une couleur mate. Une réalisation dans une couleur claire sur fond sombre est, bien entendu, possible.

Diaper patterns with reeds and bamboo
Tapetenmuster mit Schilf-, Bambus und gebogenen Blättern
Motifs de tapisserie à roseaux, bambous et feuilles incurvées

This plate shows two examples of vegetal decoration. The pattern on the left has stylized bamboo stalks, forming a scale-like basic pattern. This is decorated with a composition of extended bamboo leaves. The picture on the right shows stylized reeds, bent as if by the wind. Here too, a scale-like basic pattern is created. Both patterns are derived directly from Japanese ornamental design, and the effect is one of lightness and simplicity. These designs are suitable for the decoration of wall surfaces or paneled areas. The gold can be replaced with another color, for example a warm brown or matt red.

Hier sind zwei Beispiele vegetabilen Dekors dargestellt. Auf der linken Abbildung sieht man stilisierte Bambusstäbe, die ein schuppenförmiges Grundmuster bilden. Dieses wird von einer Komposition weit ausgreifender Bambusblätter geziert. Die rechte Abbildung zeigt vom Wind gebogene, schilfartige Blätter, die sich ebenfalls zu einem schuppenförmigen Grundmuster zusammenfügen. Beide Muster sind direkt von der japanischen Ornamentik abgeleitet und wirken leicht und unkompliziert. Diese Entwürfe eignen sich als Verzierung von Wandflächen oder Täfelungen. Die Farbgebung in Gold lässt sich auch durch einen anderen Farbton ersetzen, so zum Beispiel durch ein warmes Braun oder ein mattes Rot.

Cette planche présente deux exemples de décors végétaux. Dans l'illustration de gauche, des cannes de bambous stylisées constituent le motif de base en forme d'écailles. Ce motif est orné de feuilles de bambous largement déployées. L'illustration de droite présente des feuilles de roseaux courbées par le vent, également associées à un motif de base en forme d'écailles. Les deux motifs sont directement dérivés de l'ornementation japonaise et créent une impression de légèreté et de simplicité.
Ces motifs serviront à décorer des surfaces murales ou des lambris. Une autre teinte peut remplacer la couleur dorée, par exemple un brun chaud ou un rouge mat.

Rosettes
Rosetten
Rosaces

This plate depicts various highly stylized rosettes in gold on black. They are distributed over the surface either in pairs or singly. The chrysanthemum motif at the upper right deserves particular attention. It can be seen, paired with another, on the left of the picture in the middle. In Japanese art the chrysanthemum or "kikumon" is used as the imperial emblem.
Any color can be used for these designs, but that illustrated here is the most effective.

Hier sieht man verschiedene, stark stilisierte Rosetten in Gold auf schwarzem Grund. Sie sind paarweise oder einzeln in größeren Abständen auf der Fläche verteilt. Besondere Aufmerksamkeit verdient das Chrysanthemenmotiv oben rechts, das noch einmal in paarweiser Anordnung am linken Bildrand in der Mitte zu sehen ist. In der japanischen Kunst wird die Chrysantheme (Kikumon) als Emblem des Kaisers von Japan verwendet.
Bei diesen Mustern ist jede Farbgebung möglich, am effektvollsten wirken sie aber in der hier gezeigten Umsetzung.

Ce motif présente diverses rosaces très stylisées en doré sur fond noir qui sont dispersées sur la surface à intervalles assez grands, par deux ou individuellement. Le motif de chrysanthème en haut à droite qui réapparaît avec un autre motif au milieu et sur le bord gauche mérite une attention particulière. Dans l'art japonais, le chrysanthème (Kikumon) est en effet l'emblème de l'empereur du Japon. Toutes les combinaisons de couleurs sont possibles pour ces motifs, mais le meilleur effet sera obtenu avec les tons présentés ici.

Masonry pattern of bamboo stalks and semi-rosettes
Ziegelmuster aus Bambusstängeln mit Halbrosetten
Motif de briques à cannes de bambous et demi-rosaces

This design shows how the typically oriental motifs of bamboo and reeds can be arranged to form a masonry pattern. The continuous lines of a standard masonry pattern are here replaced by robust bamboo stalks, tied together in the oriental fashion. The rectangular areas are decorated by overhanging bamboo leaves and branches. To give the composition strength and expressivity, each rectangular has a stylized chrysanthemum in the form of a semi-rosette.

This design is suitable for the decoration of large halls and staircases, especially if it is used above a dark monochrome or simply ornamented base zone. The effect is enhanced by a larger-scale execution where each "brick" is more than 30 centimeters long. Other vegetal patterns can be worked out on the basis of this design. Any other color can be used in place of gold.

Dieses Muster zeigt, wie die typisch asiatischen Motive Bambus und Schilf nach Art eines Ziegelmusters arrangiert werden können. An die Stelle der durchgehenden Linien des Ziegelmusters treten hier kräftige Bambusstäbe, die nach asiatischer Art mit Riemen verbunden sind. Die rechteckigen Flächen werden von überhängenden Bambuszweigen und -blättern ausgeschmückt. Um der Komposition Kraft und Ausdruck zu verleihen, wurde ihr die stilisierte Chrysantheme in Form einer Halbrosette zugeordnet.

Der vorliegende Entwurf ist zur Dekoration von Sälen und Treppenhäusern geeignet, besonders wenn er oberhalb einer dunklen einfarbigen oder einer schlicht ornamentierten Sockelzone angebracht wird. Eine vergrößerte Ausführung mit einer Seitenlänge der Felder von über 30 cm verstärkt die Wirkung. Nach Art dieses Entwurfes lassen sich weitere vegetabile Muster entwickeln. Statt Gold kann auch jede andere Farbe verwendet werden.

Cette planche présente une disposition possible en briques de motifs typiquement asiatiques, à savoir des bambous et des roseaux. De puissantes cannes de bambous liées par des lanières à la manière asiatique remplacent les lignes continues du motif de briques. Les surfaces rectangulaires sont ornées de tiges et de feuilles de bambous en surplomb. Le chrysanthème stylisé prenant ici la forme d'une demi-rosace confère force et caractère à la composition.

Ce motif servira à décorer des pièces et des cages d'escaliers, surtout s'il est placé au-dessus d'un soubassement monochrome foncé ou légèrement décoré. Un agrandissement du motif pour un panneau de plus de 30 cm de côté renforcera cet effet. On réalisera d'autres motifs végétaux à partir de ce modèle. L'utilisation d'une autre couleur à la place du doré est bien sûr possible.

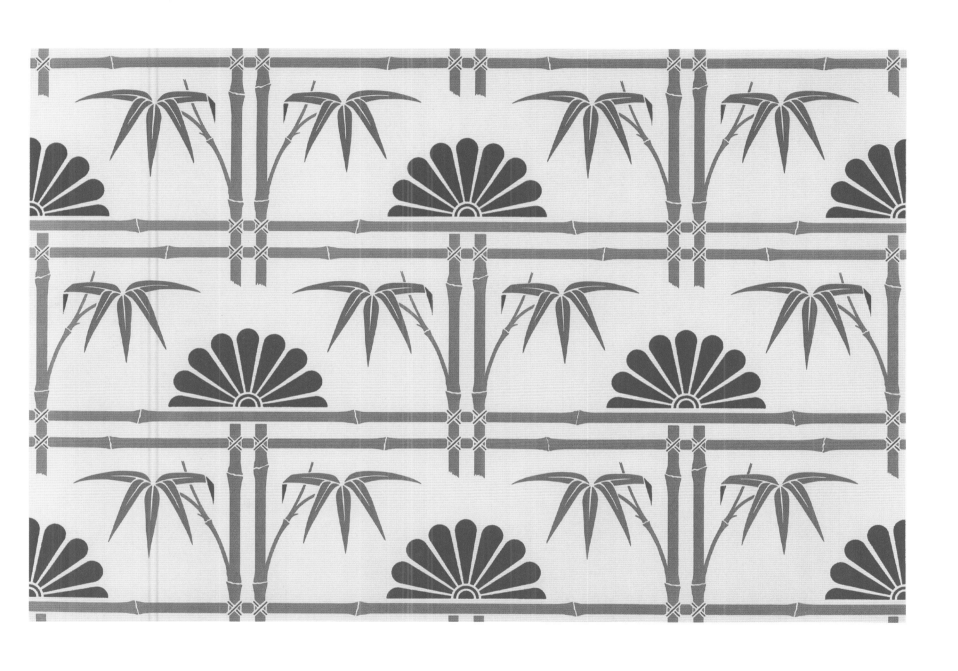

Diaper pattern with roses
Tapetenmuster mit Rosen
Motif de tapisserie avec roses

This design shows rose stems with flowers, leaves and buds, scattered over the surface in no recognizable arrangement. This informal "powdering" is characteristic of Japanese ornamental art. It conveys a friendly impression, which is further enhanced by the different colors of the blossoms.
This pattern can also be executed using other plants, allowing an even greater variety of shape and color. Where the latter is concerned, there are no restrictions.

Der vorliegende Entwurf zeigt Rosenzweige mit mehreren Blüten und Knospen, die ohne erkennbares Ordnungsprinzip über die Fläche verteilt sind. Eine solche zwanglose Anordnung ist für die japanische Ornamentik charakteristisch. Sie vermittelt einen lieblichen Eindruck, der durch die unterschiedlichen Blütenfarben noch verstärkt wird.
Dieses Muster lässt sich auch mit anderen Pflanzen umsetzen, wodurch eine noch größere Farb- und Formenvielfalt erreicht werden kann. Hinsichtlich der farblichen Gestaltung gibt es keinerlei Beschränkungen.

Ce motif présente des tiges de roses à plusieurs fleurs et boutons, réparties sur la surface sans ordre apparent. Une telle liberté est typique de l'art ornemental japonais. Elle produit un charmant effet que renforcent les différentes teintes des fleurs.
Ce motif est également réalisable avec d'autres plantes, ce qui permet d'élargir l'éventail de couleurs et de formes. La composition des couleurs n'est soumise à aucune limitation.

Stylized chrysanthemums on a partly diapered ground with fret
Tapetenmuster mit stilisierten Chrysanthemenblüten und flächigen Mäandern
Motif de tapisserie à fleurs de chrysanthèmes stylisées et méandres plats

This (part-)diaper pattern is dominated by the "powdering" of stylized chrysanthemums, some of which have a quatrefoil frame. Here too, the chrysanthemum should be seen as the Japanese imperial emblem. A particularly striking feature of this design is the background. It is not plain, but has its own pattern of diagonal frets. This decorative pattern does not cover the whole ground, but itself has a zigzag edge. The particular charm of this design lies in the interplay of geometric background and floral foreground. The color scheme can be chosen according to taste.

Dieses Tapetenmuster wird von stilisierten Chrysanthemen bestimmt: Zweige mit stilisierten Chrysanthemenblüten sowie von einem Vierpass gerahmte Blüten sind ohne bestimmte Ordnung über die Fläche verteilt. Auch hier ist die Chrysantheme als Emblem des japanischen Kaisers zu interpretieren. Besonders auffällig an diesem Entwurf ist der Hintergrund. Er ist nicht einfarbig gehalten, sondern enthält ein eigenes Ornament. Schräg gestellte Mäanderbänder werden zu einer spitzzackigen Fläche zusammengefügt. Im Zusammenspiel von geometrischem Hintergrund und floralem Vordergrund liegt der besondere Reiz dieses Entwurfs, dessen farbliche Gestaltung frei gewählt werden kann.

Des chrysanthèmes stylisés prédominent dans ce motif de tapisserie: des tiges aux fleurs de chrysanthèmes stylisées, ainsi que des fleurs incluses dans un médaillon quadrilobe sont réparties sur la surface sans organisation définie. Ici aussi, il convient d'interpréter le chrysanthème comme l'emblème de l'empereur du Japon. Le fond est particulièrement frappant dans ce motif: il n'est pas monochrome, mais possède son propre ornement. Des bandeaux de méandres obliques forment des zigzags par endroits. L'attrait particulier de ce motif à l'infinie variété de couleurs réside dans l'association d'un fond géométrique et d'un premier plan floral.

Diaper pattern with stylized chrysanthemums and paulownia blossoms
Tapetenmuster mit stilisierten Chrysanthemen und Poloniablüten
Motif de tapisserie à chrysanthèmes et fleurs de paulownia stylisés

This design has stylized chrysanthemums on a golden ground, either alone or in combination with stylized paulownia blossoms, whose fruits are shown here in white. Like the chrysanthemum, the blossom of the paulownia tree has an emblematic function in Japanese art as a badge of the nobility, especially the samurai caste of warriors. The gold background has a very elegant effect in combination with these symbolic motifs, although other color schemes are also possible.

Dieser Entwurf präsentiert stilisierte Chrysanthemen auf goldenem Grund. Sie werden allein oder in Verbindung mit stilisierten Blüten des Poloniabaumes, dessen Fruchtstände hier weiß dargestellt sind, abgebildet. Auch die Blüte des Poloniabaumes werden in der japanischen Kunst als Emblem des japanischen Adels, insbesondere der Samurai-Kämpfer, verwendet. Der goldene Hintergrund wirkt im Zusammenhang mit diesen symbolträchtigen Motiven sehr edel, wenngleich auch andere Farbgestaltungen möglich sind.

Cette planche présente des chrysanthèmes stylisés sur fond doré. Ceux-ci sont seuls ou associés à des fleurs de paulownia stylisées, dont les fruits sont représentés en blanc. L'art japonais utilise également la fleur de paulownia comme emblème de la noblesse japonaise, notamment des samouraïs. Le fond doré avec ces motifs chargés de symboles donne un air de noblesse à la composition ; d'autres combinaisons de couleurs sont, bien sûr, possibles.

Floral Style
Floraler Stil
Le style floral

Flowers have formed part of the inventory of decorative elements in architecture, painting and the crafts since the High Middle Ages. In these genres they have been used in all conceivable forms up to the present day. Toward the end of the 16th century, in the late Renaissance, veritable fashions in flowers developed; these increased in importance, especially in the various crafts, during the 17th century with the appearance of Baroque parks and gardens. Mirror frames, marquetry, and tapestries were all increasingly decorated with floral motifs. Gold and silversmiths likewise used floral motifs, as did the makers and decorators of glassware and porcelain, and the printers of ornamental editions of

Seit dem hohen Mittelalter gehören Blumen zum festen Formenschatz von Architektur, Malerei und Kunstgewerbe. In diesen Kunstgattungen sind sie in allen nur denkbaren Formen bis in die Gegenwart immer wieder verwendet worden. Gegen Ende des 16. Jahrhunderts entwickelten sich zur Spätzeit der Renaissance regelrechte Blumenmoden, die im 17. Jahrhundert mit dem Aufkommen der barocken Park- und Gartenanlagen noch stärker ausgeprägt wurden und sich vor allem im Kunstgewerbe bemerkbar machten. Spiegelrahmen, Möbelintarsien und Tapisserien wurden zunehmend mit floralen Motiven verziert. Ebenso finden sich Blumendarstellungen bei Gold- und Silberschmiedearbeiten, auf Porzellan,

Depuis le haut Moyen Âge, les fleurs appartiennent au catalogue des formes utilisées en architecture, peinture et arts décoratifs. Dans ces genres artistiques, elles ont été utilisées jusqu'à présent dans toutes les formes concevables. C'est vers la fin du XVIe siècle que se sont développées des modes florales caractéristiques de la Renaissance finissante, qui devinrent encore plus marquantes au XVIIe siècle avec l'apparition des aménagements de parcs et jardins baroques et se manifestèrent notamment dans les arts décoratifs. Les encadrements de miroirs, les meubles en marqueterie et les tapisseries s'ornèrent de plus en plus de motifs floraux. Des représentations florales se retrouvent aussi sur les pièces

Section of garden of Augustusburg Palace, Brühl, 1728
Baroque garden design was characterized by long axial lines of sight oriented toward the main body of the house. These lines of sight were accented by broad footpaths, fountains, and artistically trimmed hedges. The hedges illustrated here, forming a floral pattern of their own, are particularly prettily trimmed.

Gartenanlage von Schloss Augustusburg, Brühl, 1728
In der barocken Gartenarchitektur legte man große Sichtachsen an, die auf den Haupttrakt des Schlosses ausgerichtet waren. Sie wurden durch breite Gehwege, Springbrunnenanlagen und kunstvoll beschnittene Hecken akzentuiert. Besonders auffällig sind hier die Hecken, die ein eigenes florales Muster bilden.

Jardins du château Augustusburg, Brühl, 1728
L'architecture baroque de jardin comportait de grands axes qui menaient à l'aile principale du château. Ces axes étaient mis en valeur par de larges allées, des jets d'eau et des haies taillées avec art. Les haies représentant un motif floral sont particulièrement frappantes.

books. During the neoclassical period of the 18th century, and throughout the generally "Revivalist" 19th century, flowers are found as decorative motifs on porcelain and textiles, and from the mid-19th century onward, also on industrially produced wallpaper. In technologically advanced England, floral decoration was increasingly used in industrial design, and came to be used on objects of everyday use, which, thus "improved", came to rival more expensive hand-made and one-off pieces.

The general interest in floral ornamentation reflected public taste, and was particularly popular in England. The predilection for vegetal motifs can be seen in the context of the English landscape garden, which having made its appearance and enjoyed its heyday in the 18th century, remained popular throughout in the 19th. The landscape garden was in fact so popular that it was imitated even in

bei Glaswaren und im Buchdruck bei den „ornamentalen Drucken". Im 18. Jahrhundert zur Zeit des Klassizismus sowie im gesamten 19. Jahrhundert, jener Epoche, die sich im Rahmen des Historismus auf „historische" Stile zurückbesann, finden sich Blumendarstellungen als Dekor von Porzellan, Textilien und den seit Mitte des 19. Jahrhunderts industriell gefertigten Tapeten. Im technisch weit entwickelten England fand der Blumendekor zunehmenden Eingang in das Industrie-Design und zierte nun auch Alltagsgegenstände, die auf diese Weise veredelt in Konkurrenz zu aufwändigeren Manufakturprodukten und Einzelstücken traten.

Das allgemeine Interesse an floralen Ornamenten entsprach dem Geschmack des Volkes und erfreute sich gerade in England großer Beliebtheit. Die Vorliebe für pflanzliche Dekore ist in engem Zusammenhang mit dem englischen Landschaftsgarten zu sehen, der im

d'orfèvrerie en or et en argent, sur la porcelaine, le verre et dans l'imprimerie, sur les « gravures ornementales ». Au XVIIIe siècle, époque du néoclassicisme, et pendant tout le XIXe siècle, période qui se réfère aux styles « historiques » avec le mouvement appelé « historisme », les représentations florales décorent la porcelaine, les textiles et, dès le milieu du XIXe siècle, les tapisseries de fabrication industrielle. Dans l'Angleterre fortement industrialisée, le décor floral se répand de plus en plus dans le design industriel et orne désormais aussi des objets d'utilisation courante qui, ainsi ennoblis, concurrencent les produits manufacturés et les pièces uniques plus coûteux.

Les ornements floraux qui suscitèrent l'intérêt général correspondaient au goût du peuple et jouissaient, en Angleterre précisément, d'une grande popularité. Il faut voir un lien étroit entre cette prédilection pour les décors

Landscape garden with neoclassical temple, near Wörlitz, c. 1790
The English landscape garden inspired garden design throughout Europe. Thus Duke Friedrich Franz of Anhalt-Dessau, inspired by his travels in England, had one laid out on his own estate. The little Temple of Flora is named for the Roman goddess of flowers, and was intended to put the beholder in sentimental mood.

Landschaftsgarten mit klassizistischem Tempel bei Wörlitz, um 1790
Der englische Landschaftsgarten beeinflusste die Gartenarchitektur in ganz Europa. So ließ Fürst Friedrich Franz von Anhalt-Dessau, inspiriert durch seine Englandreisen, einen solchen Garten in seiner Heimat anlegen. Der kleine Floratempel ist nach der römischen Blumengöttin benannt und sollte den Besucher in eine sentimentale Stimmung versetzen.

Jardin anglais avec temple néoclassique près de Wörlitz, vers 1790
Le jardin anglais a influencé l'architecture de jardin dans toute l'Europe. Le prince Friedrich Franz von Anhalt-Dessau, inspiré par ses voyages en Angleterre, a fait par exemple aménager un de ces jardins sur son domaine. Le petit temple Flora, du nom de la déesse romaine des fleurs, devait transporter le visiteur dans une atmosphère sentimentale.

distant Munich, where one was laid out under the name of the "English Garden". Characteristic of this type of garden is its extent, and the fact that natural countryside is consciously integrated into the design, so that the visual boundaries between garden and landscape disappear. This effect is reinforced by planting of clumps of trees apparently at random throughout the garden. In addition, monuments, artificial ruins, and little pavilions are set up around the garden, with a view to putting visitors into sentimental mood. And of course, no garden could be without its flowers, which were planted here and there in small beds. This preference for different-colored flower-beds finds its expression not only in the magnificent grounds of English stately homes, but also in the beautifully designed front gardens of 19th century English suburban terraced houses. Not surprisingly, then, people brought these flowers into their homes, both in the form of bunches of real flowers, and in the form of floral decoration. This development was given particular impetus by the work of

18. Jahrhundert seine Blütezeit erlebte und bis ins 19. Jahrhundert sehr beliebt war. Seine Beliebtheit reichte so weit, dass er sogar im fernen München im „Englischen Garten" Nachahmung fand. Bezeichnend für den englischen Garten ist seine weitläufige Anlage, die bewusst die natürliche Landschaft in die Gestaltung des Gartens integriert, so dass die Grenzen zwischen Garten und freier Landschaft verschwinden. Dieser Effekt wird dadurch gesteigert, dass man immer wieder Gruppierungen von Bäumen wie zufällig in den Garten pflanzte. Außerdem wurden Denkmäler, künstliche Ruinen und kleine Pavillons im Garten verteilt, die den Besucher in eine sentimentale Stimmung versetzen sollten. Und natürlich durften in einem Garten Blumen nicht fehlen, die immer wieder hier und da in kleinen Beeten angelegt wurden. Diese besondere Vorliebe für farbig unterschiedlich gestaltete Blumenbeete drückt sich nicht nur in den herrschaftlichen Gärten englischer Schlösser und Landsitze aus, sondern auch in den liebevoll gestalteten Vorgärten englischer Reihenhäuser, die im 19. Jahrhundert

végétaux et le jardin paysager anglais qui connut son apogée au XVIIIᵉ siècle et fut très en vogue jusqu'au XIXᵉ siècle. Il était si populaire à cette époque qu'il a même été imité dans le « Jardin anglais » de la lointaine Munich. Le jardin anglais se caractérise par son aménagement spacieux qui intègre délibérément le paysage naturel dans l'organisation du jardin de façon à faire disparaître les limites entre ce dernier et le paysage naturel. On intensifia cet effet en plantant et replantant comme au naturel des bouquets d'arbres. On y disposa en outre des monuments, ruines artificielles et petits pavillons qui devaient plonger le visiteur dans une atmosphère romantique. Et bien sûr, un jardin était inconcevable sans fleurs qu'on plantait ici et là dans de petits parterres. Cette prédilection particulière pour des parterres de fleurs aux couleurs différentes ne s'exprime pas seulement dans les somptueux jardins de châteaux et manoirs anglais, mais aussi dans les jardinets devant les maisons individuelles anglaises décorées avec soin au XIXᵉ siècle. Il était donc logique que les fleurs fassent

Baroque table-top with marble inlay, Florentine workshop, Villa Poggio Imperiale, Florence, c. 1650
Floral decoration became increasingly important during the Baroque period. Mirror frames, furniture inlays, and tapestries were ever more frequently decorated with vegetal forms. The table-top illustrated here shows a floral motif enclosed within a cartouche. Roses, fruits and acanthus leaves rolled up in scroll-like fashion fill out the remaining space.

Barocke Tischplatte mit Stuckmarmorintarsien, Florentiner Werkstatt, Villa Poggio Imperiale, Florenz, um 1650
Im Barock gewann der florale Dekor zunehmend an Bedeutung. Spiegelrahmen, Möbelintarsien und Tapisserien wurden verstärkt mit vegetabilen Formen geziert. Die hier abgebildete Tischplatte zeigt ein Blumenmotiv, das von einer Kartusche gerahmt wird. Als Füllformen erkennt man Rosen, Früchte und Akanthusranken, die sich volutenförmig zusammenrollen.

Dessus de table baroque avec incrustations de marbre artificiel, Atelier florentin, Villa Poggio Imperiale, Florence, vers 1650
Le décor floral fut très en vogue à l'époque du baroque. Les cadres de glaces, meubles en marqueterie et tapisseries s'ornaient en abondance de formes végétales. Le dessus de table illustré ici présente un motif floral encadré d'un cartouche. Des roses, des fruits et des entrelacs d'acanthe qui s'enroulent en formant des volutes s'inscrivent entre les motifs principaux.

William Morris, who already in his own lifetime gained a reputation, extending far beyond England's shores, for his decorative wall-hangings with their purely vegetal ornamentation. What is less well-known is that Morris also ran a company producing wallpapers, furniture and fabrics in his own factory, and thus had close links to design for the real world. He held the opinion that an artist should not only design, but also execute his designs himself, and thereby advocated a fusion of art and craft which led in England to the movement which was called precisely that: "Arts and Crafts". This movement, to the fringes of which the Audsleys also belonged, exercised a fundamental reforming influence on applied art.
While Morris' early ornamental designs were permeated by a deep feeling for nature, giving way over the years to increasing stylization,

errichtet wurden. So lag es nahe, dass sich die Menschen diese Blumen ins Haus holten, sei es in Form von Schnittblumen oder in Form von Dekor.
Besonders geprägt wurde diese Entwicklung durch die Arbeiten von William Morris, der schon zu Lebzeiten mit seinen dekorativen Wandbehängen mit rein vegetabilen Ornamenten einen Ruf erlangte, der weit über die Grenzen Englands hinausging. Möglicherweise weniger bekannt ist, dass William Morris auch Tapeten, Möbel und Stoffe in eigener Manufaktur herstellte und somit dem Gebrauchsdesign eng verbunden war. Er vertrat die Ansicht, ein Künstler solle nicht nur entwerfen, sondern seine Entwürfe auch selbst ausführen. Damit setzte er sich für eine Verbindung von Kunst und Handwerk ein, die in England letztendlich zur „Arts-und-Crafts-Bewegung" führte, unter deren Einfluss das Kunstgewerbe

leur entrée dans les maisons, sous la forme de fleurs coupées ou de décors.
Cette évolution a été fortement marquée par les travaux de William Morris qui, avec ses tentures murales décoratives aux ornements purement végétaux, s'est forgé de son vivant une réputation qui a largement dépassé les frontières de l'Angleterre. Fait peut-être moins connu : William Morris fabriquait aussi des tapis, des meubles et des étoffes dans sa propre manufacture et il était de cette façon étroitement associé au design utilitaire. Il représentait l'idée selon laquelle un artiste doit non seulement concevoir, mais aussi mettre ses concepts à exécution ; avec ce principe, il s'est fait le défenseur d'une fusion de l'art et de l'artisanat qui, en Angleterre, a finalement donné naissance au mouvement « Arts and Crafts » ; ce courant, dans la sphère

Two wallpaper designs by William Morris, Victoria and Albert Museum, London, late-19th century
The English designer and theorist William Morris is regarded as the pioneer of the Arts-and-Crafts movement. His textile and wall-paper designs are characterized by highly stylized floral motifs, which seem already to herald Art Nouveau.

Zwei Tapetenentwürfe von William Morris, Victoria and Albert Museum, London, spätes 19. Jh.
Der englische Künstler William Morris gilt als Wegbereiter der Arts-und-Crafts-Bewegung. Seine Textil- und Tapetenentwürfe zeigen ein stark stilisiertes florales Design, das bereits auf den Jugendstil zu verweisen scheint.

Deux esquisses de tapisseries de William Morris, Victoria and Albert Museum, Londres, fin du XIXᵉ siècle
L'artiste anglais William Morris est considéré comme le pionnier du mouvement Arts-and-Crafts. Ses esquisses de tapisseries et de textiles présentent des motifs floraux très stylisés qui semblent déjà annoncer l'art nouveau.

the Audsleys remained loyal to traditional floral design. Their patterns take their inspiration from the art of both the Middle Ages and the early Renaissance. A striking feature of their work is that their leaves and flowers are not only highly naturalistic, but can even be identified with particular plants. Thus one sees vine and chestnut leaves, roses, thistles and oaks. These close ties with one's native flora are characteristic of medieval ornamental design. Other motifs, by contrast, such as the bindweed and jasmine seen on page 245 and, in particular, the broad ornamental band with irises depicted on page 247, already give a hint of the approach of Art Nouveau, a development which was coming

grundlegend reformiert wurde und deren entferntem Umfeld auch die Audsleys zuzuordnen sind.
Während die Ornamententwürfe von Morris in seiner Frühphase von einem tiefen Naturverständnis durchdrungen sind, das mit den Jahren einer immer stärker werdenden Stilisierung wich, blieben die Audsleys dem traditionellen floralen Design verbunden. Ihre Entwürfe nehmen sowohl Anregungen von der mittelalterlichen Kunst als auch von der Früh-Renaissance auf. Auffällig ist, dass die meisten ihrer Entwürfe nicht nur naturnahe Blatt- und Blütenformen erkennen lassen, sondern sogar bestimmten Pflanzen zugeordnet werden können. So sieht man Weinlaub- und Kastanienblätter, Rosen, Disteln, Eicheln und Busch-

éloignée duquel s'inscrivent les Audsley, a fondamentalement réformé les arts appliqués.
Si, à ses débuts, Morris a empreint ses esquisses ornementales d'une profonde compréhension de la nature qui céda la place à une stylisation de plus en plus forte au fil des ans, les Audsley sont par contre restés attachés au design floral traditionnel. Leurs esquisses s'inspirent autant de l'art médiéval que de la Renaissance primaire. Le plus frappant c'est que la plupart de leurs esquisses présentent non seulement des formes de feuilles et de fleurs proches de la nature, mais qu'elles peuvent aussi se regrouper en espèces déterminées. On rencontre ainsi des feuilles de vigne et de châtaignier, des roses, des

St Nikolai Church in Jüteborg, ceiling fresco in the south chapel, 14th–15th century
This late-Gothic groin vault is decorated in its entirety with slender tendrils and fantastical calyxes, which form the decorative background for the four medallions with the symbols of the four evangelists.

St.-Nikolai-Kirche in Jütebog, Deckenfresko der südlichen Kapelle, 14./15. Jh.
Dieses spätgotische Rippengewölbe wird vollflächig von feingliedrigen Ranken und großen, phantasievollen Blütenkelchen ausgeschmückt. Sie bilden einen dekorativen Grund, von dem sich die vier Medaillons mit den Evangelistensymbolen abheben.

Église St. Nikolai de Jütebog, fresque de plafond de la chapelle sud, XIVᵉ/XVᵉ siècles
Cette voûte à nervures de style gothique flamboyant est décorée sur toute sa surface par de délicats entrelacs et de grands calices originaux. Ces motifs constituent le fond décoratif dont se détachent les quatre médaillons aux symboles évangéliques.

to the fore in late-19th-century Europe, but which George Ashdown Audsley, having emigrated to the United States to work as a theoretician and practitioner of the art of organbuilding, did not pursue.

rosen. Diese starke Annäherung an die heimische Pflanzenwelt ist charakteristisch für die mittelalterliche Ornamentik. Andere Motive hingegen, wie zum Beispiel die Winden- und Jasminsträucher auf Seite 245 und besonders das breite Ornamentband mit den Schwertlilien auf Seite 247, lassen bereits Anklänge des Jugendstils erkennen, eine Entwicklung, die sich in Europa gegen Ende des 19. Jahrhunderts anbahnte, die aber George Ashdown Audsley aufgrund seiner Emigration in die Vereinigten Staaten und seiner dortigen Tätigkeit als Orgelbauer und -theoretiker nicht weiter verfolgte.

chardons, des chênes et des anémones. Ce recours systématique au règne végétal indigène est caractéristique de l'ornementation médiévale. Cependant d'autres motifs, par exemple les tiges de liseron et de jasmin à la page 245 et surtout le large bandeau ornemental à iris à la page 247, rappellent déjà l'art nouveau, un mouvement amorcé en Europe vers la fin du XIXe siècle, mais dans lequel George Ashdown Audsley n'a pas persévéré car il émigra aux États-Unis et y exerça l'activité de facteur d'orgues et de théoricien ce métier.

Vault of the nave of the parish church in Kötschach, 14th century
This Austrian parish church is notable for the rich decoration of its ceiling, whose ornamentation is derived from Gothic tracery, which seems to be stretched across the vault like a net.

Gewölbe des Mittelschiffs der Pfarrkirche von Kötschach in Kärnten, 14 Jh.
Diese österreichische Pfarrkirche besticht durch die ornamentale Ausschmückung ihrer Decken: Ein vom gotischen Maßwerk abgeleitetes Ornament, das an florale Formen erinnert, scheint das Gewölbe netzartig zu überspannen.

Voûte de la nef centrale de l'église paroissiale de Kötschach en Carinthie, XIVe siècle
Cette église paroissiale autrichienne séduit par le décor de ses plafonds : un ornement dérivé de la dentelle de pierre gothique et qui rappelle les formes florales semble couvrir la voûte d'une sorte de résille.

Stylized roses
Stilisierte Rosen
Roses stylisées

The central motif shows a large, highly stylized rose whose radial shoots bear leaves and buds. The whole design forms a square. This pattern is primarily suited to the decoration of square panels or square ceiling coffers. Other examples of rose blossoms are illustrated in the corners of the plate. These motifs can be used in a whole variety of ways. Stylistically, the roses are probably derived from the Stuart rose, the emblem of the Kings of Scotland. This emblem can occasionally be seen as stucco decoration in Scottish palaces. Color-wise, any scheme is possible; the roses can be executed in dark colors on a light ground, or vice versa. Gold is also conceivable as a background color.

Das zentrale Motiv zeigt eine große, stark stilisierte Rose mit radial ausgreifenden Zweigen, Knospen und Blättern, die ein Quadrat bilden. Dieser Entwurf eignet sich vor allem für die Ausschmückung quadratischer Paneele oder quadratischer Deckenkassetten. Weitere Beispiele von Rosenblüten sind in den Ecken der Tafel dargestellt. Diese Motive lassen sich vielfältig verwenden. Stilistisch sind die Rosen vermutlich von der Stuart-Rose abgeleitet, dem Emblem der schottischen Stuart-Könige. Dieses Emblem ist gelegentlich als Stuckdekor in schottischen Palastbauten zu finden.
Farblich ist jede Art der Umsetzung möglich; die Rosen können in dunklen Farben auf hellem Grund oder in hellen Farben auf dunklem Grund ausgearbeitet werden. Auch eine Verbindung mit Gold als Hintergrundfarbe ist denkbar.

Le motif central présente une grande rose très stylisée avec des tiges, boutons et feuilles qui se déploient dans un mouvement radial en formant un carré. Ce motif sert à décorer des panneaux carrés ou des caissons carrés de plafonds. D'autres exemples de roses sont représentées dans les coins de la planche. Ces motifs peuvent s'utiliser dans de multiples applications. Le style des roses est, selon toute vraisemblance, dérivé de la rose Stuart, emblème des rois d'Écosse. On retrouve parfois cet emblème sous la forme de décor en stuc dans certains palais écossais.
Toutes les transpositions de couleurs sont possibles ; les roses peuvent être réalisées dans des couleurs sombres sur un fond clair ou dans des couleurs claires sur un fond sombre. Une association avec du doré comme couleur de fond est également envisageable.

Ornamental bands with vine-leaf and floral decoration
Ornamentbänder mit Weinlaub- und Blumenranken
Bandeaux ornementaux à feuilles de vigne et entrelacs de fleurs

The pattern at the top features two undulating vines, staggered so that the crests of one "wave" correspond to the troughs of the other. The places where the two vines cross are marked by bunches of grapes, and the intermediate spaces each filled with a large vine-leaf. The pattern at the bottom depicts wild roses, sprouting from a horizontal stem at the bottom, and accompanied by buds and heavily toothed leaves.

The two designs are suitable as ornamental bands above a colored base zone, and as the motif for any other horizontal bands. They can be used both in secular buildings and in churches, provided these are not austerely Classical in style, in which case it would be more in keeping to use Greek or neoclassical designs. The color scheme shown here could be replaced by any other, either monochrome or polychrome.

Im oberen Muster sieht man gegenläufige Wellenranken, die Trauben und Weinlaubblätter tragen. Das untere Muster zeigt Heckenrosen, die sich von einem liegenden Stamm her aufrichten und von stark aufgefiederten Blättern sowie Knospen begleitet werden.

Die beiden Entwürfe eignen sich als Ornamentband oberhalb einer farbigen Sockelzone sowie als Motiv für jegliche andere horizontale Bänder. Sie können sowohl in profanen als auch in sakralen Gebäuden angebracht werden, sofern diese nicht im streng klassizistischen Stil errichtet sind. In diesem Fall würde sich die Verwendung von Entwürfen des griechischen oder neu-griechischen Ornamentstils anbieten. Anstelle der hier gezeigten Farbgebung wäre jede andere ein- oder mehrfarbige Ausführung möglich.

Le motif du haut présente des entrelacs de vagues contrariés portant des grappes et des feuilles de vigne. Dans le motif du bas, des églantines accompagnées de feuilles pennées déployées et de bourgeons se détachent d'une tige horizontale.

Les deux motifs serviront de bandeau ornemental au-dessus d'un soubassement de couleur, ainsi que de décor pour d'autres bandeaux horizontaux. Ils peuvent s'utiliser dans des édifices tant profanes que religieux dans la mesure où ceux-ci ne sont pas de style purement néo-classique. Dans ce cas, l'utilisation de motifs du style ornemental grec ou néo-grec s'imposerait. Une exécution monochrome ou polychrome peut remplacer la combinaison de couleurs présentée ici.

Ornamental bands with leaves and tendrils
Ornamentbänder mit Blattranken
Bandeaux ornementaux à entrelacs de feuilles

The pattern at the top shows an undulating stem, from which sprout chestnut leaves and rose blossoms. The pattern at the bottom consists of two intertwining stems, one of which is decorated with calyx-shaped flowers, while the other sprouts large leaves.
These designs are particularly suited to the ornamentation of horizontal or vertical bands. They require a reticent color scheme.

Das Muster oben zeigt eine Wellenranke, von der sich Kastanienblätter und Rosenblüten abspalten. Das untere Muster besteht aus zwei unterschiedlichen Wellenranken, die sich umeinander winden. Während eine der Ranken von Kelchblüten geziert wird, entwachsen der anderen große Blätter.
Diese Entwürfe eignen sich besonders für die Ausschmückung horizontaler oder vertikaler Bänder. Sie verlangen nach einer zurückhaltenden Farbgebung.

Le motif du haut présente un entrelacs de vagues accompagné d'une ondulation de feuilles de marronnier et de roses. Le motif du bas se compose de deux entrelacs de vagues différents, aux nombreuses circonvolutions. L'un est orné de fleurs s'ouvrant en calice et l'autre de feuilles de grande taille.
Ces motifs serviront à décorer des bandeaux horizontaux ou verticaux. Une combinaison de couleurs discrètes est recommandée.

Leaf and flower compositions
Kompositionen aus Blättern und Blüten
Compositions de feuilles et de fleurs

These six patterns show compositions of flowers or fruits with their appropriate leaves – thistle, wild rose and oak, for example. This kind of pattern can be used to decorate square panels or ceiling coffers.

With only minor changes to the leaves, these compositions could also be used to decorate round panels. Any color can be chosen, but design and ground must in each case be different shades of the same color. Similar designs can be seen on page 115.

Diese sechs Muster zeigen Kombinationen von Blüten oder Früchten mit deren Blättern. So sind zum Beispiel Disteln, Buschrosen und Eicheln zu erkennen. Diese Art von Mustern ist für die Ausschmückung quadratischer Paneele oder Deckenkassetten bestimmt. Bei geringfügiger Veränderung der Blätter können diese Kompositionen auch als Dekor von runden Feldern verwendet werden. Unter der Voraussetzung einer Ton-in-Ton-Umsetzung lassen sie sich in jeder beliebigen Farbe ausführen. Ähnliche Entwürfe werden auf Seite 115 präsentiert.

Ces six motifs présentent des combinaisons de fleurs ou de fruits avec leurs feuilles. On y reconnaît par exemple des chardons, des anémones et des glands. Ce type de motif convient à la décoration de panneaux carrés ou de caissons de plafonds.

Ces compositions serviront aussi à décorer des panneaux ronds, mais il faudra dans ce cas modifier légèrement les feuilles. Une transposition dans d'autres couleurs est possible, à condition que celles-ci soient ton sur ton. Des motifs similaires sont présentés à la page 115.

Broad ornamental bands with jasmine and bindweed
Breite Ornamentbänder mit Jasminsträuchern und Winden
Larges bandeaux ornementaux larges à bouquets de jasmin et liserons

Two elaborate designs for horizontal bands are illustrated here. The top one features stylized jasmine branches, while in the lower pattern the jasmine is replaced by bindweed. The reticent coloration of the leaves in combination with the ground gives these motifs a light, friendly character.

Patterns like these are appropriate for crestings and for the ornamentation of narrow friezes. In the latter application, they can be executed in several colors using a stencil, and touched up at the end by hand. The accompanying bands should be given a warm color tone.

Hier werden zwei aufwändig gestaltete horizontale Ornamentbänder präsentiert. Während bei dem Muster oben stilisierte Jasminsträucher zu sehen sind, treten beim unteren Entwurf Winden an deren Stelle. Die zurückhaltende farbliche Behandlung der Blätter in Verbindung mit dem hellen Untergrund verleiht diesen Motiven einen leichten und freundlichen Charakter.

Solche Entwürfe eignen sich als bekrönende Schmuckbänder sowie als Zierde schmaler Friese. In letzterer Anwendung können sie in mehreren Farben mit der Schablone aufgetragen und anschließend mit der Hand retuschiert werden. Die begleitenden Bänder sollten in einem warmen Farbton gehalten sein.

Cette planche présente deux somptueux bandeaux ornementaux horizontaux. Le motif du haut se compose de bouquets de jasmin stylisés et celui du bas, de liserons. La coloration discrète des fleurs associées au fond clair confère à ces motifs légèreté et charme.

Ces motifs serviront de bandeaux décoratifs en couronne, ainsi que de décor pour des frises étroites. Dans le cas de cette dernière application, une réalisation au pochoir est possible avec plusieurs couleurs retouchées ensuite à la main. Un ton chaud sera utilisé pour les bandeaux qui les accompagnent.

Broad ornamental band with bulrushes and irises
Breites Ornamentband mit Binsen und Schwertlilien
Large bandeau ornemental à joncs et iris

This design features bulrushes and irises emerging from wavy lines symbolizing the surface of a pond. The fine lines of the vegetal motifs, in combination with a light ground, brings out the ornamental character of the design to good effect. The irises and bulrushes can be replaced by any other plant with long, straight, slender stalks, for example tulips, poppies, sunflowers, cereals, or grasses.
If a polychrome color scheme is chosen, the starting point should be the natural color of the plant, albeit avoiding the bright colors of the flowers. The vegetal forms should always be stylized, to lend them their ornamental character. This ornamental band is suitable as the cresting frieze of a dark monochrome or patterned base zone. As designs in their own right, patterns like these can also be used to decorate a whole wall.

Der vorliegende Entwurf zeigt Binsen und Schwertlilien, die einem durch Wellenlinien angedeuteten Gewässer entwachsen. Die Darstellung besticht durch die feine Linienführung der vegetabilen Formen in Verbindung mit dem hellen Untergrund, der diese Ornamente eindrucksvoll zur Geltung bringt. Die Binsen und Schwertlilien können auch durch andere Pflanzen wie zum Beispiel Tulpen, Mohn- und Sonnenblumen sowie Getreidehalme und Gräser ersetzt werden. Diese Pflanzen zeichnen sich ebenfalls durch schlanke, gerade wachsende Blattstängel aus. Bei einer mehrfarbigen Gestaltung sollte man von der natürlichen Farbe der Pflanzen ausgehen, wobei aber die leuchtenden Farben der Blüten zu meiden sind. Die vegetabilen Formen sollten stets stilisiert wiedergegeben werden, um ihnen einen ornamentalen Charakter zu verleihen. Dieses Ornamentband eignet sich als bekrönender Fries einer dunkleren, einfarbigen oder gemusterten Sockelzone. Als eigenständiger Entwurf können solche Muster auch eine ganze Wand verzieren.

Cette planche présente des joncs et des iris qui s'élèvent d'un plan d'eau suggéré par des lignes ondulantes. Le motif séduit par le fin tracé des formes végétales sur un fond clair qui met ces ornements en valeur. D'autres plantes, caractérisées par des tiges élancées et droites peuvent remplacer les joncs et iris : par exemple des tulipes, des coquelicots et des tournesols, ainsi que des épis et des herbes. Pour réaliser ce motif en plusieurs couleurs, on s'inspirera de la couleur naturelle des plantes, mais on évitera d'utiliser des couleurs vives pour les fleurs. Les formes végétales doivent toujours être stylisées afin de conserver leur caractère ornemental. Ce bandeau ornemental servira de frise formant une couronne sur un soubassement plus foncé, monochrome ou à motifs. Pris individuellement, ces motifs pourront aussi servir à décorer tout un pan de mur.

Floral ornaments for vertical panels
Florale Ornamente für vertikale Paneele
Ornements floraux pour panneaux verticaux

This plate illustrates two designs for ornamental floral bands. The pattern on the left shows a central stem with stylized roses and rose-leaves, arranged alternately on each side. In the right-hand design, the roses and rose-leaves are replaced by stylized marguerites and their leaves. Unlike the rose design, the marguerites and their leaves are arranged symmetrically on the central stem.

These patterns are intended for the ornamentation of vertical panels and pilaster-like architectural elements. They can also be used for intrados or timber beams. If the patterns are executed on a larger scale, in quiet dark colors on a light ground, they can also be used to decorate the spaces between the rafters in church roofs (see also pages 105 and 117 in this connection).

Hier werden zwei Entwürfe für florale Ornamentbänder präsentiert. Beim linken Muster sieht man einen Zentralstamm mit stilisierten Rosenblüten und -blättern, die alternierend angeordnet sind. Beim rechten Entwurf sind die Rosenelemente durch stilisierte Margeriten und deren Blätter ersetzt. Im Gegensatz zu den Rosenelementen links, die versetzt dargestellt sind, spiegeln sich links die Margeritenelemente am Zentralstamm.

Diese Muster sind zur Verzierung vertikaler Paneele und vorspringender Gebäudeteile bestimmt. Sie können auch Bogenlaibungen und Holzbalken schmücken. Setzt man die Muster in einem größeren Maßstab um und trägt sie in ruhigen und gedeckten Farben auf hellem Grund auf, lassen sie sich zur Verzierung der Zwischenräume von Sparren eines Kirchendachs verwenden (siehe hierzu auch die Seiten 105 und 117).

Cette planche présente deux motifs pour des bandeaux ornementaux floraux. Dans le motif de gauche, des fleurs et feuilles de roses stylisées sont disposées de façon asymétrique de chaque côté d'une tige centrale. Dans le motif de droite, des marguerites stylisées et leurs feuilles remplacent les roses. Contrairement aux roses de gauche, les marguerites de droite sont symétriques sur la tige centrale.

Ces motifs serviront à décorer des panneaux verticaux et des éléments en saillie de bâtiments. Ils peuvent aussi orner des arcs et des poutres en bois. Agrandis et transposés dans des couleurs tendres et mates sur fond clair, ces motifs serviront à décorer les intervalles entre les chevrons d'un toit d'église (voir aussi les pages 105 et 117).

Floral motifs as corner decorations
Pflanzenornamente als Eckverzierungen
Ornements végétaux comme décorations d'angles

These four designs show floral motifs, which, while stylized, are still clearly derived from natural roses, lilies, thistles and chrysanthemums respectively.
The motifs are suitable for decorating the corners of large panels, and also for ceilings. The color scheme shown here can be replaced by a polychrome coloration, using strong colors, or indeed any other color scheme, as desired.

Diese vier Entwürfe zeigen stilisierte Pflanzenornamente, die sich stark an den natürlichen Formen von Rosen, Lilien, Disteln und Chrysanthemen orientieren.
Diese Motive eignen sich als Eckverzierungen großer Paneele sowie als Dekor von Decken. Anstelle der hier dargestellten Ausführung kann auch eine mehrfarbige Umsetzung in kräftigen Farben oder jede andere farbliche Gestaltung gewählt werden.

Ces quatre motifs présentent des ornements floraux stylisés qui ressemblent à s'y méprendre aux formes naturelles de roses, lis, chardons et chrysanthèmes.
Ces motifs serviront à décorer des angles de panneaux de grande dimension, ainsi que des plafonds. Une réalisation polychrome dans des teintes vives ou dans d'autres couleurs que celles présentées ici est, bien sûr, possible.

Masonry pattern with rose decor
Ziegelmuster mit Rosendekor
Motif de briques à décor de roses

This design shows a masonry pattern whose rectangular fields are decorated with stylized roses. The masonry pattern is characteristic of medieval ornamental style, and is shown here in a further variation. The roses are placed centrally in each field, giving a formal and very balanced effect, due in part to the quiet background, against which the lines between the "bricks" stand out well.
To attain a good effect, the leaves can be executed in irregularly graduated greens and browns, while the flowers themselves should be executed in mixed shades. Dark on a light ground, or vice versa, are equally effective.

Dieser Entwurf zeigt ein Ziegelmuster, dessen rechteckige Felder von stilisierten Rosen geziert werden. Das Ziegelmuster ist für den mittelalterlichen Ornamentstil charakteristisch und wird hier in einer weiteren Variante vorgestellt. Die im Zentrum der Felder stehenden Rosen wirken formal und farblich sehr ausgewogen, da ein ruhiger Hintergrund gewählt wurde, auf dem sich die Linien des Ziegelmusters gut abheben.
Um eine effektvolle Wirkung zu erzielen, können die Blätter in unregelmäßig abgestuften Braun- und Grüntönen ausgearbeitet werden, während für die Blüten selbst Mischtöne verwendet werden sollten. Eine dunkle Farbe auf hellem Grund wie auch eine helle Farbe auf dunklem Grund wirkt gleichermaßen ansprechend.

Cette planche présente un motif de tuiles dont les panneaux rectangulaires sont décorés de roses stylisées. Le motif de briques est caractéristique du style ornemental médiéval; il est proposé ici dans une autre variante. Les roses disposées au centre des panneaux contribuent à créer un très grand équilibre par leur forme et leurs couleurs, car on a choisi un fond discret qui met en valeur les lignes du motif de briques.
Le dégradé irrégulier de bruns et de verts des feuilles sera du plus bel effet, tandis que les fleurs elles-mêmes devront conserver des tons légèrement fondus. Le motif sera tout aussi séduisant dans une couleur foncée sur fond clair que dans une couleur claire sur fond sombre.

Diaper pattern of arches with lilies and crowns
Wandmuster aus Bögen mit Lilien und Kronen
Motif mural composé d'arcs avec lis et couronnes

This all-over design consists of arches, each formed from four arcs, which together generate a lozenge-like pattern. The vertices of the lozenges are decorated with small rosettes. The structure of this design is reminiscent of the sebka ornamentation common in Islamic art, which is likewise constructed from small arches of this shape. Patterns like these were probably familiar to the Audsleys through Owen Jones' two-volume book of patterns from the Alhambra. The Islamic influence in the design illustrated here is combined with three lilies – encircled by a crown – which fill each lozenge. The lily is the symbol of purity, which in Christian iconography is an attribute of the Virgin Mary. For this reason, the pattern is recommended for use in churches and chapels dedicated to Our Lady.

This pattern permits numerous variations. The lilies can be replaced by other flowers, such as roses, marguerites, fuchsias, dahlias, anemones or passion flowers. The color scheme in gold illustrated here is particularly effective, although other colors are certainly possible.

Dieser flächendeckende Entwurf zeigt kleine Halbbögen, die annähernd rautenförmige Grundelemente bilden. Die Verbindungspunkte der Elemente werden von kleinen Rosetten geziert. Der Aufbau dieses Musters erinnert an das in der islamischen Kunst übliche Sebka-Ornament, das sich aus kleinen Blattbögen zusammensetzt. Derartige Muster waren den Audsleys vermutlich durch Owen Jones' zweibändiges Vorlagenwerk zur Alhambra bekannt. Der islamisch beeinflusste Ornamentaufbau wird bei vorliegendem Entwurf mit drei Lilien als Füllformen kombiniert, die durch eine Krone zusammengehalten werden. Die Lilie ist das Symbol der Reinheit, das in der christlichen Ikonographie ein Attribut der Jungfrau Maria ist. Aus diesem Grund wird das Ornament als Dekor für Marienkirchen und -kapellen empfohlen.

Dieses Muster lässt vielfältige Variationen zu. Anstelle der Lilien können auch andere Blumen verwendet werden, wie zum Beispiel Rosen, Margeriten oder Fuchsien wie auch Dalien, Anemonen oder Passionsblumen. Der hier vorgestellte Entwurf in Gold ist besonders ansprechend, wenngleich auch andere Farben gewählt werden können.

Ce motif qui occupe toute la surface comprend des demi-arcs de petite taille disposés en losanges. Les points d'intersection des éléments sont ornés de petites rosaces. Ce motif rappelle le sebka, ornement courant dans l'art islamique, composé de petites feuilles incurvées. Les Audsley connaissaient probablement ces motifs pour les avoir rencontrés dans les modèles en deux volumes qu'Owen Jones avait réalisés pour l'Alhambra. La composition ornementale d'influence islamique est associée ici à trois lis aux formes pleines, maintenues par une couronne. Le lis, symbole de la pureté, est un attribut de la Vierge Marie dans l'iconographie chrétienne. Cet ornement est donc recommandé pour décorer les églises et chapelles dédiées à la Vierge.

Ce motif permet de multiples variations. D'autres fleurs peuvent remplacer les lis, par exemple des roses, des marguerites ou des fuchsias, des dahlias, des anémones ou des passiflores. Le motif réalisé ici en doré est particulièrment esthétique, mais il est, bien sûr, possible d'utiliser d'autres couleurs.

Do it yourself
Schritt für Schritt
Guide pratique

Introduction

The development of new materials and utensils in the course of the 20th century, and above all the importance which accrued to mass-esthetics and cheap construction throughout most of Europe in the postwar period, have meant that ornamentation, and with it traditional painting techniques, have increasingly fallen into oblivion. It was only with the revival of "bourgeois" values and the rise of Postmodernism that, towards the end of the century, there was a renewed interest in the decorative arts, particularly as applied to buildings. Historical ornaments and artistic techniques were rediscovered first and foremost in the private sphere, and in particular the colors and shapes of the late-19th century have since enjoyed great popularity.

The following part of the book is designed

Einleitung

Durch die Entwicklung neuer Werkstoffe und Arbeitsmittel im Verlauf des 20. Jahrhunderts, vor allem aber durch die Bedeutung, die in der Nachkriegszeit Massenästhetik und Billigbauweise in den meisten Gesellschaften Europas erlangten, sind die Ornamentik und mit ihr die alten Malertechniken zunehmend in Vergessenheit geraten. Erst durch die allgemeine Rückbesinnung auf bürgerliche Werthaltungen und im Gefolge der Postmoderne wuchs gegen Ende des 20. Jahrhunderts das Interesse an Baudekor und Ornamentik wieder. Historische Ornamente und künstlerische Techniken wurden vor allem im privaten Bereich wieder entdeckt, und insbesondere die Farb- und Formgebung des späten 19. Jahrhunderts freut sich seither großer Beliebtheit.

Der folgende praxisorientierte Buchteil

Introduction

C'est par le développement de nouveaux matériaux et outils de travail au XXᵉ siècle et surtout par l'importance qu'ont prise une esthétique de masse et une méthode de construction bon marché dans la plupart des sociétés européennes pendant l'après-guerre, que l'art ornemental et, avec lui, les anciennes techniques de peinture sont progressivement tombés dans l'oubli. Le décor architectural et l'art ornemental ne connurent un regain d'intérêt que vers la fin du XXᵉ siècle grâce à la réminiscence générale de valeurs bourgeoises et sous l'influence du postmodernisme. On redécouvrit les ornements historiques et les techniques artistiques surtout dans le domaine privé et depuis lors, les combinaisons de couleurs et de formes de la fin du XIXᵉ siècle jouissent d'une grande faveur.

Ceiling painting, Library, Château Malmaison, France, 1803
The ceiling painting in the library is a Romantic interpretation of the style of Classical Antiquity. Against a white and pale-green background, friezes and bands around the edges serve to frame freehand paintings of Classical motifs and figures. The bands with their olive-leaf motifs are likewise reminiscent of Greek Antiquity. Bands such as these were usually applied by means of a stencil and edged with straight lines. Gilded individual motifs could be combined with them (for example flowers and other details). The intrados of the arches are decorated with the same motif, in the manner of a coffered ceiling. To set off the dark walls, a ceiling was chosen which grows lighter with increasing height: the effect is to create a light and airy impression and to make the room look higher. The details shown here could also be used to tasteful effect in a modern room.

Deckenmalerei, Bibliothek, Schloss Malmaison, Frankreich, 1803
Die Deckenmalerei der Bibliothek empfindet den klassischen Stil der Antike romantisierend nach. Auf weißem und hellgrünem Untergrund finden sich an Kanten und Flächenanschlüssen rahmende Friese und Bänder. Diese Ornamentformen werden überdies zur Rahmung von freihändig gemalten klassischen Motiven und Figuren eingesetzt. Die Blattbänder in Olivenblattform erinnern ebenfalls an die griechische Antike. Bänder wie diese wurden in aller Regel schabloniert und mit Linierungen gerahmt. Hierzu könnten vergoldete Einzelmotive (Blüten und andere Details) kombiniert werden. Die Innenseiten der Durchgangsbögen sind mit den gleichen Motiven kassettenförmig bemalt. Zur dunklen Wandgestaltung wurde eine nach oben hin heller werdende Decke gewählt, um einen offenen, luftigen Eindruck zu vermitteln und den Raum optisch zu erhöhen. Die hier gezeigten Einzelelemente können auch in modernen Räumen geschmackvoll eingesetzt werden.

Peinture de plafond, Bibliothèque, Château de Malmaison, France, 1803,
La peinture des plafonds de la bibliothèque est inspirée du style classique de l'Antiquité tout en présentant des éléments romantiques. Des frises et bandeaux sur fond blanc et vert pâle ornent les angles et les raccords. Ces formes ornementales encadrent en outre des motifs et figures classiques peints à main levée. Les bandeaux de feuilles rappelant celles de l'olivier s'inspirent également de l'Antiquité grecque. Des bandeaux tels que ceux-ci ont été en général réalisés au pochoir et entourés de rangées de lignes. Il aurait été toutefois possible d'associer ici des motifs individuels dorés (fleurs et autres détails). Les faces intérieures des arcades sont peintes avec les mêmes motifs en forme de caissons. Pour les murs de couleurs sombres, on a choisi un plafond qui devient plus clair vers le haut afin de créer à la fois une impression d'espace et d'air et de donner l'illusion que la pièce est plus élevée. Les différents éléments présentés ici peuvent aussi s'intégrer subtilement dans des pièces modernes.

to be of practical use. It is hoped that it will help readers to implement historical motifs. Old techniques can certainly be executed using modern materials and contemporary color schemes; historical patterns and forms, when used with sensitivity, harmonize very well with modern interior decorating and furnishing. With a little courage and practice, even interested beginners will succeed. Traditional techniques are highly versatile; you may want to recreate Ludwig II's throne-room in your parlor, you might want to zizz up your bathroom with gilt lilies or simply apply a pretty ornamental border to the wallpaper in the nursery – but whatever the case, nothing brings greater pleasure than doing it yourself.

We start with a theoretical section to give a brief overview of the possibilities of interior decoration and color schemes and of the pigments and binding agents you will need. In the practical section, we shall describe,

dient zur Unterstützung bei der Umsetzung von historischen Motiven. Alte Techniken können durchaus mit modernen Werkstoffen und zeitgemäßer Farbgebung eingesetzt werden, denn historische Materialien und Formen harmonieren bei sensiblem Einsatz sehr gut mit moderner Raumgestaltung und Innenausstattung. Mit ein wenig Mut und Übung gelingen die Arbeiten auch interessierten Anfängern. Ob man das Wohnzimmer als Thronsaal Ludwigs II. gestaltet, das Bad mit vergoldeten Lilien veredelt oder einfach ein hübsches Ornamentband auf die Tapete im Kinderzimmer schabloniert – die Freude am Umgang mit alten Techniken ist vielseitig.

Ein theoretischer Teil gibt zunächst einen kurzen Überblick über die Möglichkeiten der Raumgestaltung und der Farbgebung sowie über die dabei benötigten Pigmente und Bindemittel. Im praktischen Teil werden neben den verschiedenen Möglichkeiten der Gestaltung des Untergrunds die

La partie pratique de ce livre explique comment transposer des motifs historiques. Il est bien entendu possible d'utiliser des techniques anciennes avec des matériaux modernes et des couleurs contemporaines, car les matériaux et formes historiques s'harmonisent très bien avec une configuration moderne de pièces, à condition de procéder avec délicatesse. Avec un peu d'audace et d'entraînement, la réalisation de ces travaux est à la portée même de débutants. Qu'il s'agisse de transformer le salon en salle du trône de Louis II, d'apporter une touche de raffinement à la salle de bains avec des lis dorés ou de pocher simplement un joli bandeau ornemental sur la tapisserie d'une chambre d'enfants – l'utilisation de techniques anciennes procure de multiples joies.

Une partie théorique donne d'abord un bref aperçu des possibilités de configuration de pièces et de combinaison de couleurs, ainsi que des pigments et liants

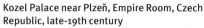

Kozel Palace near Plzeň, Empire Room, Czech Republic, late-19th century

The designer of this room attached particular importance to clear, austere lines and to the structuring of space. The frames of the oil-paintings harmonize with the wall painting and thus appear taller. Particularly striking are the ornamental bands framing the blue wall-mirrors. In order to underline the three-dimensional appearance of the fields, and thus to enhance the framing effect, the mirrors are outlined in a darker blue. The wall is crested with a pale stucco molding. The light ceiling helps to soften the otherwise severe effect of the decor.

Schloss Kozel bei Pilsen, Empirezimmer, Tschechien, Ende 19. Jh.

Bei der Gestaltung dieses Raumes wurde Wert auf klare, strenge Linienführung und Raumaufteilung gelegt. Die Rahmen der Ölgemälde korrespondieren mit der Wandmalerei und und werden dadurch erhöht. Besonders auffällig sind dabei die ornamentalen Bänder, die die blauen Wandspiegel rahmen. Um die Tiefenwirkung der Felder zu unterstreichen und so den rahmenartigen Eindruck zu verstärken, wurden die Spiegel mit dunklerem Blau liniert. Den Wandabschluss bildet eine hell gefasste Stuckleiste. Die helle Decke vermittelt dem Raum trotz der formalen Strenge eine gewisse Leichtigkeit.

Château de Kozel près de Plzeň, salle de l'Empire, République tchèque, fin du XIXe siècle

Lors de la décoration de cette pièce, on a mis l'accent sur la réalisation de lignes claires et strictes et sur la division de l'espace. Les cadres des tableaux peints à l'huile sont en harmonie avec la peinture murale qui met ceux-ci en valeur. Ce qui frappe surtout, ce sont les bandeaux ornementaux servant d'encadrement aux glaces murales bleues. Pour souligner l'effet de profondeur des panneaux et renforcer l'impression produite par les cadres, les glaces sont délimitées par une ligne bleue plus foncée. Les murs se terminent par un listel de couleur claire. Le plafond, également de couleur claire, confère à la pièce une certaine légèreté malgré la rigueur des formes.

along with the various possibilities of background-design, the historical techniques of line-drawing, freehand drawing and gilding. There is a detailed section on the technique of using stencils – a technique which proved very useful in the interior decoration of large rooms in historic buildings, and was consequently widely used.

When decorating a room with ornamental motifs it is sometimes better to have some things done by a professional before embarking on the project oneself or after one has done some of the preliminary work. Ideally, this professional should be active in the conservation area, as the traditional techniques and knowledge of materials have been preserved or relearned by firms specializing in such work.

Do-it-yourselfers will have to obtain a fair number of materials and tools. Some can be found in the DIY store, but for the great

historischen Techniken des Linierens, der Freihandmalerei und der Vergoldung vorgestellt sowie Arbeitsanleitungen und Tipps gegeben. Ein ausführlicher Abschnitt behandelt die Dekorationstechnik des Schablonierens. Diese Technik war bei der Innenraumgestaltung großräumiger historischer Bauwerke besonders zweckmäßig und wurde daher häufig eingesetzt.

Bei der Verzierung eines Raumes mit Ornamenten kann es manchmal sinnvoll sein, einige Arbeiten von einem Fachmann ausführen zu lassen, bevor man selbst mit der Dekoration beginnt oder nachdem man bereits einige Vorarbeiten erledigt hat. Idealerweise sollte dieser Fachmann im Bereich der Denkmalpflege tätig sein, da die alten Techniken und Materialkenntnisse in Betrieben mit dieser Ausrichtung erhalten geblieben sind oder wieder erlernt wurden. Für die eigene Arbeit sind eine Vielzahl von Materialien und Utensilien zu besorgen.

nécessaires. La partie pratique présente, en dehors des diverses possibilités de réalisation du fond, les techniques historiques du tracé de lignes, de la peinture à main levée et de la dorure et dispense directives et conseils. Une partie est consacrée à la technique de la décoration au pochoir. Cette technique, qui convenait parfaitement à la décoration intérieure de bâtiments historiques spacieux, a été fréquemment utilisée.

Lors de l'application des ornements dans une pièce, il est plus raisonnable de confier quelques travaux à un professionnel avant d'entamer soi-même la décoration. L'idéal serait que ce professionnel soit un spécialiste de l'entretien de monuments, car les techniques anciennes et les connaissances des matériaux ont été conservées ou redécouvertes dans ce genre de travaux spécifiques.

Pour le travail proprement dit, il convient

Here, the stencil technique helps to harmonize old premises with modern furnishings and fittings. The band with its leaf motif forms a bridge insofar as a traditional pattern has been combined with a fashionable color scheme. In order to emphasize the intense colors of the base zone and frieze, pure white was chosen as the background color for the walls and ceiling.

Hier bringt die Technik des Schablonierens alte Räumlichkeiten mit moderner Einrichtung in Einklang. Das Blattband schlägt dabei eine Brücke, indem das Muster zwar traditionell, die Farbe hingegen modisch gewählt wurde. Um die intensive Farbigkeit von Sockel und Fries hervorzuheben, wurde ein reines Weiß als Grundfarbe von Wand und Decke gewählt.

La technique du pochoir allie ici le style ancien des pièces et l'aménagement moderne. Le bandeau de feuilles sert de raccord tandis que, pour le motif sans doute traditionnel, on a choisi une couleur à la mode. Un blanc pur utilisé comme couleur de fond pour les murs et le plafond met en valeur les couleurs intenses des soubassements et frises.

majority you will have to go to a dealer specializing in artists' supplies, or even conservation equipment.

Before beginning with the work, some basic factors need to be taken into account. Most of the recommended paints, as long as they haven't dried, can be washed off with water, so it is always advisable to have a bucket of the stuff not far away, with a rag and a sponge. If the size of the room warrants it, there may be some point in having a movable scaffolding. For covering surfaces which are not going to be painted, you will need sticky tape and plastic sheeting, although old rags do the job better for floors, as they absorb drops of paint. In order to illuminate the room as completely as possible without shadows, daylight lamps with a sufficient length of flex are to be recommended. As a matter of principle, when painting, you should ensure that the room is well ventilated.

Einiges findet man im Baumarkt, den überwiegenden Teil des Bedarfs kann jedoch nur der Künstler- oder Denkmalpflegefachhandel bereitstellen.

Bevor man mit der Arbeit beginnt, sollte man einige grundsätzliche Dinge beachten: Es ist ratsam, stets einen Wassereimer mit Lappen und Schwamm griffbereit zu haben, da die meisten der zu verwendenden Farben vor dem Trocknen mit Wasser abzuwaschen sind. Für das Abdecken nicht zu bearbeitender Flächen benötigt man Klebeband und Folie, zum Schutz des Bodens sind dagegen alte Tücher besser geeignet als Folie, da sie die herabtropfende Farbe absorbieren. Um den Raum möglichst vollständig und schattenarm auszuleuchten, sind Tageslichtlampen mit ausreichender Kabellänge zu empfehlen. Generell muss beim Streichen auf eine ausreichende Lüftung des Raumes geachtet werden.

de se procurer une multitude de matériaux et d'ustensiles. On en trouvera certains chez les fournisseurs de matériaux de construction, mais seuls les magasins spécialisés dans les arts et l'entretien des monuments seront à même de proposer la majeure partie des fournitures nécessaires.

Avant de se mettre au travail, il convient de respecter quelques principes élémentaires : il est en effet judicieux d'avoir portée de la main un seau d'eau ainsi que des chiffons et une éponge, la plupart des peintures à utiliser étant lavables à l'eau à condition de ne pas être sèches. Une bande adhésive et un film serviront à recouvrir les surfaces à ne pas traiter ; de vieux chiffons protégeront mieux le sol qu'une feuille plastique. L'utilisation de lampes à halogène est conseillée pour éclairer la pièce le plus largement et avec le moins d'ombre possible. La pièce devra être suffisamment aérée pendant l'application de la peinture.

In this bathroom too, the combination of historical pattern with modern coloration provides a link between the ceiling with its rustic beams and the contemporary interior. The dark-blue outline of the tiles takes on the function of a frame. The pale-blue base zone and band at the top provide a frame for the otherwise white walls. The white stenciled ornamentation on the band reflects the white of the walls. All in all, color harmony is achieved through the combination of cool tones and tiles with the warm tones of the wood. There is practically no limit to what can be done by way of experimentation with old motifs and techniques.

Auch in diesem Badezimmer fungiert das historische Muster in moderner Farbgebung als Mittler zwischen der rustikalen Blakendecke und dem zeitgenössischen Interieur. Die dunkelblaue Fliesenrahmung übernimmt die Funktion einer rahmenden Linierung. Hellblauer Sockel und Wandabschlussband rahmen die weiß gehaltenen Wände. Das weiß schablonierte Ornament auf dem Band korrespondiert mit der weißen Wandfläche. Insgesamt wird eine ausgleichende Farbharmonie durch die Kombination von kühler Farbe und Fliesen mit den warmen Holztönen erreicht. Der Experimentierfreudigkeit mit den alten Motiven und Techniken sind nahezu keine Grenzen gesetzt.

Dans cette salle de bains, le motif historique réalisé dans des couleurs modernes sert de transition entre le plafond rustique et l'intérieur contemporain. Les raccords bleu foncé du carrelage forment un quadrillage. Le soubassement bleu clair et le bandeau qui délimite les murs encadrent les parois restées blanches. L'ornement blanc réalisé au pochoir sur le bandeau correspond à la surface blanche du mur. La fraîcheur des couleurs associée à la chaleur des teintes bois du carrelage créent un équilibre harmonieux. Les possibilités multiples qu'offrent les motifs et techniques anciens procurent des joies infinies.

Planning the Design

Before starting the actual work of applying paint and paper, you should plan how you want the room in question to look. This involves deciding on what sort of decorative elements you want to use (individual ornamental motifs, bands running round the room, corner elements, base zones etc.) as well as on the actual motifs and color scheme. Once you've made your decision, it is a good idea to make a sketch of the complete room using watercolors of the required shades, in order to get a preliminary idea of the effect of the chosen design using a particular color scheme.

Some proportions or divisions have a particularly pleasant effect – thus the base zone, for example, should not take up more than one-third of the total height of the wall. Bands and friezes should be placed a short distance above the base zone, and can be used as frames for windows and doors, as crestings for walls, or simply instead of a base zone. There should be a space of at least 10 centimeters between the cresting and the ceilin, to avoid the band appearing cramped. Small-scale individual motifs can be distributed over a particular surface. If they are larger (20–30 centimeters), they should be centered or else placed in the corners. Lines have the function of separating different color fields or designs, whether they themselves are autonomous design elements or simply serve to delineate bands and friezes.

Planung der Raumgestaltung

Bevor man mit den praktischen Arbeiten beginnt, sollte man planen, wie der betreffende Raum gestaltet werden soll. Dazu gehört neben der Entscheidung über die anzubringenden Verzierungselemente (Einzelornamente, umlaufende Bänder, Eckelemente, Sockelzone etc.) auch die Festlegung der entsprechenden Motive und Farben. Ist man sich über die zu verwendenden Elemente im Klaren, ist es sinnvoll, eine Skizze anzufertigen, die bei der Suche nach den geeigneten, mit dem Raum harmonierenden Farbtönen sehr hilfreich sein kann.

Einige Proportionen oder Aufteilungen wirken im Raum besonders angenehm – so sollte zum Beispiel die Sockelzone nicht mehr als 1/3 der Wandhöhe betragen. Bänder und Friese werden mit geringem Abstand über dem Sockel angebracht oder als Rahmungen von Fenstern und Türen, als Wandabschlussfries oder aber statt eines Sockels verwendet. Wandabschlussfriese sollten einen Abstand von mindestens 10 cm zur Decke einhalten, damit das Band nicht zu gedrungen wirkt. Kleinformatige Einzelornamente können über eine bestimmte Fläche verteilt werden. Sind sie etwas größer (20–30 cm), so sollten sie mittig auf der Fläche oder aber in den Ecken positioniert werden. Linierungen haben die Funktion, Farben zu trennen und Formen zu begrenzen, gleichgültig, ob sie als selbstständige Gestaltungselemente oder zur Rahmung von Bändern und Friesen dienen.

Configuration de la pièce

Avant d'entamer les travaux pratiques, on déterminera la configuration de la pièce concernée. On choisira les éléments de décoration à utiliser (ornements individuels, bandeaux en pourtour, éléments d'angle, soubassement, etc.), mais aussi les motifs et couleurs correspondants. Une fois le choix effectué, il sera judicieux de réaliser une esquisse qui se révèlera être une aide précieuse dans la recherche de tons s'harmonisant avec la pièce.

Certaines proportions et répartitions produisent un effet très agréable dans la pièce – le soubassement ne doit pas, par exemple, représenter plus d'un tiers de la hauteur du mur. Bandeaux et frises seront disposés au-dessus du soubassement en laissant un intervalle réduit ou encadreront des fenêtres et des portes, délimiteront les murs, ou encore tiendront lieu de soubassement. Les frises qui délimitent les murs doivent se trouver à 10 cm au moins du plafond afin que le bandeau ne soit pas trop compressé. Des ornements individuels de petite taille peuvent être répartis sur une surface déterminée. S'ils sont un peu plus grands (20 à 30 cm), il conviendra de les positionner au milieu de la surface ou dans les angles. Les lignes ont pour rôle de séparer les couleurs et de délimiter les formes, qu'il s'agisse d'éléments autonomes ou de cadres pour des bandeaux et des frises.

Sketch of the room
After the whole room has been measured, sketch it out to scale in pencil on a sheet of watercolor paper. Fixtures (e.g. stove) and existing furniture should also be entered. This sketch can be used to subdivide the walls and to establish the position and composition of the individual ornamental elements. The next step is to color in the sketch (using watercolors of the required shades) to obtain a preliminary impression of the effect of the ornamentation with a given choice of colors. Conspicuous colors in the existing furnishings must be taken into account: here, the green of the stove is reflected in the green of the leaves in the ornamental band.

Die Raumskizze
Nachdem man den kompletten Raum vermessen hat, wird er mit Bleistift maßstabsgetreu auf ein Blatt Aquarellpapier übertragen. Auch festgelegte Raumelemente (Öfen) und Möbel sollten berücksichtigt werden. In dieser Skizze wird neben der Wandaufteilung auch die Komposition und Position der einzelnen Ornamentteile festgelegt. Anschließend aquarelliert man die Bleistiftskizze in den gewünschten Farbtönen, um zunächst die Wirkung der ornamentalen Gestaltung bei einer bestimmten Farbwahl zu sehen. Markante Farbtöne in der Möblierung müssen dabei berücksichtigt werden: Hier findet sich das Grün des Ofens im Blattgrün des Ornamentbandes wieder.

Le croquis d'une pièce
Après avoir mesuré toute la pièce, on transférera les mesures au crayon sur une feuille de papier pour aquarelle en respectant l'échelle. On tiendra également compte des éléments fixes (poêle) et des meubles. Dans ce croquis, on déterminera non seulement la répartition des cloisons, mais aussi la composition et l'emplacement des différents ornements. On peindra ensuite à l'aquarelle le croquis au crayon dans les teintes désirées afin de constater l'effet produit par la décoration avec les couleurs choisies. Il faudra alors tenir compte des teintes spécifiques de l'ameublement : dans cette illustration, le vert du poêle se retrouve dans le bandeau ornemental.

Change of proportion

The selected ornament may have to be adjusted in scale in accordance with the design. A slide projector or episcope can be used to project the motif onto the wall in the desired size, and the outline can then be roughly sketched in. Copying machines can also be used to scale designs up or down. These methods do however harbor the danger that the logical structure of the motif will lose its clarity, with the result that corrections will have to be made afterwards – at worst, on the wall itself. More time-consuming, but more precise, is the traditional squaring up method, also known as the grid technique. It is used more often to change proportions than simply to change the scale of a motif, in other words it serves mainly to "stretch" or "squeeze" a design. Such changes in proportion are rarely carried out for purely esthetic reasons; more probably, they are necessary to make a particular motif fit precisely or to give an ornamental band an appropriate finish. In order to fit a repeat to the surface in question, there is also the possibility of extending or omitting a part of the motif, finding particular corner solutions by redesigning the motif, or altering the intervals between different elements.

Proportionsveränderung

Das ausgewählte Ornament muss gegebenenfalls auf die im Konzept festgelegte Größe gebracht werden. Mittels Diaprojektor oder Episkop kann man das Motiv direkt in der gewünschten Größe auf die Wand bringen und die Umrisse grob nachziehen. Auch mit einem Kopiergerät sind Größenveränderungen möglich. Bei diesen Methoden besteht allerdings die Gefahr, dass Struktur und logischer Aufbau des Motivs undeutlich werden, so dass anschließend eine Korrektur des Ornaments – im ungünstigsten Fall sogar an der Wand – nötig ist. Exakter, aber aufwändiger, ist die traditionelle Rastertechnik. Sie wird häufiger zur Proportionsveränderung als zur Vergrößerung oder Verkleinerung eingesetzt, d. h., sie dient vornehmlich zur Streckung oder Stauchung eines Ornaments. Eine solche Proportionsveränderung wird selten aus rein ästhetischen Gründen durchgeführt, vielmehr kann sie notwendig werden, um die Zusammenstellung der gewählten Motive passgenau zu machen oder ein Ornamentband stimmig abschließen zu lassen. Um den Rapport der Fläche anzupassen, gibt es daneben auch die Möglichkeit, einen Teil des Motivs zu verlängern oder wegzulassen, durch Umgestaltung des Motivs bestimmte Ecklösungen zu entwickeln oder die Abstände zwischen Ornamentteilen zu verändern.

Adaptation des proportions

Il conviendra le cas échéant d'adapter l'ornement choisi à la taille définie dans le concept. Il suffira pour cela de projeter directement le motif dans la taille désirée sur un mur à l'aide d'un projecteur de diapositives ou d'un épiscope et d'en retracer grossièrement les contours. On pourra aussi modifier le format à l'aide d'un photocopieur. Mais avec ces méthodes, la structure et la composition logique du motif risquent de devenir floues et de nécessiter une correction a posteriori de l'ornement, voire, dans le pire des cas, sur le mur. La technique traditionnelle de la trame est plus exacte, mais plus compliquée. On l'utilise plus souvent pour modifier les proportions que pour agrandir ou réduire un motif, c'est-à-dire qu'elle sert surtout à étirer et tasser un ornement. Il est rare qu'une telle modification des proportions ait lieu pour des raisons purement esthétiques ; elle peut, au contraire, s'avérer nécessaire pour adapter au plus juste la composition des motifs choisis ou faire coïncider la fin d'un bandeau. Il existe d'autres possibilités d'adapter le motif récurrent à la surface : prolonger ou ignorer une partie du motif, trouver des solutions particulières pour les angles en transformant le motif ou en modifiant les intervalles entre les éléments de l'ornement.

The squaring up technique
In order to change the proportions of an ornamental element, in other words "stretch" or "squeeze" it either horizontally or vertically, the procedure is as follows: first draw horizontal and vertical lines at equal intervals over the pattern and number them; the result will be a grid of squares. This grid can then be transferred to another piece of paper, but squeezed either horizontally or vertically, so that the squares become rectangles. The motif can then be redrawn, field by field, onto the new grid.

Die Rastertechnik
Will man mit der Rastertechnik die Proportionen eines Ornaments verändern, das Ornament also schmaler, breiter, flacher oder höher darstellen, so muss man nummerierte Linien in gleichmäßigen Abständen vertikal und horizontal über die Vorlage ziehen, so dass sich ein Gitter von Quadraten ergibt. Dieses Gitter oder Raster wird in Breite oder Höhe verändert auf ein Papier übertragen, so dass nicht wieder Quadrate, sondern Rechtecke entstehen. Anschließend zeichnet man das Motiv Feld für Feld in das veränderte Raster ein.

La technique de la trame
Si on veut modifier les proportions d'un ornement à l'aide de la technique de la trame, c'est-à-dire représenter l'ornement plus étroit, plus large, plus plat ou plus haut, on devra tracer des lignes numérotées directement sur le modèle, verticalement ou horizontalement et à intervalles réguliers de façon à obtenir une grille de carrés. On transférera cette grille ou trame modifiée en largeur ou en hauteur sur un papier afin d'obtenir, non pas des carrés, mais des rectangles. On dessinera enfin le motif panneau par panneau dans la trame modifiée.

Hints on Color Schemes

People's perception of different colors depends upon subjective criteria such as sensitivity to light, interior design and lighting, as well as each person's mood. Taste in color and color coordination also changes with fashion. However, each color can be classed objectively and systems like the color wheel have been developed for this purpose.

The colors around us give the environment a particular atmosphere. With basic knowledge about colors and the ways they can be combined anybody can attempt to create the preferred color atmosphere. In the end, only those who practise and experiment can develop a feeling for colors.

Wall surface – basic color

Before deciding on a color scheme, you should take account of the different effects of individual colors. So-called cold tones, like blue, green and their mixtures have a

Hinweise zur Farbgestaltung

Die Empfindung einer Person zu bestimmten Farben hängt ab von subjektiven Kriterien wie der Empfindlichkeit der Augen, den Lichtverhältnissen und der Wohnungseinrichtung sowie der persönlichen Stimmung. Der Farb- und Farbkombinationsgeschmack ändert sich auch mit dem Stil der Mode. Dennoch kann eine Farbe auch objektiv bewertet werden, wozu Systeme wie der Farbkreis entwickelt worden sind. Mit seiner Hilfe lassen sich Farbwerte erkennen und Mischbarkeiten ableiten.

Die Farben, mit denen der Mensch sich umgibt, verleihen der Umgebung eine gewisse Atmosphäre. Mit der Grundkenntnis über Farben und deren Mischverhalten kann jeder selbst versuchen, die persönlich bevorzugte Farbatmosphäre zu erzeugen. Letztendlich kann nur Gespür für Farben entwickeln, wer mit Übung und stetem Ausprobieren seine eigenen Erfahrungen macht.

Wandfläche – Grundton

Bevor man sich für eine Farbkombination entscheidet, sollte man die unterschiedliche Wirkung der einzelnen Farben in die Überlegungen einbeziehen. So genannte

Comment associer les couleurs

La perception individuelle de certaines couleurs dépend de critères subjectifs, tels que la sensibilité des yeux, la lumière ambiante et l'ameublement de même que l'humeur personelle. L'apppréciation des couleurs et de leurs nuances varie également selon les modes. Pourtant, toute couleur peut être considerée objectivement grâce à la mise au point de méthodes comme le cercle chromatique. Ce système permet de discerner les tons de couleurs et d'en dériver les combinations possibles.

Les coloris que l'homme place dans son environnement confèrent à celui-ci une réelle atmosphère. À condition d'avoir une connaissance élémentaire des teintes et de leurs variantes possibles, chacun est à même de réaliser à son goût la palette de ses couleurs préférées. En fait, seuls l'entraînement et la pratique permanente d'expériences individuelle sont garants d'une véritable intuition des couleurs.

Surface de mur – nuance de fond

Avant de choisir une combinaison de couleurs, on s'interrogera sur l'effet produit par les différentes couleurs. Ce qu'on appelle les couleurs froides comme le bleu, le

The color wheel

There are a number of ways of arranging colors in some systematic order. The simplest arrangement is known as the color wheel. Yellow, red and blue are the three primary colors. If any two of these are mixed, the secondary colors are obtained. Yellow and red produce orange, yellow and blue produce green, while red and blue produce violet. The primary and secondary colors lying opposite each other on the color wheel are referred to as complementary colors. Complementary colors are generally regarded as particularly harmonious and one member of each pair is thus suitable for toning down the other – in other words a pure color which is felt to be too strong or strident can be made softer or easier on the eye by mixing it with its complement. If a secondary color is mixed with a primary color once more, a new mixed tone will result. Thus blue and green produce turquoise, green and yellow produce greenish-yellow, yellow and orange produce yellowish-orange, etc.

Der Farbkreis

Für die systematische Ordnung der Farben gibt es verschiedene Ansätze. Die einfachste Anordnung der Spektralfarben ist der so genannte Farbkreis. Gelb, Rot und Blau sind die drei Grund- oder Primärfarben. Mischt man zwei von ihnen miteinander, so erhält man die Sekundärfarben: Aus Gelb und Rot wird Orange, Gelb und Blau ergeben Grün und aus Blau und Rot entsteht Violett. Primär- und Sekundärfarben liegen sich im Farbkreis gegenüber und werden als Komplementär- oder Ergänzungsfarben bezeichnet. Sie gelten im Allgemeinen als besonders gut miteinander harmonierend und eignen sich aus diesem Grund zum Abtönen des jeweils anderen Farbtons: Orange mit Blau, Grün mit Rot sowie Violett mit Gelb und umgekehrt. Abtönen bedeutet, dass man den möglicherweise zu kräftig oder zu grell erscheinenden reinen Farbton mit anderen Farben sanfter und gefälliger macht. Mischt man die Sekundärfarben mit einer weiteren Grundfarbe, so entsteht ein neuer Mischton: aus Blau und Grün wird zum Beispiel Türkis, aus Grün und Gelb Gelbgrün, aus Gelb und Orange Gelborange etc.

Le cercle chromatique

Il existe plusieurs méthodes de classification des couleurs, la plus simple étant l'organisation spectrale également appelée cercle chromatique. Le jaune, le rouge et le bleu sont les trois couleurs principales ou primaires. Si on en mélange deux, on obtient les couleurs dites secondaires: jaune + rouge = orange, jaune + bleu = vert et bleu + rouge = violet. Les couleurs primaires et secondaires se font face dans le cercle chromatique et sont qualifiées de couleurs complémentaires. Elles s'harmonisent en général bien entre elles et nuancent ainsi à la perfection la teinte correspondante: orange et bleu, vert et rouge, violet et jaune et viceversa. Nuancer signifie adoucir et atténuer avec d'autres couleurs une teinte qui peut paraître trop vive ou trop criarde. Si on mélange les couleurs secondaires à une autre couleur primaire, on obtient un nouveau mélange: par exemple, un bleu turquoise avec du bleu et du vert, un bleu vert avec du vert et du jaune, un jaune orangé avec du jaune et de l'orange, etc.

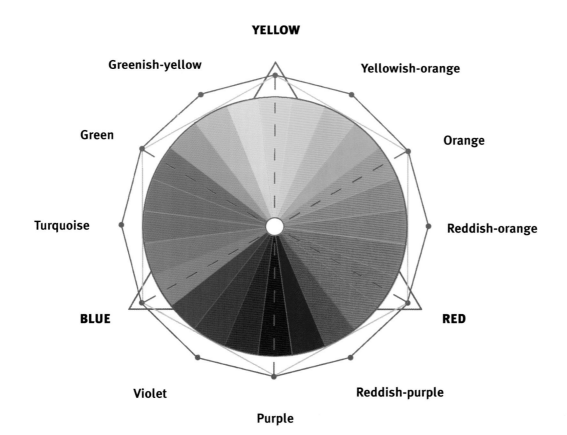

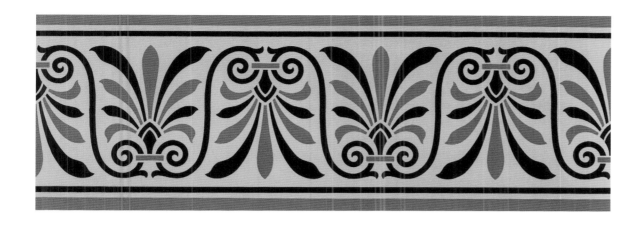

Different color combinations

In the ornamental band reproduced here once again (see page 49), as in almost all of their designs, the Audsleys attached great importance to a harmonious color scheme which would bring out the motif. The shape of the ornament is underlined by the color combination. As is demonstrated by the other color schemes, however, there are other possibilities. Thus the form of the motif can be made to take second place to the color scheme by emphasizing the background or varying the intensity of the color combination. For this reason, when choosing a color scheme for an ornamental design, you should always bear in mind what it is that you want to come across as the main feature.

Verschiedene Farbkombinationen

Wie bei fast allen ihren Entwürfen haben die Audsleys auch bei dem hier noch einmal abgebildeten Ornamentband (siehe Seite 49) größten Wert auf eine harmonische Farbgebung gelegt, die das Motiv selbst in den Vordergrund treten lässt. Die Form des Ornaments wird durch die Farbkombination besonders hervorgehoben. Wie die weiteren Farbentwürfe zeigen, lässt sich jedoch auch anders verfahren: So kann die Form des Motivs z.B durch die Betonung des Hintergrundes oder durch die Intensität der Farbkombination völlig hinter den Farbeindruck zurücktreten. Daher sollte man bei der Farbgebung eines Ornaments stets bedenken, was den Hauptcharakter des Musters ausmachen soll.

Diverses combinaisons de couleurs

Comme dans presque toutes leurs esquisses, les Audsley ont accordé une très grande importance à l'harmonie des couleurs qui met le motif en valeur. C'est le cas du bandeau ornemental illustré ici (voir page 49). La forme de l'ornement dépend tout particulièrement de la combinaison de couleurs. Comme le montrent les autres esquisses en couleurs, il existe toutefois de multiples procédés : la forme du motif peut, par exemple, être totalement refoulée à l'arrière-plan par un fond accentué ou par des couleurs intenses. Il faudra donc se demander ce qui fera l'originalité du motif lors du choix des couleurs d'un ornement.

calming, restrained effect, while the effect of warm tones like red, orange and yellow is stimulating. The more intense a color, the stronger its effect. Less intense colors are felt to be more pleasant.

The basic background color of the wall should not be too strong, or else the decorations will lose their effect. If the decorations are to be exuberant, it is best to choose a quiet background tone on a ground without much structure. If on the other hand you intend to have only bands and lines, several colors can be applied to the wall surface itself using glazing, ragging or sponging techniques. In general, off-white or any pale shade will be suitable. Earth colors, e.g. ocher, iron-oxide red or umber, are particularly good for blending. White by contrast is not suitable for mixing with strongly colored paints in order to make them brighter; all it will do is make them paler. White added to red, for example, will produce pink, not bright red. Likewise black should not be used to make colors darker, as there is a danger that the effect will be merely dirty. It is better to use complementary colors for darkening, although one should beware of using too many colors. The more different colors you mix,

kalte Farbtöne wie Blau, Grün und deren Mischungen wirken zurückhaltend und beruhigend, während warme Farbtöne wie Rot, Orange und Gelb anregende und wärmende Wirkung haben. Je intensiver eine Farbe ist, desto stärker ist ihre Reizwirkung. Ist ihre Intensität geringer, so wird sie als angenehmer empfunden.

Für den Wandfarbton sollten keine allzu kräftigen Farbtöne zum Einsatz kommen, da die Dekorationen sonst ihre Wirkung verlieren. Werden üppige Dekorationen eingesetzt, empfiehlt sich ein ruhiger Farbton auf einem strukturarmen Untergrund. Sollen hingegen lediglich Bänder und Striche gezogen werden, kann der Untergrund auch mit mehrtöniger Lasur, Wickel- oder Schwammtechnik gestaltet werden. Generell sind abgetöntes Weiß sowie alle hellen Farben geeignet. Erdfarben empfehlen sich besonders zur Abtönung: Ocker, Eisenoxydrot oder Umbra. Weiß eignet sich hingegen nicht zur Aufhellung von Volltonfarben, der jeweilige Ton wird unter der Beimischung von Weiß lediglich pasteliger, d. h., wenn man zum Beispiel Rot mit Weiß mischt, ergibt das Rosa, aber nicht Hellrot. Analog dazu sollte Schwarz nicht zum Abdunkeln der Farben verwendet

vert et leurs mélanges sont discrètes et apaisantes, tandis que des couleurs chaudes comme le rouge, l'orange et le jaune créent une atmosphère stimulante et excitante. Plus une couleur est intensive, plus son pouvoir stimulant est fort. À l'inverse, plus son intensité est faible, plus elle provoque une sensation agréable.

Il convient de ne pas utiliser de tons trop vifs pour les murs, sinon les décorations perdent de leur effet. Dans le cas de décorations surchargées, il est recommandé d'utiliser une teinte neutre sur un fond peu structuré. Si on se contente de tracer des bandeaux et des traits, on pourra aussi couvrir le fond en appliquant un glacis de plusieurs couleurs, au rouleau ou à l'éponge. Un blanc cassé et toutes les couleurs claires conviennent en général parfaitement. Les couleurs de terre sont particulièrement recommandées pour créer des dégradés : ocre, oxyde rouge de fer ou terre d'ombre. Toutefois, le blanc ne convient pas pour éclaircir des couleurs homogènes ; avec l'ajout de blanc, la teinte concernée devient simplement plus pastel, c'est-à-dire que si on mélange par exemple du rouge et du blanc, on obtient du rose et non du rouge clair. De la même façon, il ne faut pas

Colors for the decorative elements
The color schemes for the decorative elements should match those of the main wall surfaces. They can be taken from the color wheel using the complementary or toning-down colors. Here, the two complementary colors yellow and green have been deliberately used together. The yellow background of the walls was mixed with blue to achieve the green of the ornamentation and window framing.

Die Farbgebung der Dekorationen
Die Farben der Dekorationen sollten mit dem Farbton der Wandfläche korrespondieren. Sie können aus dem Kreis von dessen Abtönfarben stammen oder durch die dazugehörigen Komplementärfarben ergänzt werden. Hier wurden bewusst die beiden Komplementärfarben Gelb und Grün gegeneinander gesetzt. Für die Ornamente und die Fensterrahmungen wurde der gelbe Grundton der Wände mit Blau zu Grün gemischt.

La coloration des ornements
Les couleurs des ornements doivent s'harmoniser avec celles des murs. On peut les choisir dans le cercle de leurs dégradés ou leur adjoindre les couleurs complémentaires correspondantes. Dans cette illustration, les deux couleurs complémentaires que sont le jaune et le vert ont été délibérément opposées. Au fond jaune des murs a été mélangé du bleu afin d'obtenir le vert des ornements et des cadres de fenêtres.

the more the end result will resemble grayish-brown. Black can be used within the ornamental motifs or for accompanying lines.

Base zones and "frames"

The base zone can, indeed should, be painted in a stronger color than the background color of the wall. To establish a suitable color for the base zone, one of the colors used to blend the background color can be used, or else a stronger version of the background color itself. The paints used for the wall and the base zone should be of the same material to avoid incompatibility.

An harmonious total impression will be produced if the ceilings are lighter than the wall background, and the "frames" around windows and doors darker.

werden, da dabei die Gefahr besteht, dass die Töne schmutzig wirken. Das Abdunkeln mit Komplementärfarben ist vorzuziehen, wobei man darauf achten sollte, möglichst wenige verschiedene Farben zu verwenden. Je mehr Farben zusammengemischt werden, desto stärker geht die Farbe ins Grau-Braun. Schwarz kann innerhalb von Ornamenten oder für Begleitstriche eingesetzt werden.

Sockel und Rahmungen

Die Sockelgestaltung kann und soll farbintensiver ausfallen als der Grundton. Um einen passenden Sockelton zu ermitteln, kann man eine Farbe aus den Abtönfarben des Grundtones herausgreifen oder den Grundton selbst etwas kräftiger gestalten. Die Farben, die für Wand und Sockel verwendet werden, sollten aus dem gleichen Material bestehen, damit Unverträglichkeiten vermieden werden.

Ein harmonischer Gesamteindruck entsteht, wenn die Decken heller, die Fenster- und Türrahmungen hingegen dunkler als der Grundton der Wände gehalten sind.

utiliser de noir pour foncer des couleurs, sinon les teintes risquent de paraître sales. Il est préférable d'utiliser dans ce cas-là des couleurs complémentaires et on veillera alors à utiliser le moins possible des couleurs différentes. Plus on mélange de couleurs, plus le résultat obtenu paraît gris brun. Il est possible d'utiliser du noir à l'intérieur d'ornements ou pour tracer des traits secondaires.

Soubassement et encadrements

La couleur du soubassement peut et doit paraître plus soutenue que celle du fond. Pour trouver un ton approprié au soubassement, on peut en choisir un dans les dégradés de la couleur de fond ou prendre cette dernière et la rendre un peu plus soutenue. Les couleurs utilisées pour le mur et le soubassement doivent être réalisées dans le même matériau afin d'éviter des incompatibilités.

L'ensemble paraîtra harmonieux si les plafonds sont plus clairs et si, par contre, les encadrements de fenêtres et de portes sont plus foncés que la couleur de fond des murs.

Above: The cool appearance of the white staircase has been alleviated by coloring the base zone to match the woodwork. The gradations of earth or ocher shades in the brownish-beige base zone create a very harmonious effect.

Oben: Das kühl wirkende weiße Treppenhaus wurde mit einer farblich auf das Holzwerk der Treppe abgestimmten Sockelgestaltung aufgelockert. Der braun-beige Sockel wirkt durch Abstufungen von Erdfarben (Ockertöne) sehr harmonisch.

En haut: La cage d'escalier blanche d'où émane une impression de fraîcheur a été agrémentée d'un soubassement dont les couleurs sont en harmonie avec le bois de l'escalier. Brun beige avec des dégradés de couleurs de terre (ocres), il donne une impression de très grand équilibre.

Left: The warm red tone of the wall in combination with the two bands in yellow and white and the red-and-green design stenciled on it creates a Mediterranean ambience.

Links: Der warme rote Grundton der Wand erzeugt in Verbindung mit den beiden Bändern in gelb und weiß sowie dem darauf schablonierten rot-grünen Muster ein südländisches Ambiente.

À gauche: Le fond rouge chaud du mur crée une atmosphère méridionale, avec les deux bandeaux jaune et blanc et le motif rouge vert peint par-dessus au pochoir.

Pigments and Binders

In principle there are two ways of obtaining the paints you need: you can buy them ready-made, or make them yourself. If you want to create your own individual colors and exploit the multitude of powder pigments available, you should first take time to consider how paints are made.

A paint consists of binder, pigment, solvent, thinner, and possibly certain other additives. Binders are the basic substance of the paint; they bind the various pigments together and ensure that the color sticks to the surface to which it is applied. Pigments in powder form produce the actual color and opacity. Solvents dissolve the binder, which is usually supplied in solid form, and turn it into a thick liquid which can be easily worked. Thinners are often identical with solvents. They change the consistency of the paint, allowing it to be applied to the surface. The binders referred to in this chapter are water-soluble, and water is also the appropriate thinner. For this reason they are also known as aqueous binders. Additives change a paint's properties; they include preservatives, fillers (gypsum, chalk), or substances which change the paint's structure (e.g. quartz sand). All the materials listed here are generally suitable for use on walls.

Materials

Pigments can be subdivided into organic and inorganic substances. While natural organic pigments are derived from animal or vegetable ingredients, inorganic pigments are obtained from minerals. Since the 19th century, pigments have also been made synthetically. The pigments illustrated are largely of inorganic origin, and have been used for painting walls for centuries.

A vast number of colors is commercially available; the pigment powders illustrated form but a sample. They are all lightfast, resistant to lime and aging, and are compatible with all the binders mentioned.

Suitable binders include casein and natural organic glues. They can be bought ready mixed, but you can also make them yourself. The binders available for this purpose

Pigmente und Bindemittel

Grundsätzlich gibt es zur Bereitstellung der benötigten Farben zwei Möglichkeiten: Man kann entweder Fertigfarben verwenden oder die Farben selber herstellen. Will man eigene Farbtöne kreieren und die Vielfalt der erhältlichen Pulverpigmente nutzen, so sollte man sich zunächst mit der Zusammensetzung von Farben beschäftigen. Eine Farbe besteht aus Bindemittel, Pigment, Lösungs- und Verdünnungsmittel sowie gegebenenfalls einigen Zusatzstoffen. Bindemittel sind die Grundsubstanz der Farbe, sie verbinden Pigmente miteinander und bewirken, dass die Farbe auf dem Untergrund haftet. Die Pigmente in Pulverform sorgen für Farbigkeit und Deckkraft. Lösungsmittel lösen das zumeist in fester Form vorliegende Bindemittel auf und machen es zu einer verarbeitbaren Masse. Verdünnungsmittel sind häufig identisch mit dem Lösungsmittel. Sie verändern die Konsistenz der Farbmasse und geben der Farbe ihre Streichfähigkeit. Die in diesem Kapitel aufgeführten Bindemittel werden schlicht mit Wasser gelöst oder verdünnt, man spricht daher von einem Bindemittel auf wässriger Basis. Zusatzstoffe verändern die Eigenschaften der Farbe; es kann sich dabei um Konservierungsmittel, Füllstoffe (Gips, Kreide) oder auch Zusätze zur Veränderung der Farbstruktur handeln (z. B. Quarzsand). Alle hier aufgeführten Materialien sind generell für die Verwendung an der Wand geeignet.

Material

Pigmente lassen sich in organische und anorganische Stoffe aufteilen. Während organische Pigmente aus pflanzlichen und tierischen Grundstoffen bestehen, werden anorganische Pigmente aus Gesteinen und Erden gewonnen. Außerdem werden Pigmente seit dem 19. Jahrhundert auch synthetisch hergestellt. Die auf den Abbildungen gezeigten Pigmente sind größtenteils anorganischen Ursprungs und kommen seit Jahrhunderten in der Wandmalerei zum Einsatz.

Im Handel ist eine überaus große Vielzahl von Farbtönen erhältlich, von der die gezeigten Pigmentpulver lediglich eine Auswahl darstellen. Sie sind lichtecht sowie kalk- und alterungsbeständig und mit allen aufgeführten Bindemitteln verträglich.

Als Bindemittel dienen etwa Kaseine und

Pigments et liants

Il existe en principe deux possibilités pour la réalisation des coloris nécessaires : choisir des peintures prêtes à l'emploi ou élaborer ses propres couleurs. Si on veut créer ses propres teintes et profiter de la grande variété de pigments en poudre disponibles, on se penchera d'abord sur la composition des couleurs.

Une peinture se compose de liants, de pigments, de solvants et de diluants, ainsi que de quelques additifs éventuels. Les liants représentent la substance de base de la peinture ; ils lient les pigments et veillent à ce que la peinture accroche sur le fond. Les pigments en poudre constituent la base de la couleur et de son pouvoir couvrant. Les solvants dissolvent le liant, qui se présente le plus souvent sous une forme compacte, et en font une masse malléable. Les diluants sont souvent identiques aux solvants. Ils modifient la consistance de la matière colorante et confèrent à la peinture sa capacité à s'étendre. Les liants présentés dans ce chapitre se dissolvent ou se diluent facilement dans l'eau, c'est pourquoi on parle d'un liant aqueux. Les additifs modifient les propriétés de la peinture ; il peut s'agir de conservateurs, de pigments de charge (plâtre, craie) ou d'additifs qui modifient la structure chromatique (par exemple, du sable siliceux). Tous les matériaux présentés ici conviennent en général pour le traitement des murs.

Matériaux

Les pigments se divisent en matières organiques et inorganiques. Si les pigments organiques se composent de substances végétales et animales, les pigments inorganiques proviennent par contre de pierres et de terres. Les pigments sont en outre fabriqués aussi synthétiquement depuis le XIXe siècle. Les pigments montrés sur les illustrations sont en grande partie d'origine inorganique et sont utilisés depuis des siècles dans la peinture murale.

On trouve dans le commerce un vaste éventail de teintes, dont les pigments présentés ici ne constituent qu'une petite partie. Ils résistent à la lumière, au calcaire et au vieillissement et sont compatibles avec tous les liants mentionnés.

La caséine et la colle peuvent, le cas échéant, servir de liants. On peut se procurer de

Above: The ready-mixed paints illustrated here are available in a broad variety. They come either ready-pigmented or they can be blended using white and a color concentrate.

Oben: Die in einem vielfältigen Sortiment vorliegenden Fertigfarben sind entweder bereits pigmentiert oder sie können mit einer weißen Grundfarbe und Farbkonzentraten (Abtönfarben) abgetönt werden.

En haut : Les couleurs toutes prêtes qui existent dans de nombreuses variétés sont déjà pigmentées ou peuvent être nuancées par une peinture de fond blanche et des mélanges colorés (dégradés).

Opposite page: The most important ready-mixed painting materials are silicate paints, acrylic and emulsion paints, poster paints, tempera and gouache paints (photo).

Gegenüberliegende Seite: Die wichtigsten fertig gemischten Malmaterialien sind: Silikatfarben, Acryl- und Dispersionsfarben, Plakafarbe, Tempera und Gouachefarben (Foto).

Page ci-contre : Les principales peintures déjà mélangées sont : Peintures aux silicates, peintures acryliques et au latex, médiums à la cire, tempera et gouaches (photo).

Right: Binders used in the making of paints: 1 Bone glue in granulate form. 2 Cellulose powder. 3 Mowiol (polyvinyl alcohol) powder. 4 Slaked lime (hydrated lime, calcium hydroxide). 5 egg/oil tempera. 6 casein binder.

Rechts: Bindemittel zum Herstellen von Farbe: 1 Knochenleim in Graupeln. 2 Cellulosepulver. 3 Mowiolpulver (Polyvinylalkohol). 4 Sumpfkalk (Kalkhydrat, Löschkalk). 5 Ei-Öl-Tempera. 6 Kaseinbindemittel.

À droite : Liant pour la création de couleurs : 1 Osséine en grains. 2 Poudre de cellulose. 3 Poudre à base d'alcool polyvinylique (demander conseil à un spécialiste). 4 Chaux des marais (hydrate de chaux, chaux éteinte). 5 Tempera à base d'œuf et d'huile. 6 Liant à la caséine.

in powder form have to be soaked in cold water, where they will swell up. This jelly-like mass should then be warmed up until it becomes a viscous fluid. As glues based on animal or vegetable products remain water-soluble, paints that are bound with glue cannot be painted over with another water-soluble paint, as the two would dissolve into each other.

One traditional, very cheap and easy-to-renovate binder is lime. One part slaked lime (hydrated lime or calcium hydroxide) should be stirred or whisked with two to three parts water. The application should be carried out in humid conditions if possible, the substrate should be moistened first, and the coat allowed to dry slowly. Lime coatings are from a biological and physical point of view highly recommendable, and do not get dirty easily. If you want to renovate them, the only preparation needed is robust treatment with a dry brush. Slaked lime can also be used as a white paint if no pigment is added. If a colored coat is required, about 5–7% pigment should be added to the lime. Because it cannot absorb much pigment, paints bound with lime always have a semi-transparent glaze-like character. In order to increase the quantity of pigment absorbed, you can make lime-casein by simply adding about 100 milliliters of casein or low-fat curd cheese to 10 liters of lime-based paint.

Leime. Leime sind fertig angemacht erhältlich, können aber auch selbst hergestellt werden. Die zu diesem Zweck in Pulverform vorliegenden Bindemittel werden in kaltem Wasser eingeweicht und dadurch zum Quellen gebracht. Anschließend wird die gallertartige Masse erwärmt, bis sie zähflüssig geworden ist. Da Leime, die auf tierischer oder pflanzlicher Basis beruhen, wasserlöslich bleiben, müssen Farben, die mit Leim als Bindemittel hergestellt wurden, vor einem Überstreichen mit einer ebenfalls wasserlöslichen Farbe von der Wand entfernt werden, da sich der Altanstrich ansonsten lösen würde.

Ein sehr preiswertes und renovierungsfreundliches Material ist das althergebrachte Bindemittel Kalk. Sumpfkalk (Kalkhydrat) wird mit 2–3 Teilen Wasser verrührt bzw. verquirlt. Der Anstrich sollte bei möglichst feuchtem Raumklima mehrmals nass in nass erfolgen und langsam trocknen. Kalkanstriche sind baubiologisch und bauphysikalisch empfehlenswert und verschmutzen wenig. Will man sie überarbeiten, genügt zur Vorbereitung ein kräftiges, trockenes Abbürsten. Kalkhydrat ist ohne Pigmentzusatz auch als weißer Anstrich verwendbar. Für einen farbigen Anstrich kann man dem Kalkhydrat 5–7% Pigment zusetzen. Durch das geringe Pigmentaufnahmevermögen erhält die Kalkfarbe immer einen lasurartigen Charakter. Um den Pigmentzusatz zu erhöhen, lässt sich Kalkkasein herstellen. Dazu wird der Kalkfarbe einfach Kasein oder Magerquark zugefügt, ca. 100 ml pro 10 Liter Kalkfarbe.

la colle prête à l'emploi ou la préparer soi-même. Les liants prévus à cet effet, présentés sous forme de poudre sont amollis dans de l'eau froide jusqu'à ce qu'ils gonflent. Puis la masse gélatineuse est chauffée afin de devenir visqueuse. Comme les colles, qui sont d'origine animale ou végétale, sont solubles dans l'eau, il convient d'éliminer du mur les peintures fabriquées à base de colle (liant) avant d'appliquer une nouvelle couche de peinture également soluble dans l'eau, sinon l'ancienne couche risque de se dissoudre.

La chaux, liant traditionnel, est un matériau bon marché et idéal pour les travaux de rénovation. On mélange en remuant ou en fouettant la chaux des marais (hydrate de chaux) dans environ deux tiers d'eau. Dans un climat ambiant humide, on humectera plusieurs fois la couche et on la laissera sécher lentement. Les enduits de chaux sont recommandés du point de vue biologique et physique de la construction et salissent peu. Pour effectuer des retouches, il suffit de brosser la surface énergiquement et à sec afin de la préparer. L'hydrate de chaux peut aussi servir d'enduit blanc, sans ajout de pigment. Il est possible d'ajouter 5 à 7 % de pigment à l'hydrate de chaux pour obtenir un enduit de couleur. La peinture à la chaux a toujours un aspect de glacis. Une préparation de caséine de chaux permet d'ajouter davantage de pigment. On ajoutera dans ce cas de la caséine ou du fromage blanc maigre à la peinture à chaux, dans la proportion de 100 ml environ pour 10 litres de peinture à la chaux.

1   2   3   4   5   6   7   8

9   10   11   12   13   14   15   16

17   18   19   20   21   22   23   24

Making your own paint

If you want to make your own paint, the first step is to soak the powdered pigments in water until they have a dough-like consistency. At this stage, the resulting mass can be added to the thinned binder. Binders should be thinned according to the manufacturer's instructions: mostly this involves diluting them with three to four parts water. If too little binder has been used, the pigments can be wiped off, and the paint is said to flake. It is always possible, though, to add more binder or thinner to the paint. If too much binder has been used, however, the result is either a glaze, or the whole coating can come away from the substrate. The composition of the paint is, alongside the choice of binder, responsible for whether the effect is transparent or opaque. It is in any case a good idea to apply a trial coat, first to paper and then to an inconspicuous place on the wall.

Ready-made paints

Among the best-known ready-mixed products are emulsion and acrylic paints. The advantages of these paints are that they are easy to use, they can be washed, and

Die Farben selbst herstellen

Will man Farben selbst herstellen, so werden zunächst Pulverpigmente in wenig Wasser aufgelöst. Ist ein Farbbrei entstanden, wird er dem verdünnten Bindemittel zugefügt. Die meisten Bindemittel werden nach Herstellerangabe, meist im Verhältnis 1:3 oder 1:4, mit Wasser verdünnt.

Ist zu wenig Bindemittel verwendet worden, lassen sich die Pigmente abwischen, die Farbe „kreidet". Es ist jedoch möglich, der Farbe nachträglich noch mehr Bindemittel oder Verdünnungsmittel zuzufügen. Ist hingegen zuviel Bindemittel enthalten, kann es zu Glanzbildung oder zum Abplatzen der Malschicht kommen. Die Zusammensetzung der Farbe ist neben der Wahl des Bindemittels dafür verantwortlich, ob eine Farbe lasierend oder deckend wird. Probeanstriche, erst auf Papier, dann auf einer verdeckten Stelle an der Wand, sind in jedem Fall zu empfehlen.

Die fertigen Farben

Zu den bekanntesten fertig gebundenen und gemischten Produkten gehören Dispersions- und Acrylfarben. Die Vorteile dieser Farben liegen in der einfachen Hand-

Préparer ses propres couleurs

Pour préparer ses propres couleurs, on laissera d'abord tremper une pâte réalisée avec des pigments en poudre et un peu d'eau. La masse de couleur obtenue sera ajoutée au liant dilué. La plupart des liants sont dilués avec de l'eau selon les indications du fabricant, souvent dans la proportion 1:3 ou 1:4.

Si on n'utilise pas assez de liant, les pigments disparaissent et la couleur devient « crayeuse ». Il est toutefois possible d'ajouter a posteriori une plus grande quantité de liant ou de diluant. Si la quantité de liant est par contre excessive, on risque d'obtenir une surface brillante ou de voir la couche de peinture s'écailler. Le pouvoir couvrant et la qualité de glacis d'une peinture dépendent non seulement du choix du liant, mais aussi de la composition de cette peinture. Il est recommandé en tout état de cause de faire des essais d'application, d'abord sur papier, puis sur un endroit moins visible du mur.

Les peintures prêtes à l'emploi

Les peintures au latex et acryliques sont les produits déjà liés et mélangés les plus connus. Leur application facile, leur lavage à l'eau, ainsi que leur prix relativement faible

Pigments

1 Nickel titanium yellow. 2 Lime yellow, permanent. 3 Cadmium yellow, lemon. 4 Naples yellow, light. 5 Cadmium yellow, light. 6 Cadmium yellow, deep. 7 Lime orange, permanent. 8 Cadmium orange-red. 9 Cadmium light red. 10 Cadmium medium red. 11 Cadmium deep red. 12 Brillant Green, permanent. 13 Permanent green. 14 Chromium oxide green, dark. 15 Chromium oxide green, fiery. 16 Chromium oxide green, matt. 17 Ultramarine, light. 18 Ultramarine, medium. 19 Ultramarine, dark. 20 Smalt, standard 21 Cobalt blue, light. 22 Ultramarine violet. 23 Sienna, natural. 24 Sienna, burnt.

Pigmente

1 Nickeltitangelb. 2 Kalk Echtgelb. 3 Kadmium Gelb Zitron. 4 Neapelgelb hell. 5 Kadmium Gelb hell. 6 Kadmium Gelb dunkel. 7 Kalk Echtorange. 8 Kadmium orangerot. 9 Kadmium rot hell. 10 Kadmium rot mittel. 11 Kadmium rot dunkel. 12 Kristall echtgrün. 13 Echtgrün. 14 Chromoxydgrün dunkel. 15 Chromoxydgrün feurig. 16 Chromoxydgrün stumpf. 17 Ultramarin hell. 18 Ultramarin mittel. 19 Ultramarin dunkel. 20 Smalte Standard. 21 Kobaltblau hell. 22 Ultramarin violett. 23 Terra di Sienna natur. 24 Terra di Sienna gebrannt.

Pigments

1 Jaune de titane et de nickel. 2 Jaune solide de chaux. 3 Jaune citron de cadmium. 4 Jaune de Naples clair. 5 Jaune de cadmium clair. 6 Jaune de cadmium foncé. 7 Orange solide de chaux. 8 Rouge orange de cadmium. 9 Rouge clair de cadmium. 10 Rouge moyen de cadmium. 11 Rouge foncé de cadmium. 12 Vert solide de cristal. 13 Vert solide. 14 Vert de chrome foncé. 15 Vert de chrome chaud. 16 Vert de chrome mat. 17 Outremer clair. 18 Outremer moyen. 19 Outremer foncé. 20 Smalt standard. 21 Bleu de cobalt clair. 22 Outremer violet. 23 Terre de Sienne nature. 24 Terre de Sienne brûlée.

they are comparatively cheap. But they do have a downside: they form a closed layer on the wall surface, and thus reduce the wall's ability to "breathe". Also, the paints tend to flake after a number of years, or if overpainted too often, they are difficult, and sometimes impossible, to strip. The same generally applies to the oil and tempera paints popular in the 19th century. If you do want to use these paints, they should be restricted to small areas, such as the ornamentation itself. They can only be used for the wall background if this has previously been covered with woodchip paper or with lining-paper.

Alternatives to acrylic or emulsion paints include mineral-based paints such as silicate paints or lime paints. Mineral-based paints are easy to renovate, do not flake and create a pleasant indoor climate. Pure silicate paints consist of liquid waterglass and pigment; they are first mixed into a viscous mass by the user, before being thinned for use. They combine with the plaster substrate and create a high-grade, albeit not particularly cheap, alternative to lime.

habung, der Abwaschbarkeit sowie im vergleichsweise geringen Preis. Sie haben allerdings den Nachteil, dass sie eine geschlossene Schicht auf der Wandoberfläche bilden und somit die Atmungsaktivität der Wand herabsetzen. Außerdem blättert die Farbe nach mehreren Jahren oder bei mehrfachen Anstrichen ab, ein Entfernen ist schwierig, mitunter sogar überhaupt nicht möglich. Ähnliche Eigenschaften haben die besonders im 19. Jahrhundert beliebten Ölgemische wie Öl- und Temperafarben. Möchte man diese Farben zum Einsatz bringen, sollten sie nur für kleine Bereiche wie die Ornamente selbst verwendet werden. Für die gesamte Wandfläche kommen sie nur in Frage, wenn die Wand mit Raufaser oder der so genannten Makulatur, einer glatten Untertapete, vorbehandelt ist.

Als Alternative zu Acryl- und Dispersionsfarben bieten sich mineralische Farben (Silikatfarben, Kalkfarben) an. Sie sind renovierungsfreundlich, blättern nicht und bieten ein angenehmes Raumklima. Reine Silikatfarben bestehen aus flüssigem Wasserglas und Pigment und werden erst vom Anwender zu einem Brei angerührt und dann verdünnt. Sie verbinden sich mineralisch mit dem Putzuntergrund und bieten eine hochwertige, wenn auch nicht ganz preiswerte Alternative zum Kalkanstrich.

constituent des avantages indéniables, mais elles présentent toutefois un inconvénient : elles forment une couche hermétique sur la surface murale et empêchent de ce fait le mur de respirer. De plus, la peinture s'écaille au bout de quelques années ou s'élimine et après la superposition de couches appliquées, il est difficile de la faire disparaître. Les mélanges à l'huile si prisés au XIXe siècle, comme les peintures à l'huile et à la détrempe, ont des propriétés similaires. Si on voulait utiliser ces peintures, il faudrait limiter leur application à des surfaces restreintes comme celles des ornements. Elles ne peuvent entrer en ligne de compte pour tout un mur que si celui-ci est préparé avec de l'ingrain ou ce qu'on appelle de la maculature, c'est-à-dire un papier peint de fond.

Des peintures minérales aux silicates ou à la chaux, peuvent remplacer les peintures acryliques ou au latex. Elle sont idéales pour les travaux de rénovation, ne s'écaillent pas et créent une atmosphère agréable. Les pures peintures aux silicates se composent de verre soluble et de pigment ; l'utilisateur les malaxera d'abord pour en faire une pâte, puis les diluera. Elles se lient par un procédé minéral à l'enduit de fond et constituent, même si elles ne sont pas très économiques, une alternative de qualité supérieure à l'enduit à la chaux.

25 Gold ocher, light. 26 Gold ocher, burnt. 27 Gold ocher, dark. 28 yellow ocher. 29 Green earth (Terre verte). 30 Green earth, burnt. 31 Bohemian earth, pure. 32 Bohemian earth. 33 Verona green. 34 Venetian red. 35 Pompeian red. 36 Caput mortuum, light. 37 Caput mortuum, reddish. 38 Caput mortuum, dark. 39 Russet. 40 Umber, greenish. 41 Burnt umber. 42 Raw umber. 43 Lithopone (60% ZnS). 44 Titanium white. 45 Zinc white. 46 Ivory black. 47 Iron-oxide black. 48 Grape black.

25 Goldocker hell. 26 Goldocker gebrannt. 27 Goldocker dunkel. 28 Lichter Ocker französisch. 29 Grüne Erde. 30 Grüne Erde gebrannt. 31 Böhmische Grüne Erde rein.32 Böhmische Grüne Erde geschönt. 33 Veroneser Grüne Erde geschönt. 34 Venetianisch rot. 35 Pompejanisch rot. 36 Caput mortuum hell. 37 Caput mortuum rötlich. 38 Caput mortuum dunkel. 39 Rehbraun Deutsch. 40 Umbra grünlich. 41 Umbra gebrannt deutsch. 42 Umbra natur deutsch. 43 Lithopone Silbersiegel. 44 Titanweiß Rutli. 45 Zinkweiß. 46 Elfenbeinschwarz. 47 Eisenoxydschwarz. 48 Rebschwarz.

25 Ocre jaune clair. 26 Ocre jaune brûlé. 27 Ocre jaune foncé. 28 Ocre clair français. 29 Terre verte. 30 Terre verte brûlée. 31 Terre verte de Bohême, pure. 32 Terre verte de Bohême, avivée. 33 Terre de Vérone avivée. 34 Rouge de Venise. 35 Rouge pompéien. 36 Caput mortuum clair. 37 Caput mortuum rougeâtre. 38 Caput mortuum foncé. 39 Brun fauve allemand. 40 Verdâtre terre d'ombre. 41 Terre d'ombre brûlée, allemande. 42 Terre d'ombre nature, allemande. 43 Sceau d'argent lithopone. 44 Blanc de titane rutile. 45 Blanc de zinc. 46 Noir d'ivoire. 47 Oxyde noir de fer. 48 Noir de jais.

Preparing the Substrate

In order to ensure durability for the patterns, before the ornaments are applied it is essential to investigate the nature of the substrate or ceiling and if necessary, prepare it. In order to apply the paint to the wall, the latter must be clean, firm, free of dust, and dry. What kind of surfaces do we usually find in practice? In the mid-19th century, the traditional mineral plasters (lime and gypsum) were joined by cements, and in the 1970s by synthetic plastering materials. In addition, wall and ceiling surfaces are often clad in plasterboard of one kind or another. These various substrates demand different preliminary treatment before the paint is applied. Thus a primer is often required, for example, in order to create a smooth seal for a porous surface and hence decreasing absorption. Here it is best to ask an expert which operations should be carried out in view of the planned painting. On principle, plaster, pre-treatment and paint should be considered together to produce an acceptable result. Thus mineral paints (lime, silicate) produce good results on lime plaster when the latter is first etched – in other words when its surface is roughened to make it "take" the paint.

If you intend to apply a new coat of paint to an old surface, any flaking or water-soluble layers must first be removed. Existing coats of emulsion or acrylic paint can be painted

Untergrund-vorbereitung

Um eine lange Haltbarkeit der Muster zu gewährleisten, ist es vor der Ornament-übertragung nötig, die Beschaffenheit des Untergrundes (Decke, Wand) zu prüfen und ihn gegebenenfalls vorzubereiten. Um den Endanstrich auf den Untergrund auf-bringen zu können, muss dieser tragfähig, d. h. sauber, fest, staubfrei und trocken, sein. Welche Untergründe findet man in der Regel vor? Zu den üblichen mineralischen Putzen (Kalk und Gips) kamen Mitte des 19. Jahrhunderts Zementputze und in den 70er-Jahren des 20. Jahrhundert Kunst-stoffputze hinzu. Darüber hinaus sind Wand- und Deckenflächen häufig mit Gips-karton oder Gipsfaserplatten verkleidet. Die verschiedenen Untergründe erfordern unterschiedliche Vorbereitungsmaßnah-men für den sichtbaren Endanstrich. So wird zum Beispiel oftmals eine Grundie-rung erforderlich, um die Saugfähigkeit einer porösen Oberfläche herabzusetzen. Hier fragt man am besten einen Fachmann, welche Vorarbeiten für die vorgesehenen Anstriche günstig sind. Grundsätzlich soll-ten Putzuntergrund und Anstrich aufeinan-der abgestimmt werden, um ein akzepta-bles Gesamtergebnis zu erzielen. So eig-nen sich z. B. mineralische Anstriche (Kalk, Silikat) gut für Kalkputz, der vorher geätzt werden muss. Beim Ätzen wird die Ober-fläche des Putzes aufgeraut, um sie auf-nahmefähig für den Anstrich zu machen.

Préparation du fond

Il est nécessaire de vérifier la nature du fond (plafond, mur) et de préparer celui-ci le cas échéant avant d'y transposer des or-nements afin de garantir la durabilité des motifs. Le fond doit être correct, c'est-à-dire propre, solide, sans poussière et sec pour recevoir la couche de peinture finale. Quels genres de fonds trouve-t-on en général? Aux enduits minéraux habituels (chaux et gypse) sont venus s'ajouter les enduits au ciment au milieu du XIXe siècle et les enduits synthétiques dans les années 1970. De plus, les surfaces des murs et plafonds sont souvent revêtues de placoplâtre ou de plaques de staff. Les dif-férents fonds exigent des préparations di-verses pour l'application de la couche de peinture finale. Un apprêt s'impose donc souvent afin de diminuer la capacité d'ab-sorption d'une surface poreuse. Il vaut mieux demander dans ce cas à un spécia-liste quels sont les travaux préparatoires les plus appropriés pour les enduits prévus. En principe, le fond crépi et l'enduit devraient être compatibles afin de donner un résultat global acceptable. Des enduits minéraux (chaux, silicate) conviennent, par exemple, pour un enduit de chaux qui de-vra être préalablement poncé. Le ponçage rendra la surface de l'enduit rugueuse, ce qui lui permettra d'absorber la peinture.

Si on veut appliquer une nouvelle couche sur des surfaces anciennes, il convient

1 Striper
2 and 3 Flat brushes
4 and 5 Fitches
6 Mottler
7 Varnish brush
8 Flat brush
9 Long-bristled flat brush

1 Ringstrichzieher
2 und 3 Plattpinsel
4 und 5 Ringpinsel
6 Modler
7 Firnispinsel
8 Flachpinsel
9 Vertreiber

1 Tire-filet à anneau
2 et 3 Pinceaux plats
4 et 5 Pinceaux à anneaux
6 Pinceau plat et droit (grainure)
7 Pinceau pour vernis
8 Pinceau plat à virole métallique
9 Pinceau pour estomper les couleurs

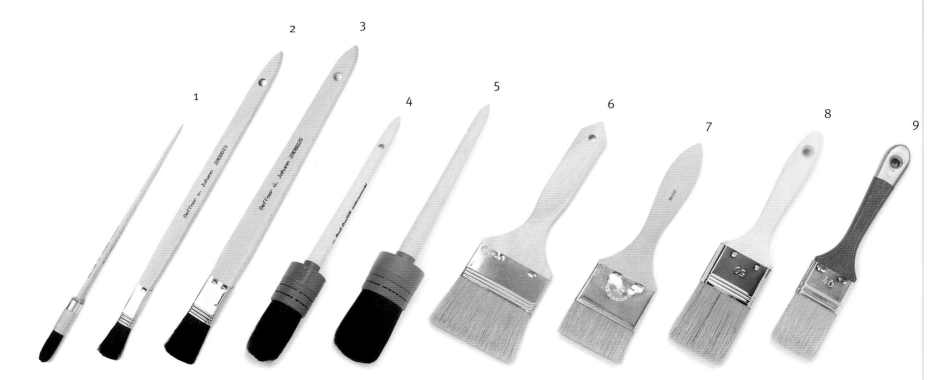

Right: In order to draw the straight lines demarcating base zones, and the frames for doors and windows, you will need a ruler (1), a spirit-level (2) and a reel of string ("chalking string") (3).

Rechts: Um Sockel, Spiegel, Fenster- und Türrahmungen und später die Bänder, Friese und Linierungen auf der Grundfarbe anzuzeichnen benötigt man einen Zollstock (1), eine Wasserwaage (2) und eine Schlagschnur (3).

À droite : Un mètre pliant (1), un niveau à bulle (2) et un cordeau à marquer (3) permettront de délimiter le soubassement, les encadrements de fenêtres et de portes, puis les bandeaux, frises et lignes sur la couleur de fond.

Below:

1 Lime brush

2 Special lime flat wall-brush ("hake")

3 Lime brush, round

4 Special lime facade brush, oval

Unten:

1 Kalkbürste

2 Spezial-Kalkflächenstreicher

3 Kalkquaste, rund

4 Spezial-Flächenstreicher, oval (Fassadenbürste)

En bas :

1 Brosse à chaux

2 Pinceau spécial pour surfaces enduites à la chaux

3 Blaireau pour surfaces enduites à la chaux, rond

4 Pinceau spécial pour surfaces enduites à la chaux, ovale (brosse pour façades)

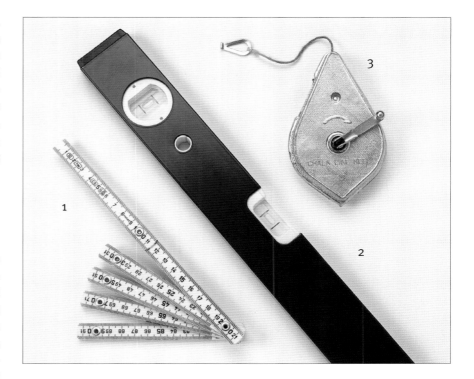

over, but only with paints of the same type. However, they do tend to flake, so it is generally advisable to remove such coats rather than try to treat them. If you would rather not apply your chosen ornamentation directly to the wall, because for example you will be using hard-to-remove oil paints, it is a good idea to paper the wall first with a fine woodchip wallpaper or smooth lining paper.

Painting techniques for the background color

Depending on the desired effect, there are various techniques which can be used to paint a wall. The paint can be applied opaquely or transparently. If what you want is opacity, the paint can be applied with a roller or a brush. If you use a brush, the brush strokes will remain visible ; depending on the type of paint, the surface will come across as anything from open to cloudy. If you prefer an even coating, it is better and quicker to use a roller. However, this is not always easy or possible with traditional binders (lime, mineral, casein). Use of a transparent rather than an opaque coating allows the substrate to shimmer through, and this in turn will visually enlarge the room. If this is what you choose, the substrate must be even, or given an undercoat. Transparency is achieved by using more thinner when mixing the paint. The usual technique is to apply the paint crosswise (i.e. making an X with the brush) using the "wet-in-wet" technique. Apart

Will man einen Neuanstrich auf alte Flächen auftragen, sollten nicht tragfähige, blätternde Schichten sowie wasserlösliche Altanstriche entfernt werden. Vorgefundene Dispersionen und Acrylfarben können nur mit demselben Material überarbeitet werden, neigen aber generell zum Abblättern. Es ist daher ratsam, solche Schichten komplett abzutragen, anstatt sie zu bearbeiten. Will man die ausgewählten Ornamente nicht direkt auf die Wand applizieren, weil zum Beispiel mit schwer entfernbaren Ölfarben gearbeitet werden soll, so empfiehlt sich eine Vorbereitung der Wand mit feiner Raufasertapete oder glatter Makulatur (Malervlies).

d'éliminer les couches fragiles qui s'écaillent, ainsi que d'anciennes couches solubles dans l'eau. Les peintures latex et acryliques découvertes ne peuvent être retouchées qu'avec le même matériau, mais elles ont en général tendance à s'écailler. Il vaut donc mieux éliminer totalement ces couches plutôt que de les traiter. Si on ne veut pas appliquer les ornements choisis à même le mur, parce qu'on doit utiliser par exemple des peintures à l'huile difficiles à éliminer, on préparera le mur avec un papier ingrain fin ou une maculature lisse (toison de peintre).

Maltechniken für den Grundton

Je nach gewünschter Wirkung kann der Untergrund in verschiedenen Techniken gestrichen werden. So kann man die Farbe entweder deckend oder lasierend aufbringen. Entscheidet man sich für einen deckenden Anstrich, lässt sich mit der Bürste oder mit der Rolle arbeiten. Verwendet man eine Bürste, bleibt die Pinselschlagstruktur (Duktus) leicht erhalten; je nach Farbmaterial wirkt der Untergrund in diesem Fall aufgelockert bis wolkig. Zieht man gleichmäßige Flächen vor, ist das Streichen mit der Rolle zweckmäßiger und schneller. Dies ist allerdings mit den meisten historischen Bindemitteln (Kalk, Mineralfarbe, Kasein) nur bedingt möglich.

Im Gegensatz zu deckenden Farben hat der

Techniques de peinture pour le fond

Il existe diverses techniques pour peindre le fond, quel que soit l'effet désiré. On pourra, par exemple, appliquer une peinture couvrante ou un glacis. Dans le premier cas, on utilisera une brosse ou un rouleau. Avec une brosse, la structure du coup de pinceau demeure légère et le fond donne l'impression d'être aéré, voire nuageux, selon la peinture utilisée. L'utilisation d'un rouleau sera plus appropriée et rapide si on veut obtenir des surfaces régulières. Cela ne sera toutefois possible que dans certaines conditions avec la plupart des liants traditionnels (chaux, peinture minérale, caséine).

Contrairement aux peintures couvrantes, le glacis est transparent. Le fond étant

from ordinary brushes, flat wall-brushes ("hake" brushes), sponges or cloths can be used.

In the technique known as graining, a special brush known as a mottler is used. Only the tip of the brush is dipped into the paint, and the strokes are applied crosswise to the wall with light pressure. The strokes remain after the paint has dried.

If you use the sponge technique, dip a natural sponge into the paint and dab it over the surface. The "ragging" technique involves dipping a cloth in the paint, wringing it out and rolling it on the wall.

All the techniques mentioned can be executed in the same color, in different colors or in alternate light and dark colors.

Whichever technique you use, make sure that the composition of the background color is compatible with that of the colors you intend to use later for the ornamentation. In case of doubt, use the same binder throughout, or ask the product manufacturer's advice.

Anstrich mit der Lasur einen transparenten Charakter, der den Raum erweitert wirken lässt. Da der Untergrund leicht durchschimmert, sollte er für diese Technik gleichmäßig sein oder mit einer Grundfarbe vorgestrichen werden. Lasurfarben werden hergestellt, indem man beim Anmischen der Farben mehr Verdünnungsmittel zusetzt. Als Werkzeuge für diese Technik eignen sich Bürste oder Flächenstreicher, gearbeitet wird meist nass in nass im Kreuzschlag (die Pinselstriche ergeben ein X). Alternativ lassen sich hier auch Schwamm oder Lappen einsetzen.

Bei der Technik des Granierens wird ein so genannter Modler (Pinselart) eingesetzt. Nachdem man nur dessen Spitzen in die Farbe getaucht hat, wischt man die Pinselstriche kreuzweise mit leichtem Druck an die Wand. Der Duktus bleibt nach dem Trocknen erhalten.

Zum Schwammstupfen wird ein Naturschwamm in Farbe getaucht und auf die Fläche getupft. Bei der Wickeltechnik wird ein Lappen in Farbe getaucht, ausgewrungen und auf der Wand entrollt.

Alle genannten Techniken kann man mit gleichen Tönen, verschiedenen Farbtönen oder im Hell-Dunkel-Wechsel ausführen.

Bei jeder der aufgeführten Techniken ist darauf zu achten, dass die Zusammensetzung der Grundfarbe und der Farben für die späteren Dekorationen aufeinander abgestimmt sind. Im Zweifelsfall verwendet man dasselbe Bindemittel oder erkundigt sich beim Hersteller nach den Verträglichkeiten.

légèrement diaphane, la pièce paraît plus grande. C'est pourquoi il doit être régulier ou déjà peint d'un couleur de fond. Pour créer un glacis, il suffit d'ajouter davantage de diluant au mélange de couleurs. La brosse et le rouleau conviennent parfaitement pour cette technique ; on travaillera le plus souvent sur une surface humide en entrecroisant les coups de brosse (en X). L'utilisation d'une éponge ou d'un chiffon est également possible ici.

La technique de la grainure exigera l'utilisation d'un pinceau plat et droit. Après en avoir trempé la pointe dans la peinture, on estompera les coups de pinceau en croix en exerçant une légère pression sur le mur. Les traits ainsi formés subsistent après le séchage.

Dans le cas de la peinture à l'éponge, on trempera une éponge naturelle dans la peinture et on en tamponnera la surface. De la même façon, on trempera un chiffon dans la peinture, avant de le tordre et de le dérouler sur le mur.

Toutes les techniques évoquées peuvent être utilisées avec les mêmes teintes, des tons différents ou avec une alternance de couleurs claires et foncées.

On veillera dans tout cas à ce que la composition de la couleur de fond et les couleurs réservées à la décoration ultérieure s'harmonisent entre elles. En cas de doute, on utilisera le même liant ou on se renseignera auprès du fabricant pour connaître les compatibilités des produits.

Left: All the surfaces are painted in the background color. Dip the bristles of the moistened brush into the paint, and apply the paint in short strokes. Do not wipe.

Links: Sämtliche Flächen werden mit der Grundfarbe gestrichen. Die angefeuchtete Bürste wird dabei mit den Borsten in Farbe getaucht und kurz ausgeschlagen (nicht abstreifen).

À gauche : Toutes les surfaces sont recouvertes de la peinture de fond. On trempera la brosse humide dans la peinture et on l'égouttera rapidement (sans l'essorer).

Right: Apply the brush in short even strokes crosswise or as a horizontal figure 8 all over the surfaces. Use loose wrist movements.

Rechts: Die Bürste wird in gleichmäßigen kurzen Schlägen in Kreuzform oder als horizontale 8 über die Fläche gestrichen, wobei locker aus dem Handgelenk gearbeitet wird.

À droite : Passer la brosse par petits coups réguliers et en forme de croix ou de 8 horizontal sur la surface, en gardant le poignet souple.

The application of guide lines

Once the background paint is dry, guide lines for the base zones, the frames and the frieze can be drawn. For this purpose you can use a ruler or some other straight-edge, a spirit-level, and a pencil. For longer lines and for the base zone, it is worth using a reel of string in a case (a "chalking string"), as follows.

First fill the casing with dry earth pigments, so that the string picks up the paint as it is drawn out. Then tense the string; you will need either a second person, or a nail, to hold one end to the wall. Pull the tight string briefly away from the wall with your fingers. When it is released, it will twang against the wall, leaving a straight colored line. Any surplus powder can be brushed off. Once you have delineated the base zone in this manner, paint it using whatever technique you have decided on. After that, you can proceed with the application of the decoration.

Das Anbringen von Hilfslinien

Ist die Grundfarbe trocken, werden Hilfslinien für Sockel, Rahmungen und Friese angelegt. Dazu kann man Zollstock, Wasserwaage, Malerlineal und Bleistift verwenden. Bei längeren Linien und am Sockel ist die Verwendung einer Schlagschnur sinnvoll: Die Schlagschnurbox füllt man zunächst mit Erdpigmenten, so dass sich die Schnur beim Herausziehen einfärbt. Anschließend wird sie gespannt, wobei eine zweite Person oder ein Nagel in der Wand das Schnurende fixiert. Die straff gespannte Schnur wird mit den Fingern kurz von der Wand weggezogen. Lässt man sie los, schnellt sie gegen die Wand und hinterlässt dort eine gerade pigmentierte Linie. Überschüssiges Pulver kann trocken abgekehrt werden. Hat man den Sockel auf diese Weise optisch abgetrennt, wird er in der gewünschten Technik farbig angelegt. Anschließend kann mit der Dekorationsmalerei begonnen werden.

Le tracé de lignes auxiliaires

Dès que la peinture du fond est sèche, on trace des lignes auxiliaires pour le soubassement, les cadres et les frises. Un mètre pliant, un niveau à bulle, une règle de peintre et un crayon sont les instruments requis pour cette opération. L'utilisation d'un cordeau à marquer est conseillée pour des lignes plus longues et pour les soubassements: on remplit d'abord le récipient du cordeau avec des pigments de couleur terre afin que la ficelle s'en imprègne, puis on tend la ficelle et on fixe l'autre extrémité au mur avec un clou ou on demande à quelqu'un de la tenir. On retire ensuite rapidement du mur la ficelle tendue. Si on la lâche, elle rebondit sur le mur en laissant une ligne pigmentée. Le surplus de poudre sec pourra être éliminé. Si le soubassement est délimité de cette façon, on peut y appliquer de la peinture selon la technique désirée. On passera ensuite à la peinture décorative.

Left: Use a string to draw a straight line demarcating the base zone.

Links: Mit Hilfe der Schlagschnur wird eine gerade Linie angebracht, die den Sockelbereich optisch abtrennt.

À gauche : Le cordeau à marquer permet de tracer une ligne qui se détache du soubassement de façon très visible.

Right: Paint the base zone using the technique you have chosen. The color of the base zone should as a rule be darker than the background color of the main part of the wall.

Rechts: Der Sockelbereich wird in der gewünschten Maltechnik gestrichen. Der Sockel sollte sich in der Regel dunkel vom Grundton abheben.

À droite : Le soubassement sera traité selon la technique de peinture désirée. Il sera en général de couleur foncée afin de trancher sur le fond.

Accompanying Lines and Bands

Lines and bands are often used in interior decoration. They demarcate the base zone and door or window areas from the rest of the wall surface, or else they are used to frame areas of decoration, including friezes and borders. A line can frame an ornamental band, or it may simply edge it above or below. A line above the band is suitable for "hanging" motifs, while one below the band is suitable for "standing" motifs. In a combination of various breadths and colors, lines can also be used as autonomous design features.

Substrate and materials

In principle, the smoother the surface of the substrate, the cleaner the line. To draw the line, it is best to use a chalking string, especially for longer lines. Alternatively, you can join up pencil marks placed at regular intervals. For bands, marks will be needed both for the top and bottom edges. To draw the lines, you will need brushes known as stripers. These are narrow brushes whose bristles are cut obliquely. They are available in various sizes and forms. In order to paint a band, i.e. the space between two lines, the best sorts of brushes, depending on the breadth of the band, are flat brushes or mottlers.

Begleitstriche und Bänder

Begleitstriche und Bänder werden in der Dekorationsmalerei häufig verwendet. Sie trennen Sockel, Fenster- und Türbereiche von den restlichen Wandflächen oder rahmen und begleiten Füllungsfelder, Friese und Borten. Eine Linierung kann ein Ornamentband rahmen oder lediglich darüber oder darunter angebracht sein. Eine Linierung über dem Band bietet sich bei hängenden, eine Linierung unter dem Band bei stehenden Ornamenten an. In verschiedenen Breiten und Farben kombiniert lassen sie sich auch als selbstständiges Schmuckelement verwenden.

Untergrund und Material

Grundsätzlich gilt: je glatter die Oberfläche des Untergrundes, desto sauberer der Strich. Um die Linie für den Strich zu markieren, ist bei längeren Linien die Verwendung einer Schlagschnur am zweckmäßigsten. Man kann sich aber auch mit Bleistiftmarkierungen in regelmäßigen Abständen behelfen. Für Bänder werden am oberen und unteren Rand Markierungslinien benötigt.
Zum Linieren verwendet man so genannte Strichzieher. Diese schmalen, schräg geschnittenen Pinsel sind in verschiedenen Größen und Ausführungen erhältlich. Um ein Band, die Fläche zwischen zwei Linien, auszumalen, sind je nach Bandbreite Plattpinsel, Flachpinsel oder Modler geeignet.

Traits auxiliaires et bandeaux

Les traits auxiliaires et bandeaux sont fréquemment utilisés dans la peinture décorative. Ils séparent les soubassements, fenêtres et portes du reste du mur ou encadrent et complètent des zones de raccords, frises et bordures. Une ligne peut encadrer un bandeau ornemental ou simplement être appliquée au-dessus ou en dessous du bandeau. Elle convient, dans le premier cas, pour des ornements verticaux et dans le deuxième cas, pour des ornements horizontaux. Dans une combinaison de différentes largeurs et couleurs, des lignes serviront aussi d'élément de décoration individuel.

Fond et matériaux

Il est un principe selon lequel plus la surface du fond est lisse, plus le trait est propre. L'utilisation du cordeau à marquer sera la plus appropriée pour tracer des lignes, notamment des lignes assez longues. Mais on peut aussi faire des marques au crayon à intervalles réguliers. On devra tracer des lignes de repère sur le bord supérieur et inférieur des bandeaux. L'instrument appelé « tire-filet » sert à tracer des lignes. Ces pinceaux étroits et biseautés existent dans des tailles et modèles divers. Pour peindre une bande, c'est-à-dire la surface entre deux lignes, on utilisera des pinceaux plats, des pinceaux plats à virole métallique ou des pinceaux plats et larges (grainure) selon la largeur du bandeau.

Below, left: To draw the line, put some fairly thin paint in a vessel. The liner must be well wiped on the edge of the dish to ensure a clean line.

Unten links: Zum Strichziehen wird etwas dünnflüssige Farbe in ein Gefäß gefüllt. Der Strichzieher muss am Rand gut abgestreift werden, damit der Strich sauber wird.

En bas, à gauche : Remplir le récipient avec une peinture très fluide pour tracer des traits. Retirer la règle à filet du bord afin que le trait soit propre.

Below, middle left: Horizontal lines are drawn from left to right. The edge of the bristles is drawn along the ruler. The ruler should not lie directly on the wall.

Unten Mitte links: Waagerechte Striche werden von links nach rechts gezogen. Der Pinsel wird mit dem Borstenrand am Lineal entlanggeführt. Das Lineal liegt nicht vollständig an der Wand auf.

En bas, au milieu à gauche : Tracer des traits horizontaux de gauche à droite. Passer le pinceau sur toute la longueur de la règle. La règle n'est pas entièrement posée contre le mur.

Below, center right and right: In order to create a broader stripe, known as a band, the dges are marked with string or with a pencil, the upper and lower edges then drawn as described, and the space between painted in with a flat brush.

Unten Mitte rechts und rechts: Um einen breiteren Farbstreifen, ein so genanntes Band, zu ziehen, werden die Ränder mit der Schlagschnur oder dem Bleistift markiert, die obere und untere Kante liniert und das Feld dazwischen mit dem Flachpinsel ausgemalt.

En bas, au milieu à droite et à droite : Marquer les bords avec le cordeau ou le crayon pour réaliser un bandeau, bande de peinture plus large, puis tracer le bord supérieur et inférieur et peindre le raccord intermédiaire avec le pinceau plat à virole métallique.

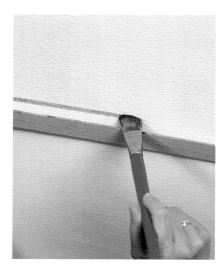

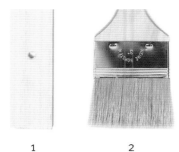         

1   2   3   4   5   6   7   8   9   10   11

Line-drawing technique

The line can be opaque or transparent, but when marking the course of the line, you must use thin paint, or the line will not be clean. It should drip easily from the brush. The brush itself must be well wiped; the bristles should not stand off, but lie flat. Now lay the ruler along the line you have

Die Technik des Linierens

Eine Linierung kann deckend oder lasierend ausgeführt werden. Die Farbe muss dünn sein, da sie nur so gut und sauber laufen kann. Nach dem Eintauchen sollte sie leicht vom Pinsel tropfen. Der Pinsel muss abgestreift werden, die Borsten sollten nicht abstehen, sondern glatt am Pinsel anliegen.

La technique du tracé de lignes

Le tracé de lignes peut être réalisé avec une peinture couvrante ou un glacis. La peinture doit avoir peu de consistance, sinon elle ne pourra pas s'étendre correctement. Après avoir trempé le pinceau dans la peinture, on l'essorera légèrement et on lissera les poils dans l'alignement du pinceau.

Above: 1 Ruler. 2 + 3 Mottlers. 4 + 5 Flat brushes. 6 + 7 Flat brushes. 8–11 Stripers in various sizes.

Oben: 1 Malerlineal. 2+3 Modler. 4+5 Flachpinsel. 6+7 Plattpinsel. 8–11 Strichzieher-Pinsel in verschiedenen Größen.

En haut : 1 Règle de peintre. 2 + 3 Pinceaux larges et plats (grainure). 4 + 5 Pinceaux plats à virole métallique. 6 + 7 Pinceaux plats. 8 à 11 Pinceaux tire-filet dans différentes tailles.

  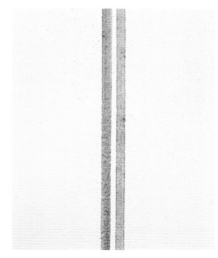 

already marked. If the line is horizontal, hold it at the left-hand end; if it is vertical, at the top. Use your index finger to hold the ruler a short distance away from the wall, in order to prevent paint seeping under it and making a mess.
Apply the liner carefully to the wall, and draw it smoothly along the ruler. It is particularly important that the brush is applied perpendicular to the wall so that the whole of the obliquely cut edge of the bristles touches the surface. Even pressure will ensure that the line is evenly broad; move the brush with your whole arm, not with your wrist. At the beginning and end of the line, somewhat less pressure should be applied, in order to avoid irregular joins. Draw the line for as long as you can comfortably do so, then move the ruler and continue.

Nun legt man das Lineal an der zuvor markierten Linie an. Das Lineal sollte mit Hilfe des Zeigefingers auf leichten Abstand zur Wand gebracht werden, damit die Farbe darunter nicht unsauber verlaufen kann.
Der Strichzieher wird gleichmäßig am Lineal entlanggezogen. Besonders wichtig ist das gerade Aufsetzen des Pinsels, die gesamte, schräg geschnittene Borstenkante muss auf der Wand aufliegen. Gleichmäßiger Druck auf den Strichzieher verhindert, dass die Linie unregelmäßig breit wird, das Handgelenk bleibt ruhig, die Bewegung erfolgt mit dem ganzen Arm. Beim Ansetzen und Auslaufen der Linie sollte man etwas weniger Druck auf den Pinsel ausüben, um unregelmäßige Übergänge zu vermeiden. Der Strich wird nur so weit gezogen, wie der Arm bequem reicht, dann wird das Lineal zum Fortsetzen der Linie erneut angelegt.

On posera alors la règle tout contre la ligne préalablement marquée. On laissera un léger écart avec le mur en maintenant la règle avec l'index, pour empêcher la peinture de couler.
On appliquera la règle à filet délicatement sur la surface et on la fera glisser régulièrement le long de la règle. Il est important de tenir le pinceau droit et de laisser reposer toute l'arête des soies coupées en biseau contre le mur. Tandis qu'une pression régulière sur la règle filet empêche la ligne d'avoir une largeur irrégulière, le poignet reste immobile et le mouvement s'effectue avec tout le bras. En commençant, puis en traçant la ligne, il convient d'exercer un peu moins de pression sur le pinceau pour éviter les raccords irréguliers. On prolongera le trait en tendant le bras, puis on déplacera de nouveau la règle pour continuer.

Left: The line is drawn cleanly using even pressure from top to bottom, with no wrist movement relative to the arm.

Links: Der Strich wird sauber und mit gleichmäßigem Druck von oben nach unten gezogen, das Handgelenk bleibt ruhig.

À gauche : Tracer le trait proprement et avec une pression régulière de haut en bas ; le poignet reste dans ce cas immobile.

Center: Should the line not be clean, or if you want a stronger line than the one you have drawn, the operation can be repeated. In this case, it is advisable to draw it in the opposite direction, in order to even out irregularities.

Mitte: Ist der Strich unregelmäßig geworden oder soll die Linie stärker oder farbkräftiger werden, kann noch einmal nachgezogen werden. In diesem Fall ist es sinnvoll, den Strich in entgegengesetzter Richtung zu ziehen, damit Unebenheiten ausgeglichen werden.

Au milieu : Repasser sur le trait si celui-ci est devenu irrégulier ou si la ligne doit être plus épaisse ou d'une couleur plus soutenue. Il est conseillé de tracer le trait dans la direction opposée afin d'éliminer les inégalités.

Right: There are numerous things one can do with lines. Just two parallel lines, for example, in different colors, can produce a decorative motif which by itself can serve as a frame for windows or doors, or simply as a border around the room.

Rechts: Die Möglichkeiten des Linierens sind vielfältig. So ergeben zum Beispiel schon zwei nebeneinander liegende, verschiedenfarbige Linien eine Verzierung, die als Rahmung für Fenster oder Türen oder auch nur als umlaufende Bordüre dienen kann.

À droite : Les possibilités de tracer des lignes sont multiples. Deux lignes de couleurs différentes et juxtaposées créent, par exemple, un ornement pouvant servir de cadre pour fenêtres ou portes ou simplement de bordure.

Freehand Painting

When applying ornamental motifs, freehand painting is an alternative to using a stencil. Freehand painting requires guide marks on the wall, indicating the contours of the relevant motifs. These contours are then filled in by hand. Freehand painting is particularly suitable for filigree, detailed, multicolored or varying motifs, while stencils are most useful for repeating patterns. Compared with the stippling technique used with stencils, freehand painting is more difficult as it requires a certain amount of practice. On the other hand, freehand painting entails almost limitless possibilities for creativity. Even in the case of repeating patterns, no two ornamental motifs painted freehand are ever exactly alike, and for this reason the effect is livelier than with the stencil technique. For practice, a piece of paper can be attached to the wall and some trial motifs painted.

Preparation

First enlarge an ornamental motif selected from a pattern book to the required scale. This can be done manually using the traditional grid technique, or else by using a copying machine. Next, it is a good idea to touch up the enlargement, because the

When touching up the design, keep retracing, using new sheets of tracing paper, until you have obtained the desired appearance.

Freihandmalerei

Bei der Applikation von Ornamenten ist die Technik des Freihandmalens eine Alternative zum Schablonieren. Die Freihandmalerei benötigt Hilfspunkte auf der Wand, die die Konturen des anzubringenden Ornaments vorgeben. Diese Konturen werden mit der freien Hand ausgemalt. Das Freihandmalen bietet sich bei besonders filigranen, detailreichen, vielfarbigen oder variierenden Mustern an, während das Schablonieren vor allem bei sich wiederholenden Mustern sinnvoll ist.
Im Vergleich zur Stupftechnik mit der Schablone ist das freie Malen anspruchsvoller, denn die Technik erfordert ein wenig Übung. Dafür sind jedoch die Gestaltungsmöglichkeiten nahezu unbegrenzt. Ein mit freier Hand gemaltes Ornament ist auch bei wiederholtem Muster an keiner Stelle identisch und wirkt daher lebendiger als eine Schablonierung. Zu Übungszwecken kann ein Blatt Papier an der Wand befestigt und bemalt werden.

Vorbereitung

Das aus einem Vorlagenbuch ausgewählte Ornament wird auf das gewünschte Maß vergrößert. Dies kann manuell in der traditionellen Rastertechnik oder auch maschinell mit einem Kopiergerät durchgeführt werden. Anschließend ist es sinnvoll, die

Bei der Überarbeitung des Ornaments wird so lange ein neues Blatt Pergamentpapier auf die Übertragung gelegt und diese korrigierend durchgezeichnet, bis das Ornament das gewünschte Aussehen erhalten hat.

Peinture à main levée

Dans l'application d'ornements, la technique de la peinture à main levée peut remplacer le pochoir. Pour la peinture à main levée, il convient de marquer des points de repère sur le mur qui esquisseront les contours de l'ornement à réaliser. Ces contours sont peints à main levée. Cette méthode convient parfaitement pour les motifs en filigrane, riches en détails, polychromes ou présentant des variantes, tandis que la technique du pochoir se prête avant tout à la réalisation de motifs répétés.
Par rapport à la technique des points avec le pochoir, la peinture à main levée est plus délicate, car elle exige un peu d'entraînement. Les possibilités de réalisation sont toutefois pratiquement illimitées. Un ornement peint à main levée n'est jamais reproduit de façon identique, même s'il est répété et il a donc l'air plus vivant qu'un motif au pochoir. On pourra fixer une feuille de papier au mur pour la peindre à titre d'exercice.

Préparation

L'ornement choisi dans un recueil de modèles est agrandi à l'échelle désirée. On pourra le reproduire à la main selon la technique traditionnelle de la trame ou à l'aide d'un photocopieur. Il est utile de retoucher ensuite le modèle agrandi, car les contours

Au moment de retoucher l'ornement, poser une nouvelle feuille de papier sulfurisé sur le transfert et le décalquer en y apportant des corrections jusqu'à l'obtention de l'effet désiré.

The desired ornamental design, enlarged to its final size, is transferred to tracing paper.

Das gewünschte und auf die Endgröße gebrachte Ornament wird auf ein Pergamentpapier übertragen.

Transférer l'ornement désiré et converti à la dimension définitive sur du papier sulfurisé.

specific contours of the motif can easily get blurred during the enlargement process. In this connection, particular attention must be paid to the organic structure of the ornament: the contours of a plant run smoothly from the tips of the leaves to the base of the stem. Corners and edges would spoil the organic effect and thus the visual image of the whole design. Not only must the contours of the leaves be redrawn, but also the logical continuation of invisible lines, in the case of knots and twists, for example, and also the hidden parts of plants.

The corrected outline is then pricked out

vergrößerte Vorlage zu überarbeiten, da die spezifischen Konturen des Ornaments im Zuge der Vergrößerung häufig undeutlich werden. In diesem Zusammenhang ist besonders auf den organischen Verlauf des Ornaments zu achten: Die Struktur einer Pflanze verläuft in weichen Linien von der Spitze der Blätter bis zum Stumpf. Ecken und Kanten stören den organischen Verlauf und damit das optische Erscheinungsbild des gesamten Ornaments. Nicht nur die Blattkonturen müssen nachgezogen werden, auch der logisch richtige Fortlauf von unsichtbaren Linien, zum Beispiel bei Kno-

spécifiques de l'ornement deviennent souvent flous en raison de l'agrandissement. Dans ce contexte, on prêtera une attention particulière à l'évolution organique de l'ornement : la structure d'une plante évolue en lignes molles, de la pointe des feuilles à la souche. Les angles et arêtes gênent l'évolution organique et, par conséquent, l'effet optique produit par l'ornement dans son ensemble. Il faut non seulement retracer les contours des feuilles, mais aussi respecter le tracé logiquement exact des lignes invisibles, par exemple dans les nœuds et bandeaux entrelacés ou plantes.

Left: Use the final corrected version to create a pricked-out outline. Use a thick needle to prick out the lines, with holes half a centimeter to a centimeter apart.

Links: Aus der letzten Korrekturzeichnung wird die Lochpause gefertigt. Mit einer dicken Nadel werden die Linien im Abstand von 0,5–1,0 cm nachgestochen.

À gauche : Le calque à trou est réalisé à partir du dernier tracé de corrections. Repiquer les lignes à des intervalles de 0,5 à 1,0 cm à l'aide d'une grosse aiguille.

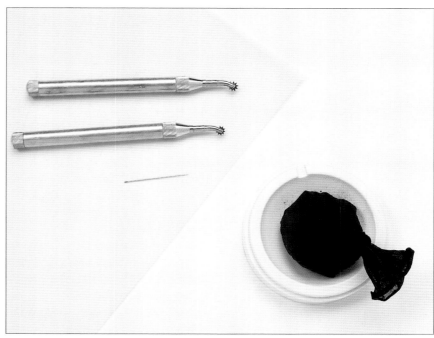

with a fairly large needle. A firm but not too hard underlay is needed, for example a piece of polystyrene, but a baby's diaper will do. In order to reproduce details correctly, or places where the lines are close together, the needle pricks should not be too far apart, but otherwise a distance of between half a centimeter and one centimeter between the pricks is sufficient. For simple lines or larger motifs, tracing wheels are easier to use than a needle.

In order to transfer the pricked out contour to the wall, you need a tracing bag. To make one, take a stocking made of silk or similarly fine material. For a light wall color, fill the bag (stocking) with the ash from a burnt newspaper, while for a dark wall color, take white pigment of some sort (e.g. chalk).

ten und verschlungenen Bändern oder Pflanzen, ist wichtig.

Die fertige Korrektur wird an den Linien entlang mit einer größeren Nadel gestupft. Als halbfeste Unterlage zum Durchstechen eignen sich Styropor oder Babywindeln. Um Details oder Stellen mit eng zusammenliegenden Linien sauber herauszuarbeiten, muss enger gestupft werden, ansonsten genügt ein Abstand von 0,5–1,0 cm zwischen den Einstichen. Bei einfacheren Linien oder größeren Formaten sind Pausrädchen zweckmäßiger als eine Nadel. Um die Lochkonturen des Ornaments auf die Wand zu übertragen, wird ein Pausbeutel benötigt. Zur Herstellung des Beutels sollte ein Seidenstrumpf oder ein ähnlich dünner Stoff verwendet werden. Der Beutel wird bei einem hellen Wandton mit Asche aus verbranntem Zeitungspapier gefüllt, bei einem dunklen Wandton ist weißes Pigment (Kreide) besser geeignet.

On marquera la correction terminée le long des lignes à l'aide d'une aiguille assez grande. Du polystyrène ou des couches pour bébés serviront de support semi-dur pour enfoncer l'aiguille. Pour retoucher certains détails ou endroits où les lignes sont serrées, on fera des marques plus rapprochées, sinon un intervalle de 0,5 à 1,0 cm entre les piqûres suffit. Dans le cas de lignes plus simples ou de formats plus grands, il sera préférable d'utiliser des roulettes à décalquer plutôt qu'une aiguille. Afin de reporter les contours des trous de l'ornement sur le mur, on utilisera une pochette à décalquer. On prendra un bas ou une matière fine similaire pour confectionner cette pochette qui sera remplie de cendre de papier journal carbonisé s'il s'agit d'un mur clair, et de pigment blanc (calcaire) s'il s'agit d'un mur sombre.

Right: For larger patterns or straight lines, use tracing-wheels of different sizes. Then make a tracing-bag by filling a silk stocking with newspaper ash.

Rechts: Bei größeren Ornamenten oder geraden Linien können Pausrädchen in unterschiedlichen Stärken verwendet werden. Um einen Pausbeutel herzustellen, wird die Asche von Zeitungspapier in einen Seidenstrumpf gefüllt.

À droite : Si les ornements sont assez grands ou que les lignes sont droites, utiliser des roulettes de décalquage dans différentes épaisseurs. Pour fabriquer une pochette de décalquage, remplir un bas avec de la cendre de papier journal.

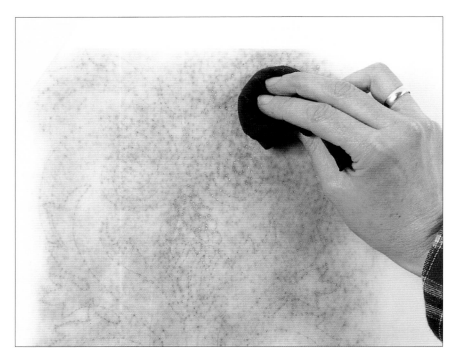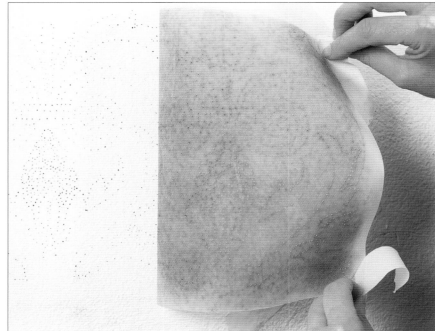

Transfer of the ornamental design

First attach the pricked out tracing securely to the wall with adhesive tape. If it is not securely fastened, the paper may slip, and the result will be doubled or blurred lines. If you are dealing with a continuous or multi-part ornament, you need guide lines over the area to be decorated so that the tracing paper is attached in the right place each time. To transfer the pattern to the wall, knock and rub the filled stocking against the wall.

Freehand painting

For painting decorative motifs, almost any brush with long natural or synthetic bristles is suitable. In general, you can use paints based on any binder (e.g. casein, lime casein, polyvinylalcohol, natural glue), but the paint should be thin. Transparent paints can give a particularly filigree look.
To paint, stand upright at a sufficient distance from the wall. Hold the brush at the top end of the handle. A mahlstick can be used to steady the hand. By varying the pressure on the brush, you can obtain a broader or narrow stroke. The direction of the brush-stroke is controlled by twisting the wrist. The hand itself should remain relatively immobile, arm movements being controlled from the shoulder. The brush-stroke should be attuned to the organic line of the motif. The brush should be placed at

Die Übertragung des Ornaments

Die Lochpause muss mit Klebestreifen sicher auf der Wand fixiert werden. Ist sie nur unzureichend befestigt, kann das Papier verrutschen, so dass die Linien möglicherweise doppelt erscheinen oder verwischen. Falls es sich um ein fortlaufendes oder mehrteiliges Ornament handelt, müssen über die ganze zu gestaltende Fläche hinweg Markierungspunkte oder -linien für das Anlegen der Pause angebracht werden. Zur Übertragung auf die Wand wird die Beutelfüllung des Pausbeutels auf die Pause aufgeklopft und verrieben.

Das Freihandmalen

Zum Aufmalen der Ornamente sind nahezu alle langhaarigen Kunst- oder Naturhaarpinsel geeignet. Generell kommen auch alle Bindemittel (z. B. Kasein, Kalkkasein, Polyvinylalkohol, Leim) in Frage, allerdings sollte die Farbe dünnflüssig sein. Lasuren sehen besonders filigran aus.
Gemalt wird in gerader Haltung mit ausreichendem Abstand zur Wandfläche, der Pinsel wird am oberen Stielende gefasst. Als Hilfe für eine ruhigere Hand kann ein Malstock verwendet werden. Durch Veränderung des Drucks auf den Pinsel wird der Pinselstrich breiter oder schmaler, man spricht vom so genannten Duktus. Durch Drehung des Handgelenkes wird der Pinsel geführt. Die Hand selbst bleibt beim Malen relativ unbeweglich, die Bewegung des Armes sollte vom Schultergelenk aus erfolgen.

Le transfert de l'ornement

On fixera le calque à trous sur le mur à l'aide d'un ruban adhésif. S'il est mal fixé, le papier risque de glisser et les lignes pourront apparaître en double ou s'estomper. S'il s'agit d'un ornement continu ou en plusieurs parties, il faudra tracer des points ou des lignes de repère pour poser le calque sur toute la surface à traiter. Pour effectuer le transfert sur le mur, on tapotera la pochette pour en vider le contenu et l'étendre en frottant.

La peinture à main levée

Presque tous les pinceaux à soies longues artificielles ou naturelles conviennent pour peindre des ornements. On peut en général utiliser tous les liants (par exemple, caséine, caséine de chaux, alcool polyvinylique, colle), mais la peinture doit être fluide. Les glacis ont un aspect de filigrane.
On peindra en position droite à une distance suffisante du mur et on tiendra le pinceau par l'extrémité supérieure du manche. On pourra utiliser un bâton de peintre pour maîtriser sa main. Une variation de pression sur le pinceau permettra d'obtenir un trait plus large ou plus étroit ; on parle alors de « coup de pinceau ». Le pinceau sera dirigé par un mouvement pivotant du poignet. La main elle-même reste relativement immobile en peignant, le mouvement du bras devrait s'effectuer

Left: Fasten the paper with the pricked-out outline to the wall by means of adhesive tape. Transfer the outline to the wall by knocking the bag against the paper and rubbing some of the ash through.

Links: Die Lochpause wird auf der Wand mit Klebestreifen rutschfest fixiert. Zum Durchpausen der Lochpunkte klopft man mit dem Pausbeutel etwas Asche auf das Papier und verreibt sie mit dem Beutel.

À gauche : Fixer le calque à trou sur le mur à l'aide d'une bande adhésive. Pour décalquer les points de repère, tapoter la pochette de décalquage pour répandre un peu de cendre sur le papier et étendre celle-ci en frottant avec la pochette.

Right: In order not to blur the ash dots, the tracing paper must be removed carefully. If the pattern is continuous or has more than one section, complete each section before attaching the paper for the next.

Rechts: Das Abnehmen der Pause sollte vorsichtig erfolgen, damit die Aschepünktchen nicht verwischen. Ist das Ornament fortlaufend oder mehrteilig, wird erst der aufgebrachte Teil fertig gestellt und dann die Pause an der nächsten Stelle neu angebracht.

À droite : Retirer le calque avec précaution afin de ne pas effacer les petits points de cendre. Si l'ornement est continu ou en plusieurs parties, terminer d'abord la partie appliquée sur le mur, puis appliquer le calque à l'emplacement suivant.

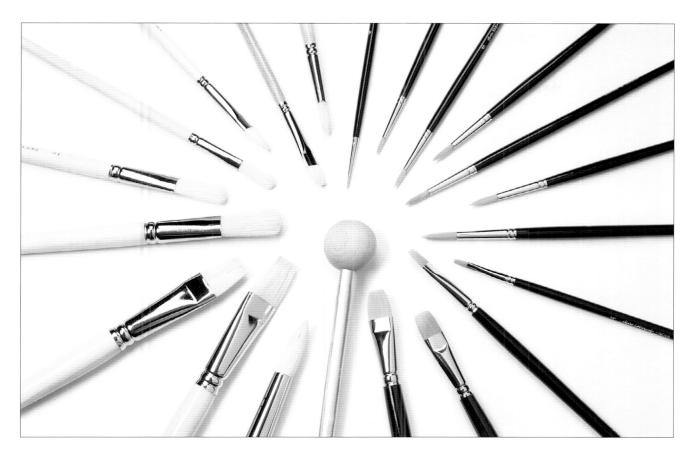

For painting ornamental motifs, almost any long-bristled brushes, with either natural or synthetic bristles, can be used. Vegetal ornaments are best painted with pointed brushes.

Zur Ornamentübertragung eignen sich nahezu alle langhaarigen Kunst- oder Echthaarpinsel. Für Pflanzenornamente sind Spitzpinsel vorzuziehen.

Presque tous les pinceaux à poils longs, synthétiques ou en véritables soies de porc conviennent pour transférer des ornements. Utiliser de préférence des pinceaux pointus pour les ornements floraux.

Below, left: To paint a leaf, place the brush on the tip, and draw it toward the stalk.

Unten links: Um ein Blatt zu malen, wird der Pinsel an der Blattspitze angesetzt und in Richtung Stiel gezogen.

En bas, à gauche : Placer le pinceau sur la pointe d'une feuille pour peindre celle-ci et déplacer le pinceau vers la tige.

Below, center: When painting a curved section of leaf or stalk, use the wrist to control the direction of the brush.

Unten Mitte: Beim Malen einer Rundung des Blattes oder des Stiels wird die Richtung des Pinsels durch Drehung des Handgelenks gesteuert.

En bas, au milieu : Pour peindre l'arrondi de la feuille ou de la tige, diriger le pinceau en tournant le poignet.

Below, right: After the paint has dried, the guide dots – where not already overpainted – can be completely removed using a broad, soft brush.

Unten rechts: Nach Trocknung der Farbe können die Hilfspunkte, soweit sie nicht übermalt wurden, mit einem weichen breiten Pinsel rückstandslos entfernt werden.

En bas, à droite : Dès que la peinture est sèche, éliminer les résidus des points de repère, dans la mesure où ils n'ont pas été retouchés, à l'aide d'un pinceau large et souple.

the tip of the design, for example the leaf or petal, and drawn along the line of the motif until the paint runs out. You should avoid starting a brush stroke in the middle of the design, and likewise you should avoid overlaps. It is not necessary to keep to the exact course of the guide lines – the shape should be determined by the sweep of the brush!

Der Pinselstrich muss dem organisch verlaufenden Ornament angepasst werden. Der Pinsel wird an der Spitze des Ornamentteiles, zum Beispiel des Blattes oder der Blüte, angesetzt und bis zum Auslaufen der Farbe in der Linie des Ornaments geführt. Sowohl Ansätze mitten im Ornament als auch Überschneidungen sollten vermieden werden. Es ist nicht notwendig, sich an die exakte Linienführung der Hilfspunkte zu halten, der Schwung des Pinsels bestimmt die Form!

depuis l'articulation de l'épaule. Il conviendra d'adapter le coup de pinceau à l'évolution organique de l'ornement. Le pinceau partira de la pointe de l'élément ornemental et sera mené dans la ligne de l'ornement jusqu'à ce qu'il n'y ait plus de peinture sur le pinceau. Il faudra éviter de commencer par le milieu de l'ornement et d'entrecroiser les coups de pinceau. Il n'est pas nécessaire de respecter la ligne exacte des points de repère, c'est l'élan donné au pinceau qui détermine la forme !

Stenciling

The transfer of decorative motifs by stencil is one of the world's very oldest decorative painting techniques, and today, by virtue of the wide variety of design possibilities which it provides, it is once more playing an important part in interior decoration. The stencil is an aid for the multiple transfer of an ornament or a text. Repeating stencil patterns include wall patterns, borders and friezes. Stencil patterns are frequently framed by bands and lines, and combined with freehand painting techniques.

While stippling the paint on to the substrate through the stencil is a relatively easy process to learn, the production of the stencil itself demands a degree of design skill. The countless combinations of forms which the technique allows mean that the imagination is subject to practically no constraints. Ready-made stencils represent an acceptable alternative, particularly as these days there are many attractive motifs commercially available, and moreover, manufacturers will produce stencils on the basis of customers' ideas.

Materials

To apply the paint by stippling, it is best to use firm, short-bristled stencil brushes (with stiff, straight bristles), or else round fitches whose bristles have been "shortened" by binding them with adhesive tape. Synthetic and natural sponges are also used, as are stippling brushes with somewhat longer, rounded bristles. These latter are used to apply paint in circular movements working inward from the outside.

Schablonieren

Bei der Übertragung von Dekorationen mit Schablonen handelt es sich um eine der ältesten Maltechniken für die Ornamentierung überhaupt, die heute aufgrund ihrer vielfältigen Gestaltungsmöglichkeiten wieder eine wesentliche Rolle in der Innendekoration spielt. Die Schablone dient als Hilfsmittel zur mehrfachen Übertragung eines Ornaments oder einer Schrift. Zu Schablonenmustern mit Rapport (Wiederholung desselben Musters) zählen Wandmuster, Borten und Abschlussfriese. Schablonierungen werden häufig von Bändern und Strichen (Linierarbeiten) gerahmt und mit Freihandmalerei kombiniert.

Während das Stupfen der Farbe durch die Schablone auf den Untergrund ein relativ leicht zu erlernendes Verfahren ist, setzt die Herstellung einer Schablone gestalterisches Können voraus. Durch die unzähligen Kombinationsmöglichkeiten der Formen sind der Phantasie hierbei keine Grenzen gesetzt. Vorgefertigte Schablonen bieten eine brauchbare Alternative, zumal heute viele schöne Motive im Handel sind und die Hersteller darüber hinaus Schablonen nach den Ideen der Kunden anfertigen.

Material

Zum Farbauftrag, dem Stupfen, verwendet man kurzhaarige, feste Schablonierpinsel (steife und gerade Borsten) oder mit Klebeband kurzhaarig abgeklebte Ringpinsel. Verwendet werden auch Kunststoff- und Naturschwämme sowie Stupfpinsel mit etwas längeren, gerundeten Borsten zum Streichen der Schablonierung in kreisenden Bewegungen von außen nach innen. Als Malmittel kommen sowohl wasser- als

Peindre au pochoir

Le transfert d'ornements avec des pochoirs est une des plus anciennes techniques de peintures, notamment dans l'art ornemental, qui revient au goût du jour dans la décoration intérieure en raison des nombreuses possibilités de réalisations qu'elle offre. Le pochoir est un instrument qui sert à transférer plusieurs fois un ornement ou une inscription. Les ornements au pochoir à motifs récurrents (répétition du même motif) comprennent des décors muraux, des bordures et des frises de séparation. Les pochoirs sont souvent encadrés par des bandeaux et des traits (lignes de repère) et associés à la peinture à main levée. Si l'application de la peinture sur le fond par petites touches à l'aide du pochoir est un procédé relativement simple à apprendre, la fabrication d'un pochoir exige par contre des talents de créateur. Les combinaisons possibles de formes laissent libre cours à l'imagination. Les pochoirs prêts à l'emploi constituent une alternative valable, d'autant plus qu'on trouve aujourd'hui de beaux motifs dans le commerce et que les fabricants réalisent en outre des pochoirs en s'inspirant des idées de leur clientèle.

Matériaux

Des pinceaux pour pochoir solides et à poils courts (soies raides et droites) ou des pinceaux à virole et à poils courts maintenus par un ruban adhésif, servent à appliquer la peinture par petites touches. Des éponges naturelles et synthétiques, ainsi que des pinceaux à pochoir avec des soies assez longues et arrondies permettent de peindre au pochoir avec des mouvements circulaires, de l'extérieur vers l'intérieur.

1–4 Stenciling brushes and stippling brushes in various shapes and sizes
5 Porcelain dish with stippling paint
6 Adhesive crepe tape for attaching the stencil onto the wall
7 Stencil-cutting knife with various blades
8 Round fitch; for stippling, the long bristles can be "shortened" and straightened with adhesive tape.
9 Pencil
10 Scalpel
11 Stencil card
12 Plastic film for making stencils
13 Ready-made plastic stencil (ivy band)

1–4 Schablonierpinsel und Stupfpinsel in unterschiedlichen Größen und Ausführungen
5 Porzellanschale mit Stupffarbe
6 Krepp-Klebeband zum Abkleben und zum Befestigen der Schablone auf der Wand
7 Schablonenmesser mit verschiedenen Klingen
8 Ringpinsel, zum Stupfen werden die langen Borsten mit Klebeband kurz und gerade abgeklebt
9 Bleistift
10 Skalpell
11 Schablonenpapier (Karton)
12 Kunststoff-Folie zur Herstellung einer Schablone
13 Fertigschablone aus Kunststoff (Efeuband)

1 à 4 Pinceaux à pochoir et pochoirs à tamponner dans des tailles et réalisations diverses
5 Coupe en porcelaine avec peinture tamponnée
6 Bande adhésive en crêpe pour coller et fixer le pochoir au mur
7 Couteau à pochoir à lames différentes
8 Pinceau à anneau ; pour tamponner, les longues soies sont maintenues droites avec un ruban adhésif et raccourcies
9 Crayon
10 Cutter
11 Papier à pochoir (carton)
12 Film plastique pour la fabrication d'un pochoir
13 Pochoir en plastique prêt à l'emploi (bandeau de lierre)

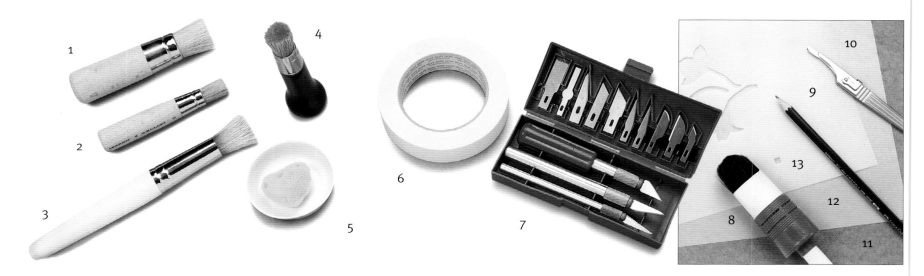

Paints can be either water-soluble or based on some other solvent. If a water-soluble binder (e.g. natural glue or casein) or a mineral-based paint (silicate) is chosen, this makes the stencils easier to clean. In any case, the chosen binder should be quick-drying so that the stencil plate can be re-applied to the wall without too long a wait.

Commercially available stencil plates include both the traditional stippling stencil and modern adhesive stencils. These allow a choice not only of a variety of motifs, but also of size. Ready-made stencils are usually made of plastic film.

Adhesive stencils are stuck to the wall and painted or sprayed over. Stippling stencils are attached to the wall with adhesive tape (they can also be stuck using a soluble spray-on adhesive applied to the back). In this way, the edges of the motifs are flush with the wall, and the contours of the finished result are sharp.

Making a stencil

If you want to make your own stencils, the best materials to use are stiff card or plastic film. Card must be soaked in shellac or a linseed-oil varnish before being cut in order to prevent fraying at the edges. After cutting, it should be painted with oil paint or gloss paint to stop it warping when paint is applied to the wall.

Next, transfer the design to the stencil plate in the desired size. This can be done with carbon paper, or in the case of plastic film, simply traced. A particularly sharp knife or scalpel should be used to cut out the pattern. When cutting straight lines, use a

auch lösemittelverdünnbare Farbe in Betracht. Verwendet man ein wasserlösliches Bindemittel (Leim, Kasein) oder eine mineralische Farbe (Silikat), sind die Schablonen leichter zu reinigen. Das verwendete Bindemittel sollte schnell trocknen, damit die Schablone rasch weiter gesetzt werden kann.

Als Fertigschablonen sind sowohl die klassischen Stupfschablonen als auch moderne Klebeschablonen im Handel. Neben einer Vielzahl von Motiven kann auch die Größe ausgewählt werden. Fertigschablonen sind in der Regel aus Kunststoff-Folie gefertigt.

Klebeschablonen werden auf die Wand aufgeklebt und mit Farbe bestrichen oder besprüht. Die Stupfschablone wird mit Klebeband auf der Wand fixiert oder kann auf der Rückseite auch mit wieder lösbarem Sprühkleber versehen werden. So schließen die Ränder der Motive plan mit der Wand ab und der Farbauftrag erhält scharfe Konturen.

Anfertigung einer Schablone

Will man eine Schablone selbst herstellen, so verwendet man als Grundmaterial entweder starkes Schablonenpapier (Karton) oder eine Kunststoff-Folie. Karton muss vor dem Zuschneiden mit Leinölfirnis oder Schellack getränkt werden, damit die Ränder beim anschließenden Schneiden nicht fransen. Nach dem Schneiden sollte sie mit Ölfarbe oder Lack gestrichen werden, damit sie sich beim Farbauftrag nicht wellt.

Auf das Grundmaterial wird das Ornament in der gewünschten Form und Größe aufgepaust (Kohlepapier) oder durchgezeichnet (Kunststoff-Folie). Zum Ausschneiden des

On pourra envisager d'utiliser des peintures diluables tant dans l'eau que dans un solvant. Si on choisit un liant soluble dans l'eau (colle, caséine) ou une peinture minérale (silicate), les pochoirs seront plus faciles à nettoyer. Le liant utilisé doit sécher rapidement afin que les pochoirs puissent resservir presque aussitôt.

On trouve dans le commerce des pochoirs prêts à l'emploi, c'est-à-dire les pochoirs à tamponner traditionnels ou des pochoirs adhésifs modernes. Il existe une gamme étendue de motifs, mais aussi de tailles. Les pochoirs tout prêts se présentent en général sous la forme d'une feuille en plastique.

On colle les pochoirs adhésifs sur le mur et on les recouvre ou les asperge de peinture, tandis qu'on fixe les pochoirs à tamponner au mur à l'aide d'une bande adhésive ou qu'on pulvérise une colle faible sur le dos de ces pochoirs. Les bords des motifs seront donc plans avec le mur et la couche de peinture aura des contours nets.

Réalisation d'un pochoir

Si on veut fabriquer un pochoir soi-même, on choisira du papier à pochoir épais (carton) ou une feuille de plastique comme support. On imprégnera le carton de vernis à l'huile de lin ou de gomme-laque avant de le découper, afin que les bords ne s'effrangent pas pendant le découpage. On le badigeonnera de peinture à l'huile ou de vernis après l'avoir découpé pour que la couche de peinture ne le fasse pas gondoler.

L'ornement est décalqué (papier carbone) ou dessiné (film plastique) sur le support dans la forme et la taille désirées. Pour dé-

Left: The outlines of the motif are traced on to the plastic-film stencil in the desired size.

Links: Die Umrisse des Schablonenmotivs werden in gewünschter Größe und Form auf die Kunststoff-Schablone durchgezeichnet.

À gauche : Décalquer les contours du motif au pochoir dans la taille et la forme désirées sur le pochoir en plastique.

Center: With a sharp knife, the elements of the design are cut out. As an underlay, a glass plate or some hard flooring is suitable.

Mitte: Mit einem scharfen Messer werden die Ornamentteile ausgeschnitten. Als Unterlage eignet sich eine Glasplatte oder ein harter Bodenbelag.

Au milieu : Découper les éléments ornementaux avec un couteau bien affilé. Utiliser une plaque de verre ou un revêtement de sol dur comme support.

Right: The cut out elements are carefully removed.

Rechts: Die ausgeschnittenen Teile werden vorsichtig entfernt.

À droite : Retirer soigneusement les éléments découpés.

Left, top: The stencil is fastened to the desired surface using adhesive tape or spray-on adhesive. If there is no existing edge such as a window frame or skirting board, a line should be drawn in pencil with the help of a spirit level.

Links oben: Die Schablone wird auf der gewünschten Fläche mittels Klebeband oder Sprühkleber fixiert. Ist keine Kante zum Anlegen der Schablone gegeben (Sockel, Fensterrahmen), sollte die Ansatzlinie mit der Wasserwaage ausgewogen und mit Bleistift leicht angezeichnet werden.

À gauche, en haut : Fixer le pochoir sur la surface désirée avec un ruban adhésif ou de la colle faible pulvérisée. S'il n'y a pas d'arête pour poser le pochoir (soubassement, cadre de fenêtre), utiliser le niveau à bulle comme ligne de base et la tracer légèrement au crayon.

Left, bottom: Place a little paint, which should be of creamy consistency, in a dish. When working, you should have just a little paint on the tip of the brush. Surplus paint must be wiped or dabbed off before stenciling begins.

Links unten: Ein wenig Schablonierfarbe in cremiger Konsistenz wird in eine Schale gegeben. Zum Arbeiten sollte sich nur wenig Farbe an den Borstenspitzen des Pinsels befinden. Überschüsse müssen vor Beginn des Schablonierens abgestreift oder abgestupft werden.

À gauche, en bas : Déposer un peu de peinture à pochoir de consistance crémeuse dans une coupelle. Tremper légèrement le bout du pinceau dans la peinture. Éliminer le surplus de peinture ou égoutter le pinceau avant de commencer à peindre.

Right: Holding the brush perpendicular to the wall, dab the paint evenly on to the surface. When using glazing, work from the outside to the center. The surround of the painted surface can be pressed against the wall freehand.

Rechts: Mit dem Schablonierpinsel wird die Farbe gleichmäßig im rechten Winkel auf die Fläche gestupft. Verwendet man Lasuren, wird von außen nach innen gestrichen. Mit der freien Hand kann man die Umgebung des zu stupfenden Motivs andrücken.

À droite : Tamponner régulièrement la peinture dans l'angle droit de la surface avec un pinceau à pochoir. Si on utilise des glacis, il faut peindre de l'extérieur vers l'intérieur. Appuyer avec la main libre tout autour du motif à tamponner.

metal ruler. Small dots can be punched out using a punch bought from the hardware shop. At the top or bottom edges small rectangular alignment or "registration" marks should be cut out so that the stencil can be placed in exactly the right place for the next repeat of the pattern. The marks are not stenciled, but simply hinted at in pencil. Sometimes small elements of the design itself can fulfill this purpose. For multiple stencils (cf. p. 287), the marks also serve to indicate where the individual stencil plates are to be placed.

Musters sollte ein besonders scharfes Messer (Schablonenmesser) oder ein Skalpell verwendet werden. Beim Schneiden gerader Kanten nimmt man ein Metalllineal zu Hilfe. Kleine Punkte lassen sich mit Stanzeisen aus dem Eisenwarenhandel ausschlagen. An den oberen oder unteren Ecken der Schablone werden kleine viereckige Markierungen (Ansatz- oder Passmarken) ausgeschnitten, mittels derer die Schablone für den nächsten Rapport exakt weiter versetzt werden kann. Die Passmarken werden nicht mit schabloniert, sondern nur leicht mit Bleistift angedeutet. Gelegentlich können auch kleine Ornamentteile als Passmarken fungieren. Bei mehrschlägigen Schablonen dienen sie darüber hinaus zum Platzieren der einzelnen Schläge (Lagen).

couper le motif, on utilisera un couteau particulièrement aiguisé (couteau à pochoir) ou un cutter et pour couper les rebords en ligne droite, on se servira d'une règle métallique. Pour réaliser les petits points, on utilisera des poinçons en vente dans les quincailleries. De petits repères carrés seront découpés dans les coins supérieurs ou inférieurs du pochoir (point de départ ou empreintes) ; ils permettront de déplacer le pochoir avec précision pour réaliser le motif récurrent suivant. Les repères d'empreintes ne seront pas pochés, mais indiqués légèrement avec un crayon. De petits éléments ornementaux peuvent aussi servir à l'occasion de repères d'empreintes. Dans le cas de pochoirs à plusieurs couches, ces éléments servent en outre à disposer les différentes couches.

Measuring the repeats

If you intend to stencil an ornamental band onto a wall, you should first measure the repeats and draw them in. For this purpose, measure the wall and calculate how often the motif will repeat in the relevant area. Measuring the wall is also necessary if an individual motif is to be placed centrally or as part of a grid pattern. In the case of bands and friezes, draw a light marker line

Das Ausmessen der Rapporte

Will man ein Ornamentband auf eine Wand schablonieren, sollten vorher die Rapporte ausgemessen und eingezeichnet werden. Dazu wird die Wandfläche gemessen und anschließend errechnet, wie oft sich das Muster im ausgesuchten Bereich wiederholt. Das Vermessen der Wand ist ebenfalls nötig, wenn ein Einzelobjekt mittig oder im Raster angebracht werden soll. Bei

Mesure de motifs récurrents

Si on veut peindre un bandeau ornemental au pochoir sur un mur, on doit mesurer au préalable les motifs récurrents et les dessiner. On mesurera pour cela la surface du mur, puis on calculera la fréquence à laquelle le motif se répète dans l'espace choisi. Il faudra aussi mesurer le mur pour appliquer un seul objet au milieu de la surface ou dans la grille. S'il s'agit de

Left: The stencil should be removed immediately the paint has been applied. When removing the stencil, first look on one side to see if the motif is complete.

Links: Die Schablone wird gleich nach dem Farbauftrag vorsichtig entfernt. Bei der Abnahme sollte zuerst an einer Seite kontrolliert werden, ob das gewünschte Motiv vollständig ist.

À gauche : Retirer le pochoir délicatement juste après l'application de la peinture. Vérifier d'abord sur un côté si le motif désiré est complet.

Right: Once the paint has dried, move the stencil to the right for the next repeat. Use registration marks for this purpose.

Rechts: Ist das Motiv getrocknet, setzt man die Schablone nach rechts zum nächsten Rapport an der markierten Passmarke an.

À droite : Si le motif est sec, déplacer le pochoir vers le repère à droite pour exécuter le motif suivant.

Bottom: When the stenciled band is complete, it can be framed with lines or narrow bands.

Unten: Ist das schablonierte Band fertig, kann es von Bändern oder Begleitstrichen gerahmt werden.

En bas : Si le bandeau poché est terminé, on peut l'encadrer de bandeaux ou de traits auxiliaires.

to show where the stencil is to be placed. Individual motifs can be positioned with the help of a plumb line.

To get an ornamental band round a corner, you can push the stencil into the corner. A more elegant solution however would be to ensure that the ornamentation finishes at the corner and starts again on the adjoining wall. It does not look good for a band to end in the middle of the design. The "finale" can be created by adapting an element of the design (leaf, branch etc.) or by creating a special corner element. A further possibility would be to stretch or squeeze the whole ornamental band by enlarging or reducing the spaces between the elements. Alternatively, to obtain a clean end to the band, individual elements can be added or omitted.

Bändern und Friesen wird mit Bleistift eine leichte Markierungslinie zum Ansetzen der Schablone aufgetragen. Einzelmotive können mit einem Lot ausgerichtet werden.

Um ein Ornamentband über Eck laufen zu lassen, kann man die Schablone in die Ecke drücken. Eleganter wirkt es jedoch, wenn das Ornamentband vor der Ecke abschließt und auf der anschließenden Wandfläche erneut beginnt, denn für einen weichen Ausklang sollte das Ornament nicht mitten im Muster enden. Der Abschluss kann durch Abwandlung eines Ornamentteils (Blatt, Zweig) oder durch ein spezielles Eckornament gebildet werden. Eine weitere Möglichkeit bietet die Streckung bzw. Stauchung des gesamten Ornamentbands, wobei die Zwischenräume der Ornamentteile vergrößert oder verkleinert werden. Außerdem können zugunsten eines sauberen Abschlusses Ornamentteile hinzugefügt oder weggelassen werden.

bandeaux et de frises, on tracera une légère ligne de repère pour commencer le pochoir. Un fil à plomb permettra d'aligner les motifs individuels.

Si un bandeau ornemental doit passer par un angle, on appuiera le pochoir dans l'angle concerné. L'effet obtenu sera toutefois plus élégant si le bandeau ornemental se termine avant l'angle et reprend sur le mur suivant, car pour être harmonieux, l'ornement ne doit pas se terminer au milieu du motif. Un bandeau peut se terminer par une alternance d'ornements (feuille, branche) ou par un ornement d'angle spécifique. Il existe une autre possibilité : l'extension ou la déformation de tout le bandeau ornemental, auquel cas il faut agrandir ou réduire les espaces intermédiaires des éléments ornementaux. On peut en outre ajouter des éléments ornementaux pour terminer un bandeau proprement ou les ignorer totalement.

The Multiple Stencil

With multiple stencils, the basic pattern is applied throughout for the individual motif or repeat with the first stencil. Once the first stage is completely finished and dry, the second stage can begin with the second stencil. The different colors as well as light and shade in the design are built up through the different stencils. In order to align the stencils correctly, registration marks must be included in every stencil. These marks can be either ad hoc, or existing elements in the design. As different stencils may overlap, it is important to use the stencils in the same order each time (number your stencils).

Die mehrschlägige Schablone

Bei der mehrschlägigen Schablone wird mit der ersten Lage das Grundmuster durchgängig für den Rapport oder das Einzelmotiv (Hauptschablone) angelegt. Ist die erste Lage komplett fertig und getrocknet, kann mit der zweiten Lage der Schablone begonnen werden. Durch die einzelnen Schläge werden unterschiedliche Farben sowie Licht und Schatten im Ornament gesetzt. Damit die Lagen im Motiv aufeinander passen, werden Markierungslinien (Passmarken) auf jedem Schlag angebracht. Diese Marken können auch aus Punkten oder Teilen des Ornaments bestehen. Da verschiedene Schläge im Motiv überlappen können, ist die Einhaltung der Reihenfolge des Auftragens wichtig (Schablonen nummerieren).

Le pochoir à plusieurs couches

Dans le cas d'un pochoir à plusieurs couches, poser le motif principal avec la première couche pour le motif récurrent ou le motif individuel (pochoir principal). Si la première couche est tout à fait terminée et sèche, passer à la suivante. Les multiples couches permettent d'intégrer des couleurs différentes dans l'ornement, ainsi que des lumières et des ombres. Pour que les couches se superposent dans le motif, tracer des lignes de repères (empreintes) sur chaque couche. Ces repères peuvent être aussi des points ou des éléments de l'ornement. Comme diverses couches peuvent se chevaucher dans le motif, il est important de respecter l'ordre d'application (numéroter les pochoirs).

Stippling

In order to familiarize yourself with the technique, and to create the right consistency of the paint, it is a good idea to carry out trials on prepared cardboard or on wallpaper. In this way you can also test the combination of selected techniques and paints with the desired ornamental motif. Paint the cardboard in the background color of the wall and simply attach it to the wall with adhesive tape.

In the subsequent work direct on the wall, you should always make sure that the surface is smooth; if it is not, the edges of the motifs are unlikely to be quite sharp. When you carry out the stenciling, there should only be a little paint on the tip of the brush. Stippling is facilitated by applying a paint of creamy consistency with an almost dry brush. To be on the safe side, the brush can first be dabbed on a piece of card. For detailed work, it is best to use a thin, transparent paint. In this case, the brush must first be well wiped on the rim of the paint pot.

Stippling should proceed from left to right and from the outside of the field inward. Press the surround of the stencil onto the wall somewhat with your fingers. Before removing the stencil, look hard for any unpainted patches and rectify them.

If a simple motif is composed of several colors, individual parts of the stencil can be covered and these subsequently treated with a different color. Small errors can be retouched with a pointed brush.

The stencil plate should be removed as soon as the paint has been applied. It is a good idea to release the stencil at one end first, and to lift it up to inspect the quality of

Das Stupfen

Um sich mit der Technik vertraut zu machen und um die Konsistenz der Farbe abzustimmen, sind Musterflächen auf grundierter Pappe oder Tapete sinnvoll. Auf diese Weise kann man auch die Kombination der ausgewählten Techniken und Farben mit dem gewünschten Ornament testen. Die im Wandton grundierte Pappe wird hierzu einfach mit Klebeband an der Wand fixiert.

Bei der anschließenden Arbeit direkt an der Wand sollte stets auf einen glatten Untergrund geachtet werden, da die Motivränder bei rauen Oberflächen meist nicht ganz scharf werden. Zum Schablonieren sollte nur wenig Farbe an den Pinselspitzen sein. Eine Farbe von cremiger Konsistenz mit fast trockenem Pinsel erleichtert das Stupfen. Zur Sicherheit kann man den Pinsel auf einer Pappe erst etwas abstupfen. Für feine Dekorationen sollte man am besten eine Lasur (dünne Farbe) verwenden. Hierbei muss der Pinsel am Rand des Gefäßes sehr gut abgestreift werden.

Gestupft wird von links nach rechts und von der Außenkante des Ornamentteiles nach innen. Mit den Fingern drückt man das Umfeld der Schablone etwas an. Vor Abnahme der Schablone wird noch einmal nach Fehlstellen im Auftrag gesucht und gegebenenfalls nachgestupft.

Soll ein einfaches Ornament aus mehreren Farben zusammengesetzt werden, kann man einzelne Bereiche der Schablone abdecken und diese dann mit einer anderen Farbe stupfen. Kleine Fehler werden mit dem Spitzpinsel retuschiert.

Nach dem Farbauftrag wird die Schablone sofort entfernt. Es ist sinnvoll, die Schablone zunächst nur an einem Ende zu lösen

Le tamponnage

Pour se familiariser avec la technique et harmoniser la consistance de la peinture, il sera utile de réaliser des motifs sur du carton ou du papier peint qui servira de fond. On pourra aussi tester de cette façon la combinaison des techniques et des couleurs sélectionnées avec l'ornement désiré. Le carton servant de fond qui a la teinte du mur y sera simplement fixé à l'aide d'un ruban adhésif.

Lors des opérations suivantes effectuées directement sur le mur, il faudra toujours veiller à avoir un fond lisse, car en général, les bords des motifs ne tranchent pas nettement sur des surfaces brutes. Pour peindre au pochoir, on trempera très légèrement le bout du pinceau dans la peinture. Une peinture de consistance crémeuse avec un pinceau presque sec facilite le tamponnage. On peut, par mesure de précaution, commencer par tamponner un peu le pinceau sur un carton. S'il s'agit de décorations délicates, on utilisera de préférence un glacis (peinture fluide) et dans ce cas, on égouttera bien le pinceau sur le bord du pot.

On tamponnera de gauche à droite et du bord extérieur de l'élément ornemental vers l'intérieur. On appuiera légèrement avec les doigts sur les pourtours du pochoir. Avant de retirer le pochoir, on cherchera encore une fois les défauts dans l'enduit et on les tamponnera le cas échéant.

Si un ornement simple se compose de plusieurs couleurs, on peut couvrir diverses zones du pochoir et les tamponner avec une autre couleur. Les petites imperfections seront retouchées avec le pinceau pointu.

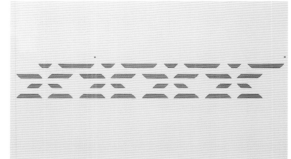
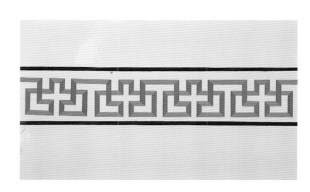

the work. After every application, the back of the stencil should be cleaned with a rag to ensure that any paint which may have run underneath does not smear the wall at the next repeat. The stencil cannot be attached to the wall again until the overlapping section has dried. This process can be speeded up with a hair-drier.

After the work is finished, or if it is going to be interrupted for some time, the stencil should be cleaned with whatever solvent has been used to thin the paint (for aqueous binders, use warm water, for acrylics, white spirit). The stencil should be laid flat to dry between two cloths to make sure it does not warp.

Multiple stencils

For complicated patterns or where there are a number of colors one above the other, multiple stencils are used. This means multiple layers of stencils, with each stencil plate corresponding to one color and its shape in the motif (cf. caption on page 286).

und anzuheben, um die Qualität der Schablonierung zu überprüfen. Nach jedem Arbeitsgang wird die Rückseite einer Schablone mit dem Lappen gereinigt, damit untergelaufene Farbreste beim nächsten Rapport nicht die Wand verschmieren. Die Schablone kann erst weiter versetzt werden, wenn der überlappende Teil trocken ist – dieser Prozess kann mit einem Fön beschleunigt werden.

Nach Beendigung oder längerer Unterbrechung der Arbeit wird die Schablone mit dem Lösemittel der Farbe gereinigt (bei wässrigen Bindemitteln verwendet man dazu warmes Wasser, bei Acrylfarbe Spiritus). Die Schablone sollte zum Trocknen glatt zwischen Tüchern liegen, damit sie sich nicht verzieht.

Mehrschlägige Schablonen

Bei komplizierteren Mustern oder mehreren und übereinander liegenden Farben werden so genannte mehrschlägige Schablonen verwendet. Hierbei werden mehrere Lagen von Schablonen hergestellt, bei denen jede Lage (Schlag) einer Farbe und deren Form entspricht (Bildtext Seite 286).

Après avoir appliqué la couche de peinture, on retirera le pochoir en prenant soin de le détacher d'abord à une seule extrémité et de le soulever pour vérifier la qualité de la peinture. Après chaque opération, on nettoiera le dos du pochoir avec un chiffon, afin que les résidus de peinture qui ont coulé ne salissent pas le mur lors de l'exécution du motif suivant. On ne pourra déplacer le pochoir que si la partie qui chevauche est sèche – un sèche-cheveux pourra accélérer ce processus.

À la fin du travail ou après une interruption assez longue, on nettoiera la peinture du pochoir avec le solvant (eau chaude pour éliminer les agents aqueux et alcool pour la peinture acrylique). On laissera sécher le pochoir à plat entre des morceaux de tissu pour éviter les déformations.

Pochoirs à plusieurs couches

Dans le cas de motifs compliqués ou de couches de peinture multiples et superposées, on utilisera ce qu'on appelle des pochoirs à plusieurs couches, chacune correspondant à une couleur et à une forme (voir légende page 286).

Top, left: With the use of two stencils, a fret pattern can be given a three-dimensional effect by using one for the basic color and the other for the shading.

Oben links: Mittels zweier Schläge kann man ein Mäanderband durch verschiedene Farbtöne, dem Grund- und dem Schattenton, mit räumlicher Wirkung schablonieren.

En haut, à gauche : Il est possible de peindre avec deux pochoirs, un bandeau de méandres aux teintes différentes, la couleur du fond et l'ombre, pour créer une impression d'espace.

Top, center: First use the stencil with the lighter main color.

Oben Mitte: Zuerst wird der Schlag mit dem helleren Grundton aufgebracht.

En haut, au milieu : Appliquer d'abord la couche avec la couleur de fond plus claire.

Top, right: After the first color has dried, repeat the operation with the more intensive shading color. This will give a three-dimensional effect. Finally, it can be framed with lines.

Oben rechts: Nach der Trocknung wird der zweite Schlag mit dem intensiveren Schattenton ausgeführt, so dass das Band einen plastischen Charakter erhält. Abschließend kann es mit Linien gerahmt werden.

En haut, à droite : Dès que la première couche est sèche, appliquer la deuxième couche avec la couleur d'ombre pour créer un effet de relief pour le bandeau, que l'on encadra de lignes.

Gilding

Gilding is used in the main to complete the decoration of friezes and stucco contoured elements. It is also frequently used to highlight individual motifs, elements or letters. The most widely used technique is known as oil-gilding.

Oil-gilding is a relatively easy-to-learn technique, but it does require a certain amount of practice. Oil-gilding lasts for years with no loss of quality, and it can easily be cleaned with soft bread or a dry sponge and polished with cotton-wool.

Materials

The gold used in oil-gilding comes in a wide variety of forms. There is gold leaf, which also comes in transfer and ribbon form; additionally, there is gold powder, which is also available ready-mixed with a binder.

Gold leaf mostly comes in books of 24 leaves measuring 80 millimeters square. The degree of purity is expressed in carats. Depending on the metal with which it is alloyed, and in what proportion, gold is sometimes referred to as red, orange or white gold.

Transfer gold leaf is gold leaf backed with tissue, which makes it easier to work. It can be cut with scissors into the desired

Vergolden

Vergoldungen werden in der Regel zur abschließenden Verzierung von Friesen und Stuckleisten eingesetzt. Häufig verwendet man sie auch zur Hervorhebung einzelner Ornamente oder Buchstaben sowie zur Betonung bestimmter Ornamentteile. Am weitesten verbreitet ist die Technik der so genannten Ölvergoldung.

Die Ölvergoldung ist eine relativ leicht zu erlernende Technik, die jedoch etwas Übung erfordert. Eine Ölvergoldung ist über Jahre ohne Qualitätsverlust haltbar und kann leicht mit weichem Brot oder einem Trockenreinigungsschwamm gereinigt und mit Watte poliert werden.

Material

Das bei der Ölvergoldung zu verarbeitende Gold liegt in den verschiedensten Formen vor. So ist neben Blattgold auch Transfer- und Rollengold sowie Gold in Pulverform oder als gebundenes Pulver erhältlich.

Blattgold ist meist im Format 80 x 80 mm in Heften zu 24 Blatt erhältlich. Der Reinheitsgrad des Goldes wird in Karat angegeben. Je nach Anteil der zugefügten Metalle spricht man z B. von Rot-, Orange- oder Weißgold.

Transfer-Blattgold (Sturmgold) ist auf Seidenpapier gepresst und daher leichter zu verarbeiten. Es kann mit der Schere in entsprechende Stücke geschnitten und von Hand bequem auf die zu vergoldende

Dorure

Les dorures terminent en général la décoration de frises et de moulures en stuc. On les utilise souvent pour mettre en valeur des ornements individuels ou des lettres, ainsi que pour souligner certains éléments ornementaux. La technique la plus répandue est celle de la dorure à l'huile.

La dorure à l'huile est une technique relativement simple à apprendre qui exige toutefois un peu de pratique. Une dorure à l'huile se conserve pendant des années sans perdre de sa qualité ; elle se nettoie facilement avec de la mie de pain ou une éponge sèche et peut être polie avec de l'ouate.

Matériaux

La feuille d'or à traiter avec la technique de la dorure à l'huile se présente sous les formes les plus diverses. On trouvera, en dehors de la feuille d'or, de l'or à transférer ou en rouleaux, ainsi que de l'or en poudre ou en poudre agglomérée.

La feuille d'or mesure le plus souvent 80 x 80 mm et se présente dans des cahiers de 24 feuilles. Le degré de pureté de l'or est indiqué en carats. Selon le pourcentage de métaux ajoutés, on parle par exemple d'or rouge, orange ou blanc.

La feuille d'or à transférer est pressée sur un papier de soie et devient donc plus facile à travailler. On peut découper des morceaux correspondants avec des ciseaux et

Left: Adhesive agents
In order to stick the gold to the surface to be gilded, you can use either an oil-based size (1) tinted with oil paint (2), or a water-based size (3), which are applied with brushes (4). For porous substrates, a primer (5) is needed. Oil-size is applied with synthetic-bristle brushes (6) and wiped clean with a silk stocking (7).

Links: Anlegemittel
Damit das Gold auf der zu vergoldenden Stelle haftet, verwendet man Anlegeöl (1), gefärbt mit Ölfarbe (2), oder Anlegemilch (3), die mit Anlegepinseln (4) aufgebracht werden. Auf porösen Untergründen ist eine Grundierung (5) notwendig. Anlegeöl wird mit Kunsthaarpinseln (6) aufgetragen und mit einem Seidenstrumpf (7) abgezogen.

À gauche : Matériaux pour l'application de couches
Pour que l'or tienne sur la surface à dorer, utiliser de l'huile (1), teintée avec de la peinture à huile (2) ou du lait (3), appliquée avec des pinceaux (4). Une couche de fond (5) sera nécessaire pour les fonds poreux. Appliquer l'huile avec des pinceaux à poils synthétiques (6) et l'égaliser avec un bas de soie (7).

Right: Gilding tools
For the preparation of gold leaf you need a gilder's pad (or cushion) (1), a gilding knife (2) and various gilder's tips (3).

Rechts: Vergolderwerkzeuge
Für die Verarbeitung von Blattgold benötigt man ein Vergolderkissen (1), ein Vergoldermesser (2) sowie verschiedene Anschießer und Anlegepinsel (3).

À droite : Outils de doreur
Pour travailler la feuille d'or, disposer d'un coussin de doreur (1), d'un couteau de doreur (2), ainsi que de divers pinceaux (3).

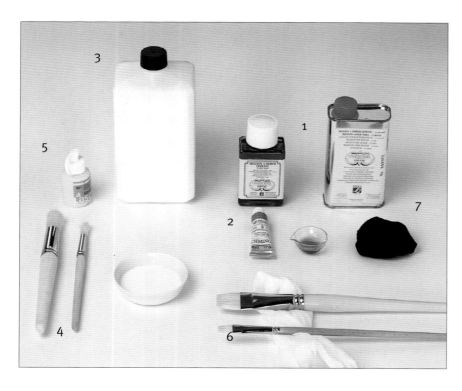

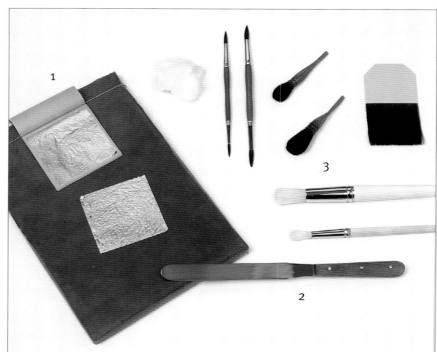

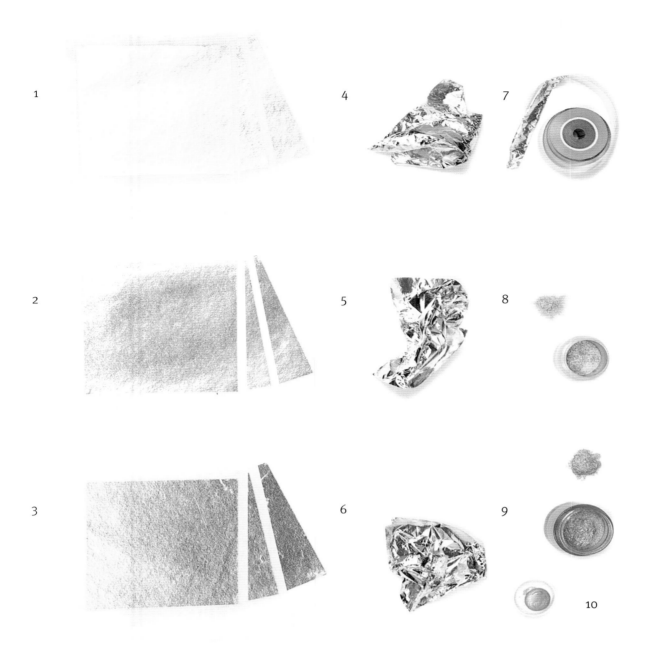

shape, and easily placed by hand onto the surface to be gilded. After brief pressure, the paper can be peeled off. These properties make transfer gold leaf particularly suitable for a variety of external applications. Transfer gold leaf can also be obtained as ribbon gold, available in rolls between 3 and 100 millimeters broad and backed with tissue paper. Gold leaf in this form facilitates the gilding of borders, lines and edges of stucco profiles and the like.

Gold powder is used for particularly small areas. The powder can also be obtained ready-bound (shell gold), in which case it can be treated as paint. Alternatively there is so-called imitation gold, which is also a powder, but not real gold. The visual effect is less striking than real gold, however.

There are gold substitutes in the form of

Fläche aufgelegt werden. Nach kurzem Andrücken lässt sich das Papier abziehen. Aufgrund dieser Eigenschaften wird Transfergold zumeist in der Außenvergoldung verwendet. Transfer-Blattgold ist auch als so genanntes Rollengold erhältlich. Dieses auf Seidenpapier gepresste und aufgerollte Blattgold kann in der gewünschten Breite geliefert werden (3–100 mm). Rollengold wird für die leichtere Vergoldung von Rändern, Linien und Kanten z. B. an Stuckprofilen eingesetzt.

Goldpulver wird für besonders kleinteilige Bereiche eingesetzt. Das Pulver ist auch fertig gebunden erhältlich (Muschelgold) und kann wie eine Farbe verarbeitet werden. Als Alternative kann das ebenfalls in Pulverform vorliegende unechte Malergold eingesetzt werden. Das optische Erscheinungsbild ist allerdings weniger eindrucksvoll als bei echtem Gold.

les poser facilement à la main sur la surface à dorer. Après une légère pression, le papier s'enlève facilement. On utilise la plupart du temps la feuille d'or à transférer pour la dorure extérieure en raison de ces propriétés. La feuille d'or à transférer est également disponible en rouleaux. Cette feuille d'or pressée sur du papier de soie et enroulée peut être fournie dans la largeur désirée (3 à 100 mm). On utilisera des feuilles d'or en rouleaux pour la dorure plus facile de bordures, de lignes et d'arêtes, par exemple sur des profils en stuc.

La poudre d'or est utilisée pour des zones particulièrement petites. On trouve aussi de la poudre agglomérée toute prête (or moulu) et on peut la travailler comme une peinture. Autre solution : le faux or d'applique sous forme de poudre. L'effet optique est toutefois moins impressionnant que lorsqu'il s'agit d'or véritable.

alloys of copper and tin, known as Schlagmetal or Dutch metal. These substitutes are cheaper than gold leaf; they also usually come in larger sheets (160 millimeters square) and are easier to use because the leaves are thicker. However, these metals oxidize, which causes them to go darker or to blacken. If this effect is not wanted, they should be coated with shellac after application. This shellac coating will form a protective layer against oxidation.

Gold leaf is attached to the substrate by means of adhesive size, based on linseed oil, or by a water-size.

Additives ensure that oil-size starts to dry quickly, but remains tacky for some time (known as the "open time"). The best time to apply the gilding is before the size is completely dry and while it is still slightly tacky. It comes in forms which (assuming a temperature of 20° Celsius) dry in 3, 12 or 24 hours. A simpler alternative to oil-size is water-size, which can be directly worked with hair or bristle brushes; gilding can proceed after a brief drying period.

If you are working with transfer gold leaf, all you need is a gilding brush. Plain gold leaf by contrast requires a number of tools. The gilder's cushion or pad is a wooden board with soft upholstery and a suede cover. As the gold leaf is cut to size on the pad, it is particularly important to keep it clean and free of dust.

The gold leaf is cut with a gilding knife, a two-edged flat knife with a round tip. It

Die so genannten Schlagmetalle sind Legierungen aus Zinn und Kupfer und fungieren als Goldersatz. Sie sind preiswerter als Blattgold, haben zumeist ein größeres Format (160 x 160 mm) und sind wegen einer höheren Schichtdicke leichter zu verarbeiten. Diese Metalle oxidieren jedoch, d. h. sie dunkeln nach oder verschwärzen. Ist dieser Effekt nicht gewünscht, so sollten sie nach dem Auflegen mit Schellack überzogen werden, der vor Oxidation schützt.

Als Haftmittel eignen sich das Anlegeöl auf Leinölbasis (Mixtion) und die Anlegemilch auf wässriger Basis (Acrylat).

Durch Zusätze wurde erreicht, dass die Mixtion zwar schnell antrocknet, aber einige Zeit benötigt, um klebefrei zu werden. Der beste Zeitpunkt zum Vergolden ist erreicht, wenn die Mixtion noch nicht komplett trocken ist, sondern noch geringe Klebkraft aufweist. Das Anlegeöl ist als 3-Std.-, 12-Std.- und 24-Std.-Mixtion erhältlich (Trocknungszeit bis zum Anlegen bei 20 °C). Eine vereinfachte Alternative zur Mixtion bietet die so genannte Anlegemilch, eine Acryldispersion auf wässriger Basis, die direkt mit Haar- oder Borstenpinseln verarbeitet werden kann und schon nach kurzer Trocknung die Vergoldung erlaubt.

Wird mit Transfer-Blattgold gearbeitet, reicht ein Vergoldepinsel aus. Soll allerdings loses Blattgold verwendet werden, sind einige Werkzeuge notwendig: Das Vergoldekissen ist ein Holzbrett mit weicher Polsterung und Wildlederüberzug. Da auf dem Kissen das Blattgold zugeschnitten

Ce qu'on appelle les métaux battus (au marteau-pilon) sont des alliages d'étain et de cuivre et un substitut de l'or. Ils sont moins chers que les feuilles d'or, ont souvent un format supérieur (160 x 160 mm) et sont plus faciles à travailler en raison de leur plus forte épaisseur. Ces métaux s'oxydent toutefois, c'est-à-dire qu'ils foncent ou noircissent. Si cet effet est indésirable, il conviendra de les recouvrir de gomme-laque qui les protégera de l'oxydation.

L'huile à base d'huile de lin (mixtion) et le lait à base aqueuse (acrylate) servent de substances adhésives.

Des adjuvants permettent à la mixtion de sécher rapidement, mais il faudra un certain temps pour qu'elle ne soit plus collante. Le meilleur moment pour réaliser une dorure est celui où la mixtion n'est pas encore tout à fait sèche, mais présente un pouvoir agglutinant réduit. L'huile existe en mixtions de 3 heures, 12 heures et 24 heures (temps de séchage jusqu'à l'application à une température de 20 °C). Il existe une solution plus simple pour remplacer la mixtion : le lait, dispersion acrylique à base aqueuse qui peut être directement travaillée avec des pinceaux à poils ou à soies et permet d'exécuter des dorures après une courte période de séchage.

Si on utilise une feuille d'or à transférer, un simple pinceau à dorure suffit. Mais si on utilise une feuille d'or, quelques outils s'avéreront nécessaires : le coussin à dorer est un capiton mou avec une enveloppe en daim. Comme on découpe la feuille d'or sur ce coussin, il est particulièrement

Below, left: After the substrate has been prepared for gilding, draw the ornamental element which you wish to gild on the wall with the help of a stencil.

Unten links: Nachdem der Untergrund für eine Vergoldung vorbereitet wurde, zeichnet man das zu vergoldende Ornamentteil mit einer Schablone auf die Wandfläche.

En bas, à gauche : Après avoir préparé le fond pour la réalisation d'une dorure, dessiner l'ornement à dorer sur la surface du mur à l'aide d'un pochoir.

Below, right: Using a synthetic-bristle brush, apply the tinted size to the areas which are to be gilded.

Unten rechts: Mit einem Kunsthaar-Flachpinsel wird die eingefärbte Mixtion auf die zu vergoldenden Stellen aufgetragen.

En bas, à droite : Appliquer la mixtion teintée sur les endroits à dorer à l'aide d'un pinceau plat à poils synthétiques.

Opposite page, top: This detail shows an eagle, part of an overall repeating pattern by the Audsleys, who liked an exuberant use of gold in their designs.

Gegenüberliegende Seite oben: Dieser Ausschnitt zeigt einen Adler aus einem flächendeckenden, rapportierenden Muster der Audsleys, die in ihren Entwürfen gern und ausgiebig Gold verwendet haben.

Page ci-contre, en haut : Cette illustration montre un aigle provenant d'un motif décoratif récurrent des Audsley qui ont largement privilégié le doré dans leurs esquisses.

Below, left: When the size is completely dry, use the gilder's tip to place the piece of cut gold leaf on the surface, and press lightly.

Unten links: Ist die Mixtion vollständig getrocknet, hält man die zurechtgeschnittenen Goldblättchen mit dem Anschießer auf die entsprechenden Flächen und drückt sie leicht an.

En bas, à gauche : Dès que la mixtion est entièrement sèche, maintenir les feuilles d'or découpées à l'aide du pinceau sur les surfaces correspondantes en exerçant une légère pression.

Below, right: The pieces of gold leaf are added from bottom to top, overlapping. After an adequate drying period, the surplus gold can be swept up with a soft brush (gilder's mop) and polished with cotton wool.

Unten rechts: Die Blättchen werden überlappend nebeneinander von unten nach oben angelegt. Nach ausreichender Trocknung kann das überschüssige Gold mit einem weichen Vergoldepinsel eingekehrt und mit Watte poliert werden.

En bas, à droite : Poser les feuilles côte à côte et de bas en haut en les faisant se chevaucher. Après un temps de séchage suffisant, recueillir le surplus de doré avec un pinceau pour dorure souple et polir la surface avec de l'ouate.

should be sufficiently sharp to cut the gold leaf without tearing it.

The gilder's tip is a brush used to apply the gold leaf to the surface to be gilded. They are available in various forms, and consist of badger or camel hair.

Surplus gold is removed with a gilder's mop. The hairs or bristles (mostly squirrel hair) must be soft and rounded.

Preparing the substrate

For oil gilding, it is particularly important to have a clean substrate, free of grease and dust, because the gilding can only gleam insofar as the substrate permits it to do so. Generally speaking, any existing coats must be removed, and any holes or cracks filled in. Porous substrates, such as plaster or stucco, for example on contoured profiles, must be primed with shellac. This priming is adequate if it forms a closed layer. If not, the size will seep into the depths of the substrate. Priming is not absolutely necessary if water-size is applied to a painted substrate.

wird, ist es besonders wichtig, es stets sauber und fettfrei zu halten.

Das Vergoldemesser, ein beidseitig geschärftes, flaches Messer, das vorne gerundet ist, benötigt man für den Zuschnitt des Blattgolds. Das Messer sollte scharf genug sein, die Goldblätter zu schneiden, ohne dass sie reißen.

Der so genannte Anschießer oder Anlegepinsel dient zum Anlegen des Goldblättchens auf die zu vergoldende Fläche. Anschießer sind in verschiedenen Ausführungen erhältlich und bestehen aus Dachs- oder Kamelhaar.

Zum Entfernen des überschüssigen Goldes wird ein Vergoldepinsel, auch Einkehrer genannt, verwendet. Die Haare oder Borsten des Einkehrpinsels müssen weich und gerundet sein. Meist handelt es sich um einen Pinsel aus Eichhörnchen- oder Fehhaar.

Die Untergrundvorbereitung

Um eine Ölvergoldung vorzunehmen, ist ein sauberer, fett- und staubfreier Untergrund besonders wichtig, da die Vergoldung nur so glänzend werden kann, wie der Untergrund es zulässt. Generell müssen alte Anstriche entfernt sowie Risse und Löcher geschlossen werden. Auf porösen Putz- oder Stuckuntergründen, z. B. an Profilen, wird mit Schellack vorgestrichen. Die Grundierung ist dann ausreichend, wenn der Anstrich eine geschlossene Schicht bildet. Ist dies nicht der Fall, versackt das Anlegeöl für die anschließende Vergoldung in den Vertiefungen des Untergrundes. Eine

important que celui-ci soit toujours propre et sans graisse.

Le couteau à dorer, plat, affilé des deux côtés et arrondi à l'avant, sert à découper la feuille d'or. Il doit être suffisamment affûté pour couper les feuilles d'or sans les déchirer.

Le pinceau dit « appuyeux » sert à appliquer la petite feuille d'or sur la surface à dorer. Il existe divers modèles d'appuyeux en poils de blaireau ou de chameau.

Pour éliminer le surplus de dorure, on utilisera un pinceau appelé « mouilleux ». Les poils ou soies de ce pinceau doivent être souples et arrondis. Il s'agit le plus souvent d'un pinceau en poils d'écureuil ou de petit-gris.

La préparation du fond

Pour procéder à une dorure à l'huile, il est particulièrement important d'avoir un fond propre, sans graisse ni poussière, car la dorure ne pourra être brillante que si le fond le permet. En général, il convient d'éliminer les anciennes couches et de boucher les fentes et trous. On passera une première couche de gomme-laque sur des fonds poreux en crépi ou en stuc, par exemple des profils. Ce fond sera alors suffisant si l'enduit constitue une couche fermée. Dans le cas inverse, l'huile qui servira à exécuter la dorure s'accumule dans les cavités. Un fond de ce type n'est pas indispensable si

It can in any case be applied directly over wall paint.

Applying the size

After the substrate has been prepared, all the areas to be gilded must be treated with the transparent size. In order to see the coating better, a drop of artist's oil-paint (e.g. iron-oxide red) can be added. To ensure that on the one hand all the relevant places are reached, but on the other, that no surplus is applied, it is important to apply the size as thinly and evenly as possible. A flat brush with synthetic bristles is particularly suitable. Gold will not adhere to places where there is no size, while if there is too much, the size penetrates the gold, giving rise to a patchy effect later. Wiping with a silk stocking after application will ensure an even coating.

Gilding itself should not start until the size has lost most of its tackiness. The finger test is reliable: if you draw your finger across the dry size coating, you must be able to hear a slight squeak. The gold should not be applied earlier, otherwise it will not adhere.

If you are using water-size, a relatively even coating is also important. In contrast to working with oil-size, you do not have to wait before proceeding to apply the gold. This easier process is recommended for porous plaster substrates for indoor stuccos or for very small ornamental elements.

Applying the gold

First cut the gold leaf into the pieces you want, using a dry, grease-free gilding knife. Each cut should be made in one movement. When the piece is cut, it should be picked up using the bristles of the gilder's tip, placed in the required position and pressed into place. To improve the electrostatic attraction between the gilder's tip and the gold, the bristles should first be stroked lightly across the forehead.

solche Grundierung ist nicht unbedingt erforderlich, wenn Anlegemilch auf dem gestrichenen Untergrund verwendet wird. Die Milch kann direkt auf die Wandfarbe aufgetragen werden.

Der Auftrag des Anlegemittels

Nach der Untergrundvorbereitung werden alle zu vergoldenden Flächen mit der transparenten Mixtion behandelt. Um den Schichtauftrag besser sehen zu können, wird der Mixtion ein Tropfen Künstlerölfarbe (z. B. Eisenoxydrot) hinzugefügt. Um zu gewährleisten, dass einerseits alle relevanten Stellen erreicht werden und andererseits nirgendwo ein Mixtionsüberschuss entsteht, ist es wichtig, das Anlegeöl so dünn und gleichmäßig wie möglich aufzutragen. Ein Kunsthaar-Flachpinsel ist dazu besonders geeignet. An Stellen ohne Mixtion würde das Gold nicht haften, an zu starken Auftragsstellen würde die Mixtion das Gold durchdringen, so dass später Flecken auftreten würden. Ein anschließendes Abstreifen mit einem Seidenstrumpf garantiert einen gleichmäßigen Auftrag.

Vergoldet wird erst, nachdem die Mixtion nahezu klebefrei angetrocknet ist. Ein sicherer Test ist die Fingerprobe: Fährt man mit dem Finger über die getrocknete Mixtionsschicht, muss ein leichtes Quietschen zu hören sein. Nur zu diesem Zeitpunkt sollte das Gold angelegt werden, da das Gold sonst nicht haftet.

Auch bei der Arbeit mit Anlegemilch sollte ein relativ gleichmäßiger Auftrag gewährleistet sein. Im Unterschied zur Mixtion kann man hier sofort nach dem Trocknen mit der Vergoldung beginnen. Besonders zur Vergoldung auf porösen Putzuntergründen und von Stuck im Innenbereich oder bei kleinteiligen Ornamentstücken ist diese weniger schwierige Variante zu empfehlen.

Das Anschießen

Zunächst schneidet man das Blatt mit dem trockenen und fettfreien Vergoldemesser in passende Stücke. Das Messer wird einmal pro Schnitt angesetzt und durchgezogen. Ein zugeschnittenes Goldblättchen wird zum Anlegen mit den Haarspitzen des Anschießers aufgenommen, auf die zu vergoldende Stelle gehalten und leicht angedrückt. Um die Haftung des Blattes auf dem Anschießer zu verbessern, streicht man sich zuvor mit dem Pinsel über die Stirn.

on applique une couche de lait sur le fond badigeonné. Le lait peut être appliqué directement sur la peinture du mur.

L'application de couches

Après avoir préparé le fond, on traitera toutes les surfaces à dorer avec la mixtion transparente. On ajoutera une goutte de peinture à l'huile (par exemple de l'oxyde rouge de fer) afin de mieux voir la couche. Il est essentiel d'appliquer l'huile en une couche aussi mince et régulière que possible afin de s'assurer que, d'une part, tous les endroits importants sont atteints et qu'il n'y a, d'autre part, aucun excédent de mixtion. Un pinceau plat à poils synthétiques est idéal pour cette opération. Aux endroits sans mixtion, le doré ne peut pas prendre et aux endroits saturés, la mixtion risque de traverser le doré, ce qui entraînera la formation ultérieure de taches. En frottant la surface avec un bas de soie, on obtient une couche régulière.

On n'utilisera la technique de la dorure que si la mixtion est presque sèche et ne colle pas. Pour s'en assurer, il suffit de passer le doigt sur la couche de mixtion sèche ; on doit alors entendre un léger crissement. C'est à ce moment-là seulement qu'il conviendra d'appliquer le doré, sinon il n'accrochera pas.

Même en utilisant du lait, on doit s'assurer que la couche est relativement régulière. Contrairement à la mixtion, la dorure peut commencer tout de suite après le séchage. Cette variante moins difficile est particulièrement recommandée pour réaliser des dorures sur des fonds de crépi poreux et du stuc dans des intérieurs ou sur de petits ornements.

La dorure

La procédure est la suivante : découper d'abord les morceaux appropriés dans la feuille avec le couteau pour dorure ; engager le couteau une fois par entaille et tirer vers soi ; prendre une feuille d'or coupée sur mesure pour l'appliquer avec la pointe des poils du pinceau, la maintenir à l'endroit approprié en exerçant une légère pression. Pour améliorer l'adhérence de la feuille sur le pinceau à dorure, on se frottera auparavant légèrement le front avec le pinceau.

Above: Mistakes in the preparation of the substrate make themselves known through a still porous, insufficiently primed surface which is rough and cracked. If the size is too thin or has been absorbed by the substrate, the gold will not stick.

Oben: Fehler in der Untergrundvorbehandlung zeigen sich durch einen noch saugenden, nicht ausreichend grundierten Untergrund und eine raue, rissige Fläche. Ist die Mixtion zu dünn oder in den Untergrund eingesackt, haftet das Gold nicht.

En haut : Des défauts de traitement préalable du fond se manifestent par un fond encore absorbant et insuffisamment enduit et par une surface rêche et craquelée. Si la mixtion est trop mince ou accumulée dans le fond, le doré n'accroche pas.

Below: Another mistake is to apply too much size. Too little is better than too much. If too much has been applied, the size penetrates the gold and dulls it.

Unten: Ein weiterer Fehler ist der zu satte Auftrag der Mixtion, hier gilt: weniger ist mehr. Ist die Mixtion zu dick aufgetragen oder erfolgt die Vergoldung zu früh, dringt die Mixtion durch das Gold und lässt es stumpf aussehen.

En bas : Autre défaut, l'application excessive de mixtion ; il faut de la mesure dans toutes choses. Si la couche de mixtion est trop épaisse ou si la dorure a lieu trop tôt, la mixtion traverse le doré et donne à celui-ci un aspect terne.

When using transfer gold leaf or ribbon gold, the cut piece is laid (using the fingers or the gilder's tip) on the surface to be gilded gold side down, and pressed in place with stroking movements. Then the tissue paper is removed from the back of the gold leaf.

If you are using gold powder, hold a dish beneath the surface to be gilded to catch the surplus. Then apply the powder with a soft, round gilding brush.

Imitation gold can be applied either by hand or with a brush. Any surplus can be torn off.

In general, oil gilding proceeds from bottom to top to make sure that any gold which falls down does not adhere where it is not wanted.

Beim Transfer-Blattgold und beim Rollengold wird das zurechtgeschnittene Blättchen bzw. der Rollenabschnitt mit den Fingern oder dem Vergoldepinsel auf die Goldseite gelegt und streichend angedrückt. Dann wird das Seidenpapier von der Rückseite abgenommen.

Verwendet man Pulvergold, hält man ein Schälchen zum Auffangen des überschüssigen Materials unter die zu vergoldende Stelle. Dann trägt man das Pulver mit einem weichen, runden Vergoldepinsel satt auf.

Schlagmetall kann von Hand und mit dem Pinsel auf die angelegte Stelle gedrückt werden, überschüssige Reste werden abgerissen.

Vergoldet wird bei der Ölvergoldung generell von unten nach oben, damit kein herabfallendes Goldmaterial an unerwünschter Stelle haften bleibt.

S'il s'agit de feuilles d'or à transférer ou en rouleaux, on posera le morceau découpé avec les doigts ou le pinceau à dorer sur le côté doré et on le lissera en appuyant dessus. On retirera ensuite le papier de soie du verso.

Si on utilise de l'or en poudre, on tiendra une coupelle en dessous de l'endroit à dorer afin de récupérer l'excédent de matériau. On appliquera ensuite la poudre avec un pinceau à dorer souple et rond.

On pourra appliquer du métal battu à la main et avec le pinceau à l'endroit enduit et on retirera les excédents.

Pour dorer une surface avec de la dorure à l'huile, on procédera en général de bas en haut afin que des déchets indésirables ne restent pas accrochés à la surface.

Mopping

After allowing an adequate drying period of at least a day, the surplus gold can be brushed off with a soft brush. Slight folds can be carefully and gently rubbed smooth with cotton-wool, as can the joins. The freshly gilded surface should then be left to harden for a week.

Das Einkehren

Nach ausreichender Trocknung von mindestens einem Tag kann das überschüssige Gold mit einem weichen Pinsel eingekehrt werden. Kleine Falten sowie die Anschlüsse der Blätter werden mit Watte vorsichtig und leicht glatt gerieben. Danach sollte die frisch vergoldete Fläche eine Woche durchhärten.

Le mouilleux

Après un temps de séchage suffisant d'au moins un jour, on peut recueillir le surplus de doré avec un pinceau souple. On lissera délicatement et légèrement les petits plis, ainsi que les raccords des feuilles avec de l'ouate. On laissera la surface fraîchement dorée durcir pendant une semaine.

Staircase in the Regional Courthouse, Berlin (Mitte precinct), 1896–1905
As in many major buildings of its time throughout Europe, the staircase in this Regional Courthouse in Berlin uses an ornamental band with an extravagant use of gold-leaf decoration. Previously reserved for stately homes or public buildings, ordinary people can now use gold leaf to decorate their own homes at no great expense.

Treppenhaus des Landgerichts Berlin-Mitte, 1896-1905
Wie in vielen historischen Gebäuden in ganz Europa lässt sich auch im Treppenhaus des Landgerichts Berlin-Mitte ein mit Blattgold aufwändig verziertes Ornamentband entdecken. Was in früheren Zeiten lediglich in Prunkpalästen oder öffentlichen Gebäuden zu finden war, kann man heute für wenig Geld im eigenen Heim selbst ausführen: die Vergoldung.

Cage d'escalier du tribunal de grande instance de Berlin, 1896-1905
Comme dans de nombreux bâtiments historiques d'Europe, on peut découvrir un bandeau ornemental richement décoré à la feuille d'or dans la cage d'escalier du tribunal de grande instance de Berlin. Il est désormais possible de réaliser chez soi à moindre coût ce qu'on ne trouvait jadis que dans de somptueux palais ou dans des bâtiments publics : la dorure.

Glossary

Terms in *italics* refer to further entries in the glossary.

acanthus Mediterranean species of thistle, whose characteristic feature is its large heavily indented leaves which roll slightly inwards towards the tip. In *Antiquity*, the acanthus was already the model for the capitals of Corinthian columns and other decorative elements, for example, the *frieze*. During the *Renaissance*, *Baroque* and *neoclassical* periods, this decorative device was once more widely used in architecture.

acroterion pedestal placed on the *pediment* of a Classical temple

anthemion Classical ornamental border depicting *lotus* blossoms and *palmettes*. It was often used in ancient Greek vase-painting and architecture.

Antiquity the period of ancient Greek and Roman civilization, beginning in the 2nd millennium BC. with the first wave of Greek immigration and conventionally deemed to end in the West in AD 476 with the deposition of the Western Roman emperor Romulus Augustulus, and in the East in AD 529 with the closure of the Platonic Academy in Athens by Emperor Justinian.

arcade row of arches supported on columns or pillars

architrave in the architecture of *Antiquity*, the main horizontal beam, which, supported on columns, itself supported the roof. In the *Renaissance*, *Baroque* and *neoclassical* periods, the architrave was increasingly used in architecture once more.

archivolt the ornamental band surrounding an arch. In the architecture of *Antiquity*, a frequent decorative element in triumphal arches, city gates, and the like. Used once again in the *Renaissance* and *neoclassical* periods.

Art Nouveau a style of decorative art (and to a lesser extent, architecture) current around 1900, characterized in particular by sinuous vegetal forms, and marked asymmetry. There was also a more geometric variant, which placed an emphasis on vertical lines. The German and Austrian manifestations are often known as "Jugendstil" and "Sezessionsstil" respectively.

Arts-and-Crafts movement a late-19th-century movement in England to counteract what was seen as the depressing effect of industrial mass-production on the quality of goods. It aimed, as its name implies, at an integration of art and handicraft.

astragal in the art of Classical *Antiquity*, a narrow ornamental *molding* consisting of small spheres or ovals reminiscent of beads or pearls. The astragal is not usually found alone, but in conjunction with *leaf-and-tongue* and *egg-and-dart* patterns as an accompanying subelement in cornice moldings.

baldaquin a rooflike structure or ornamental canopy of embroidered silk fabric; later, also a stone or wooden protective roof over an altar, throne, pulpit, statue etc.

band a stripe, mostly colored or decorated, dividing or ornamenting a surface

Baroque the style of art and architecture prevalent in Europe during the 17th and early-18th centuries. It was characterized by dynamic forms, curved figures and sometimes *grotesque* ornamentation. Typical Baroque architectural features are broken semicircular *pediments* and twisted columns.

billet molding a *molding*, usually in *Norman* buildings, consisting of staggered cylindrical elements. See *cubed molding*

blind arch, blind arcade an arch-like decoration on a wall, without an actual opening. A blind arcade is a series of such arches.

border ornamental *band* acting as an edge to some other area

calyx the cup-like outer covering of a flower

capital projecting topmost element of a column or pillar, often decorated

cartouche a scroll-shaped architectural ornament, often used for inscriptions

Celtic style a style of decoration, which, though it dates from earlier, is associated in particular with the British Isles in the early Middle Ages (7th to 9th centuries). It is characterized by intricate plaited and knotted designs and stylized mythical birds and beasts. The finest examples are probably illuminated manuscripts such as the "Book of Kells", but the style is also seen in jewelry, liturical objects and household utensils.

cinquefoil a stylized five-leaved clover pattern, often used as decoration in *Gothic* stonework. See *trefoil*, *quatrefoil*

Classical period in general terms, the same as *Antiquity*. In a narrower sense, the term is sometimes applied to Greece (and especially Athens) between 500–386 BC.

Classicism the forms and styles of Classical *Antiquity*, or a style inspired by these. Conscious imitation is usually called *neoclassicism*.

coffered ceiling an ornamental wooden ceiling consisting of individual fields known as coffers. Very widespread in ancient Roman architecture, and used in the *Renaissance* in particular for the ceilings of palaces. Occasionally encountered in the *Baroque* period and in *neoclassical* buildings, but largely replaced here by decorative plasterwork.

console an architectural element, projecting from a wall as a bracket to support a *cornice* or some other element

corinthian the most decorative of the "orders" of Classical architecture, characterized in particular by fluted columns with a *capital* of (usually) three rings of sculptured *acanthus* leaves. (The Diric column has a plain capital, while the capital of the Ionic column takes the form of a scroll.)

cornice projecting horizontal, usually molded, element in architecture, typically the uppermost element of an *entablature*

crenellation the battlements on a fortified castle, or a decorative imitation thereof

cresting the ornamentation of the top member of some element

crocket *Gothic* vegetal decorative element that appears to creep along a *gable*, *groin* or the like

cubed frieze, cubed molding a *molding* or *frieze*, usually in *Norman* buildings, consisting of staggered cuboid elements. See *billet molding*

Decorated style the name given to the second (roughly 14th century) phase of the *Gothic* style in England

diaper pattern an all-over pattern consisting of repeated units of design connected with each other

Early English style the name given to the first (roughly 13th century) phase of the *Gothic* style in England, characterized in particular by narrow windows, often in groups of three

egg-and-dart also known as egg-and-tongue, or egg-and-anchor. An ornamental design consisting originally of an egg-shaped motif alternating with a roughly triangular figure, and used to decorate a *cornice* or *molding*.

engaged column in *Gothic* architecture, a column-like projection from a wall supporting the *ribs* of a *groin vault*, or the profiles of a *blind arch*

entablature system of horizontal elements between wall and roof. In Classical architecture, consisting of *architrave*, *frieze* and *cornice*. Rediscovered by the architects of the *Renaissance* and *neoclassicism*.

Etruscan style style reminiscent of the art of the ancient Etruscans. The Etruscans were a people who migrated from Greece and inhabited the region of Etruria in Italy until about the 4th century BC. The Etruscan style is similar to that of ancient Greece, but enjoyed its heyday later. Particularly well-known is Etruscan pottery, painted ox-blood, ocher and black.

fan vaulting A style of *vaulting* used in the late-*Gothic Perpendicular styl*e in England in which the individual *ribs* spread out in fan-like fashion

fascia in Classical architecture, three, or less commonly two, stripes, one above the other, which subdivide an architrave horizontally

finial decorative element in *Gothic* architecture: a narrow pyramid forming the upper extremity of a pinnacle or *gable*, crowning a flying buttress, or flanking a gable above a window or door.

flamboyant the characteristic late *Gothic* style of France, characterized in particular by flame-like patterns in the *traceries*

fresco a *mural* or ceiling-painting executed by applying the paint to wet plaster ("fresco" being the Italian for "fresh"), causing the paint and plaster to form a durable combination.

fret also known as "Greek key". An ornamental device consisting of small straight bars meeting (usually) at right angles in some continuously repeating pattern. Used very widely in Classical art and architecture. See *meander*

frieze horizontal decorative band, sometimes in *relief*, forming the upper border of a wall. Used by the Audsleys as the crowning element or as the border of decorated interior walls.

functionalism a late-19th-century architectural movement, which later spread to the design of artifacts. It argued that a building or artifact should be designed primarily with its function in mind, rather than its appearance. The result was often a conscious renunciation of any decoration whatever.

gable the termination of a pitched roof. At the front of a building, often a vehicle for decoration. Originally simply a triangular cross section of the roof, it is often given a more elaborate shape. By extension, a similarly-shaped element over a door or window. In Classical architecture, or styles based on Classical architecture, the equivalent element is called a *pediment*.

Gothic period of art and architecture in medieval Europe, following immediately on the *Romanesque* period. Gothic appeared in the mid-12th century in France, from where it

gradually spread to the whole of Europe. Characteristic of Gothic architecture are the cathedrals of the period with their pointed arches and vertically accented clustered pillars. Gothic varied considerably from place to place both in style and in duration. While in Italy it had been replaced by the *Renaissance* by 1400, late-Gothic continued in England, Spain and Germany until about the end of the 15th century.

Gothic revival also known as neo-Gothic. In English art history, the rediscovery and very widespread use of *Gothic* forms from about 1840 until well into the 20th century.

groin vault See *vault*

grotesque in decorative art, fanciful or bizarre forms of humans or animals, often interwoven with floral or vegetal elements

ground the basic surface of a relief, or the surface on which a picture or decoration is painted. See *substrate*

grounding an undercoat applied to a *ground* before the decoration is painted. Different grounds require their specific grounding.

iconography the study and description of the meaning or significance of particular elements in pictures

Imari ware a style of Japanese porcelain named for the town where it was made, and characterized by a design of stylized vegetation and rocks in red, green, and blue.

impost a block on top of a pillar or column which takes the weight of an arch or vault and conducts it into the supporting column or pillar. Often combined with a *capital*.

intrados the interior curve of an arch or vault

jamb a projecting columnar part of a wall

keystone topmost stone in the center of an arch. While often given decorative emphasis, the keystone has no greater structural importance than any of the other stones in the arch.

kikumon the Japanese name for the imperial emblem, a stylized chrysanthemum. Often encountered as a motif on Japanese porcelain.

kirimon the Japanese name of the Paulownia tree, common in Asia. Its leaves and fruit were used in Japanese art as the emblem of the Japanese nobility, in particular the samurai warrior caste.

lanceolate of leaves: long, thin, and pointed, like a lance

leaf-and-tongue also known as leaf-and-dart. A pattern consisting of alternating stylized leaves and narrow tongue or dart-like elements.

lotus a kind of water-lily. In stylized form, a frequent motif in Egyptian art and in *Revivalist* styles based thereon.

mahlstick stick used by a painter to steady the hand

manueline a highly elaborate style of late-*Gothic* with *Renaissance* elements confined to Portugal c. 1480–1530

marquetry decorative process whereby patterns of thin carved wood, ivory, mother-of-pearl or sometimes metal are inlaid in wood of a different color. If the patterns are of straight lines, the process is known as *parquetry*.

masonry pattern a *diaper pattern* in which the alternate rows of motifs are staggered so as to produce an effect like bricks in a wall

meander in the context of this book, the same as a *fret*

medallion round or oval decorative element

molding a continuous narrow contoured surface, or a plane or curved strip (e.g. of wood), used for decorative effect

monogram the initials of a name combined to form a decorative element

mural a wall-painting

neoclassicism a style or period in art or architecture characterized by imitation of the forms of Classical *Antiquity*. In this sense, the *Renaissance* was a neoclassical period, though it is not normally referred to as such. The word is mainly applied to the Classical *Revival* of the late-18th and early-19th centuries, which followed the *Baroque* and *Rococo* periods and was itself replaced by other forms of *Revivalism*. Neoclassical architecture tends to be monumental, and is characterized by clarity of structure and form. Typical elements are facades with columns and *pediments*, domes and decorative elements derived from Classical Greece and Rome.

neo-Greek see *neoclassicism*

Norman the *Romanesque* style in its English manifestation. Norman buildings are conspicuous by their massive walls and pillars.

palmette conventional ornament of radiating petals, of ancient origin. Frequently employed in *neoclassical* architecture.

parquetry see *marquetry*

patera a disk or medallion, usually round or oval, but also square, bearing some ornamentation, often in *relief*

pattern book book of decorative motifs which could either be simply copied or used as inspiration. With the appearance of schools of applied arts in the later 19th century, they came to be of great importance. They were a characteristic feature of the *Revivalist and Art Nouveau* periods. After the First World War, and the various economic crises that followed, they lost their importance owing to the resulting lack of artistic commissions.

pediment the equivalent of a *gable* in Classical architecture or styles based thereon

Perpendicular style specifically English form of late-Gothic (mid-14th to mid-15th century), characterized by large areas of glass, flattened arches and windows, and preponderance of vertical lines in the stone *tracery* of windows. Fan vaulting was another feature.

pilaster a rectangular pillar, almost always with base and *capital*, not free-standing but projecting from a wall. A pilaster may be load-bearing or purely decorative. In the latter case, if slender, it is known as a pilaster strip.

Postmodernism a style which came to the fore in the late 20th century as a reaction to the austere *functionalism* which characterized the Modern Movement of the mid-century. It is characterized by more fanciful, but often rather predictable, forms.

powdering a form of design where individual motifs are repeated at random over the whole surface

purlin horizontal roof member, running parallel to the ridge and supporting the *rafters*

quatrefoil a stylized four-leaved clover pattern, often used as decoration in *Gothic* stonework. See *trefoil*, *cinquefoil*

rafter sloping roof-beam, usually of wood

relief a form of sculpture consisting of raised motifs on a plane surface. "High relief" means that the sculpture stands well out from the plane surface; "low relief" is flatter.

Renaissance the period in the history of European art and culture which ended the Middle Ages. Its name derives from its being seen as a "rebirth" ("renaissance" is French for rebirth) of the civilization of Classical *Antiquity*. The Renaissance started in 14th century Italy and spread rapidly throughout Europe, reaching its climax in the 16th century. Renaissance architecture sought inspiration in Classical forms, and turned its back on *Gothic*. In the 17th century, Renaissance styles were replaced by the *Baroque*.

Revivalism a period of 19th century art history, during which various "historical" styles were revived (hence the alternative term "historicism"). In England, the style in question was usually *Gothic*, hence the term *Gothic revival*. However *neoclassicism* and neo-Baroque are also examples of revivalist styles. Revivalism was not confined to architecture, but was also characteristic of decorative art, including that of the Audsleys.

rib, rib vaulting see *vault*

Rococo highly ornamental form of late *Baroque*, prevalent in the mid-18th century. Rococo forms are lighter than those of the *Baroque*; one very characteristic feature is the avoidance of symmetry.

Romanesque the style of architecture prevalent in Europe from late *Antiquity* until the 12th century. The characteristic Romanesque feature is the (structurally highly stable) round arch derived from ancient Roman buildings. The English form of Romanesque is known as *Norman*.

rose window in *Gothic* buildings, a large round window, usually with radial *tracery*

rosette decorative motif based on a rose; it must be imagined as an open rose seen from above, and stylized. One of the most widely-used of all forms of ornamentation.

scotia molding a concave *molding* often used in Classical architecture

scrollwork architectural ornamentation in imitation of parchment scrolls

soffit the ornamental underside of a ceiling beam, *rafter* or *entablature*

spandrel the roughly triangular "left over" space which results when a roughly circular motif is placed inside a (usually) rectangular area, for example the spaces in the corners of a clock-face outside of the dial.

strapwork ornamentation composed of crossed, interlaced or plaited elements

stringcourse a horizontal band running around a building, usually on the outside

stucco high-quality plaster. While wet, it is easy to shape, and can still be finished with a sharp tool when dry. These features make it a popular material for applied sculptural decoration for walls and ceilings.

substrate the surface to which decoration, e.g. painting or gilding, is applied, usually in respect of its physical characteristics, e.g. rough, flaky, firm etc.

swag a form of ornamentation used in architecture, but also in pottery, consisting of garlands of carved or molded leaves or fruit, often combined with urns. Very characteristic of the *neoclassical* style.

swastika a cross with arms of equal length, the ends of which are turned at right angles, all in the same direction. Often used as the repeating element in a *fret*.

tesselation the all-over division of a surface into polygonal shapes

tracery decorative openwork in *Gothic* windows, or similar decoration on other surfaces

trefoil a clover-leaf pattern, often seen in the *tracery* of *Gothic* windows. See *quatrefoil*

trompe l'œil literally "deceive the eye"; a painted optical illusion, usually the creation of an illusion of depth by clever use of perspective

vault the system of arches usually forming a ceiling and supporting a roof. A structural necessity, during the *Gothic* period the vaulting was often a decorative feature as well, and developed through several stages. The earliest vault was the "barrel" vault, simply a deep round arch. By combining two of these at right-angles, a "groin" vault is formed, which has structural advantages. These two forms are characteristic of *Romanesque* architecture. While each *groin vault*, with its round arches, can only cover a square area, the pointed arches of *Gothic* allowed more flexibility; *Gothic* architects used a skeleton of arches, or *ribs*, to support the roof. Ribs were often arranged for decorative effect; the culmination of this trend was the *fan vault*.

Vitruvian scroll a decorative pattern used on *band*s and *borders*, consisting of a series of elements resembling scrolls, spirals or breaking waves (for which reason it is also called a "wave *meander*"). Sometimes also called the "running dog" pattern.

zigzag frieze a *frieze* with a zigzag pattern, commonly found in *Norman* buildings

Glossar

Die *kursiv* hervorgehobenen Begriffe sind ebenfalls im Glossar erklärt.

Abakus obere Deckplatte als Abschluss eines *Kapitells*

Akanthus Distelart im Bereich des Mittelmeeres, deren charakteristisches Merkmal große, zackige Blätter sind, die sich an den Blattspitzen leicht einrollen. Der A. wurde bereits in der Antike als Vorbild für korinthische *Kapitelle* und andere Dekorationselemente wie zum Beispiel *Friese* übernommen. In der Renaissance, im Barock und im Klassizismus wird dieses Dekorelement wieder verstärkt beim Baudekor aufgenommen.

Akroterion Giebelbekrönung antiker Tempel

Allegorie bezeichnet in der Kunst die bildliche Darstellung von abstrakten Begriffen und Vorstellungen. Meist geschieht dies durch die Personifizierung eines Begriffs (z. B. die Darstellung des Todes als Sensenmann).

Anthemion antikes Ornamentband, das abwechselnd *Lotusblüten* und Palmetten zeigt. Wurde häufig bei der antiken griechischen Vasenmalerei und Baukunst angewandt.

Architrav in der Baukunst der Antike der waagerechte Hauptbalken, der auf Säulen aufliegend den Oberbau trägt. In der Renaissance, dem Barock und dem Klassizismus wird der A. wieder verstärkt als Bauelement eingesetzt.

Archivolte Bogenlauf, d. h. bandartige, von der Mauer abgesetzte Einfassung eines Bogens. In der Baukunst der Antike häufig als Dekorationselement von Triumphbögen, Stadttoren und dergleichen zu sehen; in der Renaissance und im Klassizismus wieder verwendet.

Arkade Bogenstellung, d. h. eine Reihe von Bögen, die über Säulen oder Pfeilern ansetzen

Art Nouveau die in Frankreich übliche Bezeichnung für den Jugendstil

Arts-and-Crafts-Bewegung englische Bewegung zur Reform des Kunsthandwerks, die eine enge Zusammenführung von Kunst und Kunstgewerbe zum Ziel hatte

Astragal auch *Perlstab*; bezeichnet in der antiken Kunst ein schmales Ornamentband, das sich aus kleinen Kugeln oder Ovalen zusammensetzt, die formal an Perlen erinnern. Der A. tritt gewöhnlich nicht für sich, sondern zusammen mit Blatt- und *Eierstäben* als begleitendes Unterglied von Gesimsprofilierungen auf.

Band horizontal verlaufender Streifen, der meist farbig akzentuiert ist oder von *Ornamenten* geziert wird

Bandelwerk vielfältig gebrochener, miteinander verschlungener Rankendekor, der in flächiger Ausprägung für den Régence-Stil charakteristisch ist

Basis profilierter, ausladender Fuß einer *Säule* oder eines *Pfeilers*

Bekrönung obere, schmückende Endigung eines Bauwerks wie zum Beispiel *Bänder*, *Friese* oder andere Baudekorelemente

Beschlagwerk Ornamentform der Spät-Renaissance. Wurde um 1570 entwickelt und stellt eine flache, symmetrisch angeordnete Ornamentform dar, die ursprünglich als Dekor für Holzvertäfelungen in Innenräumen vorgesehen waren und in Stein ausgeführt zu einer der gängigsten Ornamentformen der Spät-Renaissance avancierte.

Blattwelle *Eierstab*

Bogen Überwölbung einer Maueröffnung, deren Steine zur Erhöhung der Druckfestigkeit keilförmig zugeschnitten oder verfugt sind

Bordüre Ornamentband mit begrenzendem oder abgrenzendem Charakter, vergleichbar einem Rahmen oder einer Borte

Chor der nach Osten orientierte Altarraum einer Kirche

Chorschluss auch Chorhaupt; der am Außenbau einer Kirche hervortretende Abschluss des *Chores*, dessen Grundriss halbrund, gerade oder polygonal sein kann.

Dekor Gesamtheit aller zur Ausschmückung dienenden Elemente eines Bauwerks oder anderer Kunstgegenstände

Dekoration künstlerische Ausschmückung von Bauwerken oder Gegenständen aller Art. Die D. von Gefäßen wie z. B. Fayencen oder Porzellan wird hingegen als *Dekor* bezeichnet. Im Gegensatz zum *Ornament*, das nur eine Schmuckform bezeichnet, versteht man unter D. ihre Gesamtheit.

Dienst in der gotischen Architektur hohe Halb- oder Dreiviertelsäule an Wand oder Pfeiler, die dazu bestimmt ist, *Gurte* oder *Rippen* eines Kreuzgewölbes sowie *Profile* der Arkadenbögen aufzunehmen.

Dreiecksgiebel dreieckiger *Giebel* als *Bekrönung* einer *Tempelstirnwand*

Eierstab auch Ionisches *Kymation* oder *Blattwelle*; antikes Ornamentband aus ovalen, eiförmigen Elementen, das während der Regierungszeit (117–138 n. Chr.) des römischen Kaisers Hadrian besonders häufig angewandt wurde und deshalb mitunter auch als *Hadrianischer E.* bezeichnet wird. Der E. ist rein *vegetabilen* Ursprungs. Eine Reihe von stilisierten Akanthusblättern krümmt sich unter der von ihnen zu tragenden Last und wölbt sich dabei ein, wobei eiförmige Elemente entstehen.

Emblem in der Antike verstand man unter E. zunächst eine Verzierung sinnbildlicher Art; später wurde der Begriff ganz allgemein für Sinnbild gebraucht. Ein E. besteht nach heutigem Kunstverständnis aus drei Elementen: 1.) dem Ikon (einem *allegorischen* Bild), 2.) dem Lemma (der Überschrift) und 3.) der Subscriptio (der Unterschrift).

Etruskischer Stil Stil, der an die Kunst der Etrusker erinnert. Die Etrusker, ein aus dem antiken Griechenland eingewanderter Volksstamm, lebten bis etwa ins 4. Jh. v. Chr. in der oberitalienischen Region Etrurien. Die etruskische Kunst steht der antiken griechischen Kunst nahe, erlebte ihre Entwicklungsstufen und Höhepunkte jedoch später. Bekannt ist vor allem die etruskische Töpferware, die in den Farben Ochsenblut, d. h. Dunkelrot, Ocker und Schwarz gehalten ist.

Evangeliar mittelalterliche Handschrift mit dem vollständigen Text der vier Evangelien, die, in Buchform gestaltet, für den lithurgischen Gebrauch bestimmt war

Fächergewölbe spätgotische Gewölbeform, deren dicht gereihte, meist rein dekorative *Rippen* einen fächerartigen Eindruck erwecken, der vor allem für die spätgotische Kathedralarchitektur Englands von Bedeutung ist

Faszie in der antiken Baukunst drei, seltener zwei übereinander liegende Streifen, die den *Architrav* waagerecht unterteilen

Feston Schmuckmotiv in Form einer durchhängenden Girlande, die aus Blumen, Blättern, Früchten und flatternden Bändern besteht; seit der Antike in Baukunst, Kunsthandwerk und Malerei verbreitet, avancierte das F. in der Renaissance (16. Jh.) und im Barock (17. Jh.) zu einer der charakteristischsten Ornamentformen.

Fiale architektonisches Zierelement der Gotik, das ein schlankes, pyramidenförmiges Gebilde bezeichnet, das als *Bekrönung* von Strebepfeilern sowie zur Flankierung von *Wimpergen* verwendet wird

Fischblase Ornamentform der Gotik, die für das *Maßwerk* charakteristisch ist. Die F. gleicht in ihrem Umriss der Schwimmblase eines Fisches und kann in unterschiedlicher Ausführung auftreten, so z. B. als Füllung von Fensterrosetten oder Spitzbogenfenstern. In der franz. und engl. Spätgotik wurde die F. bei den Spitzbogenfenstern vertikal aneinander gereiht, so dass der Eindruck von Flammen (franz. flamboyant – flammend) entstand. Diese Stilstufe war für das 15. Jh. prägend und wird *Flamboyant-Stil* genannt.

Flamboyant-Stil ornamentaler Stil der Spätgotik in Frankreich und England, der seinen Namen von den „flammenartigen" Motiven des *Maßwerks* ableitet; siehe hierzu auch *Fischblase*

Flechtband altes *Ornament*, das bereits seit dem 3. Jahrtausend v. Chr. in Vorderasien bekannt war und auch in der Antike verwandt wurde. In nachrömischer Zeit, in der Völkerwanderungszeit sowie im frühen Mittelalter hatte das F. seine Blütezeit; es wurde sowohl im Kunsthandwerk als auch in der Architektur angewandt und trat zuletzt in der romanischen Bauornamentik in zahlreichen Variationen auf.

Fries horizontal verlaufendes, meist plastisch ausgearbeitetes Ornamentband, das den oberen Abschluss einer Wand bildet. Von den Audsleys als bekrönendes Element oder als Abschluss ornamental gestalteter Wände in Innenräumen verwendet.

Funktionalismus Architekturtheorie gegen Ende des 19. Jh., die die enge Beziehung von Form und Funktion untersucht, um dem seit der Antike bestehenden Ideal einer Übereinstimmung von Gestalt und Aufgabe nahe zu kommen

Gebälk Balkensystem zwischen Mauer und Dach. In der klassischen Architektur aus *Architrav*, *Fries* und *Gesims* bestehend; in der Architektur der Renaissance und des Klassizismus wieder entdeckt.

Geometrischer Stil Epoche der griechischen Kunst (etwa 1.000–700 v. Chr.), die nach den vorherrschenden geometrischen Motiven der Vasenmalerei benannt ist

Gesims auch *Sims*, horizontal verlaufendes, plastisches Gliederungselement in der Architektur

Giebel meist repräsentiver, vorderer Abschluss eines Satteldachs oder *Bekrönung* eines Fensters. In der Grundform dreieckig wird sein Umriss häufig mit Ziermotiven, wie zum Beispiel skulpturalem Schmuck oder anderen *Bekrönungen* gestaltet.

Groteske Ornamentform der Renaissance (16. Jh.), die pflanzliche Formen, phantastische Tiere, bizarre menschliche Darstellungen und Fabelwesen aller Art vereint. Die Motive der G. gehen auf römische Wandmalereien zurück, die im Zeitalter der Renaissance in Höhlen (ital. grotta – Grotte) wieder entdeckt wurden.

Gurt auch Gurt*bogen*; Verstärkungs*bogen*, der quer zur Längsachse eines Gewölbes verläuft

Hadrianischer Eierstab *Eierstab*

Heraldische Motive Motive, die der Heraldik, d. h. der Wappenkunde, entnommen sind, etwa Schwerter, Schilde, häufig Löwen usw.

Hohlkehle *Kehle*

Ikonographie Lehre von den Bildinhalten

Imari-Porzellan japanisches Porzellan, das sich durch kleinteilige geometrische Muster auszeichnet

Industrie-Design Mitarbeit an industriellen Produktionen im Bereich der Gestaltung. Das I.-D. reicht heute vom manufakturellen Bereich (Textilien, Porzellan, Glas, Tafel- und Hausgerät) bis zur Entwurfsarbeit an spezifisch technischen Produkten (wie z. B. der Feinwerktechnik und dem Maschinen-, Fahrzeug- und Flugzeugbau).

Initiale Anfangsbuchstabe eines Manuskriptes, meist ornamental verziert

Intarsie(n) Einlegearbeiten aus Holz. Verschiedenfarbiges Holz, Elfenbein, Perlmutt oder auch Metall wird zur Verzierung in Holz eingelegt.

Islamische Kunst Kunst der islamischen, d. h. arabischen Welt; reicht vom 7. Jh. n. Chr. bis zur Gegenwart und erstreckt sich regional – in ost-westl. Ausrichtung – von Indien bis nach Spanien.

Kämpfer Platte, die auf einer *Säule* oder einem *Pfeiler* aufliegend die Last der *Bögen* oder des Gewölbes aufnimmt und auf die stützenden *Säulen* oder *Pfeiler* ableitet. Der K. wird häufig in Verbindung mit einem *Kapitell* verwendet.

Kapitell ausladendes Kopfstück einer *Säule* oder eines *Pfeilers*, das als *Zwischenstück* zwischen Stütze und Last vermittelt

Karnies Leiste mit s-förmig geschwungenem Profil am *Gesims*; tritt sowohl in der antiken Architektur als auch bei Gebäuden des Klassizismus auf.

Kassettendecke Zierdecke aus einzelnen, meist dekorativ gestalteten Feldern, die als Kassetten bezeichnet werden. K. waren in der römischen Antike weit verbreitet und wurden in der Renaissance vor allem bei der Gestaltung von Palastdecken verwendet. Vereinzelt trifft man auch im Barock und im Klassizismus auf K., die jedoch nach und nach durch *Stuck*decken ersetzt wurden.

Kartusche Ornamentform der Renaissance (16. Jh.), die ein medaillonförmiges, meist mit *Voluten* verziertes Rahmenwerk darstellt, das ursprünglich für Wappen und Inschriften verwendet wurde, später jedoch als reine Zierform in Architektur und Kunsthandwerk Anwendung fand

Kehle auch *Hohlkehle* genannt; konkaves *Profil* eines *Gesimses* oder eines anderen plastischen Architekturelements

Kelchkapitell *Kapitell*, das eine einfache, kelchförmige Überleitung von der runden Grundfläche der Säule zum *Abakus* bildet

Keltischer Stil Ornamentstil der Kelten, der sich durch seine reiche Flechtbandornamentik und seine schematisierten Tierdarstellungen auszeichnet. Die keltische Kunst entwickelte sich aus der Hallstatt-Kultur (5. Jh. v. Chr.) und zeichnete sich durch ihren prunkvollen Schmuck und Hausrat aus. Der K. S. erlebte seine letzte Hochblüte im frühen Mittelalter (7.–9. Jh.), als in Großbritanien kirchliche Geräte und illuminierte Handschriften (wie z. B. das „Book of Durrow" und das „Book of Kells") angefertigt wurden.

Kikumon japanische Bezeichnung für das *Emblem* des Kaisers von Japan, die stilisierte Chrysantheme. Sie ist häufig bei den Motiven japanischen Porzellans anzutreffen.

Kleeblatt(motiv) Dreipass, der formal an ein Kleeblatt erinnert. Schmuckform des mittelalterlichen Baudekors, das häufig bei Fenstern und *Maßwerk* zu sehen ist. Das K. fand auch Ausprägungen als Kleeblattfries oder Kleeblattbogen.

Konsole auch *Kragstein*; hervorspringendes Tragelement an der Wand

Kontur Umrisslinie bzw. farbig akzentuierter Rand einer geometrischen Form oder eines *Ornaments*

Korinthisches Kapitell Antiker Kapitelltypus mit plastisch herausgearbeiteten Akanthusblättern und Voluten, der ab dem 5. Jh n. Chr. verbreitet ist und in der mittelalterlichen Kunst variantenreich weiterentwickelt wurde.

Krabbe auch *Kriechblume*; *vegetabiles* Zierelement der Gotik, das an *Diensten*, *Rippen* oder Borten „entlangzukriechen" scheint

Kragstein *Konsole*

Kranzgesims Hauptgesims einer Fassade oder Wand, das deren Abschluss unter dem Dachansatz bildet (vgl. *Gesims*)

Kriechblume *Krabbe*

Kymation *Eierstab*

Lady Chapel Marienkapelle am Ostende einer englischen Kathedrale, häufig als Zentralkapelle des Umgangs ausgeprägt

Laibung innere Mauerflächen an Tür-und Fensteröffnungen sowie *Bögen* und Portalen

Längsschiff längs gerichteter, ein- oder mehrschiffiger Gebäudeteil einer Kirche, der sich zwischen der Hauptfassade und dem *Querschiff* bzw. dem *Chor* erstreckt

Laufender Hund Variation des *Mäanders*, gelegentlich auch als *Wellenband* bezeichnet

Lesbisches Kymation *Blattwelle*, die sich von der klassischen Form des *Eierstabes* ableitet

Lilie Nachtschattengewächs. In der alt-ägyptischen Kunst und der Antike als Schmuckmotiv verbreitet. In der mittelalterlichen Kunst Attribut der Jungfräulichkeit Marias. Im Jugendstil als reine Ornamentform wieder entdeckt.

Lisene leicht vortretende, vertikal verlaufende Mauerverstärkung zur Gliederung einer Fassade, im Gegensatz zum *Pilaster* ohne *Basis* und *Kapitell*

Lotusblüte Seerosengewächs. Der Lotus spielt in der Religion, der Kunst und der Kultur Ägyptens, Indiens und Ostasiens eine bedeutende Rolle. Nach ägyptischem Mythos dem Urwasser entsprossen, war der Lotus Sinnbild unvergänglichen Lebens. Er kommt häufig in der Bildkunst sowie beim Baudekor vor. Von Ägypten ausgehend verbreitete sich der Lotus als Ornamentform der Antike, wo er schöne Stilisierungen, etwa als *Lotus- und Palmettenfries (Anthemion)* erfuhr.

Lotus- und Palmettenfries *Anthemion*

Mäander Ornamentband, das aus rechtwinklig gebrochenen, fortlaufenden Linien gebildet wird. Eines der ältesten Motive der Welt, das bereits in der Vor- und Frühgeschichte, insbesondere bei der Verzierung von Keramik ausgeprägt wurde. Seinen Höhepunkt erreichte der M., dessen Name sich vom besonders windungsreichen, kleinasiatischen Fluss Maiandros ableitet, in der Antike. Der M. tritt in zahlreichen Variationen auf: M. mit eingeschriebenen Hakenkreuzen (Hakenkreuzm. oder doppelter M.); schräggestellter M.; M. verbunden mit Spiralen oder *Rosetten*; M. als flächiges Muster ausgeprägt (Flächenm.). Vom M. leitet sich auch das klassische *Wellenband* ab, umgangssprachlich als *Laufender Hund* bezeichnet.

Maßwerk gemessenes, d. h. mit dem Zirkel konstruiertes geometrisches Bauornament der Gotik. Zur Unterteilung, Füllung oder Aussteifung von Fenstern, *Giebeln*, Wandflächen, Brüstungen oder ähnlichen Bauelementen benutzt.

Medaillon rundes oder ovales Schmuckelement

Miniaturmalerei Malerei in mittelalterlichen Handschriften und Büchern, die nach der charakteristischen roten Schriftfarbe (lat. minium – Mennigfarbe) so benannt wird

Musterbuch Buch mit einer Sammlung von Mustern, die Architekten, Malern und Bildhauern als Vorlage dienten. Die ältesten M. gehen bis ins Mittelalter zurück; sie wurden vor allem von den *Miniaturmalern* in den Klöstern benutzt. Neuzeitliche M. für das Kunsthandwerk werden hingegen als *Vorlagensammlung* bezeichnet.

Ornament Schmuckmotiv als Zierde von Bauten und anderen Kunsterzeugnissen. Das Hauptmerkmal des O. ist der *Rapport*, d. h. die rhythmische Wiederholung von gleichartigen Ornamentmotiven. Diese können in Reihung oder auch als Flächenornament ausgeprägt werden, wobei fast alle Formvarianten möglich sind. Neben abstrakten O. bilden florale oder *vegetabile* O. die Haupttypen. Eine Sonderform stellen die Tierornamente dar, die häufig stilisierte Tier- und Fabelwesen mit Flechtbandmotiven und Ranken verbinden. In der *islamischen Kunst* bildete sich überdies ein eigener Ornamenttypus heraus, der aus der Schönschrift hervorgegangen ist und deshalb als Kalligraphie bezeichnet wird.

Ornamentik Sammelbegriff für *Ornamente*, die einer bestimmten Stilrichtung angehören

Ornamentale Drucke Drucke mit ornamentalen Darstellungen, die Kunsthandwerkern und Architekten als Vorlage dienten. Ursprünglich handelte es sich bei den O. D. um Kupferstiche und Zeichnungen, die Mitte des 16. Jh. mit dem Aufkommen des Buchdrucks eine schnelle Verbreitung fanden.

Paneel Tafel bzw. Vertäfelung, die meist aus Holz gefertigt ist

Papyrus der P. stammt aus Ägypten, wo er bereits seit Anfang des 3. Jahrtausends v. Chr. bekannt ist. Die aus der Papyrusstaude gewonnenen Blätter, die generell als P. bezeichnet werden, dienten als Beschreibstoff in Rollen-, Blatt- und Buchform. Die Bedeutung des P. für die alt-ägyptische Kultur lässt sich auch daran ablesen, dass er häufig in der Kunst, vielfach in Verbindung mit der *Lotusblüte*, abgebildet wurde.

Perlstab *Astragal*

Pfeiler massive, gemauerte Stütze mit rechteckigem Grundriss. Man unterscheidet frei stehende Pfeiler, die z. B. eine *Arkade* stützen, oder mit der Wand verbundene Pfeiler, die auch als *Pilaster* bezeichnet werden.

Pfette Balken, der horizontal und parallel zum First eines Daches verläuft und ein tragendes Element der Dachkonstruktion darstellt

Pilaster flacher, nur wenig aus der Wand hervortretender Wandpfeiler, der häufig mit einer *Basis* und fast immer mit einem *Kapitell* versehen ist. Er dient sowohl zur Gliederung der Wand als auch zur Verstärkung einer Mauer und kann als Träger eines *Gebälks* oder zur Rahmung von Eingangsportalen oder Fenstern verwendet werden.

Polis in der griechischen Antike Bezeichnung für den Stadtstaat sowie für ein demokratisch geprägtes Regierungssystem

Postmoderne Gegenbewegung zur klassischen Moderne, die in den 60er Jahren des 20. Jh. aufkam und sich gegen den strengen *Funktionalismus* und Rationalismus der zeitgenössischen Architektur wandte.

Profil Querschnitt eines Bauelements

Querschiff auch Transept genannt; der zwischen *Längsschiff* und *Chor* eingezogene Querbau einer Kirche. Durch das Querschiff erhält der Grundriss die Form eines Kreuzes.

Rapport systematische Wiederholung einzelner Motive, die für den Aufbau eines Musters bestimmend sind

Relief erhabenes, d. h. aus einer Fläche plastisch hervortretendes Motiv, das ein architektonisches Zierelement darstellt. Man unterscheidet nach den Graden der Oberflächenmodellierung Hoch-, Flach- und Halbrelief.

Rippe rippenartiges Konstruktionsteil eines Gewölbes, das für die Gotik charakteristisch ist

Rocaille barocke Ornamentform, die in den 30er Jahren des 18. Jh. entstand und ein muschelförmiges, sich volutenartig zusammenrollendes *Ornament* bezeichnet, das Elemente des *Akanthus* enthält. Von der R. leitet sich der Stilbegriff Rokoko ab.

Rollenfries aus waagerechten, gegeneinander versetzten Zylindern gebildetes Ornamentband der Romanik

Rollwerk auch Rollwerkkartusche genannt; Ornamentform der Renaissance und des Barock. Sammelbezeichnung für eine Rahmenform mit stilisierten Spruchbändern, Wappenschildern und *Kartuschen*, deren Enden schneckenförmig eingerollt sind und plastisch aus der Fläche hervortreten.

Römische Kunst die Kunst der Römer und die unter ihrer Herrschaft entstandene Reichskunst. Die R. K. kennzeichnete ab dem 2. Jh. v. Chr. vor allem die Verschmelzung von italienischen und griechisch-hellenistischen Elementen. Beginn und Ende der R. K. sind nicht scharf begrenzt; allg. bezeichnet man die Kunst der nachkonstantinischen Zeit bis zum Tode Justinians I. (565 n. Chr.) als spätantike Kunst; in ihr vermischen sich bereits frühchristliche und byzantinische Elemente.

Rosette Ziermotiv, das sich von einer Rose ableitet. Eine aufgesprungene Rosenblüte wird von oben wiedergegeben. Die Darstellung ist meist kreisförmig. Die Rosette stellt eines der am weitesten verbreiteten *Ornamente* dar. In der Gotik bezeichnet eine R. ein großes rundes Fenster, das sich zumeist an der Westfassade einer Kathedrale befindet.

Rundbogen halbkreisförmiger *Bogen*, meist in der Romanik vertreten, aber auch in der antiken römischen Kunst üblich. Der R. zeichnet sich durch eine besonders gute Statik aus.

Säule stützendes Glied mit rundem Grundriss, das ein *Gebälk* oder Ähnliches trägt. Die S. ist gewöhnlich in *Basis*, Schaft und *Kapitell* gegliedert. Die *Basis* besteht aus einer quadratischen Platte (Plinthe) sowie Wülsten und *Kehlen*. Die S. ist aus einem durchgängigen Stein (Monolith) oder einzelnen Steinzylindern (Trommeln) zusammengesetzt. Das *Kapitell* vermittelt zwischen S. und weiteren tragenden Elementen, wie zum Beispiel den *Bögen* oder dem *Gebälk*.

Säulenportikus die von *Säulen* getragene Vorhalle eines Tempels

Schematismus schematische, d. h. abstrahierte, sich von den Naturformen entfernende Wiedergabeform in der Kunst

Schlussstein Stein im Scheitelpunkt eines *Bogens* oder auch Stein am Hauptknotenpunkt der *Rippen* eines Gewölbes

Sims *Gesims*

Sockel(zone) unterer Abschnitt einer Wand, der meist farbig akzentuiert wird

Spitzbogen spitz endender *Bogen*, typisch für die Gotik

Ständerbau der in der traditionellen japanischen Architektur verbreitete Typus eines auf Holzpfeilern errichteten Gebäudes

Sterngewölbe spätgotische Gewölbeform, deren bestimmendstes Merkmal *Rippen* sind, die einen Stern bilden

Stil Der S. wird durch Bau- und Kunstwerke definiert, die charakteristische gleichartige Merkmale aufweisen und somit eine Gruppe bilden. Für die Ausprägung eines S. sind persönliche, regionale und epochale Gemeinsamkeiten ausschlaggebend.

Stirnziegel beim antiken Tempel ein Dachziegel mit aufrecht stehender Ansichtsfläche, der meist mit einer (reliefierten oder gemalten) Palmette geschmückt ist

Stuck mit Leimwasser angemachter Gipsmörtel, dem zwecks Haltbarkeit Kalk- und Marmorstaub beigemischt werden kann. Der gut formbare, feuchte S., der auch im trockenen Zustand nachträglich mit einem Messer oder einem anderen spitzen Gegenstand bearbeitet werden kann, bietet sich zur Herstellung frei aufgetragener, plastisch hervortretender *Dekorationen* an.

Täfelung Verkleidung einer Wand oder einer Decke mit Holzpaneelen

Tempelstirnwand auch -front oder -fassade. Die vordere Ansicht eines Tempels

Tierstil Ornamentstil zur Völkerwanderung (4.–6. Jh. n. Chr.); zeigt schematisierte Tierdarstellungen in Verbindung mit Flechtbandmotiven.

Tüpfelmuster Muster mit unregelmäßig über die Fläche verteilten *Ornamenten*, die von ihrer Anordnung wirken, als seien sie mit einem Pinsel auf die Fläche getüpfelt worden

vegetabil pflanzlich

Vierpass *Ornament*, das sich aus vier Dreiviertelkreisen zusammensetzt und ein vierblättriges Motiv bildet. Der V. wird meist kreisförmig gerahmt und man findet ihnt häufig beim *Maßwerk* gotischer Kathedralen.

Volute eingerolltes *Ornament* oder Bauelement

Vorlagensammlungen *Musterbücher* für das Kunsthandwerk; enthalten Abbildungen von *Ornamenten* sowie Details und Gesamtkonstruktionen. Das älteste Beispiel dieser Art stellen die Ornamentstiche des 15. Jh. dar, die zunehmend an Bedeutung gewannen. Ihre Breitenwirkung wurde nur noch im 19. Jh. von den *Musterbüchern* englischer Designer übertroffen.

Wandvorlage der Wand vorgelegte Mauerverstärkung in Form eines *Dienstes*, *Pilasters* oder einer *Lisene*.

Wellenband auch *Laufender Hund*; wellenförmiges Ornament

Wellenranke Ranke bzw. Blattranke mit wellenförmigem Verlauf des Blattstängels

Wimperg giebelartige *Bekrönung* in der gotischen Architektur

Würfelfries *Fries* mit würfelförmigen, plastisch hervortretenden Elementen, die eine raffinierte Licht-Schatten-Wirkung erzeugen. Für den Baudekor der Romanik von Bedeutung

Zickzack-Fries *Fries* mit Zickzack-Muster, typisch für die normannische Stilrichtung der romanischen Architektur

Ziegelmuster Muster, das den Steinverband bzw. Ziegelverband einer Mauer nachahmt, d. h. das Muster besteht aus verschiedenen Reihen rechteckiger Felder, die wie die Ziegel einer Wand angeordnet sind.

Zwickel dreiseitig begrenztes, mit der Spitze nach unten weisendes Dreieck, das eine Füllform im geometrischen Aufbau von Ornamentbändern darstellt

Zwischenstück Element, das zwischen zwei Formen vermittelt

Glossaire

Les termes indiqués en *italique* sont également définis dans le glossaire.

abaque également appelé *tailloir*. Élément en forme de tablette qui couronne le *chapiteau* d'une *colonne*.

acanthe sorte de chardon poussant dans le bassin méditerranéen, qui se caractérise par de grandes feuilles dentelées à la pointe légèrement enroulée. L'acanthe a servi de modèle dès l'*Antiquité* pour les *chapiteaux* corinthiens et d'autres éléments de décoration, par exemple les *frises*. À l'époque de la *Renaissance*, du *baroque* et du *néoclassicisme*, cet élément ornemental revint au goût du jour dans la décoration architecturale.

acrotère motif ornemental qui décore le sommet des frontons des temples *antiques*

anthémion bandeau ornemental *antique* avec une alternance de *fleurs de lotus* et de *palmettes*. Il a été fréquemment utilisé dans la peinture de vases et l'architecture de la Grèce *antique*.

antique décorer à l'antique : imiter le langage des formes de l'*Antiquité*

Antiquité époque désignant l'Antiquité gréco-romaine. L'Antiquité débute au IIe millénaire avant J.-C. avec les vagues d'immigration de peuples grecs archaïques et se termine en Occident en 476 après J.-C. avec la chute de l'empereur romain Romulus Augustule et en Orient en 529 après J.-C. avec la fermeture de l'Académie qu'avait créée Platon grâce à l'empereur Justinien.

arc voûte d'une ouverture de mur, dont les pierres ont été taillées en forme de cônes ou jointoyées pour augmenter leur résistance à la pression

arc en plein cintre *arc* en demi-cercle, surtout présent dans l'art roman, mais on le rencontre souvent aussi dans l'art romain *antique*. L'arc en plein cintre se caractérise par une excellente statique.

arcade ouverture couverte par un *arc*, c'est-à-dire une rangée d'*arcs* qui commencent au-dessus de *colonnes* ou de *piliers*

arc-doubleau *arc* de renforcement perpendiculaire à l'axe longitudinal d'une voûte

architrave dans l'architecture de l'*Antiquité*, poutre maîtresse horizontale qui repose sur des *colonnes* et supporte l'*entablement*. À l'époque de la *Renaissance*, du *baroque* et du *néoclassicisme*, l'architrave est remise au goût du jour dans l'architecture.

archivolte voussure, c'est-à-dire moulure d'un *arc* en forme de *bandeau* en saillie sur le mur. On la rencontre fréquemment dans l'architecture de l'*Antiquité* comme un élément décoratif d'*arcs* de triomphe, de portes de ville, etc. ; elle a été réutilisée à l'époque de la *Renaissance* et du *néoclassicisme*.

astragale également *bande de perles* ; dans l'art *antique*, il désigne un bandeau ornemental étroit composé de petites sphères ou d'ovales qui rappellent la forme de perles. L'astragale s'accompagne de *rinceaux* de feuilles et d'*oves* servant de soubassement à des *profils* de *corniches*.

baldaquin structure en forme de toit ou de dais d'apparat en étoffe de soie précieuse ; il se présentera plus tard sous la forme d'un auvent en pierre ou en bois au-dessus d'un autel, d'un trône royal ou épiscopal, d'une chaire, d'une statue, etc.

bandeau bande horizontale le plus souvent mise en valeur par des couleurs ou décorée d'*ornements*

bande de perles *astragale*

bande de vagues appelé également *méandre* ; bandeau ornemental en forme de vagues

bandeau de palmettes bandeau ornemental composé de *palmettes*

baroque *style* qui s'est développé aux XVIe, XVIIe et XVIIIe siècles d'abord en Italie au moment de la Contre-Réforme, puis dans de nombreux pays. Le baroque se caractérise par la liberté des formes et la profusion des *ornements*.

base pied profilé et saillant d'une *colonne* ou d'un pilier

billette *bandeau* ornemental de l'art roman, composé de cylindres horizontaux, disposés tête-bêche

bordure *bandeau* ornemental qui limite ou délimite un élément ; il est comparable à un cadre.

caissons plafond composé de *panneaux* individuels, souvent décoratifs appelés caissons. Les plafonds à caissons étaient très répandus dans l'*Antiquité* romaine et ont été surtout utilisés pour orner les plafonds des palais à l'époque de la *Renaissance*. On rencontre aussi quelques plafonds à caissons à l'époque du *baroque* et du *néoclassicisme*, mais ils ont été de plus en plus remplacés par des plafonds en *stuc*.

chapiteau partie supérieure large d'une *colonne* ou d'un *pilastre*, située entre le support et la charge

chevron pièce de charpente posée en biais, le plus souvent en bois

claveau triangle délimité sur les trois côtés, à la pointe orientée vers le bas, qui sert de *raccord* dans la composition géométrique de bandeaux ornementaux

clé de voûte pierre placée au centre d'une voûte ou à l'intersection principale des *nervures* d'une voûte

colonne support cylindrique qui soutient un *entablement* ou un élément similaire. Les trois éléments d'une colonne sont en général la *base*, le *fût* et le *chapiteau*. La *base* comprend une partie carrée (plinthe), ainsi que des *tores* et des *gorges*. La colonne se compose d'un seul bloc de pierre (monolithe) ou de plusieurs cylindres de pierre (tambours). Le *chapiteau* se trouve entre la colonne et d'autres éléments portants, par exemple les *arcs* ou l'*entablement*.

console également appelée *corbeau* ; élément en surplomb placé contre un mur

construction profane édifice destiné à une utilisation séculière, contrairement à l'édifice sacré

construction religieuse édifice consacré au culte de la religion, par exemple une église, un cloître, une cathédrale, etc.

contour ligne extérieure ou bord accentué par une couleur d'une forme géométrique ou d'un *ornement*

contrefort renforcement du mur se présentant sous la forme d'une *perche colonnette*, d'un *pilastre* ou d'une *lisière*

corbeau *console*

corniche également appelée *moulure* ; élément d'une structure architecturale horizontale et en *relief*

couche de fond application de la première couche de peinture pour réaliser un *ornement*. Chaque *fond* nécessite l'application d'une couche spécifique.

couronnement élément décoratif formant le faîte d'un bâtiment, par exemple des *bandeaux*, des *frises* ou d'autres éléments de décoration architecturale

crosse également appelée « crochet » ; élément décoratif végétal du *gothique* qui semble « ramper » le long de *perches colonnettes*, *nervures* ou *bordures*

cymaise *oves*

cymaise de Lesbos *ondulation de feuilles* dérivant de la forme classique de l'*ove*

décor floral décor végétal qui reproduit principalement des fleurs, des feuilles et des *rosaces*

Decorated Style désignation du haut *gothique* anglais (XIVe siècle)

dentelles de pierre *ornement* architectural géométrique du *gothique* tracé « au compas », qui sert à subdiviser, remplir ou étayer des vitraux, *pignons*, murs, balustrades ou d'autres éléments architecturaux similaires

disperser répartir des *ornements* irrégulièrement sur la surface, par exemple des *rosaces*

doucine moulure à deux courbures en forme de S surmontant une *corniche* ; elle apparaît aussi bien dans l'architecture *antique* que dans des édifices du *néoclassicisme*.

Early English Style désignation du premier *gothique* anglais (XIIIe siècle)

entablement système de poutres entre le mur et le toit. Dans l'architecture classique, il se compose d'une *architrave*, d'une *frise* et d'une *corniche* ; il a été redécouvert dans l'architecture de la *Renaissance* et du *néoclassicisme*.

entrelacs motif décoratif végétal

entrelacs de vagues feuilles entrelacées dont les tiges ondulent à la manière des vagues

entrelacs fourchu *entrelacs* dont les tiges se séparent

fasce dans l'architecture *antique*, trois bandes, ou plus rarement, deux bandes superposées qui subdivisent l'*architrave* dans le sens horizontal

feuille de trèfle motif trilobé qui rappelle la feuille de trèfle par sa forme. Forme ornementale du décor architectural médiéval qu'on rencontre souvent dans des fenêtres et *dentelles de pierre*. Le motif de la feuille de trèfle est aussi apparu sous la forme de *frise* à feuilles de trèfle ou d'*arc* trilobé.

fleuron *couronnement* en forme de croix d'un *pignon gothique*, d'un *pinacle* ou d'une *guimberge* qui se présente sous la forme de feuilles stylisées

fleurs de lotus et palmettes *anthémion*

fond arrière-plan en couleur d'un *ornement*

frise *bandeau* ornemental horizontal, le plus souvent en *relief*, qui constitue la limite supérieure d'un mur. Elle a été utilisée par les Audsley comme *couronnement* ou élément de finition de murs décorés dans des intérieurs.

frise à damiers *frise* à éléments en *relief* en forme de damiers qui créent un jeu raffiné d'ombres et de lumières. Elle jouait un grand rôle dans la décoration architecturale de l'art roman.

frise d'acanthe *acanthe*

frise d'anthémion *anthémion*

frise en zigzag *frise* avec motif en zigzag, caractéristique de l'influence normande dans l'architecture romane

fût partie d'une *colonne* comprise entre la *base* et le *chapiteau*

gorge également appelée *moulure concave*; *profil* concave d'une *corniche* ou d'un autre élément architectural en *relief*

Gothic Revival également appelé *néogothique* ou renaissance du *gothique* dans l'histoire anglaise de l'art; l'influence de ce mouvement sur le *style* architectural de l'*historisme* a été déterminante.

gothique époque de l'art médiéval en Europe, qui a immédiatement suivi l'art roman. Le gothique est né au milieu du XIIe siècle en France et s'est peu à peu étendu dans toute l'Europe. L'architecture gothique trouve sa plus belle expression dans la cathédrale aux *ogives* et *piliers* en faisceaux qui s'élancent vers le ciel. Dans les pays européens, le gothique connut des évolutions très diverses qui ont eu une durée variable. En Italie, la *Renaissance* a commencé dès 1400, tandis que le gothique flamboyant s'est poursuivi jusque vers la fin du XVe siècle en Angleterre, en Espagne et en Allemagne.

grotesque dans l'art ornemental, forme d'*entrelacs* de feuilles élancées où se mêlent des figures humaines ou animales souvent bizarres, des plantes, des éléments architecturaux, des emblèmes, des *médaillons* ou des *motifs héraldiques*

guimberge dans l'architecture *gothique*, sorte de *pignon* servant de *couronnement*

héraldique science des armoiries

historié désigne en général un *chapiteau* décoré de scènes qui illustrent une « histoire » empruntée par exemple aux Évangiles. Ces *chapiteaux* sont fréquents dans l'art roman.

historisme *style* du XIXe siècle qui se rapporte aux *styles* architecturaux et formes de décorations « historiques ». En Angleterre, le *gothique* revint au goût du jour dans la deuxième moitié du XIXe siècle, d'où le nom de *Gothic Revival* ou *néogothique*. Le *néogothique* se caractérise par l'utilisation de formes *gothiques* telles que les *perches colonnettes*, *pinacles* et *crosses*, ainsi que les *dentelles de pierre* et les *rosaces*. Les principes de l'historisme se reflètent aussi dans les formes décoratives de cette époque et ont donc joué un rôle décisif dans l'évolution des motifs des Audsley.

iconographie étude et interprétation des portraits

initiale première lettre d'un manuscrit, le plus souvent enluminée

intrados surfaces intérieures d'ouvertures de portes et de fenêtres, ainsi que d'*arcs* et de portails

Jugendstil désigne, en Allemagne, l'art néobaroque des années 1900. Ce mouvement également appelé « art nouveau » s'est étendu dans toute l'Europe.

Kikumon mot japonais désignant le chrysanthème stylisé, emblème de l'empereur du Japon. On le rencontre souvent dans les motifs de la porcelaine japonaise.

Kirimon mot japonais désignant le paulownia, arbre largement répandu en Asie dont les feuilles et les fruits sont, dans l'art japonais, les emblème de la noblesse japonaise, notamment des samouraïs.

L'art étrusque est proche de celui de la Grèce *antique*, mais son évolution et son apogée n'ont eu lieu que plus tard. La poterie étrusque de couleur sang de bœuf (rouge foncé), ocre et noire est particulièrement célèbre.

lambris habillage d'une cloison ou d'un plafond avec des *panneaux* de bois

lambris de couvrement habillage d'un plafond avec des *panneaux* ou des *caissons*

lisière *contrefort* d'un mur vertical, légèrement en saillie qui sert à délimiter une façade; contrairement au *pilastre*, la *lisière* n'a pas de *soubassement* ni de *chapiteau*

marqueterie incrustations en bois. Des pièces de bois de différentes couleurs, d'ivoire, de nacre ou de métal sont incrustées dans un support en bois à des fins de décoration

méandre *bandeau* ornemental composé de lignes continues, formant des angles droits. C'est un des motifs les plus anciens du monde qui était déjà utilisé dans la préhistoire et la protohistoire, notamment pour décorer des céramiques. Le méandre, dont le nom vient du fleuve d'Asie Mineure particulièrement sinueux Maiandros, a connu son apogée sous l'*Antiquité*. Il existe de nombreuses variantes du méandre: à croix gammées incorporées (*méandres à croix gammées* ou méandre double), oblique, associé à des spirales ou des *rosaces*, plat (méandre plat). La *bande de vagues* classique est aussi dérivée du méandre.

méandre à croix gammées *méandre*

médaillon élément décoratif rond ou ovale

monogramme *initiales* ou premières lettres de noms

motif de briques motif qui imite l'assemblage de pierres ou l'assemblage de briques d'un mur; le motif se compose en effet de diverses rangées de *panneaux* rectangulaires disposés comme les briques d'un mur.

motif moucheté motif dont les *ornements* sont répartis de façon irrégulière sur la surface et qui, en raison de leur disposition, donnent l'impression d'avoir été mouchetés avec un pinceau

motifs héraldiques motifs empruntés à l'*héraldique*, c'est-à-dire la science des armories, par exemple des épées, boucliers, lions, etc.

moulure concave *doucine*

néoclassicisme mouvement artistique européen qui a relayé le *baroque* et le rococo au milieu du XVIIIe siècle et s'est terminé au milieu du XIXe siècle avec l'avènement de l'*historisme*. Le néoclassicisme s'inspire de modèles classiques de l'*Antiquité* romaine et grecque. L'architecture néoclassique est monumentale et se distingue par une structure stricte et des formes claires. Les éléments caractéristiques sont les façades à *pignons* jalonnées de *colonnes*, les imposantes coupoles, ainsi que les formes décoratives empruntées à l'*Antiquité*.

néogothique *Gothic Revival*

Neo-Greek Style désignation du *néoclassicisme* dans l'histoire anglaise de l'art

nervure partie cannelée d'une voûte, caractéristique du *gothique*

ogive *arc* se terminant en pointe, caractéristique du *gothique*

ondulation de feuilles *ove*

ornement forme décorative. L'ornement sert le plus souvent à décorer des éléments architecturaux qui mettent en valeur la structure d'un édifice. On distingue en général les ornements géométriques et les ornements végétaux.

ove également appelé « cimaise ionienne » ou *ondulation de feuilles*, bandeau ornemental *antique* composé d'éléments ovales, en forme d'œufs, qui était fréquemment utilisé sous le règne de l'empereur romain Hadrien (117–138 après J.-C.) et qu'on appelle parfois aussi *ove d'Hadrien*. L'ove est d'origine purement végétale. Des feuilles d'*acanthe* stylisées se courbent sous la charge qu'elles portent et se voûtent en donnant naissance à des éléments de forme ovoïde.

ove d'Hadrien *ove*

palmette motif végétal décoratif dérivé de l'*acanthe* et largement répandu dans l'art *antique*. Cet élément décoratif était très en vogue dans l'architecture du *néoclassicisme*.

panne poutre horizontale et parallèle au faîte d'un toit et élément porteur de la construction de toit

panneau latte ou *lambris* souvent en bois

perche colonnette dans l'architecture *gothique*, *contrefort* en forme de *colonne*, qui supporte les *arcs* doubleaux ou *nervures* de la voûte à croisée d'*ogives* ou qui soutient les *profils* des *arcades*

Perpendicular Style désignation du *gothique* anglais finissant (du milieu du XIVe siècle au milieu du XVe siècle)

pignon élément de façade qui décore en général un toit en bâtière ou un *couronnement* de fenêtre. Souvent de forme triangulaire, le pignon présente souvent des motifs décoratifs sur ses rampants, par exemple des moulures ou des *couronnements*.

pilastre *pilier* de mur plat, légèrement en saillie, qui a souvent une *base* et presque toujours un *chapiteau*. Il sert à diviser un mur, mais aussi à le renforcer et peut servir de support d'*entablement* ou d'encadrement de portails d'entrée ou de fenêtres.

pilier support massif maçonné, à *base* horizontale rectangulaire. On distingue les piliers isolés qui supportent par exemple une *arcade* et les piliers également appelés *pilastres* qui font corps avec le mur.

pinacle élément ornemental architectonique du *gothique*. Il désigne une forme élancée, pyramidale qui couronne des *piliers* de *contreforts* et flanque des *guimberges*.

profil vue en coupe d'un élément architectural

quadrilobe *ornement* composé de quatre *arcs* de cercle et formant un motif à quatre feuilles. Le quadrilobe s'inscrit souvent dans un cadre rond; c'est un motif *récurrent* dans les *dentelles de pierre* des cathédrales *gothiques*.

raccord Forme qui remplit les espaces entre des motifs prépondérants

recueil de modèles ouvrage regroupant des motifs transposés ou utilisés comme modèles pour un projet d'*ornements*. Les recueils de modèles ont pris une importance considérable en Europe à partir du milieu du XIXe siècle avec l'apparition des écoles d'arts décoratifs. Jusqu'à la fin du XIXe et au début du XXe siècle, de nombreux recueils de modèles ont non seulement marqué l'époque de l'*historisme*, mais aussi le *Jugendstil*. Ce genre d'ouvrage est tombé en disgrâce après la Première Guerre mondiale en raison de la crise économique mondiale et de la diminution des commandes à caractère artistique.

récurrent un élément récurrent se compose de deux motifs qui se répètent à intervalles réguliers

relief motif saillant, c'est-à-dire en relief, qui représente un élément décoratif architectural. On distingue, selon le degré de modelé, le haut-relief, le bas-relief et le moyen-relief.

Renaissance époque qui a succédé au Moyen Âge. La Renaissance est un mouvement né en Italie au début du XIVe siècle et qui s'est très vite propagé à toute l'Europe. Elle a connu son apogée au XVIe siècle. Les idéaux de l'*Antiquité* revinrent au goût du jours dans des domaines tels que la philosophie, les arts plastiques et l'architecture. Sur le plan des formes, l'architecture de la Renaissance se réfère aux éléments architecturaux *antiques*, par exemple les *colonnes* et les *chapiteaux*, les *corniches*, les *reliefs* et les *frises*. Le *baroque* a succédé à la Renaissance au XVIIe siècle.

rinceaux bandeau ornemental entrelacé

rosace motif décoratif dérivé de la rose. La fleur de rose éclose est représentée à plat. Elle a souvent une forme circulaire. C'est un des *ornements* les plus répandus. Dans l'art *gothique*, une rosace désigne un grand vitrail rond qui se trouve en général sur la façade ouest d'une cathédrale.

sommier traverse couronnant une *colonne* ou un *pilier* supportant la charge des *arcs* ou de la voûte et la reportant sur les *colonnes* ou *piliers* de support. Le sommier est souvent utilisé avec un *chapiteau*.

soubassement partie inférieure d'une cloison, souvent mise en évidence par des couleurs

stuc mortier de plâtre gâché avec une solution de colle; on peut y ajouter de la poussière de chaux et de marbre afin de le solidifier. Le stuc humide et malléable qui, une fois sec, pourra être travaillé au couteau ou avec un autre objet pointu, est idéal pour la réalisation de décors en *relief* et aux nombreuses possibilités d'application.

style le style se définit par des édifices et des œuvres d'art qui présentent des caractéristiques similaires et forment de ce fait un groupe. Les analogies de personnes, de régions et d'époques sont déterminantes pour l'expression d'un style.

style étrusque *style* qui rappelle l'art des Étrusques. Les Étrusques, peuple à l'origine controversée, ont occupé l'Étrurie, une région de l'Italie du Nord, à peu près jusqu'au IVe siècle avant J.-C.

tailloir *abaque*

tore moulure à *profil* convexe, demi-cylindrique, qui entoure la *base* d'une *colonne*

vessie de poisson dans le *gothique* flamboyant, motif ornemental qui ressemble à la vessie natatoire d'un poisson. Elle peut aussi avoir la forme d'un S.

Photographic Credits
Bildnachweis
Crédits photographiques

Bibliography
Bibliografie
Bibliographie

W. J. Audsley: *Handbook of Christian Symbolism*, London 1865 (new edition: New York 1984).

G. A. Audsley und T. W. Cutter: *The Ornamental Arts of Japan*, Vols. I–II, London 1882–1884 (new edition: *Grammar of Japanese Ornament: Studio Library of Decorative Art*, New York 1989).

W. J. und G. A. Audsley: *Outlines of Ornament in the Leading Styles. Selected from executed ancient art works*, London 1882 (new edition: *Designs and Patterns from Historic Ornament*, New York 1993).

W. J. und G. A. Audsley: *Victorian Sourcebook of Medieval Decoration: With 166 Full-Color Designs*, New York 1991.

D. Debes: *Das Ornament. Wesen und Geschichte. Ein Schriftenverzeichnis*, Leipzig 1956.

P. Finkelstein: *L'Art du Faux*, Paris 1999.

O. Grabar: *The Mediation of Ornament*, Washington 1992.

Alain Gruber: *L'art décoratif en Europe, 3 volumes: Tome 1: Renaissance et maniérisme, Tome 2: Classique et baroque, Tome 3: Du néoclassicisme à l'art déco*, Paris 1992–1999.

G. Irmscher: *Kleine Kunstgeschichte des europäischen Ornaments seit der Frühen Neuzeit (1400–1900)*, Darmstadt 1984.

O. Jones: *The Grammar of Ornament*, London 1856 (Neuauflage in Deutsch: *Grammatik der Ornamente*, Köln 1997).

I. Maierbacher: *Schablonieren. 140 historische Vorlagen zur individuellen Raumgestaltung*, München 1997.

K. McCloud: *La décoration: guide des styles et des techniques*, Paris 1992.

F. S. Meyer: *Ornamentale Formenlehre*, Leipzig 1886 (Neuauflage: *Handbuch der Ornamentik*, Stuttgart 1995; New edition in English: *Handbook of Ornaments*, New York 1967).

M. Praz: *Histoire de la décoration d'intérieur*, Paris 1994.

A. Riegl: *Historische Grammatik der Bildenden Künste*, Graz/Köln 1966.

D. Schneider-Henn: *Ornament und Dekoration*, München 1997.

A. Sloan et K. Gwynn: *Peinture Décor: toutes les techniques pour réussir soi-même les effets, les formes, les couleurs, les harmonies*, Paris 1990.

E. Wilson: *8000 Years of Ornament. An Illustrated Handbook of Motifs*. London 1994 (deutsche Auflage: *Ornamente. Das Handbuch einer 8000 jährigen Geschichte*, Bern 1996).

S. et S. Walton: *La décoration au tampon: comment embellir facilement son cadre de vie*, Paris 1996.

Le grand livre des techniques décoratives, Paris 1997.